lonely planet

Discover
Canada

Experience the best
of Canada

This edition written and researched by

Karla

Celeste Brash, John Lee, Sarah Richards,

Brendan Sainsbury, Caroline Sieg,

Ryan Ver Berkmoes, Benedict Walker

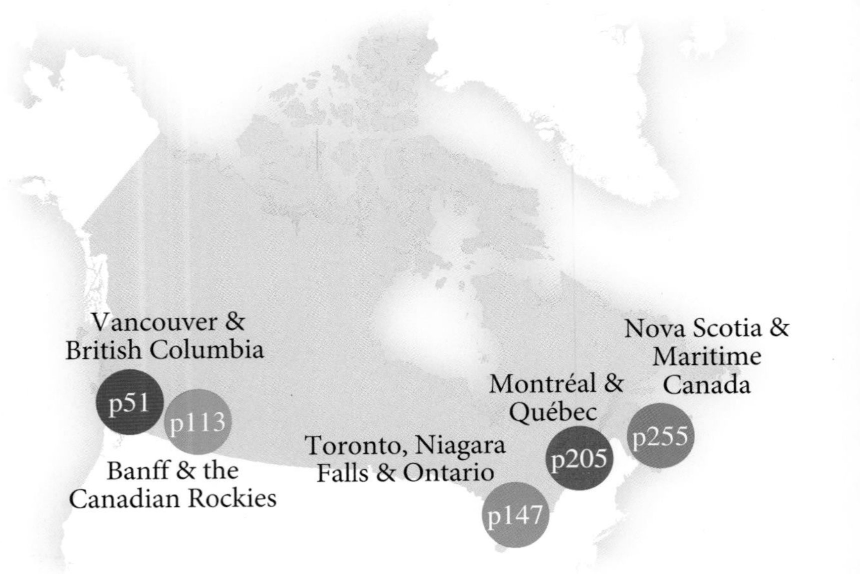

Vancouver & British Columbia

- Vancouver
- Whistler
- Victoria & Around
- Okanagan Valley
- Tofino

Banff & the Canadian Rockies

- Banff National Park
- Jasper National Park
- Athabasca Glacier
- Lake Louise
- Yoho National Park

Toronto, Niagara Falls & Ontario

- Niagara
- Toronto
- Thousand Islands
- Lake Superior Provincial Park
- Ottawa

Montréal & Québec

- Montréal Jazz Festival
- Québec City Old Town
- Wet & Wild Tadoussac
- Baie St-Paul
- Îles de la Madeleine

Nova Scotia & Maritime Canada

- Cape Breton Highlands
- Grand Manan Island
- Halifax
- Cavendish
- Digby & Annapolis Valley

Contents

Plan Your Trip

Discover

Contents

Discover Canada

This Is Canada

Canada is too polite to say so, but it's got the goods: a trio of cultured cities in Montréal, Toronto and Vancouver; an epic amount of terrain to play on outside the urban areas; and a welcoming, progressive vibe throughout.

The globe's second-biggest country has an endless variety of landscapes. Spiky mountains, glinting glaciers, spectral forests – they're all here, spread across six times zones. Wave-bashed beaches, too. With the Pacific, Arctic and Atlantic oceans on three sides, Canada has a coastline that would reach halfway to the moon, if stretched out. These landscapes form the backdrop for a big provincial menagerie: that's 'big' as in polar bears, grizzly bears, whales and everyone's favorite, shrub-nibblin' moose.

Canada is a land of action. Whether it's snowboarding Whistler's mountains, kayaking in Québec's Îles de la Madeleine or walking on Banff's glaciers, outfitters will help you gear up. Gentler adventures abound, too, such as strolling along Vancouver's Stanley Park seawall, swimming off Prince Edward Island's pink-sand beaches, or ice skating Ottawa's Rideau Canal.

Canada is a local food smorgasbord. If you grazed from east to west across the country, you'd fill your plate like this: lobster with a dab of melted butter in the Maritime provinces, poutine (golden fries soaked in gravy and cheese curds) in Québec, and wild salmon and velvety scallops in British Columbia. Tastemakers may not tout Canadian food the way they do with, say, Italian or French fare, so let's just call the distinctive seafood, piquant cheeses and off-the-vine fruits and veggies our little secret. Ditto for the bold reds and crisp whites the country's vine-striped valleys grow.

Canada parties all year long. Okanagan's ice wine festival in January, Québec City's winter carnival in February, Whistler's ski and snowboard fest in April, Montréal's jazz fest in June, Toronto's film fest in September and Niagara's Winter Festival of Lights in December all rock the calendar.

> “Canada is too polite to say so, but it's got the goods”

Lake Louise (p127), Banff National Park

Canada

150°W
140°W
130°W
120°W
110°W
100°W
90°W
80°W
70°W
60°W
ARCTIC OCEAN
Ellesmere Island
Axel Heiberg Island
Nares Strait
Sverdrup Islands
Bathurst Island
Melville Island
Cornwallis Island
Devon Island
Banks Island
Viscount Melville Sound
Beaufort Sea
Amundsen Gulf
Somerset Island
Prince of Wales Island
Victoria Island
Baffin Island
Boothia Peninsula
Gulf of Boothia
King William Island
Melville Peninsula
Foxe Basin
ALASKA
USA
Tuktoyaktuk
Inuvik
Dawson City
YUKON TERRITORY
Mackenzie Mountains
Franklin Mountains
Mackenzie River
Great Bear Lake
Whitehorse
NORTHWEST TERRITORIES
NUNAVUT
Thelon River
Southhampton Island
Juneau
Watson Lake
Nahanni National Park Reserve
Fort Simpson
Lac La Martre
Yellowknife
Baker Lake
Dubawnt Lake
Coats Island
Great Slave Lake
Spatsizi Plateau Provincial Wilderness Park
BRITISH COLUMBIA
Wood Buffalo National Park
Lake Claire
Lake Athabasca
Hudson Bay
Prince Rupert
Williston Lake
Rocky Mountains
Churchill
Haida Gwaii
Coast Mountains
ALBERTA
Athabasca R
Wollaston Lake
Reindeer Lake
Churchill R
Nelson R
Prince George
SASKATCHEWAN
Thompson
Severn R
Jasper National Park
Jasper
Edmonton
Lac la Ronge
MANITOBA
Winisk R
Vancouver Island
Whistler
Banff National Park
Prince Albert
Lake Winnipeg
Tofino
Nanaimo
Vancouver
Victoria
Banff
Calgary
Saskatoon
Yorkton
ONTARIO
Nelson
Moose Jaw
Riding Mountain National Park
Lac Seul
Lake Nipigon
Seattle
WA
Medicine Hat
Swift Current
Regina
Brandon
Winnipeg
Thunder Bay
Lake Superior Provincial Park
Lake of the Woods
Lake Superior
MT
ND
OR
MN
Sault Ste Marie
WI
ID
SD
Lake Michigan
WY
UNITED STATES OF AMERICA
NV
IA
Chicago
CA
NE
UT
IL
CO
KS
MO

25 Top Highlights

1. Banff National Park
2. Old Town, Québec
3. Vancouver
4. Niagara Falls
5. Cape Breton Highlands
6. Whistler
7. Victoria & Around
8. Toronto
9. Montréal
10. Jasper National Park
11. Grand Manan Island
12. Icefields Parkway
13. Haida Gwaii
14. Okanagan Valley
15. Thousand Islands
16. Tofino
17. Halifax
18. Cavendish
19. Lake Superior
20. Tadoussac
21. Charlevoix
22. Îles de la Madeleine
23. Ottawa
24. Churchill
25. Digby & Annapolis Valley

25 Canada's Top Highlights

Banff National Park

Holy Mother Nature! Banff (p122) is the beautiful, buxom rock star of Canada's national parks. It's impossible to describe without resorting to shameless clichés, so let's get them out of the way: placid, turquoise-tinted lakes; dagger-shaped peaks; bright, jumbled wildflower meadows; and glistening glaciers. While paddling and skiing earn raves, hiking is Banff's tour de force, especially around Lake Louise. Alpine-style teahouses pop up along the trails, so exertion is rewarded with sweet treats – and ethereal, in-the-cloud views.

1

PHILIP & KAREN SMITH/GETTY IMAGES ©

2

Old Town, Québec

Québec's capital (p234) is over 400 years old, and its stone walls, glinting cathedral spires and jazz-playing corner cafes suffuse it with romance, melancholy and intrigue on par with any European city. Soak it up by walking the Old Town's labyrinth of lanes and get lost amid the street performers and cozy inns, stopping every so often for a café au lait, flaky pastry or plate of poutine (fries smothered in cheese curds and gravy).

Vancouver

Vancouver (p60) always lands atop the 'best places to live' lists, and who's to argue? Sea-to-sky beauty surrounds the laid-back, beer-lovin' metropolis. With skiable mountains on the outskirts, beaches fringing the core and Stanley Park's forest just blocks from downtown's glass skyscrapers, it's a harmonic convergence of city and nature. It also mixes Hollywood chic (many movies are filmed here) with buzzing Chinese neighborhoods and a freewheeling counterculture (including a popular nude beach and Marijuana Party headquarters). Bottom: Stanley Park seawall (p61)

3

The Best... Jaw-Dropping Parks

BANFF NATIONAL PARK
Picture-perfect jewel with white-tipped mountains and turquoise lakes. (p122)

GWAII HAANAS NATIONAL PARK RESERVE
Ancient rainforests reveal lost Haida villages, burial caves and totem poles. (p109)

CAPE BRETON HIGHLANDS NATIONAL PARK
Misty coastal wilderness of cliffs, whales and eagles. (p274)

YOHO NATIONAL PARK
Dramatic peaks and pounding waterfalls. (p132)

STANLEY PARK
Vancouver's sea-licked forest with beaches and totem poles at down-town's edge. (p61)

The Best... Adrenaline Towns

WHISTLER
To ski or snowboard Canada's best, Whistler reigns supreme. Mountain biking takes over in summer. (p81)

TOFINO
Little Tofino offers big adventure with its surfing, kayaking and storm watching. (p100)

BANFF
In the heart of the Rockies, this place has it all: skiing, snowboarding, hiking, rafting and cycling. (p122)

THE LAURENTIANS
Sweet mountain villages speckling the landscape outside Montréal let you ski, climb and hike. (p232)

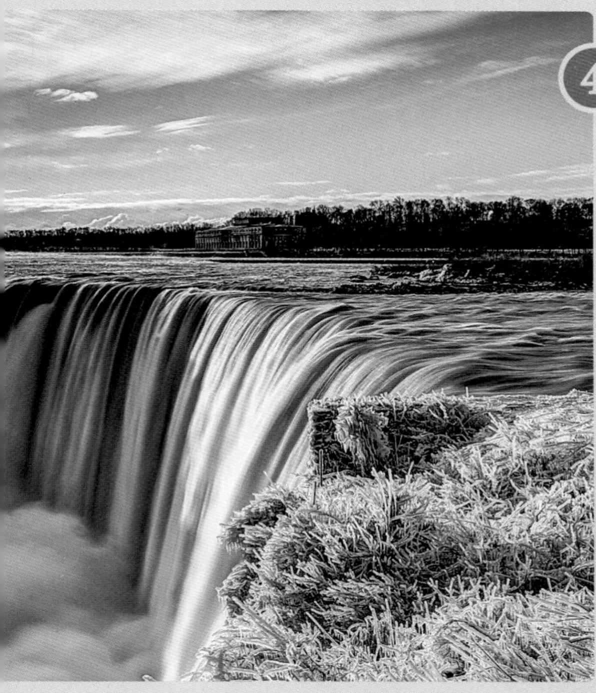

ED NORTON/GETTY IMAGES ©

4 Niagara Falls

Crowded? Cheesy? Well, yes. Niagara is short, too – it barely cracks the world's highest 50 falls. But when those great muscular bands of water arch over the precipice like liquid glass, roaring into the void below, and when you sail toward it in a misty little boat, Niagara Falls (p177) impresses. In terms of sheer volume nowhere in North America beats its thundering cascade, with more than one million bathtubs of water plummeting over the edge every second.

HENRY GEORGI/GETTY IMAGES ©

5 Cape Breton Highlands

Cape Breton Island (p273) crowns Nova Scotia, and Cape Breton Highlands National Park is the jewel in that crown. It's a heavenly, forested realm of bald eagles, migrating whales, palpable history and foot-tapping music in the wee communities that dot the perimeter. The Cabot Trail, with its scenic views, is the main vein through. The park is best explored on foot, reaching vistas overlooking an endless, icy ocean. Left: Cabot Trail (p273)

Whistler

Whistler (p81) is one of the world's most popular ski resorts. Comprising 37 lifts, 34 sq km of skiable terrain and more than 200 runs, this home to the 2010 Winter Olympics kicks up some serious snow action. But summer is also a popular time to visit, with adventure hounds lured to the lakes and crags by radical mountain biking, rafting and alpine hiking. Jolly pubs and bistros help you soothe aching muscles.

6

7

Victoria & Around

Picture-postcard Victoria (p87) is Vancouver Island's heart, beating with bohemian shops, coffee bars and hip, seasonal eateries. After exploring the excellent museums and resident castle, go orca watching, kayaking or cycling – Victoria has more bike routes than any other city in Canada. Nearby, the Cowichan Valley (p95) beckons, studded with welcoming little farms and boutique wineries, prime for wandering foodies. Just 20km from Victoria, Butchart Gardens (p92) wafts fragrant blooms and serves up afternoon tea and evening concerts.

Above: Butchart Gardens

Toronto

A truly global city, Toronto (p156) delivers the multicultural goods. About half its residents were born in another country and the city bubbles with ethnic enclaves, such as Little Italy, Chinatown, Little Korea and Little India. Nowhere is the cultural mash-up more thrilling than in Toronto's restaurants, which fill plates with everything from Korean walnut cakes to Thai curries, jerk chicken and good ol' Canuck pancakes with maple syrup. Markets, bohemian quarters and arts aplenty solidify Toronto's world-class reputation. Bottom: Chinatown, Toronto

8

The Best...
Views

CN TOWER
Rocket up the Western Hemisphere's highest structure and see Toronto in all its glory. (p160)

GROUSE MOUNTAIN
Hike (or take the gondola) up Vancouver's neighboring crag for excellent mountain-meets-sea vistas. (p79)

BANFF GONDOLA
Glide to the top of Sulphur Mountain and ogle the Rockies as they sparkle out around you. (p123)

PEYTO LAKE
Idyllic platform view across the bluest of water. (p134)

Montréal

Nowhere blends French-inspired *joie de vivre* and cosmopolitan culture like Montréal (p214), Canada's second-largest city and its cultural heart. A flourishing arts scene, an indie rock explosion, a medley of world-renowned boutique hotels, the Plateau's swank cache of eateries and a cool Parisian vibe that pervades every *terrasse* (patio) in the Quartier Latin drive the playful scene. Monster festivals add a high note – the Montréal Jazz Festival and Just for Laughs Festival foremost among them – letting the good times roll 24/7. Bottom: Montréal Jazz Festival (p43)

9

The Best... Markets

KENSINGTON MARKET, TORONTO
Have a blast rummaging through the boutiques of bohemian Toronto. (p171)

MARCHÉ JEAN TALON, MONTRÉAL
Farmers bring fruits, veggies, cheeses and sausages to Montréal's lively marketplace. (p230)

HALIFAX SEAPORT FARMERS MARKET
With 250 vendors, it's a prime place to people-watch and buy organic produce, wine and seafood. (p268)

GRANVILLE ISLAND PUBLIC MARKET, VANCOUVER
Wander through Vancouver's multisensory smorgasbord of fish, cheese, fruit and bakery treats. (p66)

10 Jasper National Park

Jasper (p122) shares the same majestic mountain-and-wilderness scenery as its sibling park, Banff, though it's farther flung and thus less visited. It offers superb hiking, and its rugged backcountry wins plaudits for vertiginous river canyons (loved by white-water paddlers) and adrenalin-charged mountain-bike trails. But it's the park's big hairy wildlife that steals the show. Bear, elk, moose and caribou are common sights on the park's slopes and around its lakes.

11 Grand Manan Island

Cue the Maritime fiddle music. As the ferry from the mainland rounds Grand Manan Island (p279), Swallowtail Lighthouse looms into view, poised atop a rocky, moss-covered cliff. Brightly painted fishing boats bob in the harbor. Clapboard houses surrounded by flower gardens unfurl along the shore. There is plenty of fresh sea air and that rare commodity: silence, broken only by the rhythmic ocean surf. Picnic while seals swim nearby, wave to the seaweed vendor, or go on a whale-watch in this quintessential setting.

12

Icefields Parkway

Hwy 93 parallels the Continental Divide for 230km between Lake Louise and Jasper Town. Did we just hear a snore? What if we tell you the road is also known as the 'Icefields Parkway' (p134) and fraught with fanning glaciers, foaming waterfalls, aquamarine lakes and hulking mountains? Then what if we say you can get up close and personal with the cold stuff at places such as Athabasca Glacier (p135), where giant-wheeled tour buses rumble onto its craggy surface, as do guided hikes? We thought that'd seal the deal.

CHRIS CHEADLE/GETTY IMAGES ©

13

Haida Gwaii

This archipelago (p107) off British Columbia's coast makes a magical trip. Colossal spruce and cedars cloak the wild, rainy landscape. Bald eagles and bears roam the ancient forest, while sea lions and orcas patrol the waters. But the islands' real soul is the resurgent Haida people, best known for their war canoes and totem poles. See the lot at Gwaii Haanas National Park Reserve, which combines lost Haida villages and burial caves with some of the continent's best kayaking.

Okanagan Valley

Vines spread across terraced hills in this 180km-long valley (p102), Canada's premier grape-growing region, which suns itself between Vancouver and Banff. More than 100 wineries lie in the lake-spattered area, filling sip-trippers' glasses with fruity whites to the north and complex reds to the south. Even non-oenophiles will enjoy the vineyards' view-worthy terraces and bistros plating regional fare. And everyone will love picking strawberries, cherries, apricots and peaches at the local orchards – or just pulling over at a roadside stand to buy.

14

The Best...
Wine Regions

OKANAGAN VALLEY ✓
In BC's lake-dotted hills, dozens of wineries pour pinot noir, pinot gris, merlot and chardonnay. (p104)

NIAGARA PENINSULA
Ontario's inn-filled grape-growing area has chardonnay, riesling and pinot noir flowing in abundance. (p184)

COWICHAN VALLEY
Vancouver Island's verdant farming region uncorks blackberry port, apple cider and pinot noir. (p96)

PRINCE EDWARD COUNTY
Off the beaten path in pastoral eastern Ontario, the county fills goblets with cooler-climate wines. (p186)

The Best... Scenic Drives

ICEFIELDS PARKWAY
Motor past fanning glaciers, weeping waterfalls, elk and bighorn sheep between Lake Louise and Jasper. (p134)

CABOT TRAIL
Snake by Cape Breton's mountain vistas, sparkling seas and dramatic cliffs. (p273)

ROUTE 199
Roll along sand dunes and fishing villages on the Îles de la Madeleine. (p250)

THOUSAND ISLANDS PARKWAY
Meander beside Ontario's misty, dreamy, island-dotted St Lawrence River. (p185)

HWY 101
Slowpoke through the convivial Sunshine Coast communities. (p74)

15

Thousand Islands

No false advertising here: the 'Thousand Islands' (p185) live up to the number, and then some. The lush archipelago's 1800 isles dot the St Lawrence River between Toronto and Ottawa (and beyond). They offer tufts of fog, showers of trillium petals, quaking tide pools, and 19th-century mansions, whose turrets pierce low-slung clouds. Whether you motor through on the scenic parkway or glide past on a boat, the mist-kissed atmosphere transports visitors to a slower, gentler era. Stately towns and inns let you tuck in overnight. Top: Boldt Castle (p185) Left: View from Skydeck (p186)

ABOVE: MARIO TUMM/IMAGEBROKER/CORBIS ©; BELOW: GLENN VAN DER KNIJFF/GETTY IMAGES ©

Tofino

16

Located on the far west coast, where a wind-bashed ocean meets a Paul Bunyan wilderness, adventurers come to this Vancouver Island outpost (p100) to surf, hike through old-growth forest to hot springs, boat out to see migrating gray whales, and storm watch as winter tempests blow in, rattling windows and spewing waves. It's also a popular destination for kayakers, who glide through the sheltered waters of Clayoquot Sound. Tofino's food trucks, bistros and guesthouses reveal its hippie spirit.

T KITCHIN & V HURST/GETTY IMAGES ©

Halifax

17

The hub of the Maritimes, with the second-largest natural harbor in the world, Halifax (p264) draws its strength from the sea. The Maritime Museum of the Atlantic showcases the *Titanic*, whose victims were brought to the city for burial. Alexander Keith's brewery sits by the harbor, slaking visitors' thirst now as it has done for two centuries. Tall-masted schooners, music-filled pubs, seafood and slow-food restaurants bob up in this nautical city, too.

Cavendish

How did the tiny town of Cavendish (p286) become one of Prince Edward Island's biggest moneymakers? It's a long story – a book actually, about a red-pigtailed orphan named Anne. Lucy Maud Montgomery wrote *Anne of Green Gables* in 1908, drawing inspiration from her cousins' bucolic farmhouse. She never would have dreamed of the groupies who descend each year to lay eyes on the gentle, creek-crossed woods and other settings. Bonus for visitors: the surrounding area bursts with fresh-plucked oysters, mussels and lobsters to crack into.

Bottom: House of Green Gables (p287)

18

The Best... Wildlife-Watching

JASPER NATIONAL PARK
Jasper boasts the Rockies' royal menagerie – grizzlies, elk, moose and caribou. (p122)

CHURCHILL
Polar bears rule the tundra at Hudson Bay's edge, while beluga whales chatter in the river. (p294)

DIGBY NECK
Rare North Atlantic right whales, blue whales and humpbacks swim offshore from Nova Scotia. (p271)

VICTORIA
Resident pods of killer whales ride the local waves. (p87)

Lake Superior

19

Whether the lake (p202) got its name from its size (it's the world's largest freshwater lake) or from its beauty, its provincial park is a stellar place to see the lake's many moods. One minute the water is ferocious enough to sink a ship, the next it's blue-green enough to be in the Caribbean (though the moose hovering nearby reminds you otherwise). The park's lonely road carries you through misty fjord-like passages braced by thick evergreens.

HENRY@SCENICFOTO.COM/GETTY IMAGES ©

The Best... Historic Sites

FORTIFICATIONS OF QUÉBEC
History wafts throughout the walled city where the French put down stakes in 1608. (p235)

LOUISBOURG
Munch soldiers' rations and bribe guards at Nova Scotia's re-created 1744 fortress. (p277)

KLONDIKE NATIONAL HISTORIC SITES
Preserved structures in the Yukon tell the gold-rush tale. (p292)

CRAIGDARROCH CASTLE
Climb the tower's 87 steps in this turreted coal baron's mansion. (p88)

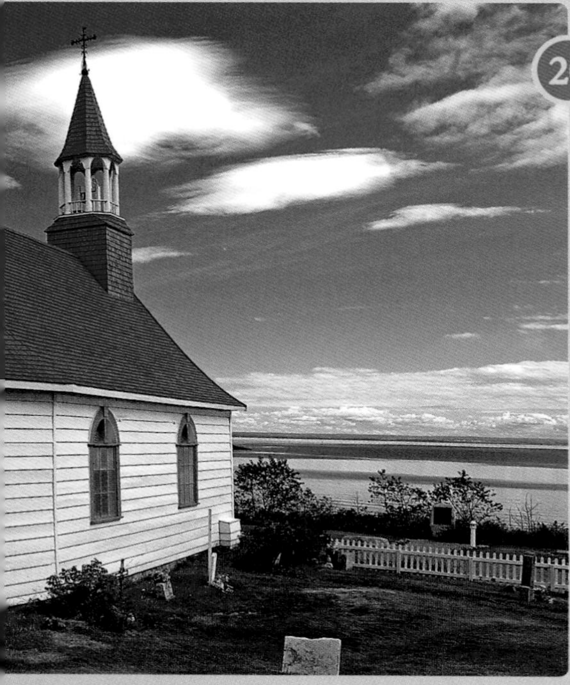

BRIGITTE MERLE/GETTY IMAGES ©

20 Tadoussac

Location, location, location. The captivating town of Tadoussac (p249) has it in spades. Parked at the foot of the Saguenay River fjord – a dramatic waterway bookended by massive cliffs – Tadoussac is perfect for hiking, paddling, vistas and whale-watching, too. Here, the warm, fresh waters of the Saguenay jet out atop the frigid, salt waters of the St Lawrence River, churning up massive volumes of krill. This in turn attracts the whales that put on a splashy show for visitors. Left: Chapel at Tadoussac

Charlevoix

A pastoral strip of rolling hills northeast of Québec City, the Charlevoix region (p246) harvests much of the province's food. Gastronomes road-trip out, knowing the produce from farms and orchards that flash by will be part of their next meal in true farm-to-table fashion. Village inns and alehouses serve the distinct, local wares: think a tomato aperitif with foie gras or pear ice wine served with fresh sheep cheese. Baie St-Paul and La Malbaie are good bases for exploration.

21

22

Îles de la Madeleine

The six largest islands of this breezy archipelago (p250) are connected by a 200km-long road that curves between white-washed lighthouses, green hills and red sandstone cliffs, all edged by the omnipresent blue sea. If you're not poking in rock pools, windsurfing or keeping your bike upright on a blustery sand spit, artists' studios and seafood huts beckon. At night, listen for wistful Acadian songs being strummed in cafes.

Ottawa

There's no time to waste in Ottawa (p187), Canada's culture-rich capital. From the uber-mod, curved-walled Canadian Museum of Civilization to the gothic-arched Canadian Museum of Nature and the glass-spired National Gallery of Canada, each attraction is an inspired architectural gesture with an intriguing exhibition space. In winter the Rideau Canal becomes the world's longest skating rink, where people swoosh by, pausing to purchase steaming hot chocolate and scrumptious slabs of fried dough known as beavertails.

Bottom: National Gallery of Canada (p192)

23

The Best... Museums

CANADIAN MUSEUM OF CIVILIZATION
Ottawa's big kahuna packs the nation's history into a rippled architectural wonder. (p190)

UBC'S MUSEUM OF ANTHROPOLOGY
Vancouver's top collection centers on soaring, beautifully carved totem poles. (p71)

NATIONAL GALLERY OF CANADA
Another Ottawa trove, this one amasses the world's largest collection of Canadian and Inuit art. (p192)

ROYAL ONTARIO MUSEUM
Toronto's architectural explosion houses new art, science and ancient civilization galleries. (p161)

Churchill

The first polar bear you see up close takes your breath away. Immediately forgotten are the two bum-numbing days on the train that took you beyond the tree zone onto the tundra, to the very edge of Hudson Bay. Churchill (p294) is the lone outpost here, and it happens to be smack in the bears' migration path. From late September to early November, tundra buggies head out in search of the razor-clawed beasts, sometimes getting you close enough to lock eyes. Bottom: Polar bears, Churchill

24

The Best... Tables for Foodies

MONTRÉAL
North America's finest French-influenced cuisine feeds a city with a Bacchanalian love for eating out. (p214)

VANCOUVER
Fork into salmon, oysters and other West Coast specialties, washed down with local wines and microbrews. (p60)

TORONTO
Canada's megacity is a wild melting pot of Asian, Greek, Italian and British flavors. (p156)

CHARLEVOIX
Rustic on-the-farm restaurants pepper Québec's organic growing region. (p246)

25

Digby & Annapolis Valley

Whales and wine are the draws of this rustic region (p270) along Bay of Fundy. Whales amass thanks to the bay's unique geography, which unleashes the most extreme tides in the world. These stir up a serious feast for fin, humpback, right and blue whales. Tour boats leave from Digby Neck, a spit of land that juts out in the thick of it. Back on shore, in the farm-studded Annapolis Valley, roads through the pretty countryside wind by welcoming vineyards known for sparkling and ice wines.

Canada's Top Itineraries

Fredericton to Québec City French Canadian Sampler

7 DAYS

Get a taste of Canada's French side on this 700km jaunt. Ease in with a night in leafy Fredericton, before moving on to whale-watching, art, history and saucy gastronomy in Québec.

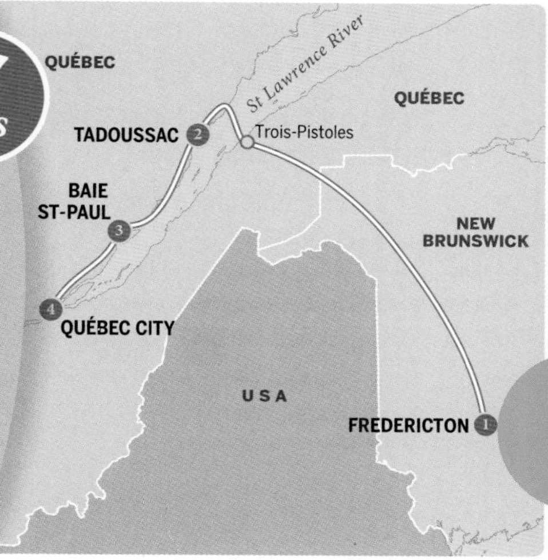

1 Fredericton (p276)

New Brunswick's capital is quaint – red-brick storefronts, rowboats on the river and concerts on the green. On Saturday, peruse the stalls at **WW Boyce Farmers Market**. Nip into **Beaverbrook Art Gallery** to see old masters and contemporary Canadian works. Sleep in a Victorian house-turned-inn on an elm-shaded street.

FREDERICTON ➔ TADOUSSAC

Car Ferry **Six and a half hours** Trans-Canada Hwy (Hwy 2) into Québec, then ferry from Trois-Pistoles.

2 Tadoussac (p249)

It's a long day of driving, and you'll need to sync with the ferry schedule to get across the St Lawrence River. Your reward is welcoming Tadoussac. It's all about **whale-watching** in this bo-ho little town. Zodiacs go out to see the humpbacks, minkes, belugas and king-of-the-sea blue whales. **Hiking** and **paddling** around the dramatic Saguenay River fjord are also big draws.

TADOUSSAC ➔ BAIE ST-PAUL

🚗 **Two hours** Hwy 138 to Hwy 362.

3 Baie St-Paul (p246)

Passing through Québec's countryside, you'll see small farms offering everything from foie gras to lamb to cheeses. Pull over for a taste or three before arriving in arty Baie St-Paul. Artists' studios, galleries and boutiques line the streets, and the **Musée d'Art Contemporain** shows contemporary works. After your arts fix, commence eating. All those farms you passed earlier supply the sublime restaurants, while local alehouses pour the drink.

BAIE ST-PAUL ➔ QUÉBEC CITY

🚗 **One and a half hours** Along Hwy 138.

4 Québec City (p234)

Romantic and history-drenched, Québec's 400-year-old walled capital enchants you into thinking you're an ocean away from North America. Walk over the old **fortifications**, photograph the turreted **Le Château Frontenac**, and sip a café au lait in the soulful **Place Royale**. Dine in the Old Lower Town before a nightcap at a jazzy corner cafe. It's easy to linger in this atmospheric city.

Left: Place Royale (p237), Québec City

7 DAYS

Halifax to Îles de la Madeleine
Island Hopper

You're never far from the sea on this 600km journey that jumps two islands (one by bridge, the other by ferry). Nova Scotia, Prince Edward Island (PEI) and Québec's Îles de la Madeleine (Magdalen Islands) are the stars.

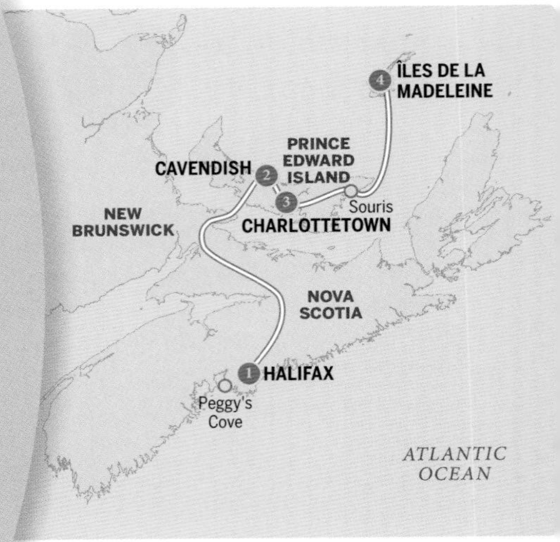

① Halifax (p264)

Wander the historic waterfront, making sure to tour **Alexander Keith's Nova Scotia Brewery** and enhance your *Titanic* knowledge at the **Maritime Museum of the Atlantic** (Halifax played a prominent role in the ship's story, as many of the dead were brought here). In the evening, fork into downtown's seafood and slow-food restaurants, then see who's playing in the live-music pubs. Make a day trip to **Peggy's Cove** for the prettiest dang lighthouse you ever did see.

HALIFAX ○ CAVENDISH

🚗 **Four hours** Hwy 102 to Hwy 104 to Hwy 16/ Confederation Bridge.

② Cavendish (p286)

After a dip into New Brunswick to access the 12.9km Confederation Bridge – presto – you're on PEI. The pastoral land mass was made famous by the 1908 novel *Anne of Green Gables,* and Cavendish is the town that pays homage to the fictional red-headed orphan. Join the groupies goggling at the gentle, creek-crossed woods and other settings, then explore the nearby **pink-sand beaches** and **Prince Edward Island National Park** bluffs. A **lobster supper** is a must; seek out one of the local community halls that sponsor them to get cracking.

CAVENDISH ○ CHARLOTTETOWN

🚗 **One hour** Along Hwy 13 and Hwy 2.

③ Charlottetown (p282)

PEI's compact, colonial capital Charlotte-town is known as the 'birthplace of Canada.' See where it all came together at **Province House National Historic Site**. Enjoy the town's inns, wharfside seafood cafes and lively pubs. The latter often host **ceilidhs** (programs of traditional Celtic music and dance).

CHARLOTTETOWN ○ ÎLES DE LA MADELEINE

Car Ferry **Six hours** Hwy 2 to Souris for ferry to islands.

④ Îles de la Madeleine (p250)

White-washed lighthouses, green hills and red sandstone cliffs dominate Québec's breezy Magdalen Islands. The ferry arrives at **Île du Cap aux Meules**, the archipelago's hub and a fine place to catch a sunset at **Cap du Phare lighthouse**. Wee Rte 199 rolls along the omnipresent blue sea and links several of the islands. **Île Du Havre Aubert** is the Magdalen's largest island, popular with kite surfers and sand-castle builders. Days are spent poking in rock pools, waving to folks in fishing villages and trying to keep your bike upright on the blustery sand spits. At night, listen for wistful Acadian songs strummed in cafes.

Left: Peggy's Cove lighthouse (p269), Nova Scotia
DMATHIES/GETTY IMAGES ©

10 DAYS

Niagara Falls to Québec City
Central Corridor

This 1100km route from Niagara Falls to Québec City swoops up Canada's largest cities, mightiest waterfalls and prettiest islands.

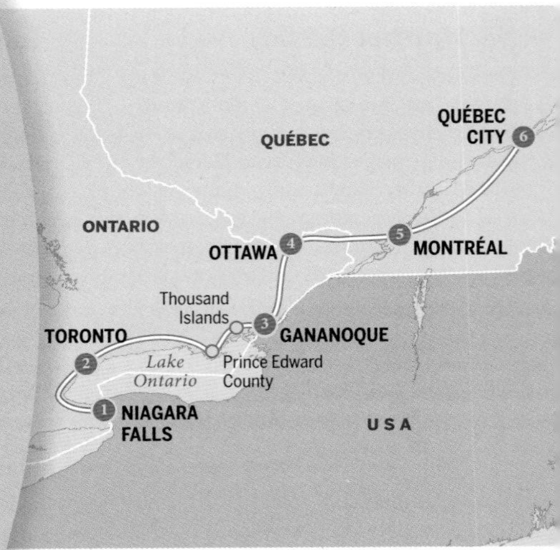

1 Niagara Falls (p177)

Kitschy but still impressive, Niagara Falls roars, pounds and spews North America's most voluminous cascade. Don a raincoat and board one of the mist-sprayed **tour boats** for a soggy full frontal, then take advantage of the region's **wineries**. More than 60 of them speckle the landscape; drive or cycle the scenic roads between vineyards.

NIAGARA FALLS ➜ TORONTO

One and a half hours Along Queen Elizabeth Way. **Two hours** Summer weekends only.

2 Toronto (p156)

Spend a few days in multicultural Toronto and wallow in the wealth of architecture, art museums, restaurants and nightclubs. Rocket up the 553m **CN Tower**, dawdle in **St Lawrence Market**, wield chopsticks in **Chinatown**, browse the vintage shops in **Kensington Market** and get a tattoo in **Queen West**.

TORONTO ➜ GANANOQUE

Three and a half hours Hwy 401 via Prince Edward County.

3 Gananoque (p185)

The misty Thousand Islands – a constellation of some 1800 rugged isles – dot the St Lawrence River. Victorian Gananoque makes a good break in their midst, where you can take **boat rides** into the archipelago. Or drive the **Thousand Islands Parkway** as it unfurls dreamy vistas. Foodies should detour to bucolic **Prince Edward County** en route.

GANANOQUE ➜ OTTAWA

Two hours Hwy 401 to Hwy 416.

Left: St Lawrence Market (p165), Toronto

4 Ottawa (p187)

Canada's vibrant capital draws applause for its museum cache. The mod, rippling **Canadian Museum of Civilization**, the fancifully arched **Canadian Museum of Nature** to the glass-walled **National Gallery of Canada** are all architectural marvels with impressive exhibits to boot. The bounteous **ByWard Market** and myriad global eateries provide sustenance.

OTTAWA ➜ MONTRÉAL

Two hours and 15 minutes Along Hwy 417 and Hwy 40. **Two hours** To Montréal's Central Station.

5 Montréal (p214)

Ah, Montréal. Canada's second-largest city is an irresistible blend of French-inspired *joie de vivre* and cosmopolitan culture. Hike up **Mont Royal**, explore the cobblestoned alleys of **Old Montréal**, and grab a seat at a boisterous **Plateau** or **Quartier Latin** cafe. Montréalers have a bacchanalian love for good food and drink, so loosen the belt.

MONTRÉAL ➜ QUÉBEC CITY

Three hours Along Hwy 20. **Three hours and 15 minutes** Montréal's Central Station to Québec City's Gare du Palais.

6 Québec City (p234)

Québec City packs unparalleled culture, history and romance into its stone walls and soulful plazas. Explore the **fortifications**, the turreted **Le Château Frontenac** and the **Old Town's** muddling maze of lanes.

2 WEEKS

Vancouver to Jasper National Park

Rocky Mountain High

Feast on a smorgasbord of scenic delights on this 1200km trek, which rises from valleys to mountains in British Columbia (BC) and Alberta.

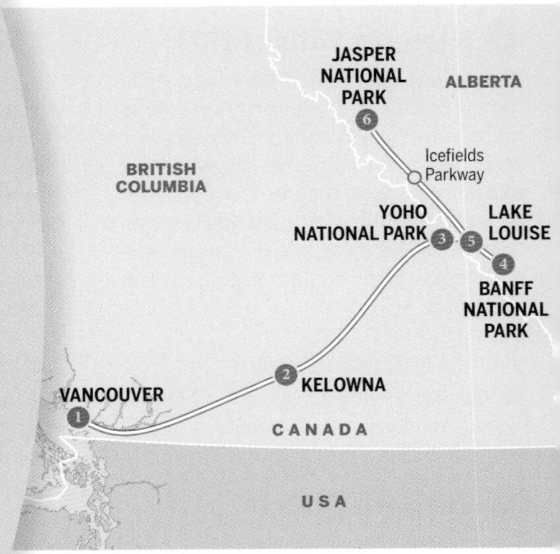

1 Vancouver (p60)

There's loads to do in mountain-meets-sea Vancouver. Hike or bike along the seawall in forested **Stanley Park**, discovering the beaches, totem poles and **Lost Lagoon**. Visit clamorous **Chinatown** for pork buns. And take your pick of freewheeling, foodie-approved restaurants and microbreweries in **Yaletown**, **Gastown** and the **West End**.

VANCOUVER ➔ KELOWNA

Five hours Hwy 1 to Hwy 5 to Hwy 97.

2 Kelowna (p105)

Make Kelowna the base for a tipple trip through the **Okanagan Valley**, famed for its 100-plus wineries and lake-speckled scenery. Check out **Summerhill Pyramid Winery**, **Quails' Gate Winery** and Syrah-licious **Mission Hill Family Estate**. Roadside fruit stands and pick-your-own cherry and peach farms line Hwy 97 in the valley's southern end.

KELOWNA ➔ YOHO NATIONAL PARK

Five and a half hours Hwy 97 to Hwy 1.

3 Yoho National Park (p132)

It may be the smallest of the Rocky Mountain national parks, but Yoho packs a big wallop of looming peaks and crashing waterfalls. **Wapta Falls** and **Lake O'Hara** are worth the hike.

YOHO NATIONAL PARK ➔ BANFF NATIONAL PARK

One hour and 15 minutes Along Hwy 1.

4 Banff National Park (p122)

Cross the border into Alberta and pull over in Banff, Canada's most-visited national park. You won't be able to stop the superlatives from flying forth: grand! majestic! awe-inspiring! Allot plenty of time for hiking, paddling, hot-springs soaking and grizzly-bear spotting (best done from a distance).

BANFF NATIONAL PARK ➔ LAKE LOUISE

45 minutes Along Bow Valley Pkwy (Hwy 1A). **One hour**.

5 Lake Louise (p127)

Bluer-than-blue Lake Louise is a must-see, surrounded by alpine-style teahouses that fuel day hikers with scones and hot chocolate. There are actually multiple lakes to hike to, including deep-teal **Moraine Lake** and **Mirror Lake**. Feeling lazy? The **Sightseeing Gondola** will do the hard work, and you'll still get those lake-and-glacier snapshots.

LAKE LOUISE ➔ JASPER NATIONAL PARK

Three hours Along Hwy 93, aka Icefields Parkway. **Four hours**.

6 Jasper National Park (p134)

Peer into extreme-blue **Peyto Lake**, gape at the gothic, glacier-strewn **Columbia Icefield** and walk over **Athabasca Glacier** – those are just the things to do on the way to Jasper. The park itself is bigger and less crowded than Banff, and offers superb hiking and bear, elk and moose watching, as well as horseback riding, mountain biking and rafting.

Left: Moraine Lake (p129), Banff National Park

MATTHEW CROWLEY PHOTOGRAPHY/GETTY IMAGES ©

Québec City to Vancouver Trans-Canada Highway

3 WEEKS

The Trans-Canada is the world's longest highway, a whopping belt of asphalt cinched around Canada's girth. Scenic stretches alternate with mundane ones. Pack patience and good tunes.

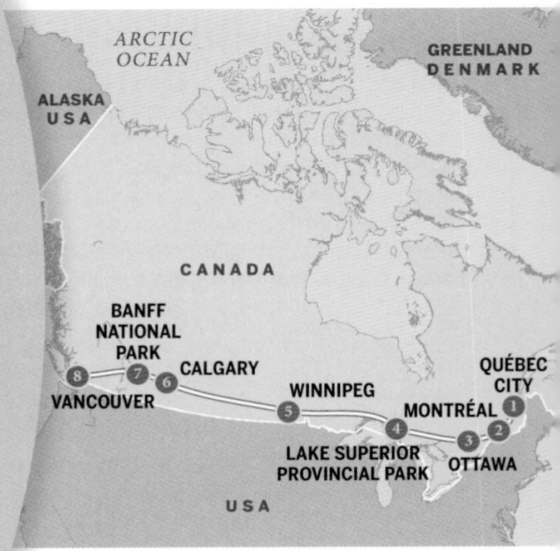

1 Québec City (p234)

Why not start where French Canada started, in Québec's 400-year-old walled capital? Check out the **fortifications**, **citadel** and turreted **Le Château Frontenac**. Walk the **Old Town's** labyrinth of lanes and get lost amid the street performers and cozy inns, stopping every so often for a café au lait, flaky pastry or heaping plate of poutine (fries covered in cheese curds and gravy).

QUÉBEC CITY ➔ MONTRÉAL

🚗 **Three hours** Along Hwy 20. 🚆 **Three hours and 15 minutes** Québec City's Gare du Palais to Montréal's Central Station.

2 Montréal (p214)

Canada's second-largest city and its cultural heart, Montréal buzzes with a mix of sophistication, playfulness and history-soaked preserved quarters. Hike up **Mont Royal**, explore **Old Montréal's** basilicas and plazas, and indulge at a happening **Plateau** or **Quartier Latin** cafe. Arrive in summer and groove to the Montréal Jazz Festival, Just for Laughs Festival or another city-enveloping event.

MONTRÉAL ➔ OTTAWA

🚗 **Two hours and 15 minutes** Along Hwy 40 and Hwy 417. 🚆 **Two hours** From Montréal's Central Station.

3 Ottawa (p187)

Go museum-crazy in Canada's striking capital, taking in the superb architectural feats of **Parliament Hill**, the **Canadian Museum of Civilization** and the **National Gallery of Canada**. For eats, fill up in the **ByWard Market** and array of international restaurants. Join the ice skaters on the **Rideau Canal** if it's winter.

OTTAWA ➔ LAKE SUPERIOR PROVINCIAL PARK

🚗 **10 hours** Along Hwy 17.

4 Lake Superior Provincial Park (p202)

The scenery turns transcendent as the road skirts Lake Superior and coasts through the eponymous provincial park. Wispy beard-like fog and shivering arctic trees give it a distinctly primeval flavor. Day hikes reward with isolated **beaches**, gushing **waterfalls** and mysterious, red-ochre **pictographs**.

Left: Downtown Calgary (p143)
WITOLD SKRYPCZAK/GETTY IMAGES ©

LAKE SUPERIOR PROVINCIAL PARK ➔ WINNIPEG

🚗 **13 and a half hours** Along Hwy 17 in Ontario, Hwy 1 in Manitoba.

5 Winnipeg (p293)

Not long after the highway enters the prairie flatlands of Manitoba, Winnipeg rockets up and provides an enlivening patch of cafes and culture. Linger over the mighty Inuit collection at **Winnipeg Art Gallery**, the riverside trails and museums of the **Forks National Historic Site**, and the impressive **fringe theater** scene.

WINNIPEG ➔ CALGARY

🚗 **13 and a half hours** Along Hwy 1. *Plane* **Two hours and 15 minutes**.

6 Calgary (p143)

Put on your cowboy boots before arriving in Calgary, a ranching center overtaken by the big new biz in town: oil. Brash and shiny, it's a good place to refuel on a thick-cut steak and peruse the intriguing western art, history and pop culture exhibits in **Glenbow Museum**.

CALGARY ➔ BANFF NATIONAL PARK

🚗 **One and a half hours** Along Hwy 1. 🚌 **Two hours**.

7 Banff National Park (p122)

Banff is Canada's most-visited national park, and it's easy to see why. Head for the turquoise lakes and white-dipped mountains and prepare to be overwhelmed by breath-catching panoramas. Hiking, paddling, hot-springs soaking and grizzly-bear spotting are the to-do's.

BANFF NATIONAL PARK ➔ VANCOUVER

🚗 **9 and a half hours** Along Hwy 1. 🚌 14 hours Along Hwy 1. 🚆 **Two days** Calgary to Vancouver on Rocky Mountaineer.

8 Vancouver (p60)

Skiable mountains rise on the outskirts of this laid-back metropolis, while beaches fringe the core. The seawalled rainforest at **Stanley Park** is perfect for hiking and biking past totem poles and the occasional seal. **Chinatown** offers tasty Asian food and one-of-a-kind shopping. **Yaletown**, **Gastown** and the **West End** are there with seafood-enriched cuisine and microbrews.

Month by Month

Top Events

Montréal Jazz Festival, June

Québec City's Winter Carnival, February

Stratford Theater Festival, April–November

Calgary Stampede, July

Celtic Colours, October

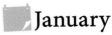

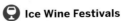

January

Ice Wine Festivals

British Columbia's Okanagan Valley (www.thewinefestivals.com) and Ontario's Niagara Peninsula (www.niagarawinefestival.com) celebrate their ice wines with good-time festivals. The distinctive, sweet libations go down the hatch amid chestnut roasts, cocktail competitions and cozy alpine-lodge ambience.

February

Chinese New Year

Dragons dance, firecrackers burst and food sizzles in the country's Chinatowns. Vancouver (www.vancouver-chinatown.com) hosts the biggest celebration, but Toronto, Calgary, Ottawa and Montréal also have festivities. The lunar calendar determines the date.

Québec City's Winter Carnival

Revelers watch ice-sculpture competitions, hurtle down snow slides, go ice fishing and cheer on their favorite paddlers in an insane canoe race on the half-frozen, ice floe–ridden St-Lawrence River. It's the world's biggest winter fest (www.carnaval.qc.ca).

Winterlude in Ottawa

At this snowy bash along the Rideau Canal, skaters glide by on the 7km of groomed ice. When not sipping hot chocolate and eating beavertails (fried, sugared dough), the townsfolk build a massive village entirely of ice (www.canadas-capital.gc.ca/winterlude).

March

Vancouver Wine Festival

Vancouver uncorks 1700 wines from 200 vintners at the Vancouver International Wine Festival

(left) February Chinese New Year
MICHAEL WHEATLEY/GETTY IMAGES ©

(www.vanwinefest.ca). You're drinking for art's sake, since the event raises funds for the city's contemporary theater company.

April

Stratford Theater Festival

Canada's Stratford, a few hours outside Toronto, nearly outdoes England's Stratford-upon-Avon. The Stratford Festival (www.stratfordfestival.ca) runs from April to November, with four theaters staging contemporary drama, music, operas and, of course, works by Shakespeare. Productions are first-rate and feature well-known actors.

World Ski & Snowboard Festival

Whistler hosts 10 days of adrenaline events, outdoor rock and hip-hop concerts, film screenings, dog parades and a whole lotta carousing (www.wssf.com). Heed the motto: Party in April. Sleep in May.

Hot Docs

Toronto hosts North America's largest documentary film festival (www.hotdocs.ca), screening 170-plus docos from around the globe.

May

Canadian Tulip Festival

After a long winter, Ottawa bursts with color – more than three million tulips of 200 types blanket the city for the Canadian Tulip Festival (www.tulipfestival.ca). Festivities include parades, regattas, car rallies, dances, concerts and fireworks.

June

Luminato

For 10 days in early June, big-name musicians, dancers, artists, writers, actors and filmmakers descend on Toronto for a celebration of creativity that reflects the city's diversity (www.luminatofestival.com).

North by Northeast

Around 1000 emerging indie bands spill off the stages in Toronto's coolest clubs. Film screenings and comedy shows add to the mix. Over its 20-year history, NXNE (www.nxne.com) has become a must on the music-industry calendar.

Montréal Jazz Festival

Two million music lovers descend on Montréal in late June, when the heart of downtown explodes with jazz and blues for 11 straight days (www.montrealjazzfest.com). Most concerts are outdoors and free, and the party goes on round the clock.

Pride Toronto

Toronto's most flamboyant event (www.pridetoronto.com) celebrates all kinds of sexuality, climaxing with an out-of-the-closet Dyke March and the outrageous Pride Parade. Pride's G-spot is in the Church-Wellesley Village; most events are free.

Elvis Festival

If you're in Penticton, BC in late June and you keep seeing Elvis, rest assured it's not because you've swilled too much of the local Okanagan Valley wine. The town hosts Elvis Fest (www.pentictonelvisfestival.com) with dozens of impersonators and open-mike sing-alongs.

July

Country Music in Cavendish

Some of the biggest names in country music come to Prince Edward Island (PEI) for the Cavendish Beach Festival (www.cavendishbeachmusic.com). They croon beachside while campers get their party on. This is one of the largest outdoor music festivals in North America, and the island swells with people.

Montréal Comedy Festival

Everyone gets giddy for two weeks at the Just for Laughs Festival (www.hahaha.com), which features hundreds of comedy shows, including free ones in the Quartier Latin. The biggest names in the biz yuck it up for this one.

Calgary Stampede

Raging bulls, chuckwagon racing and bad-ass, boot-wearing cowboys unite for the 'Greatest Outdoor Show on Earth.' A midway of rides and games makes it a family affair well beyond the usual rodeo event, attracting 1.1 million yee-hawin' fans (www.calgarystampede.com).

Winnipeg Fringe Festival

North America's second-largest fringe fest (www.winnipegfringe.com) stages creative, raw and oddball works from a global line-up of performers. Comedy, drama, music, cabaret and even musical memoirs are on tap over 12 days.

August

⭐ Edmonton Fringe Festival

North America's largest fringe bash, staging some 1600 performances of wild, uncensored shows over 11 days in mid-August. Acts are democratically chosen by lottery (www.fringetheatreadventures.ca).

◉ Canadian National Exhibition

Akin to a state fair in the USA, 'The Ex' (www.theex.com) features more than 700 exhibitors, agricultural shows, lumberjack competitions, outdoor concerts and carnivalia at Toronto's Exhibition Place. The 18-day event runs through Labour Day and ends with a bang-up fireworks display.

 September

✖ PEI Fall Flavours

This island-wide kitchen party merges toe-tapping traditional music with incredible seafood at events over the course of three weeks (www.fallflavours.ca). In Charlottetown, don't miss the oyster-shucking championships or the chowder challenge.

⭐ Toronto International Film Festival

Toronto's prestigious 10-day celebration (www.tiff.net) is a major cinematic event. Films of all lengths and styles are screened in September, as celebs shimmy between gala events and the Bell Lightbox building. Buy tickets well in advance.

⭐ Canadian Deep Roots Festival

Tune in to Mi'kmaw, Acadian, African–Nova Scotian and other unique music – all with local roots – in the fun university town of Wolfville,

Nova Scotia (www.deeprootsmusic.ca). Workshops are available with some of the performers, so you can learn to drum, strum or fiddle.

October

Celtic Colours

With foot-stompin' music amid riotous foliage, this roving festival in Cape Breton attracts top musicians from Scotland, Spain and other countries with Celtic connections (www.celtic-colours.com). Community suppers, step-dancing classes and tin whistle lessons round out the cultural celebration.

November

Canadian Finals Rodeo

If you missed the Calgary Stampede, here's your other chance to see top cowboys test their skills with bucking broncos, steer wrestling and lasso throwdowns (www.canadianfinalsrodeo.com). Held in Edmonton mid-month.

December

Mountain Time

Powder hounds hit the slopes from east to west. Whistler in BC, Mont-Tremblant in Québec and the Canadian Rockies around Banff, Alberta, pull the biggest crowds, but there's downhill action going on in every province (snowboarding and cross-country skiing, too).

Winter Festival of Lights

The family-friendly Winter Festival of Lights (www.wfol.com) in Niagara Falls gets everyone in the holiday spirit with three million twinkling bulbs and 125 animated displays brightening the town and the waterfall itself. Ice-skate on the 'rink at the brink' of the cascade.

Far left: November Canadian Finals Rodeo **Left: June** Montréal Jazz Festival

What's New

For this new edition of Discover Canada, our authors hunted down the fresh, the transformed, the hot and the happening. Here are a few of our favorites. For up-to-the-minute recommendations, see lonelyplanet.com/canada.

1 LEGACY TRAIL, ALBERTA
The paved trail between Banff and Canmore runs parallel to Hwy 1 and is ideal for people who want to undertake safe, easy cycling through splendid mountain scenery. (p123)

2 PARKBUS, ONTARIO
You no longer need to rent a car in Toronto to reach Algonquin and Killarney parks, or Tobermory on the Bruce Peninsula. Parkbus now offers a low-cost transportation alternative. (p349)

3 ROBERT BATEMAN CENTRE, BRITISH COLUMBIA
Victoria's new Robert Bateman Centre showcases the work – and campaigning environmentalism – of Canada's leading nature painter. Dozens of photo-realistic artworks capture animals and landscapes in British Columbia and beyond. (p88)

4 RIO TINTO PLANETARIUM, QUÉBEC
Making stars look sexy, Montréal's $48-million planetarium marries art and science with a theatrical light-and-sound show that makes good use of brand-new, state-of-the-art equipment. (p223)

5 YELLOWKNIFE BAY FLOATING B&B, NORTHWEST TERRITORIES
Join the houseboaters on Great Slave Lake by staying in this floating B&B: utter relaxation just a short paddle from the center of town. (867-444-8464; www.ykbayfloatingbnb.com; s/d/apt $125/150/225;)

6 RIPLEY'S AQUARIUM OF CANADA, ONTARIO
Fearsome sharks, graceful stingrays and good ol' Canadian largemouth bass are among the creatures swimming in this aquarium next to the CN Tower in Toronto. (p157)

7 HUDSON'S ON FIRST, BRITISH COLUMBIA
Set in the wee town of Duncan in the slow-food-lovin' Cowichan Valley, this little farm-to-table eatery is gaining a big reputation thanks to 'Top Chef' Daniel Hudson. (p96)

8 RELUCTANT CHEF, NEWFOUNDLAND
The dishes always vary at this little St John's restaurant, but count on an eight-course, three-hour, locally sourced feast with 30 other chowhounds under a sparkly chandelier. (p297)

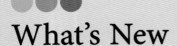

Get Inspired

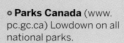

Books

- **The View from Castle Rock** (2006) Alice Munro won the 2013 Nobel Prize for literature; this book of short stories shows why.
- **Indian Horse** (2012) Richard Wagamese's novel follows a culturally displaced Ojibway boy who grows up to become a hockey star.
- **Anne of Green Gables** (1908) Lucy Maud Montgomery's tale of a spunky, pigtailed orphan has made Prince Edward Island a pilgrimage site.
- **In the Skin of a Lion** (1987) Michael Ondaatje's story of the immigrants who built Toronto c 1920.

Films

- **Incendies** (2010) Québec siblings travel to the Middle East and uncover their immigrant mother's tortured history.
- **Away from Her** (2006) Alzheimer's breaks apart a rural Ontario couple.
- **C.R.A.Z.Y.** (2005) A teen misfit in 1970s Montréal dreams of a brighter future.

Music

- **Live at Massey Hall 1971** (2007) Canadian legend Neil Young's 1971 acoustic concert in Toronto, featuring a set list of wistful classics.
- **Moving Pictures** (1981) Rush's defining prog-rock album vaulted them into the 'Limelight.'
- **Mass Romantic** (2000) The debut of Vancouver's power pop 'indie supergroup' The New Pornographers.
- **Songs of Love and Hate** (1971) Leonard Cohen's most intense album, full of acoustic guitar and poetic lyrics.

Websites

- **Environment Canada Weather** (www.weather.gc.ca) Forecasts for any town.
- **Lonely Planet** (www.lonelyplanet.com/canada) Destination information, hotel bookings, traveler forum.
- **Government of Canada** (www.canada.ca) National and regional information.
- **Parks Canada** (www.pc.gc.ca) Lowdown on all national parks.
- **Canadian Broadcasting Corporation** (www.cbc.ca) National and provincial news.

Short on time?

This list will give you an instant insight into Canada.

Read *The Apprenticeship of Duddy Kravitz* (1959) is Mordechai Richler's novel about a Jewish boy questing for success in Montréal.

Watch *Bon Cop, Bad Cop* (2006), about an Anglophone and Francophone cracking a case together, is one of Canada's top-grossing films.

Listen Arcade Fire's *Reflektor* (2013) may be long and indulgent, but the Montréal band still rocks it.

Log on The Canadian Tourism Commission (www.canada.travel) operates the country's official travel site.

Top: Street performer, Vancouver
CHRIS CHEADLE/GETTY IMAGES ©

Need to Know

Currency
Canadian dollars ($)

Language
English and French

Visas
Generally not required for stays of up to 180 days; some nationalities require a temporary resident visa.

Money
ATMs widely available. Credit cards accepted in most hotels and restaurants.

Mobile Phones
Local SIM cards can be used in European and Australian phones. Other phones must be set to roaming.

Wi-Fi
Widely available. Common in most lodgings and in cafes. Generally free.

Internet Access
Main tourist areas have internet cafes; access costs $2 to $4 per hour.

Tipping
Tipping is standard practice; about 15% to 20% of the bill.

When to Go

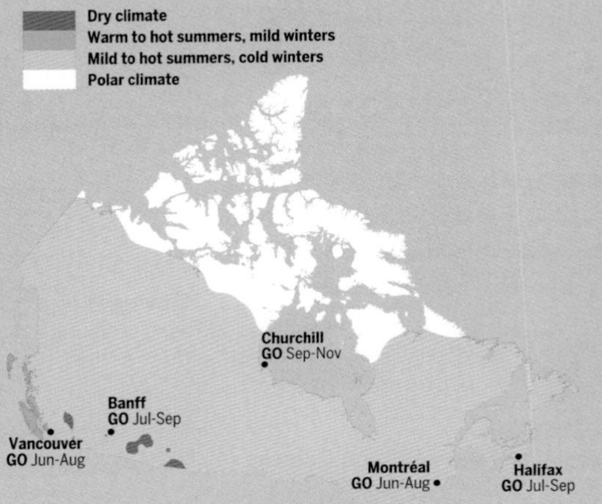

High Season
(Jun–Aug)

- Warm weather prevails; far northern regions briefly thaw
- Accommodation prices peak (30% up on average)
- December through March is busy and expensive in ski resort towns

Shoulder
(May, Sep & Oct)

- Crowds and prices drop off
- Temperatures are cool but comfortable
- Attractions keep shorter hours
- Fall foliage areas (ie Cape Breton, Québec) remain busy

Low Season
(Nov–Apr)

- Places outside the big cities and ski resorts close
- Darkness and cold take over
- April and November are good for travel bargains

Advance Planning

- **Three months before** Book accommodation and tickets for Montréal's Jazz Festival; Churchill train tickets during polar bear season; Rocky Mountain train tickets during summer.
- **One month before** Secure lodging and a rental car, especially in summer.
- **Two weeks before** Book activities in busy spots like Banff and Whistler; theater tickets in Toronto and Montréal; ferries in British Columbia (BC) and Nova Scotia.

Your Daily Costs

Budget less than $100

- Dorm bed: $25-40
- Campsite: $25-35
- Self-catered meals: $8-12

Midrange $100–250

- B&B or midrange hotel: $80-180 ($100-250 in major cities)
- Meal in a good local restaurant: from $20 plus drinks
- Rental car: $35-65 per day
- Attraction admissions: $5-20

Top end more than $250

- Four-star hotel room: from $180 (from $250 in major cities)
- Three-course meal in a top restaurant: from $50 plus drinks
- Skiing day-pass: $50-80

Exchange Rates

Australia	A$1	C$0.93
Europe	€1	C$1.38
Japan	¥100	C$1.05
New Zealand	NZ$1	C$0.81
UK	UK£1	C$1.59
USA	US$1	C$1.04

For current exchange rates see www.xe.com.

What to Bring

- **Warm clothing** Canada is one of the coldest places on the planet. Even in summer it can get chilly, especially on the coasts and in the Rockies.
- **Rain gear** Coastal BC and the Maritimes tend toward rain.
- **Binoculars** You want to see those moose, bears and whales up close, right?
- **Insect repellent** Important if you're visiting northern or woodsy regions in summer, when black flies and mosquitoes can be a major annoyance.

Arriving in Canada

- **Toronto Pearson Airport**

Express buses To downtown every 20 to 30 minutes from 6am to midnight ($28).

Taxis 45 minutes to downtown (around $60).

- **Montréal Trudeau Airport**

Buses To downtown every 10 to 12 minutes 8:30am to 8pm, every 30 to 60 minutes other times ($9).

Taxis 30 to 60 minutes to downtown (flat rate of $40).

- **Vancouver International Airport**

Trains To downtown every 6 to 20 minutes ($7.50 to $9).

Taxis 30 minutes to downtown (around $40).

- **Land Border Crossings**

The Canadian Border Services Agency (p346) posts wait times (usually 30 minutes).

Getting Around

- **Car** Extensive highway system. Major rental car companies readily available.
- **Train** Outside the Toronto–Montréal corridor, train travel is mostly for scenic journeys.
- **Ferry** Public ferry systems operate extensively in BC, Québec and the Maritime provinces.

Sleeping

- **B&Bs** (*'gîtes'* in French) Common in Canada. Standards vary; most have private bathrooms and a two-night minimum-stay requirement.
- **Hotels** Most are part of international chains, catering to high-end and business travelers. Rooms have cable TV and wi-fi.
- **Inns** Like B&Bs, but with more rooms available.
- **Motels** More common outside the big cities. Good-value rooms; typically less stylish and amenity-laden than hotels.

Be Forewarned

- **Summertime** Transportation (rental car, ferry) and sleeping reservations a must July/August.
- **Distances** Canada's immense scale means travel distances can be long and travel times slow due to single-lane highways and ferries.

Vancouver & British Columbia

British Columbia (BC) visitors need a long list of superlatives when describing their trips – the words spectacular, breathtaking and jaw-dropping only go so far. But it's hard not to be moved by towering mountains, wildlife-packed forests and dramatic coastlines that slow your heart like sigh-triggering spa treatments. Canada's westernmost province is more than just nature-hugging dioramas, though.

Cosmopolitan Vancouver fuses cuisines and cultures from Asia and beyond, while vibrant smaller communities such as historic Victoria, surf-loving Tofino and the wine-sipping Okanagan Valley lure ever-curious travelers. And for sheer character, it's hard to beat rustic Haida Gwaii or the winter wonderland of Whistler, one of the world's great ski resorts.

Wherever you head, the great outdoors will always call. Don't just point your camera at it. BC is unbeatable for the kind of life-enhancing skiing, kayaking and hiking that can easily make this the trip of a lifetime.

Downtown Vancouver
H. PIORKOWSKI/GETTY IMAGES ©

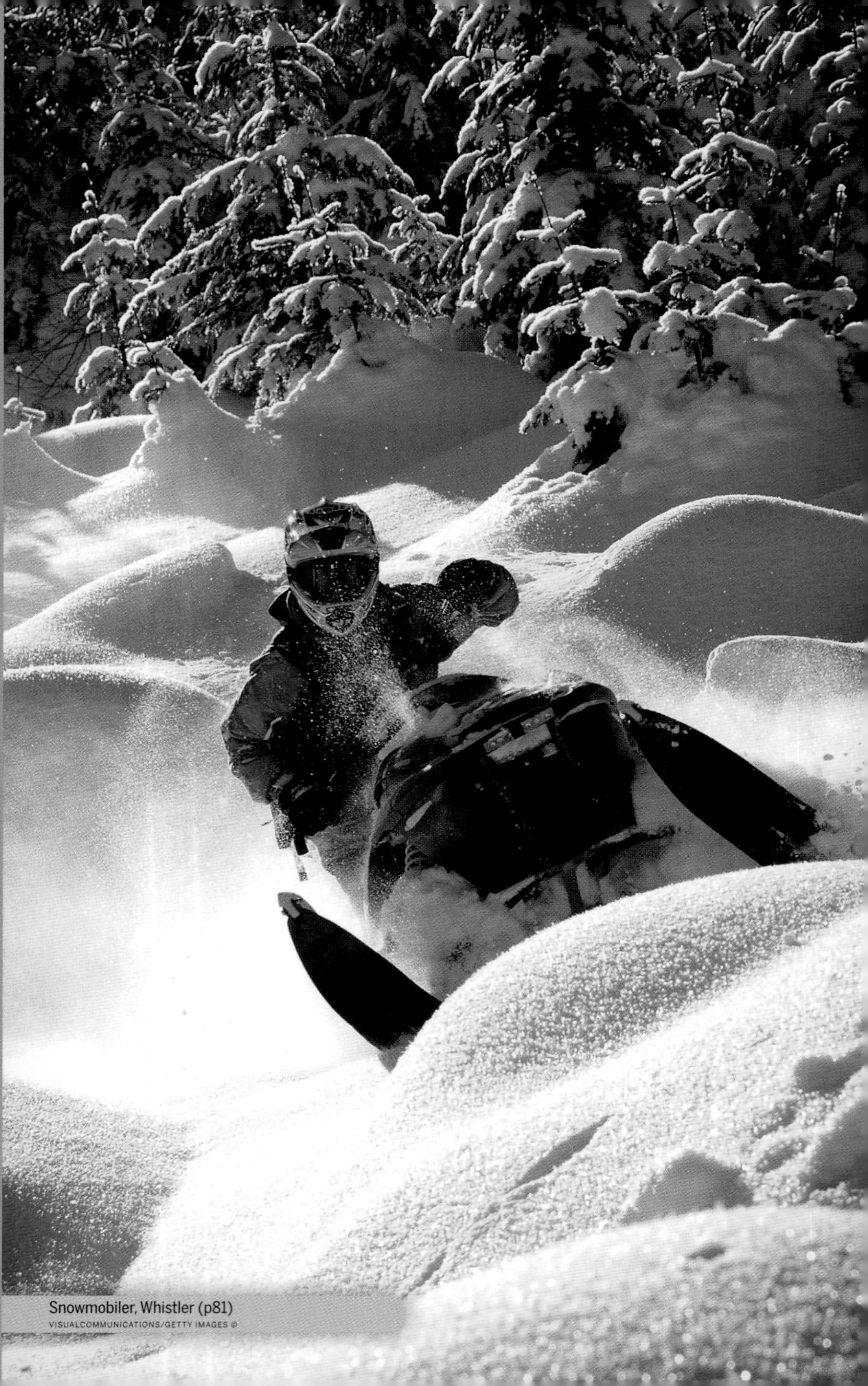

Snowmobiler, Whistler (p81)
VISUALCOMMUNICATIONS/GETTY IMAGES ©

Vancouver & British Columbia

Vancouver & BC's Highlights

Vancouver

Hip neighborhoods meet gob-smacking nature in BC's main city (p60). Ski Grouse Mountain (p79) or hike in Stanley Park's rainforest (p61) – both feel wild and remote but are within minutes from downtown. Wander Vancouver's beaches, trawl Granville Island Public Market (p66), and sample the region's abundance: wild salmon and local craft beers feature prominently.

Below: Lost Lagoon, Stanley Park (p61)

1

2

Whistler

Canada's favorite ski resort (p81) combines a gabled, Christmas-card village with jaw-dropping dual-mountain terrain that thrills everyone from beginners to grizzled veterans. Come summer, daredevils swap skis for mountain bikes to swoop down the slopes. Groovy neighborhoods like Function Junction entertain after the action, letting folks hang out over a beer to compare stories and bruises.

RANDY LINCKS/GETTY IMAGES ©

CHRIS CHEADLE/GETTY IMAGES ©

3 Victoria & Around

Fueled by an increasingly younger demographic, a quiet revolution has taken place in BC's capital Victoria (p87), transforming stodgy tourist pubs and shops into innovative restaurants and artisan markets. The vibe extends beyond city boundaries, especially in the nearby Cowichan Valley (p95), a slow-food mecca of cheese makers, chili growers, beekeepers, wineries and cideries. You can't help but relax – and eat and drink well – out here.

Right: Cherry Point Vineyards (p96), Cowichan Valley

CHRIS CHEADLE/GETTY IMAGES ©

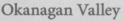

4 Okanagan Valley

The moniker 'Canada's Napa Valley' is oft repeated and somewhat apt. Once a locals-only secret, the blossoming fruit and wine region (p102) has grown to include many nationally and internationally celebrated vineyards. Most visitors weave around the tasting rooms by car or by bicycle, but the region's lakeside hills are idyllic whether or not you fancy a tipple. Orchards continue the sweet theme with their bounty of apples and peaches.

5 Tofino

A magnet for surf-loving dudes and dudettes for decades, Tofino (p100) is dramatically licked by the frothing Pacific Ocean throughout the year: hit Long Beach whether or not you have a board and you'll be sucked into one of Canada's most awe-inspiring waterfront vistas. The town itself is a hippy-chic hamlet of cool eateries and galleries and is dripping with adventures like kayaking and whale watching.

Vancouver & BC's Best...

Restaurants for Local Fare

- **Hawksworth** Vancouver's movers and shakers mingle over the seasonal tasting menu. (p73)
- **Hudson's on First** Gets its goods from the surrounding abundance of the Cowichan Valley. (p96)
- **Ulla** Victoria's cookbook-strewn eatery serves BC halibut and lamb, plus a bounty of organic veggies. (p93)
- **Araxi Restaurant & Bar** Okanagan apple cheesecake, BC halibut and Salt Spring Island cheese in Whistler. (p85)

Wineries

- **Quails' Gate Winery** Charming, mid-sized winery with excellent pinot noir. (p104)
- **Summerhill Pyramid Winery** With its own 'aging pyramid'; sparkling whites recommended. (p104)
- **Cherry Point Vineyards** Star Vancouver Island vineyard with wines – and a great patio. (p96)
- **Merridale Estate Cidery** OK, not a winery, but an inviting apple-cider producer that also makes brandy. (p96)

Waterfronts

- **Tofino** Dramatic wave-licked surf beaches. (p100)
- **Stanley Park Seawall** Forest-fringed seafront path. (p61)
- **English Bay Beach** Vancouver's favorite summertime hangout. (p61)
- **Parksville & Qualicum** Family-friendly beach-studded stretch. (p99)
- **Sunshine Coast** Idyll of little communities; popular with kayakers. (p74)

Skiing

- **Whistler** Canada's top ski resort, with an amazing array of accessible terrain and a great village vibe. (p81)
- **Big White Ski Resort** Attractively secluded 118-run resort loved by skiers and snowboarders alike. (p107)
- **Grouse Mountain** Twenty minutes from downtown Vancouver, it's the city's favorite winter playground. (p79)
- **Apex Mountain Resort** Best small ski resort in the region, with 68 runs. (p105)

Left: Kayaker, Sunshine Coast (p74); **Below:** Grouse Mountain (p79)

(LEFT) HENRY GEORGI/GETTY IMAGES ©; (ABOVE) RON WATTS/GETTY IMAGES ©

Need to Know

ADVANCE PLANNING

- **One month before** Book accommodation for summer travel.
- **Two weeks before** Book activities in busy destinations such as Vancouver and Whistler.
- **One week before** Make restaurant reservations at high-end eateries.

RESOURCES

- **BC Parks** (www.bcparks.ca) Information, resources and activities for the province's 830 parks.
- **Destination British Columbia** (www.hellobc.com) Community information, activities, guides and accommodation booking.
- **Tourism Vancouver** (www.tourismvancouver.com) Blogs, listings and accommodation bookings in BC's biggest city.
- **BC Wine Institute** (www.winebc.com) Information on wineries and festivals across BC.
- **Cycling BC** (www.cyclingbc.net) Resources for cyclists.
- **Surfing Vancouver Island** (www.surfingvancouverisland.com) Videos and tips on the region's surfing culture.

GETTING AROUND

- **Fly** Vancouver International Airport is a hub for travel across the region: services go to Victoria, Kelowna, Haida Gwaii and beyond. Floatplane services run from downtown Vancouver across the region.
- **Car** Extensive highway system links most towns, with all major hire-car companies available.
- **Ferry** World's largest public ferry system links the mainland with Vancouver Island and throughout BC.
- **Train** VIA Rail services across Canada to Vancouver via Jasper. Seasonal services from Vancouver to Whistler and Vancouver to the Rockies via Banff on *Rocky Mountaineer* (www.rockymountaineer.com).

BE FOREWARNED

- **BC Ferries** (www.bcferries.com) will reduce services on some routes, including to the Southern Gulf Islands and Haida Gwaii, in 2014. Book in advance online (usually a $15 fee) to ensure you get a spot.

Vancouver & BC Itineraries

For a taste of BC, take a three-day mainland-and-island loop covering the two main cities and many small towns. Then, visit the spectacular Okanagan wine region, sampling Canada's best tipples and finest fruit.

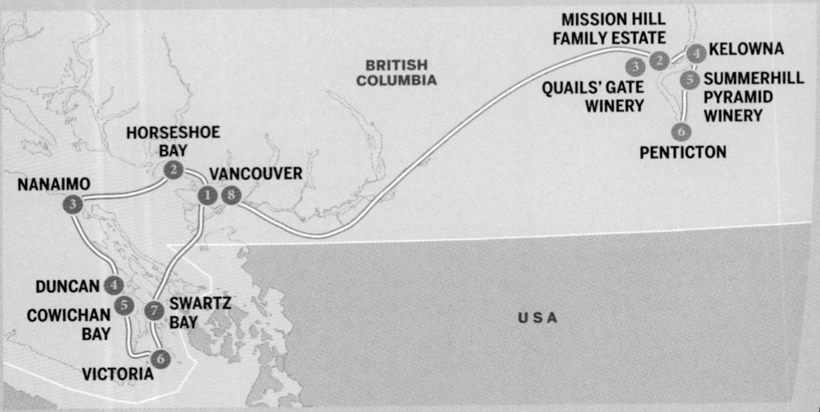

3 DAYS — VANCOUVER TO VANCOUVER
MINI BC CIRCLE TOUR

Don't leave ❶ **Vancouver** (p60) before taking a morning stroll along the seawall in Stanley Park. Then drive through the park and across the Lions Gate Bridge to West Vancouver's ❷ **Horseshoe Bay** (p80). Aboard the Nanaimo-bound ferry slide across the glassy waters to Vancouver Island. Get off at ❸ **Nanaimo** (p96), good for a museum browse and spin through the Old City Quarter, then take Hwy 1 down the island. Drop into the Cowichan Valley, known for its wineries and slow food restaurants. The valley's colorful small communities of ❹ **Duncan** (p95) and ❺ **Cowichan Bay** (p96) are good spots to pull over for the evening.

Next day, continue south to BC's capital ❻ **Victoria** (p87) for your next sleepover – two nights is recommended if you want to explore all the attractions and activities and enjoy the city's great restaurants. Conclude your circle tour with a drive to the ❼ **Swartz Bay** (p94) ferry terminal, where you'll have another idyllic sea crossing back to the mainland. From the dock, follow the signs and you'll be back in Vancouver within the hour. Toast your journey, and check out all your digital photos, over a regional microbrewed beer in ❽ **Gastown** (p76), the city's old town area.

VANCOUVER TO KELOWNA

5 DAYS

WINE WEAVE THROUGH THE OKANAGAN

Follow the three-day itinerary, then depart eastward from ❶ **Vancouver** (p60) on Hwy 1 – then Hwys 5 and 97 – through BC's farmland interior. If the Cowichan Valley gave you a taste for local wine, you're about to hit the motherlode: just make sure one of you is a designated driver. It's around 380km to the Okanagan Valley. Your first reward for the long drive awaits in the lakefront community of Westbank, home of ❷ **Mission Hill Family Estate** (p104) winery, where Bordeaux and syrah swirl in glasses.

Check out nearby ❸ **Quails' Gate Winery** (p104), then continue along Hwy 97 over the bridge into ❹ **Kelowna** (p105), a good base. From here, spend your time puttering around the verdant region. Include side trips south of Kelowna to ❺ **Summerhill Pyramid Winery** (p104) and on to ❻ **Penticton** (p102), with its beaches and inner tube floating (and Elvis impersonators, if you're visiting in June). This area grows Canada's best fresh fruit – watch for roadside markets selling peaches, apples or cherries. By this stage, you'll be considering moving here: have another glass of wine and hit the Citizenship and Immigration Canada website.

Quails' Gate Winery (p104), overlooking Okanagan Lake

Discover Vancouver & British Columbia

At a Glance

- **Vancouver** BC's main metropolis with city parks and waterfront trails.
- **Whistler** (p81) Spectacular skiing and snowboarding country.
- **Vancouver Island** (p87) Victoria, Tofino and many colorful communities in between.
- **Okanagan Valley** (p102) Verdant fruit, winery and lakefront country.
- **Haida Gwaii** (p107) Mystical northern islands with rich First Nations culture.

Totem poles in Stanley Park
AL HARVEY/GETTY IMAGES ©

VANCOUVER

Swooping into Vancouver International Airport on a cloud-free summer's day, it's easy to appreciate the idea that this is a nature-bound utopia that deserves to be recognized as one of the world's best places to live. Gently rippling ocean crisscrossed with ferry trails, the crenulated shorelines of dozens of forest-green islands and the ever-present sentinels of snow-dusted crags glinting on the horizon give this city arguably the most spectacular setting of any metropolis on the planet.

While the city's twinkling outdoor backdrop means you're never far from great skiing, kayaking or hiking, there's much more to Vancouver than appearances. Hitting the streets on foot means you'll come across a kaleidoscope of distinctive neighborhoods, each one almost like a village in itself. This diversity is Vancouver's main strength and a major reason why visitors keep coming back for more. If you're a first timer, soak in the breathtaking views and hit the verdant forests whenever you can, but also save time to join the locals and do a little exploring off the beaten track; it's in these places that you'll discover what really makes this beautiful metropolis special.

Sights

DOWNTOWN

Canada Place Landmark

(Map p64; www.canadaplace.ca; 999 Canada Place Way; M Waterfront) Vancouver's version of the Sydney Opera House, this iconic landmark is shaped like a series of sails. A cruise-ship terminal, it's also a pier where you can stroll

Vancouver for Children

Pick up a copy of the free *Kids' Guide Vancouver* flyer from racks around town and visit www.kidsvancouver.com for tips, resources and family-focused events.

Stanley Park (p61) can keep most families occupied for a full day. If it's hot, make sure you hit the water park at Lumberman's Arch or try the swimming pool at Second Beach; also consider the **Miniature Railway** (**Map p62; adult/child from $5; hours vary; 19**) for a fun trundle. The park is a great place to bring a picnic, and its beaches especially are highly kid-friendly. Save time for the Vancouver Aquarium (p61) and, if your kids have been good, consider a behind-the-scenes trainer tour.

The city's other educational family-friendly attractions – the kind where your moppets get educated without even noticing – include Science World (p63) and the HR MacMillan Space Centre (p67).

the waterfront for camera-triggering North Shore mountain vistas. The adjoining grass-roofed convention center expansion opened in 2010. The nearby plaza houses the tripod-like Olympic Cauldron from the 2010 Games.

Vancouver Art Gallery Gallery
(**Map p64; 604-662-4700; www.vanartgallery.bc.ca; 750 Hornby St; adult/child $20/6; 10am-5pm Wed-Mon, to 9pm Tue; 5**) The VAG has dramatically transformed in recent years, becoming a vital part of the city's cultural scene. Contemporary exhibitions – often showcasing Vancouver's renowned photoconceptualists – are now combined with blockbuster international traveling shows.

STANLEY PARK

The magnificent 404-hectare **Stanley Park** (**www.vancouver.ca/parks; ; 19**) combines attractions with a mystical natural aura. Don't miss a stroll or cycle around the 8.8km **seawall** (**19**): a kind of visual spa treatment fringed by a 150,000-tree temperate rainforest. The path takes you right alongside the park's camera-luring totem poles. There are bike rentals near the W Georgia St entrance. For more info on Stanley Park, see p68.

Vancouver Aquarium Aquarium
(**Map p62; 604-659-3474; www.vanaqua.org; 845 Avison Way; Jul & Aug adult/child $27/17; 9:30am-6pm; ; 19**) Stanley Park's biggest draw houses 9000 water-loving critters, including sharks, beluga whales and a rather shy octopus. There's also a small rainforest of birds, turtles and a statue-still sloth. Peruse the mesmerizing iridescent jellyfish and consider an Animal Encounter tour, where you'll learn about being a trainer. Expansion was underway on our visit, so look for changes to come.

Lost Lagoon Lake
(**Map p62; www.stanleyparkecology.ca; 19**) This forested lagoon near the park entrance is Vancouver's downtown nature sanctuary. Its perimeter pathway makes for a wonderful stroll – keep your eyes peeled for beady-eyed blue herons and duck into the excellent Lost Lagoon Nature House for exhibits on the park's multitudinous flora and fauna. Check ahead for their guided park walks and you'll spot even more.

WEST END

English Bay Beach Beach
(**Map p64; cnr Denman St & Beach Ave; 5**) Wandering south on Denman St, you'll suddenly spot a rustle of palm trees announcing one of Canada's best urban beaches. There's a party atmosphere

Vancouver City Overview

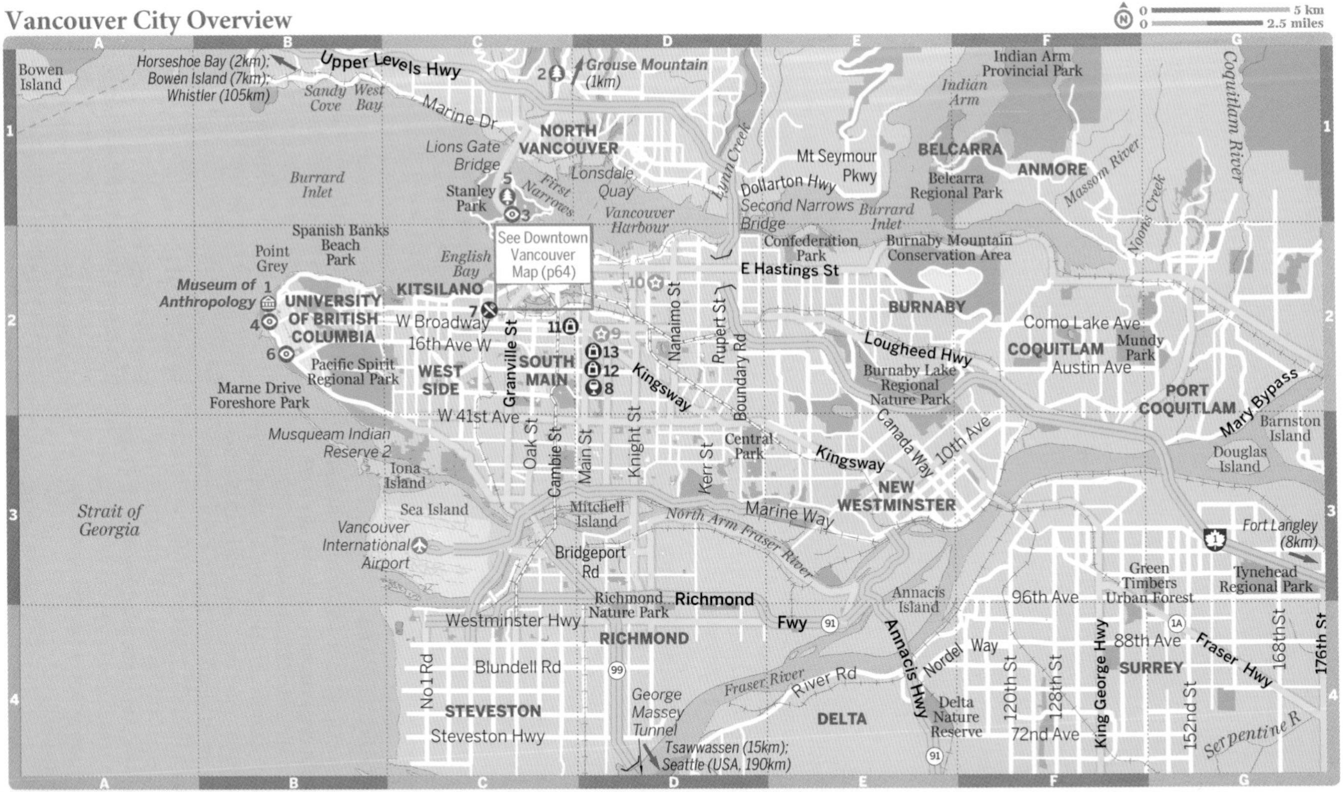

Vancouver City Overview

Don't Miss Sights

1	Museum of Anthropology	B2

Sights

2	Capilano Suspension Bridge	C1
3	Lost Lagoon	C1
	Miniature Railway	(see 5)
4	Nitobe Memorial Garden	B2
5	Stanley Park	C1
6	UBC Botanical Garden	B2
	Vancouver Aquarium	(see 5)

Eating

7	Fable	C2

Drinking & Nightlife

8	Shameful Tiki Room	D2

Entertainment

9	Biltmore Cabaret	D2
10	Cultch	D2

Shopping

11	Mountain Equipment Co-Op	C2
12	Regional Assembly of Text	D2
13	Smoking Lily	D2

here in summer as West Enders catch the rays, crowd the busker shows and check out artwork vendors...or just ogle volleyball players prancing around on the sand. Snap some pics of the laughing bronze figures – Vancouver's fave public artwork.

GASTOWN

Vancouver Police Museum — Museum

(Map p64; 604-665-3346; www.vancouverpolicemuseum.ca; 240 E Cordova St; adult/child $12/8; 9am-5pm Tue-Sat; 4) Contextualizing the city's crime-colored history, this quirky little museum is lined with confiscated weapons, counterfeit currency and a grizzly former mortuary room where the walls are studded with preserved slivers of human tissue – spot the bullet-damaged brain slices. If your interest in crime is triggered, take their excellent Sins of the City walking tour around the area.

CHINATOWN

Dr Sun Yat-Sen Classical Chinese Garden & Park — Gardens

(Map p64; www.vancouverchinesegarden.com; 578 Carrall St; adult/child $12/9; 9:30am-7pm; M Stadium-Chinatown) A tranquil break from clamorous Chinatown, this intimate 'garden of ease' illustrates Taoist symbolism through the placing of gnarled pine trees, winding covered pathways and limestone formations. Entry includes a 45-minute guided tour, where you'll learn that everything in the garden reflects balance and harmony.

If you're on a budget, check out the free park next door: not quite as elaborate as its sister, it's still a pleasant oasis of whispering grasses, a large fishpond and a small pagoda.

Chinatown Night Market — Market

(Map p64; www.vancouverchinatownnightmarket.com; Keefer St, btwn Columbia & Main Sts; 6-11pm Fri-Sun mid-May–early Sep; M Stadium-Chinatown) Recently reinvented to compete with the success of larger night markets in Richmond, Chinatown's version is well worth a summer evening visit. Cheap and cheerful trinkets still feature, but the highlight is the food – it's like a walk-through buffet of fish balls, bubble tea and tornado potatoes. Check ahead: there's an eclectic roster of entertainment, including alfresco movie screenings.

Jimi Hendrix Shrine — Notable Building

(Map p64; 207 Union St; 1-6pm Mon-Sat Jun-Sep; 3) FREE Said to occupy the building that formerly housed Vie's Chicken and Steak House – the 1960s restaurant where Hendrix' grandmother cooked and the young guitarist frequently strummed – this is worth a quick look. A quirky, homemade attraction, the red-painted shack is lined with old photos and album covers and is staffed by a chatty volunteer or two.

Science World — Museum

(Map p64; www.scienceworld.ca; 1455 Quebec St; adult/child $22.50/15.25; 10am-5pm Mon-Fri, to 6pm Sat & Sun; ; M Main St-Science World) Nestled under the city's favorite geodesic dome (OK, its only one), this recently revamped hands-on science and nature showcase brings out the kid in almost everyone. Expect to spend a half-day here as your squirts run themselves ragged learning scientific principles, especially in the new outdoor park area.

Downtown Vancouver

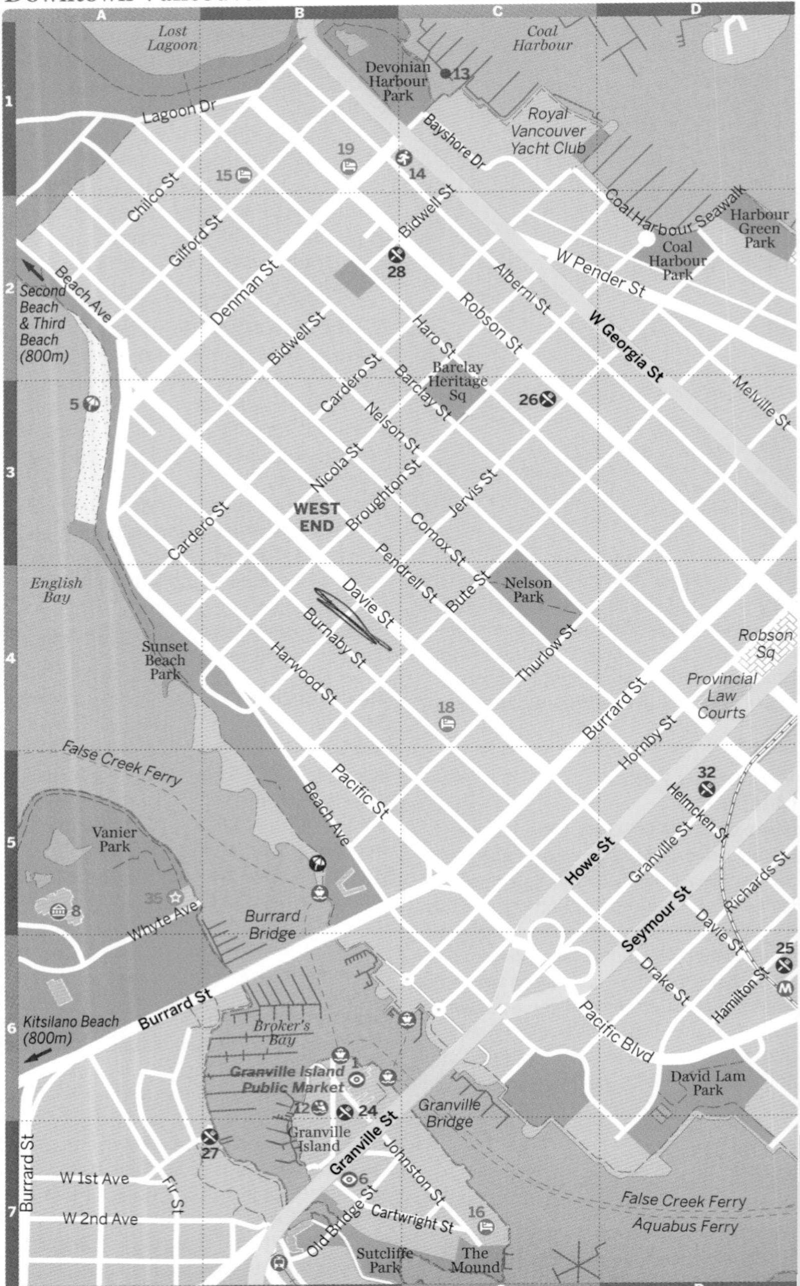
A
B
C
D
1
2
3
4
5
6
7
Lost Lagoon
Coal Harbour
Devonian Harbour Park
13
Lagoon Dr
Royal Vancouver Yacht Club
Bayshore Dr
19
15
14
Chilco St
Bidwell St
Coal Harbour Seawalk
Harbour Green Park
Gilford St
28
Coal Harbour Park
W Pender St
Second Beach & Third Beach (800m)
Beach Ave
Denman St
Alberni St
Robson St
W Georgia St
Bidwell St
Haro St
Cardero St
Barclay Heritage Sq
Barclay St
26
Melville St
5
Nelson St
Nicola St
Broughton St
Jervis St
WEST END
Cardero St
Comox St
Pendrell St
Bute St
Nelson Park
English Bay
Davie St
Thurlow St
Burnaby St
Robson Sq
Sunset Beach Park
Harwood St
Provincial Law Courts
18
Burrard St
Hornby St
False Creek Ferry
Pacific St
32
Helmcken St
Beach Ave
Vanier Park
Granville St
Howe St
Richards St
35
Seymour St
8
Whyte Ave
Burrard Bridge
Davie St
25
Drake St
Hamilton St
Burrard St
Kitsilano Beach (800m)
Pacific Blvd
Broker's Bay
1
Granville Island Public Market
David Lam Park
12
24
Granville Bridge
Granville St
27
Granville Island
Johnston St
Burrard St
W 1st Ave
Fir St
6
Old Bridge St
False Creek Ferry
Cartwright St
16
Aquabus Ferry
W 2nd Ave
Sutcliffe Park
The Mound

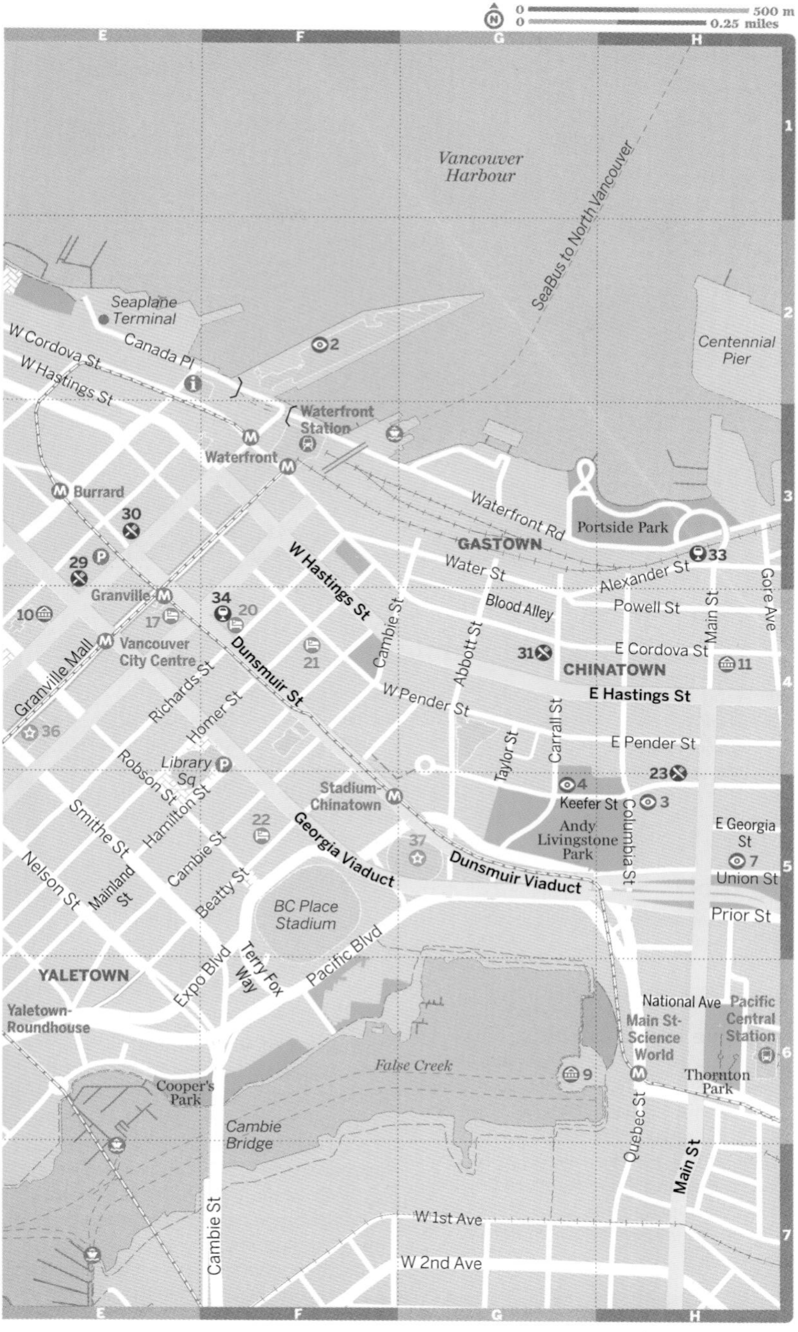

0 500 m
0 0.25 miles
E
F
G
H
1
2
3
4
5
6
7
Vancouver Harbour
SeaBus to North Vancouver
Seaplane Terminal
Canada Pl
W Cordova St
W Hastings St
2
Centennial Pier
Waterfront Station
Waterfront
Burrard
30
29
Granville
10
17
34
20
Vancouver City Centre
Granville Mall
21
Waterfront Rd
Portside Park
GASTOWN
W Hastings St
Water St
Alexander St
33
Blood Alley
Powell St
Main St
Gore Ave
Cambie St
Abbott St
31
E Cordova St
CHINATOWN
11
Dunsmuir St
W Pender St
E Hastings St
Richards St
Homer St
36
E Pender St
Carrall St
Taylor St
Robson St
Library Sq
23
Stadium-Chinatown
4
Keefer St
3
Hamilton St
Smithe St
22
Georgia Viaduct
Andy Livingstone Park
Columbia St
E Georgia St
37
7
Nelson St
Cambie St
Mainland St
Beatty St
Dunsmuir Viaduct
Union St
BC Place Stadium
Prior St
Pacific Blvd
Expo Blvd
Terry Fox Way
YALETOWN
National Ave
Pacific Central Station
Yaletown-Roundhouse
Main St-Science World
False Creek
9
Thornton Park
Cooper's Park
Cambie Bridge
Quebec St
Main St
Cambie St
W 1st Ave
W 2nd Ave

ALL CANADA PHOTOS RM/GETTY IMAGES ©

Don't Miss
Granville Island Public Market

Granville Island's highlight is the covered Public Market, a multisensory smorgasbord of fish, cheese, fruit and bakery treats. Pick up some fixings for a picnic at nearby Vanier Park (a 10-minute walk west along the seawall) or hit the little international food court (dine off-peak and you're more likely to snag a table). In summer there's also a farmers market outside.

This is a great spot to pick up unusual souvenirs for home and – if you're a true foodie – market tours are available, with samples included.

NEED TO KNOW

Map p64; www.granvilleisland.com/public-market; Johnston St; 9am-7pm; 50, miniferries

GRANVILLE ISLAND

Granville Island Brewing Brewery

(Map p64; 604-687-2739; www.gib.ca; 1441 Cartwright St; tours $9.75; tours noon, 1:30pm, 3pm, 4:30pm & 5:30pm; 50) Canada's oldest microbrewery offers half-hour tours where smiling guides walk you through the tiny brewing nook, before depositing you in the Taproom for some tasty samples, often including the summer-favorite *Hefeweizen*.

KITSILANO

Museum of Vancouver Museum

(Map p64; www.museumofvancouver.ca; 1100 Chestnut St; adult/child $12/8; 10am-5pm Fri-Wed, to 8pm Thu; ; 22) One of Vanier Park's three well-established educational attractions, the MOV has been upping its game in recent years with cool temporary exhibitions and regular late-opening parties for adults. It hasn't changed everything, though. There are still colorful displays on local 1950s pop culture and

Downtown Vancouver

Don't Miss Sights		**18** Sunset Inn & Suites	C4
1 Granville Island Public Market	B6	**19** Times Square Suites Hotel	B1
		20 Urban Hideaway Guesthouse	F4
Sights		**21** Victorian Hotel	F4
2 Canada Place	F2	**22** YWCA Hotel	F5
3 Chinatown Night Market	H5		
4 Dr Sun Yat-Sen Classical Chinese Garden & Park	G5	**Eating**	
5 English Bay Beach	A3	**23** Bao Bei	H4
6 Granville Island Brewing	B7	**24** Edible Canada at the Market	B6
HR MacMillan Space Centre	(see 8)	**25** Flying Pig	D6
7 Jimi Hendrix Shrine	H5	**26** Forage	C3
8 Museum of Vancouver	A5	**27** Go Fish	B7
9 Science World	G6	**28** Guu with Garlic	B2
10 Vancouver Art Gallery	E4	**29** Hawksworth	E3
11 Vancouver Police Museum	H4	**30** Mario's Coffee Express	E3
		31 Rainier Provisions	G4
Activities, Courses & Tours		**32** Templeton	D5
12 Ecomarine Paddlesport Centres	B6		
13 Harbour Cruises	C1	**Drinking & Nightlife**	
14 Spokes Bicycle Rentals	C1	**33** Alibi Room	H3
		34 Railway Club	F4
Sleeping			
15 Buchan Hotel	B1	**Entertainment**	
16 Granville Island Hotel	C7	**35** Bard on the Beach	A5
17 St Regis Hotel	E4	**36** Commodore	E4
		37 Vancouver Canucks	G5

1960s hippie counterculture, plus plenty of hands-on stuff for kids, including scavenger hunts and fun workshops.

HR MacMillan Space Centre Museum

(Map p64; www.spacecentre.ca; 1100 Chestnut St; adult/child $15/11; 10am-5pm; ; 22) Popular with packs of marauding schoolkids – expect to have to elbow them out of the way to push the flashing buttons – this high-tech science center illuminates the eye-opening world of space. There's plenty of fun to be had battling aliens and designing a spacecraft. There's also an observatory and planetarium; check ahead for the schedule of openings and events.

UNIVERSITY OF BRITISH COLUMBIA

UBC Botanical Garden Gardens

(Map p62; www.ubcbotanicalgarden.org; 6804 SW Marine Dr; adult/child $8/4; 9:30am-5pm; 99 B-Line, then C20) You'll find a giant collection of rhododendrons, a fascinating apothecary plot and a winter green space of off-season bloomers in this 28-hectare complex of themed gardens. The recently added Greenheart Canopy Walkway lifts visitors 17m above the forest floor on a 308m guided ecotour. Walkway tickets include garden entry.

Nitobe Memorial Garden Gardens

(Map p62; www.nitobe.org; 1895 Lower Mall; adult/child $6/3; 9:30am-5pm; 99 B-Line, then C20) Exemplifying Japanese horticultural philosophies, this verdant, tranquil oasis includes the Tea Garden – complete with ceremonial teahouse – and the Stroll Garden, which reflects a symbolic journey through life, with its little waterfalls and languid koi carp.

NORTHERN VANCOUVER

Capilano Suspension Bridge Park

(Map p62; www.capbridge.com; 3735 Capilano Rd; adult/child $34.95/12; 8:30am-8pm; ; 236 from Lonsdale Quay) As you walk gingerly onto one of the world's longest (140m) and highest (70m) suspension bridges, swaying gently over the roiling Capilano Canyon, remember that its thick steel cables are embedded in concrete. Added park attractions include a

Stanley Park

A HALF-DAY TOUR

It's easy to be overwhelmed by Stanley Park, one of North America's largest urban green spaces. But there are ways to explore this spectacular waterfront swathe – from its top sites to hidden gems – without popping any blisters.

From the Georgia St entrance, trace the seawall around the shoreline to Brockton Point's **totem poles** 1. An early arrival means getting some snaps of these brightly painted carvings without fighting crowds.

From here, continue along the seawall. You'll pass a squat, striped lighthouse before reaching the Lumberman's Arch area. Duck under the road bridge and plunge into the park's tree-lined heart. Just ahead is **Vancouver Aquarium** 2, the park's most popular attraction.

Next up, follow the path to the **Miniature Railway** 3. If you have kids in tow, take them for a trundle on this replica of the locomotive that pulled the first transcontinental passenger train into Vancouver.

From here, follow Pipeline Rd to the Tudoresque pavilion a few minutes away. In front is the **Malkin Bowl** 4, a hidden outdoor theater. Poke around the nearby manicured gardens, then continue southwards to Lost Lagoon. Follow the shoreline clockwise to **Lost Lagoon Nature House** 5, where you can learn about the park's flora and fauna.

Continue to the lagoon's western tip, then head to the ocean front ahead. Now on the park's rugged western side, follow the seawall northbound to **Third Beach** 6. Find a log perch and prepare for Vancouver's best sunset.

TOP TIPS

» When cycling the seawall, keep in mind that wheeled traffic is one-way only.

» The park is home to raccoons. Take pictures, but don't feed them.

» There are restaurants in the park if you're peckish.

» The meadow near Lumberman's Arch is a top picnic spot.

JOHN LEE ©

Third Beach
Second Beach gets the crowds but Third Beach is where the savvy locals head. This is the perfect spot to drink in a sunset panorama over the lapping Pacific Ocean shoreline.

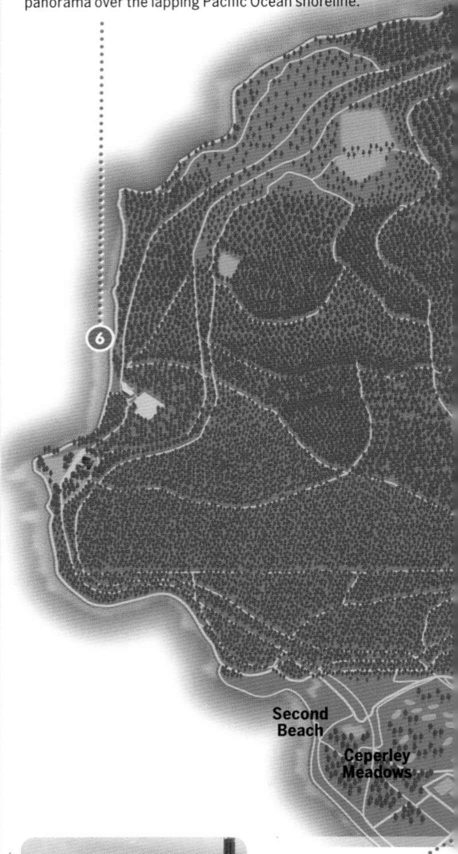

JOHN LEE ©

Lost Lagoon Nature House
The freshwater Lost Lagoon was created when the Stanley Park Causeway was built. Its shoreline Nature House illuminates the park's plant and animal life and runs guided walks.

DAVE FLEETHAM/GETTY IMAGES ©

Miniature Railway
The area occupied by this ever-popular attraction was created when dozens of trees were felled by a 1960s hurricane. It's now transformed every Christmas into a winter wonderland of fairy lights.

Vancouver Aquarium
One of Vancouver's best family-friendly attractions, the aquarium fuses education and fishy fun with memorable critters from belugas to jellyfish.

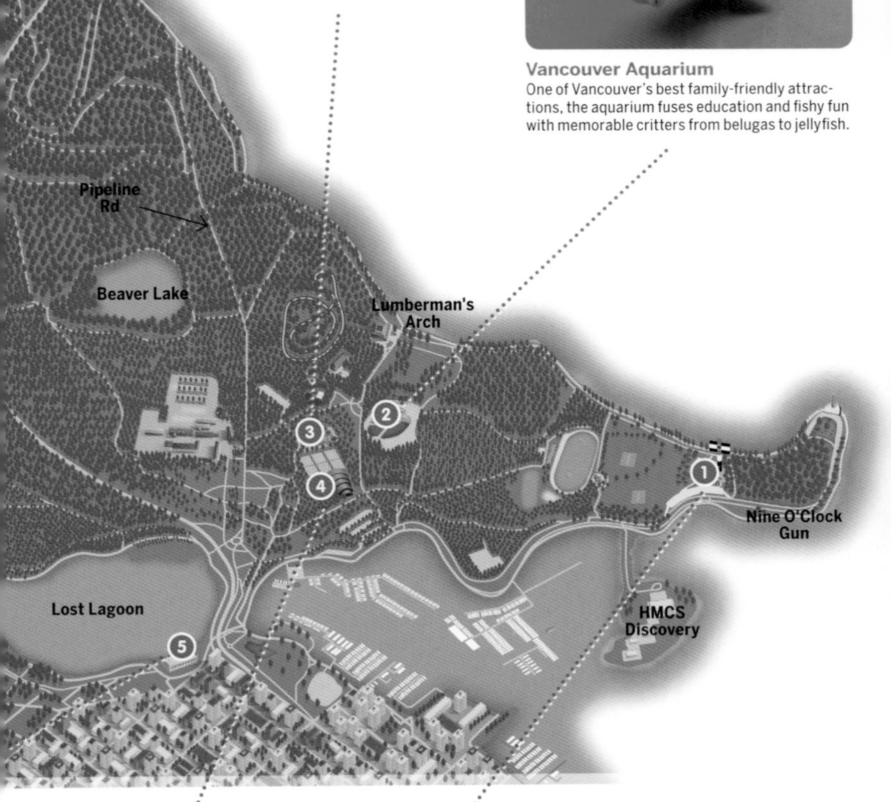

Malkin Bowl
Built by Vancouver mayor WH Malkin, this alfresco theater replaced an original bandstand. At the back of the seating area, you'll find a memorial statue to US president WG Harding.

Totem Poles
First Nations residents were still living here when Stanley Park was designated in 1888, but these poles were installed much later. The current poles are replicas of 1920s originals, carved in the 1980s.

KORINA MILLER ©

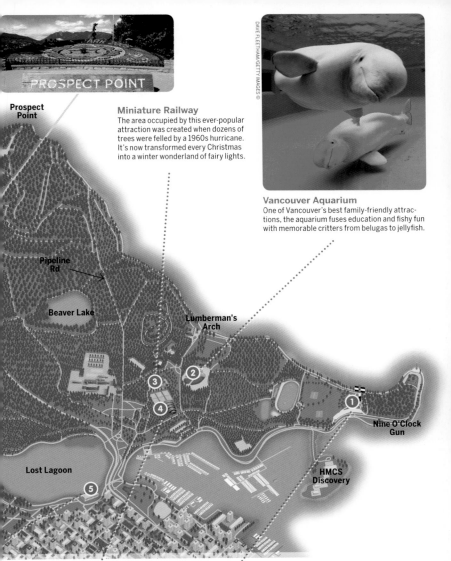

glass-bottomed cliffside walkway and an elevated canopy trail through the trees.

A hugely popular attraction (hence the summer tour buses), try to arrive early during peak months and you'll be able to check out the historic exhibits, totem poles and tree-shaded nature trails on the other side of the bridge in relative calm. From May to September, Capilano makes it very easy to get here from downtown by running a **free shuttle** from Canada Pl and area hotels.

Activities

RUNNING & CYCLING

Joggers share the busy Stanley Park seawall with cyclists (and in-line skaters), necessitating a one-way traffic system to prevent bloody pileups. The sea-to-sky vistas are breathtaking, but the exposed route can be hit with crashing waves and icy winds in winter.

There's a plethora of bike and blade rental stores near Stanley Park's W Georgia St entrance, especially around the intersection with Denman St. One of these, **Spokes Bicycle Rentals** (Map p64; www.vancouverbikerental.com; 1798 W Georgia St; adult per hr/7hr from $8.60/34.30; 8am-9pm; 5), can also arrange guided tours.

WATERSPORTS

Ecomarine Paddlesport Centres Kayaking
(Map p64; 604-689-7575, 888-425-2925; www.ecomarine.com; 1668 Duranleau St; single kayak rental per 2/24hr $39/94; 9am-6pm Sun, Mon, Wed & Thu, to 9pm Tue, Fri & Sat; 50) With headquarters on Granville Island, the friendly folk at Ecomarine Paddlesport Centres offer equipment rentals and guided tours.

Tours

Forbidden Vancouver Walking Tour
(www.forbiddenvancouver.ca; adult/concession $22/19; Apr-Nov) This quirky company offers two core, highly entertaining, tours: a delve into prohibition-era Vancouver and a poke around the seedy underbelly of historic Gastown. Not recommended for kids. Book ahead: they fill up quickly.

Vancouver Foodie Tours Guided Tour
(877-804-9220; www.foodietours.ca; tours $49-69; year-round) The perfect way to dive into the city's food scene, the two belt-busting guided tours include a street food crawl ($49) and a gourmet drink and dine tour ($69).

Harbour Cruises Boat Tour
(Map p64; 800-663-1500, 604-688-7246; www.boatcruises.com; Denman St; adult/child $30/10; May-Oct) View the city – and some unexpected wildlife – from the water on a 75-minute narrated harbor tour. Tours weave past Stanley

Capilano Suspension Bridge (p67)
TRAVELSTOCK44/GETTY IMAGES ©

BARRETT & MACKAY/GETTY IMAGES ©

Don't Miss
Museum of Anthropology

Recently renovated and expanded, Vancouver's best museum houses northwest coast aboriginal artifacts, including Haida houses and totem poles, plus non–First Nations exhibits, like European ceramics and Cantonese opera costumes. The free guided tours are highly recommended, as is the excellent artsy gift shop. Give yourself a couple of hours at this museum.

NEED TO KNOW

Map p62; www.moa.ubc.ca; 6393 NW Marine Dr; adult/child $16.75/14.50; 10am-5pm Wed-Sun, to 9pm Tue; 99B-Line

Park, Lions Gate Bridge and the North Shore mountains.

Sleeping

While rates peak in July and August, there are good deals available in fall and spring, when the weather is often amenable and the tourist crowds are reduced. Be aware that hotels charge up to $40 for overnight parking, while parking at B&Bs is typically free.

DOWNTOWN

St Regis Hotel Boutique Hotel **$$**

(Map p64; 604-681-1135, 800-770-7929; www.stregishotel.com; 602 Dunsmuir St; d incl breakfast $220; ; M Granville)
Transformed in recent years, the St Regis is now an art-lined boutique sleepover in a 1913 heritage shell. The rooms – which, befitting its age, almost all seem to be a different size – exhibit a loungey élan, complete with leather-look wallpaper, earth-tone bedspreads, flatscreen TVs and multimedia hubs. Rates include

cooked breakfast, nearby gym access and free international phone calling.

Victorian Hotel Hotel $$

(Map p64; ☎877-681-6369, 604-681-6369; www.victorianhotel.ca; 514 Homer St; r incl breakfast with shared/private bathroom $99/159; ⊜@📶; Ⓜ Granville) The high-ceilinged rooms at this popular heritage-building Euro-style hotel combine glossy hardwood floors, a sprinkling of antiques, an occasional bay window and plenty of historical charm. The best rooms are in the renovated extension, where raindrop showers, marble bathroom floors and flatscreen TVs add a slice of luxe. Rooms are provided with fans in summer.

Urban Hideaway Guesthouse Guesthouse $$

(Map p64; ☎604-694-0600; www.urban-hideaway.com; 581 Richards St; d with shared bathroom/ste $109/159; ⊜@; Ⓜ Granville) This cozy but fiendishly well-hidden home away from home is a budget word-of-mouth favorite in the heart of the city. Tuck yourself into one of the comfy rooms – the loft is recommended – or spend your time in the lounge areas downstairs. There are laundry facilities, a free-use computer and loaner bikes are also gratis. Bathrooms are mostly shared, although the loft's is private.

WEST END

Buchan Hotel Hotel $$

(Map p64; ☎604-685-5354, 800-668-6654; www.buchanhotel.com; 1906 Haro St; d with private/shared bathroom $139/99; ⊜@📶; 🚌5) The cheap and cheerful, 1926-built Buchan has bags of charm and is steps from Stanley Park. Along corridors lined with old prints of yesteryear Vancouver, its budget rooms – most with shared bathrooms – are clean, cozy and well maintained, although some furnishings have seen better days. The pricier rooms are correspondingly prettier, while the east-side rooms are brighter.

Sunset Inn & Suites Hotel $$

(Map p64; ☎800-786-1997, 604-688-2474; www.sunsetinn.com; 1111 Burnaby St; ste incl breakfast $175; ⊜❄@📶; 🚌6) A generous cut above most of the West End's self-catering suite hotels, the popular Sunset Inn offers larger-than-average rooms with full kitchenettes. Each has a balcony, while some rooms – particularly those on

Cycling the seawall, Stanley Park (p61)

TIM DRAPER/GETTY IMAGES ©

south-facing higher floors – have partial views of English Bay. Rates include rare-for-Vancouver free parking and the attentive staff are among the best in the city.

Times Square Suites Hotel Apartment $$$
(Map p64; ☎877-684-2223, 604-684-2223; www.timessquaresuites.com; 1821 Robson St; ste $225; ⊖❄📶🐾; 🚌5) Superbly located just steps from Stanley Park, this excellent West End hidden gem (even the entrance can be hard to spot) is the perfect apartment-style Vancouver sleepover. Rooms – mostly one-bedroom suites – are spacious, with tubs, laundry facilities, full kitchens and superbly well-maintained, if slightly 1980s, decor.

YALETOWN

YWCA Hotel Hostel $
(Map p64; ☎604-895-5830, 800-663-1424; www.ywcahotel.com; 733 Beatty St; s/d/tr with shared bath $73/90/117; ⊖❄@📶; M Stadium-Chinatown) This good value, well-located option offers well-maintained, if spartan, rooms of the student accommodation variety. There's a wide range of configurations, from singles to five-bed rooms that are ideal for groups. Some rooms have shared bathrooms while all have access to communal kitchens – each room also has a minifridge. Rates include access to the **YWCA Health & Fitness Centre**, a 10-minute walk away.

GRANVILLE ISLAND & KITSILANO

Granville Island Hotel Boutique Hotel $$
(Map p64; ☎604-683-7373, 800-663-1840; www.granvilleislandhotel.com; 1253 Johnston St; r $220; ⊖❄@📶🐾; 🚌50) This gracious boutique property hugs Granville Island's quiet eastern tip, enjoying tranquil views across False Creek to Yaletown's mirrored towers. You'll be a five-minute walk from the Public Market, with shopping and theater options on your doorstep. Rooms have an elegant, west coast feel with some exposed wood flourishes. There's also a cool rooftop Jacuzzi, while the on-site brewpub-restaurant has a great patio.

Food Truck Frenzy

The downtown core is home to many of the four-wheeled takeouts and, while there are lots of experimental fusion trucks, several have quickly risen to the top table: look out for local favorites **TacoFino**, **Re-Up BBQ**, **Roaming Dragon**, **Feastro**, **Fresh Local Wild**, **Yolk's Breakfast**, **Pig on the Street** and **Vij's Railway Express**. And don't miss one of the **JapaDog** locations.

For up-to-the-minute listings, opening hours and locations for street food carts, go to www.streetfoodapp.com/vancouver.

Eating

DOWNTOWN

Mario's Coffee Express Coffee $
(Map p64; 595 Howe St; mains $4-8; ⏰7am-4pm Mon-Fri; M Burrard) A java-lover's favorite that only downtown office workers seem to know about, you'll wake up and smell the coffee long before you make it through the door here. The rich aromatic beverages served up by the man himself are the kind of ambrosia brews that should make Starbucks drinkers weep – you might even forgive the 1980s Italian pop percolating through the shop.

Templeton Diner $$
(Map p64; www.thetempleton.ca; 1087 Granville St; mains $10-14; ⏰9am-11pm Mon-Wed, to 1am Thu-Sun; 👪; 🚌10) A chrome-and-vinyl '50s-look diner with a twist, Templeton cooks up plus-sized organic burgers, addictive fries, vegetarian quesadillas and perhaps the best hangover cure in town, the 'Big Ass Breakfast'. Avoid weekend peak times or you'll be queuing for ages.

Hawksworth West Coast $$$
(Map p64; ☎604-673-7000; www.hawksworthrestaurant.com; 801 W Georgia St; mains $29-39; ⏰7am-11pm) A top spot for the

Detour: Sunshine Coast

Stretching 139km along the water from Langdale to Lund, the Sunshine Coast – separated from the Lower Mainland by the Coast Mountains and the Strait of Georgia – has an independent, island-like mentality that belies the fact it's only a 40-minute ferry ride from West Vancouver's Horseshoe Bay. Hwy 101 links key communities Gibsons, Sechelt and Powell River, plus tiny Roberts Creek, and it's an easy and convivial region to explore. There are also plenty of activities to keep things lively: think ocean kayaking and spectacular wilderness hiking with a side order of artists' studios.

Your first port of call after docking in Langdale is Gibsons (pop 4400). Putter around the rows of galleries and artisan stores, especially along Marine Dr and Molly's Lane. Gourmet seafood fans shouldn't miss **Smitty's Oyster House** (www. smittysoysterhouse.com; 643 School Rd; mains $9-23; ⊗noon-late Tue-Sat, till 8pm Sun), which faces the boat-bobbling marina, for perfect fresh-catch treats.

Funky, hippie-tinged Roberts Creek is 12km northwest of Gibsons. Outdoor activity center Sechelt is another 12km onward.

Peruse the website of **Sunshine Coast Tourism** (www.sunshinecoastcanada.com) for information.

city's movers and shakers, this is the fine-dining anchor of the top-end Rosewood Hotel Georgia. But unlike most hotel restaurants, this one has a starry-eyed local following. Created by and named after one of the city's top local chefs, the menu fuses contemporary west coast approaches with clever international influences, hence dishes like soy-roasted sturgeon. The seasonal tasting menu is also heartily recommended.

WEST END & STANLEY PARK

Guu with Garlic Japanese $$
(Map p64; www.guu-izakaya.com; 1689 Robson St; small plates $4-9, mains $8-16; ⊗11:30am-2:30pm Tue-Sun & 5:30pm-midnight daily; ☐5) Arguably the best of Vancouver's many authentic *izakayas,* this welcoming, wood-lined joint is a cultural immersion. Hot pots and noodle bowls are available but it's best to experiment with some Japanese-bar tapas, such as black cod with miso mayo, deep-fried egg pumpkin balls or finger-lickin' *tori-karaage* fried chicken.

Forage West Coast $$
(Map p64; ☎604-661-1400; www.foragevancou-ver.com; 1300 Robson St; mains $17-21; ⊗6:30-10am & 5pm-midnight Mon-Fri, 7am-2pm & 5pm-midnight Sat & Sun; ☐5) ✿ A champion of the local farm-to-table scene, this sustainabil-ity-loving restaurant is the perfect way to sample the flavors of the region. Brunch has become a firm local favorite – the turkey sausage hash is recommended – but for dinner the idea is to sample an array of tasting plates. Though the menu is innovative and highly seasonal, look out for the delectable pork tongue ravioli and roast bison bone marrow.

YALETOWN

Flying Pig West Coast $$
(Map p64; www.theflyingpigvan.com; 1168 Hamil-ton St; mains $18-24; ⊗11:30am-midnight Mon-Fri, 10:30am-midnight Sat & Sun; Ⓜ Yaletown-Roundhouse) Yaletown's best mid-range restaurant has mastered the art of friendly service and excellent, savor-worthy dining. But since everyone else knows that, too, it's a good idea to dine off peak to avoid the crowds. A warm, woodsy bistro, the

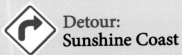

dishes focus on seasonal local ingredients and are virtually guaranteed to make you smile: scallops and halibut are perfect, and the roasted chicken is the city's best.

At the time of writing, a new, much bigger Flying Pig had just opened in Gastown.

GASTOWN

Rainier Provisions — West Coast $

(Map p64; www.rainierprovisions.com; 2 W Cordova St; mains $8-12; 11am-8pm Mon-Fri, 9am-8pm Sat & Sun; 4) Revitalizing a former Gastown hotel building, this great-value cafe-bistro is a perfect fuel-up spot. Drop in for Stumptown coffee or dive into a hearty menu, ranging from hot sandwich specials served with soup or salad to a heaping plate of roast with all the extras. The local-made sausages with roast potatoes is the winner though.

CHINATOWN

Bao Bei — Chinese $$

(Map p64; 604-688-0876; www.bao-bei.ca; 163 Keefer St; small plates $9-18; 5:30pm-midnight Mon-Sat; ; 3) Reinventing a Chinatown heritage building interior with funky flourishes, this hidden-gem Chinese brasserie is the area's most seductive dinner destination. Enjoying a local cult following, it brings a contemporary edge to Asian-style, tapas-sized dishes like *shao bing*, octopus salad and crispy pork belly.

GRANVILLE ISLAND

Go Fish — Seafood $

(Map p64; 1505 W 1st Ave; mains $8-14; 11:30am-6:30pm Tue-Sun; 50) A short stroll westwards along the seawall from the Granville Island entrance, this almost too-popular seafood stand is one of the city's fave fish-and-chips joints, offering halibut, salmon or cod encased in crispy golden batter. The smashing, lighter fish tacos are also recommended, while ever-changing daily specials, brought in by the nearby fishing boats, often include scallop burgers or ahi tuna sandwiches.

Edible Canada at the Market — West Coast $$

(Map p64; 604-682-6681; www.ediblecanada.com/bistro; 1596 Johnston St; mains $18-29; 11am-9pm Mon-Thu, to 10pm Fri-Sun; 50) Granville Island's most popular bistro delivers a short but tempting menu of seasonal dishes from across Canada,

Templeton (p73)

CHRISTOPHER HERWIG/GETTY IMAGES ©

often including perfectly prepared Alberta beef, Newfoundland fish and several BC treats – look out for slow-roasted pork belly. Consider sharing some small plates if you're feeling adventurous, perhaps topped with a naughty maple-sugar pie and a glass of ice wine. Book ahead.

KITSILANO & WEST SIDE

Fable West Coast **$$**

(Map p62; ☎604-732-1322; www.fablekitchen.ca; 1944 W 4th Ave; mains $18-28; ⏲11:30am-2pm Mon-Fri, 5:30-10pm Mon-Sat, brunch 10:30am-2pm Sat & Sun; 🚌4) One of Vancouver's favorite farm-to-table restaurants is a lovely rustic-chic room of exposed brick, wood beams and prominently displayed red-rooster logos, but looks are just part of the appeal. Expect perfectly prepared bistro dishes showcasing local seasonal ingredients, often including duck, chicken or halibut. It's great gourmet comfort food with little pretension, hence the packed room most nights. Reservations recommended.

Drinking & Nightlife

Wherever you end up imbibing, sip some of the region's excellent craft brews, including tasty tipples from Driftwood Brewing, Howe Sound Brewing and Central City Brewing.

Alibi Room Pub

(Map p64; www.alibi.ca; 157 Alexander St; ⏲5-11:30pm Mon-Fri, 10am-11:30pm Sat & Sun; 🚌4) Vancouver's best craft beer tavern, this exposed brick bar stocks an ever-changing roster of around 50 drafts from celebrated BC breweries, like Phillips, Driftwood and Crannóg. Adventurous taste trippers – hipsters and old-lag beer fans alike – enjoy the $9.50 'frat bat' of four sample tipples: choose your own or ask to be surprised. And always check the board for alternating guest casks.

Railway Club Pub

(Map p64; www.therailwayclub.com; 579 Dunsmuir St; ⏲4pm-2am Mon-Thu, noon-3am Fri, 3pm-3am Sat, 5pm-midnight Sun; Ⓜ Granville) A local-legend, pub-style music venue, the upstairs 'Rail' is accessed via an unobtrusive wooden door next to a 7-Eleven. Don't be put off: this is one of the city's friendliest bars and you'll fit right in as soon as you roll up to the bar – unusually for Vancouver, you have to order at the counter, since there's no table service. Live music nightly.

Shameful Tiki Room Bar

(Map p62; www.shamefultikiroom.com; 4362 Main St; ⏲5pm-midnight Wed-Mon; 🚌3) Slip through the curtains into this windowless snug and you'll be instantly transported to a Polynesian beach. The lighting – including glowing puffer-fish lamp shades – is permanently set to dusk and the walls are lined with Tiki masks

Alibi Room

CHRISTOPHER HERWIG/GETTY IMAGES ©

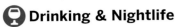

Gay & Lesbian Vancouver

Vancouver's gay and lesbian scene is part of the city's culture rather than a subsection of it. The legalization of same-sex marriages has resulted in a huge number of couples using Vancouver as a kind of gay Vegas for their destination nuptials. For more information on tying the knot, visit www.vs.gov.bc.ca/marriage/howto.html.

Vancouver's West End district – complete with its pink-painted bus shelters, fluttering rainbow flags and hand-holding locals – houses western Canada's largest 'gayborhood,' while the city's lesbian contingent is centered more on Commercial Dr.

Pick up a free copy of *Xtra!* for a crash course on the local scene, and check www.gayvancouver.net, www.gayvan.com and www.superdyke.com for pertinent listings and resources.

and rattan coverings under a straw-shrouded ceiling, but it's the drinks that rock: seriously well-crafted classics from zombies to scorpion bowls.

Entertainment

Pick up the free *Georgia Straight* or check www.straight.com for local happenings.

LIVE MUSIC

Commodore Live Music
(Map p64; www.commodoreballroom.ca; 868 Granville St; 🚌10) Local bands know they've made it when they play Vancouver's best mid-sized venue, a restored art-deco ballroom that still has the city's bounciest dance floor, courtesy of tires placed under its floorboards. If you need a break from your moshing, collapse at one of the tables lining the perimeter, catch your breath with a bottled Stella and then plunge back in.

Biltmore Cabaret Live Music
(Map p62; www.biltmorecabaret.com; 2755 Prince Edward St; 🚌9) One of Vancouver's best alternative venues, the Biltmore is a firm favorite on the local indie scene. A low-ceilinged, vibe-tastic spot to mosh to local and touring musicians, there are also regular event nights: check their online calendar for upcoming happenings or hit the eclectic monthly Talent Time, Wednesday's rave-like dance night or Sunday's ever-popular Kitty Nights burlesque show.

THEATER & CLASSICAL MUSIC

Cultch Theater
(Vancouver East Cultural Centre; Map p62; www.thecultch.com; 1895 Venables St; 🚌20) This once-abandoned 1909 church has been a gathering place for performers and audiences since being officially designated a cultural space in 1973. Following a comprehensive recent renovation, the beloved Cultch, as everyone calls it, is now one of Vancouver's entertainment jewels with a busy roster of local, fringe and visiting theatrical shows, from spoken word to touring Chekov productions.

Bard on the Beach Performing Arts
(Map p64; ☎604-739-0559; www.bardonthebeach.org; Vanier Park, Kitsilano; ⏰Jun-Sep; 🚌22) Watching Shakespeare performed while the sun sets against the mountains through the open back of a tented stage is a Vancouver summertime highlight. There are usually three Bard plays, plus one Bard-related work (*Rosencrantz and Guildenstern are Dead,* for example) to choose from during the run. Question-and-answer talks are staged after Tuesday-night performances, along with regular opera, fireworks and wine-tasting nights throughout the season.

Ferry Hopping

If you don't arrive or depart from Granville Island via one of the tiny miniferries operated by **Aquabus Ferries** (Map p64; www.theaquabus.com; adult/child from $3/1.50) or **False Creek Ferries** (Map p64; www.granvilleislandferries.bc.ca; adult/child from $3/1.50), you haven't really conducted your visit correctly. But these signature boats – the Aquabus vessels tend to be rainbow hued while the False Creek ferries are blue – don't only transport passengers from the north side of False Creek to the market on the south side. Both have several additional ports of call around the shoreline and, if you have time, a 'cruise' of the area is a great way to see the city from the water. An all-day pass on each service costs $10 to $15 (tickets are not interchangeable between the operators, who remain cutthroat rivals) and there are several highlight stop-offs to consider along the way.

SPORTS

Vancouver Canucks Hockey

(Map p64; www.canucks.com; Rogers Arena, 800 Griffiths Way; M Stadium-Chinatown) The city's National Hockey League (NHL) team toyed with fans in 2011's Stanley Cup finals before losing Game 7 to the Boston Bruins, triggering riots and looting across Vancouver. But love runs deep and 'go Canucks, go!' is still boomed out from a packed Rogers Arena at every game. Book your seat early or just head to a local bar for some raucous game-night atmosphere.

Shopping

Regional Assembly of Text Arts & Crafts

(Map p62; www.assemblyoftext.com; 3934 Main St; 11am-6pm Mon-Sat, noon-5pm Sun; 3) This ironic antidote to the digital age lures ink-stained locals with its journals, handmade pencil boxes and T-shirts printed with typewriter motifs. Check out the tiny under-the-stairs gallery showcasing zines from around the world, and don't miss the monthly letter-writing club (7pm, first Thursday of every month), where you can sip tea, scoff cookies and hammer away on vintage typewriters.

Smoking Lily Clothing

(Map p62; www.smokinglily.com; 3634 Main St; 11am-6pm Mon-Sat, noon-5pm Sun; 3) Art-school cool rules here, with skirts, belts and halter tops whimsically accented with prints of ants, bicycles and the periodic table. Men's clothing is a smaller part of the mix, with fish, skull and tractor T-shirts. It's hard to imagine a better souvenir than the silk tea cozy printed with a Pierre Trudeau likeness – ask the friendly staff for more recommendations.

Mountain Equipment Co-Op Outdoor Equipment

(Map p62; www.mec.ca; 130 W Broadway; 10am-7pm Mon-Wed, to 9pm Thu & Fri, 9am-6pm Sat, 11am-5pm Sun; 9) Grown hikers weep at the amazing selection of clothing, kayaks, sleeping bags and clever camping gadgets at this cavernous outdoors store: MEC has been encouraging fully fledged outdoor enthusiasts for years. You'll have to be a member to buy, but that's easy to arrange for just $5. Equipment – canoes, kayaks, camping gear etc – can also be rented here.

Information

Tourist Information

Tourism Vancouver Visitors Centre (Map p64; 877-826-1717, 604-683-2000; www.tourismvancouver.com; 200 Burrard St; 8:30am-6pm; M Waterfront) The Tourism Vancouver Visitors Centre is a large repository of resources for visitors, with a staff of helpful advisors ready to assist in planning your trip. Services include free maps, visitor guides, half-price theater tickets, accommodation and tour bookings.

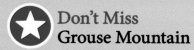

CHRISTOPHER HERWIG/GETTY IMAGES ©

Don't Miss
Grouse Mountain

Calling itself the 'Peak of Vancouver,' this mountaintop playground offers smashing views of downtown, shimmering in the water below. In summer, **Skyride** gondola tickets include access to lumberjack shows, alpine hiking, movie presentations and a grizzly-bear refuge. Pay extra for zip lining and Eye of the Wind, a 20-storey, elevator-accessed turbine tower with a panoramic viewing pod that will have your camera itching for action.

There are also restaurants up here if you fancy dining: it's an ideal sunset-viewing spot. You can reduce the gondola fee by hiking the ultra-steep Grouse Grind up the side of the mountain – you have to pay $10 to get back down on the Skyride, though. Like Capilano, Grouse lures visitors from downtown in summer by offering a **free shuttle** from Canada Pl. In winter it's all about skiing and snowboarding as Grouse become the locals' fave powder playground.

NEED TO KNOW

www.grousemountain.com; 6400 Nancy Greene Way; Skyride adult/child $39.95/13.95; 9am-10pm; ; 236 from Lonsdale Quay

Getting There & Away

Air

Vancouver International Airport (YVR; www.yvr.ca) is the main west coast hub for airlines from Canada, the US and international locales. It's in Richmond, a 13km (30 minute) drive south of downtown.

Several handy floatplane services can also deliver you directly to the Vancouver waterfront's **Seaplane Terminal** (Map p64; 604-647-7570; www.vhfc.ca; 1055 Canada Place; Waterfront). These include frequent **Harbour Air Seaplanes**

(www.harbour-air.com) services from downtown Victoria and beyond.

Boat

BC Ferries (www.bcferries.com) services arrive at **Tsawwassen** – an hour's drive south of downtown – from Vancouver Island's Swartz Bay (passenger/vehicle $15.50/51.25, 1½ hours) and Nanaimo's Duke Point (passenger/vehicle $15.50/51.25, two hours). Services also arrive here from the Southern Gulf Islands.

Ferries arrive at West Vancouver's **Horseshoe Bay** – 30 minutes from downtown – from Nanaimo's Departure Bay (passenger/vehicle $15.50/51.25, 1½ hours), Bowen Island (passenger/vehicle $11.10/31.65, 20 minutes) and Langdale (passenger/vehicle $14.55/49.05, 40 minutes) on the Sunshine Coast.

Bus

Most out-of-town buses grind to a halt at Vancouver's Pacific Central Station.

Train

Trains trundle in from across Canada and the US at **Pacific Central Station (Map p64; 1150 Station St)**. The Main Street-Science World SkyTrain station is just across the street for connections to downtown and the suburbs.

Getting Around

To/From the Airport

SkyTrain's 16-station Canada Line (adult one-way fare to downtown $7.50 to $9) operates a rapid-transit train service from the airport to downtown. Trains run every few minutes and take around 25 minutes to reach downtown's Waterfront Station.

If you prefer to cab it, budget $30 to $40 for the 30-minute taxi ride from the airport to your downtown hotel.

Public Transportation

The website for **TransLink (www.translink.bc.ca)** bus, SkyTrain and SeaBus services has a trip-planning tool. A ticket bought on any of its three services is valid for 1½ hours of travel on the entire network, depending on the zone in which you intend to travel. The three zones become progressively more expensive the further you journey.

One-zone tickets are adult/child $2.75/1.75, two-zone tickets $4/2.75 and three-zone tickets $5.50/3.75. An all-day, all-zone pass costs $9.75/7.50.

SeaBus

The aquatic shuttle **SeaBus (Map p64)** operates every 15 to 30 minutes throughout the day, taking 12 minutes to cross the Burrard Inlet between Waterfront Station and Lonsdale Quay. At Lonsdale there's a bus terminal servicing routes throughout North Vancouver and West Vancouver (take bus 236 to Grouse Mountain and Capilano Suspension Bridge).

SkyTrain

The SkyTrain rapid-transit network consists of three routes and is a great way to move around the region: consider taking a spin on it, even if you don't have anywhere to go. A fourth route, the Evergreen Line, is scheduled for 2016 completion.

Whistler village
RANDY LINCKS/GETTY IMAGES ©

Whistler

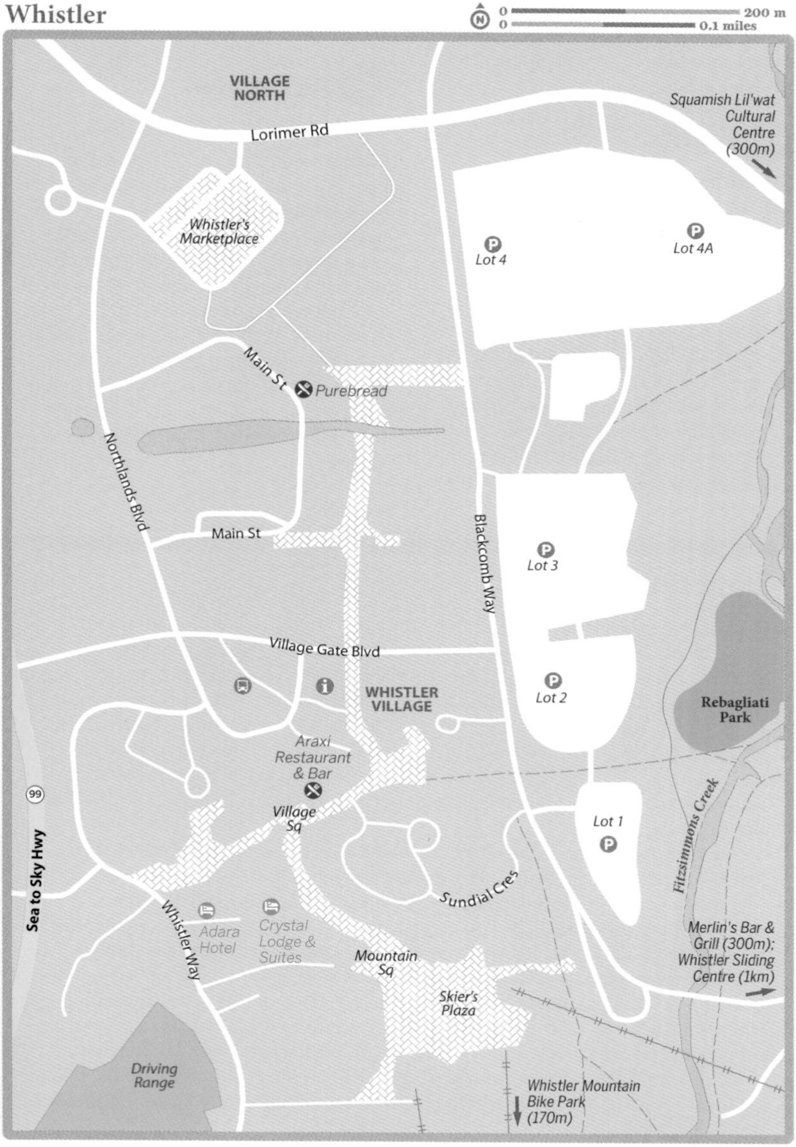

WHISTLER

Named for the furry marmots that populate the area and whistle like deflating balloons, this gabled alpine village – and 2010 Olympic and Paralympic Winter Games venue – is one of the world's most popular ski resorts. Nestled in the shade of the formidable Whistler and Blackcomb Mountains, the wintertime village has a frosted, Christmas-card look. But summer is now even more popular, with

Vancouverites and visitors lured to the region's natural charms by everything from mountain biking to scream-triggering zip-line runs.

Sights

Squamish Lil'wat Cultural Centre Museum

(www.slcc.ca; 4584 Blackcomb Way; adult/child $18/8; 9:30am-5pm) This handsome, wood-beamed facility showcases two quite different First Nations groups – one coastal and one interior based. Take a tour for the vital context behind the museum-like exhibits, including four newly carved totem poles and a new upstairs gallery that includes a 1200-year-old ceremonial bowl. Ask about the summer barbecue dinners ($58) or nip into the downstairs cafe for delicious venison chili with traditional bannock.

Activities

SKIING & SNOWBOARDING

Comprising 37 lifts and crisscrossed with over 200 runs, the **Whistler-Blackcomb** (www.whistlerblackcomb.com; 1-day winter lift ticket adult/child $98/52) sister mountains were physically linked for the first time when the resort's mammoth 4.4km Peak 2 Peak gondola opened in 2009. It takes 11 minutes to shuttle wide-eyed powder hogs between the two high alpine areas, so you can hit the slopes on both mountains on the same day. More than half the runs are aimed at intermediate-level skiers.

Function Junction

Take bus number 1 southbound from Whistler village and within 20 minutes you'll be in the heart of the locals' fave neighborhood. **Function Junction** started life as a hidden-among-the-trees area where industrial businesses carried on without affecting the Christmas card visuals of the village. But things have changed in recent years and this area now resembles the early days of Vancouver's Granville Island, its industrial units now slowly colonized by galleries and cafes. It's ideal for an afternoon of leisurely browsing, especially if you plan to dine. There are a couple of streets to explore, but the best is **Millar Creek Rd**.

Start with a late breakfast at **Wild Wood Cafe** (www.wildwoodrestaurants.ca; 1085 Millar Creek Rd; mains $6-12; 6:30am-2pm Mon-Thu, to 3pm Fri & Sat, 9am-3pm Sun;), a folkie, ever-friendly neighborhood haunt where the eggs Benedict is recommended; they also chef up great burgers if it's lunchtime. Then wander past the yarn-bombed trees en route to **White Dog Whistler Studio Gallery** (www.whitedogwhistler.com; 1074 Millar Creek Rd; 11am-6pm). Luna, the white dog in question, will be waiting to welcome you at the door of this smashing gallery where artist Penny Eder works. As well as her own work, the snob-free spot showcases the eclectic creations of dozens of local artists: look out for pottery, paintings and a glass kaleidoscope or two and ask Eder about her guided village art tours – also check to see whether one of her regular workshops is running if you fancy being creative.

If you need inspiration first, nip across the street to **Whistler Brewing Company** (www.whistlerbeer.com; 1045 Millar Creek Rd; tours $13.95; 1pm-8pm Mon-Thu, to 10pm Fri, noon-7pm Sat & Sun). You can take a tour of the facilities and try a few brews in the taproom – with any luck, the sought-after winter-only Chestnut Ale will be available.

The winter season kicks off here in late November and typically runs to April on Whistler and June on Blackcomb; December to February is the peak. If you want to emulate your fave Olympic ski heroes, Whistler Creekside was the setting for the downhill skiing events at the 2010 Games.

You can beat the crowds with an early morning Fresh Tracks ticket ($18) which must be bought in advance at Whistler Village Gondola Guest Relations. With your regular lift ticket, it gets you an extra hour on the slopes and the ticket includes breakfast at the Roundhouse Lodge up top. Night owls might prefer the evening Night Moves program, operated via Blackcomb's Magic Chair lift after 5pm.

CROSS-COUNTRY SKIING & SNOWSHOEING

A pleasant stroll or free shuttle bus away from the village, Lost Lake is a hub of wooded cross-country ski trails, suitable for novices and experts alike. Around 4km of the trail is lit for nighttime skiing until 10pm and there's a handy 'warming hut' providing lessons and equipment rentals. Snowshoers are also well served in this area: you can stomp off on your own on 10km of trails or rent equipment and guides.

MOUNTAIN BIKING

Taking over the melted ski slopes in summer and accessed via the lift at the village's south end, **Whistler Mountain Bike Park** (http://bike.whistlerblackcomb.com; 1-day pass adult/child $53/31; May-Oct) offers barreling downhill runs and an orgy of jumps, beams and bridges twisting through 200km of well-maintained forested trails. You don't have to be a bike courier to stand the knee-buckling pace: easier routes are marked in green, while blue intermediate trails and black-diamond advanced paths are offered if you want to **Crank It Up** – the name of one of the park's most popular routes.

Local Knowledge

Whistler

RECOMMENDATIONS FROM PETER SMART, GUIDE AND SKI INSTRUCTOR WITH EXTREMELY CANADIAN

1 HITTING THE SLOPES

I love the amazing access to challenging terrain here and also the great backcountry areas that are available. The caliber of the skiers on the hill has really improved in recent years but it's not all about being an advanced skier: there are some great intermediate runs such as Emerald and Symphony.

2 SKI TWO MOUNTAINS IN ONE DAY

The Peak 2 Peak Gondola is the longest lift of its kind in the world and it's an amazing engineering feat. It's a huge advantage because you can switch mountains and get two totally different experiences: hitting the spring sun on Whistler then the crispy terrain on Blackcomb on the same day. Blackcomb also has a new lift called Crystal that makes for much quicker access to Blackcomb and Horstman glaciers.

3 SNOWBOARDING PARADISE

Snowboarding has become bigger every year up here – it's right up there with skiing now and the Terrain Park is definitely one of the best in North America. If you're here for the Ski & Snowboard Festival in April, the skiers and snowboarders take over the village and there's everything from photo contests to live music and great parties.

4 APRES SKI WIND-DOWN

It's an amazing feeling to walk around the Village Stroll area in the evening with like-minded people after a hard day on the slopes. It's comfortable and laid-back and there's a great vibe with a good mix of people shopping, hitting the bars or dining in great restaurants... and maybe comparing stories and bruises from the tumbles they might have had.

Below: Whistler village; Right: Skiers, Whistler

(BELOW & RIGHT) RANDY LINCKS/GETTY IMAGES ©

HIKING

With more than 40km of flower-and-forest alpine trails, most accessed via the Whistler Village Gondola, the region is ideal for those who like nature of the strollable variety. Favorite routes include the **High Note Trail** (8km), which traverses pristine meadows and has stunning views of the blue-green waters of Cheakamus Lake.

Sleeping

Adara Hotel Hotel **$$**

(☎604-905-4009, 866-502-3272; www.adarahotel.com; 4122 Village Green; r from $149;) Unlike all those lodges now claiming to be boutique hotels, the sophisticated and centrally located Adara is the real deal. Lined with designer details, including fake antler horns in the lobby, accommodations have spa-like bathrooms and fireplaces that look like TVs. Despite the ultra-cool aesthetics, service is warm and relaxed. Check ahead for the popular summertime bike packages.

Crystal Lodge & Suites Hotel **$$**

(☎800-667-3363, 604-932-2221; www.crystal-lodge.com; 4154 Village Green; d/ste from $130/175;) Not all rooms are created equal at the Crystal, forged from the fusion of two quite different hotel towers. Cheaper rooms in the South Tower are standard style – baths and fridges are the highlight – but those in the Lodge Wing match the handsome rock-and-beam lobby, complete with small balconies. Both share excellent proximity to restaurants and ski lifts.

Chalet Luise B&B Inn B&B **$$**

(☎800-665-1998, 604-932-4187; www.chaletluise.com; 7461 Ambassador Cres; d from $125;) A five-minute trail walk from the village, this Bavarian-look pension has eight bright and sunny rooms – think pine furnishings and crisp white duvets – and

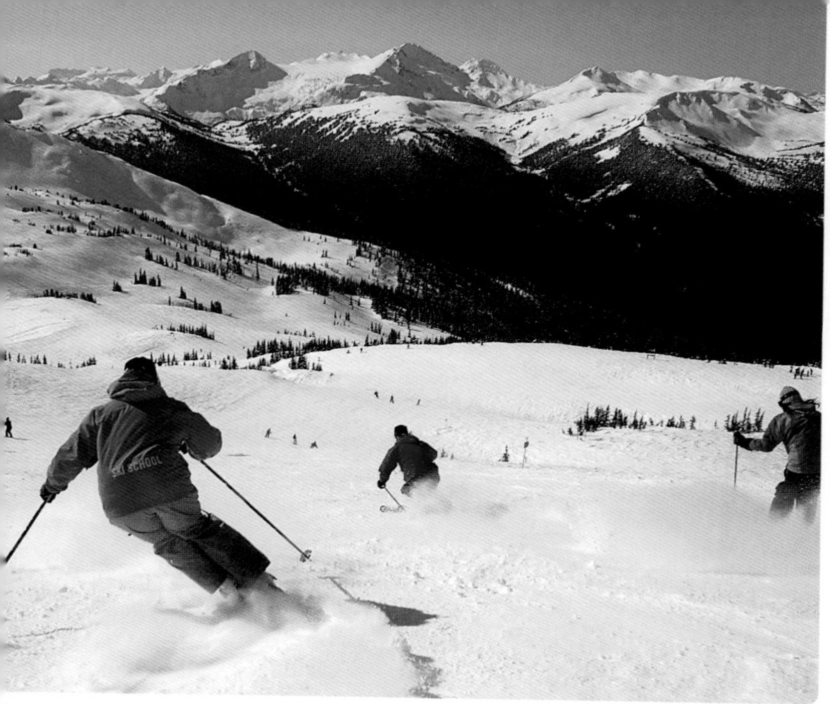

a flower garden that's ideal for a spot of evening wine quaffing. Or you can just hop in the hot tub and dream about the large buffet breakfast coming your way in the morning. Free parking.

Eating

Purebread Bakery $

(www.purebread.ca; 4338 Main St; baked goods $3-5; 8:30am-7pm) When this Function Junction legend finally opened a village branch, the locals came running, and they've been queuing ever since. They're here for the cornucopia of eye-roll-worthy bakery treats, including salted caramel bars, sour-cherry choc-chip cookies and the amazing Crack, a naughtily gooey shortbread cookie bar. There's savory here, too; go for the hearty homity pie.

Rimrock Cafe West Coast $$

(604-932-5565; http://rimrockcafe.com; 2117 Whistler Rd; mains $16-28; 5:45-9:30pm) On the edge of Creekside and accessible just off Hwy 99, the menu at this locals' favorite includes highlights like seared scallops, venison tenderloin and a recommended seafood trio of grilled prawns, ahi tuna and nut-crusted sablefish. All are served in an intimate room with two fireplaces and a large, flower-lined patio where you can laugh at the harried highway drivers zipping past.

Araxi Restaurant & Bar West Coast $$$

(604-932-4540; www.araxi.com; 4222 Village Sq; mains $24-41; 5-11pm daily, plus brunch 10am-2pm Sat & Sun) Whistler's best splurge restaurant, Araxi cooks up an inventive and exquisite Pacific Northwest menu and has charming and courteous service. Try the BC halibut and drain the 15,000-bottle wine selection but save room for dessert: a regional cheese plate or the amazing Okanagan apple cheesecake...or both.

Vancouver Island

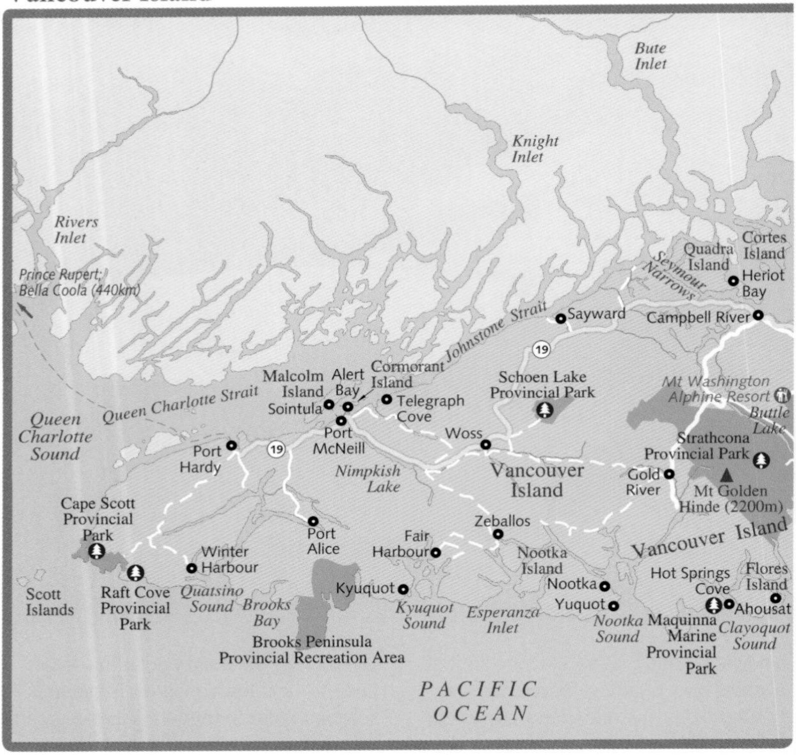

Drinking & Entertainment

Merlin's Bar & Grill Pub

(4553 Blackcomb Way; 11am-1am) The best of Whistler's cavernous ski pubs, this Upper Village local also looks the part: log-lined walls, ceiling-mounted lift cars, bra-draped moose head and a large slope-facing patio. Menus, mounted on snowboard tips, cover the pub-grub classics and, although the beer is mostly of the generic Kokanee-like variety, there's usually some tasty Whistler Brewing ales available. Regular live music during peak season.

Information

Whistler Visitors Centre (800-944-7853, 604-935-3357; www.whistler.com; 4230 Gateway Dr; 8am-10pm) Flyer-lined visitors center with friendly staff.

Getting There & Around

Pacific Coach Lines (www.pacificcoach.com) services arrive from Vancouver (from $49, two hours, five daily) and Vancouver International Airport and drop off at Whistler hotels.

Train spotters can trundle into town on Rocky Mountaineer Vacations' **Whistler Sea to Sky Climb (www.rockymountaineer.com)**, which winds along a picturesque coastal route from North Vancouver (from $169, three hours, one daily May to mid-October).

Whistler's **WAVE (www.busonline.ca)** public buses (adult/child/one-day pass $2.50/2/7) are equipped with ski and bike racks.

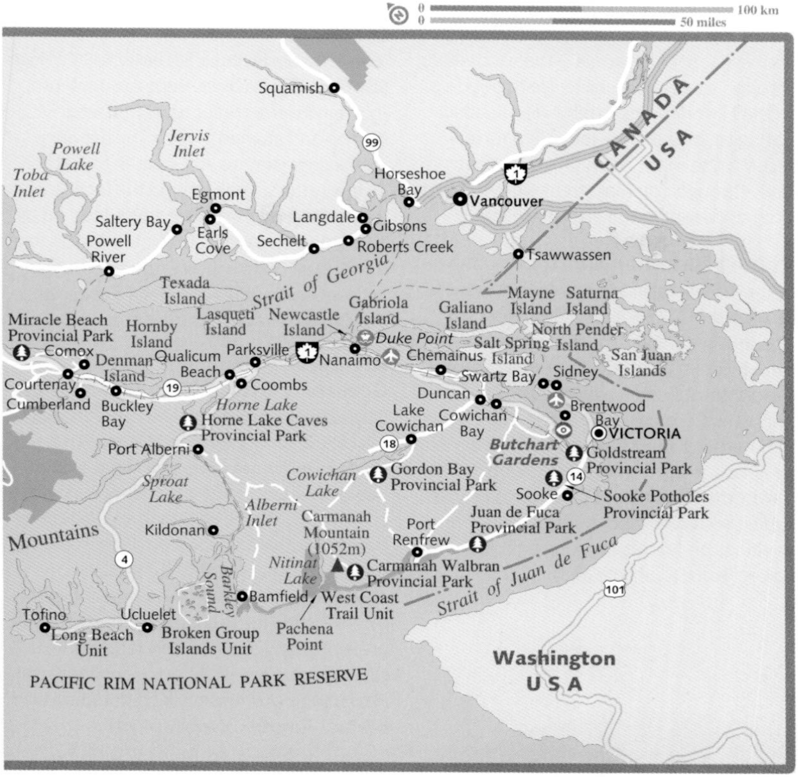

VANCOUVER ISLAND

While the history-wrapped BC capital Victoria is the first port of call for many, it should not be the only place you visit. Food and wine fans will enjoy weaving through the verdant Cowichan Valley farm region; those craving a laid-back, family-friendly enclave should hit the twin seaside towns of Parksville and Qualicum; and outdoor-activity enthusiasts shouldn't miss the surf-loving west-coast area of Tofino and beyond.

Victoria

With a wider metro population approaching 360,000, this picture-postcard provincial capital was long-touted as North America's most English city. Thankfully, the tired theme-park version of old-fashioned England has faded in recent years. Fueled by an increasingly younger demographic, a quiet revolution has seen lame tourist pubs, eateries and stores transformed into the kind of brightly painted bohemian shops, coffee bars and innovative restaurants that would make any city proud. It's worth seeking out these enclaves on foot, but activity fans should also hop on their bikes: Victoria has more cycle routes than any other Canadian city.

Sights

Royal BC Museum Museum

(Map p90; www.royalbcmuseum.bc.ca; 675 Belleville St; adult/child from $16/10; 10am-5pm Sun-Wed, to 10pm Thu-Sat) Start in the natural-history gallery on your visit to the province's best museum. Fronted by a beady-eyed woolly mammoth, it's lined with evocative dioramas – the elk peeking through trees is a favorite. Next, head up to the First Peoples exhibit with its fascinating mask gallery – look for a ferret-faced white man. The highlight is the walk-through colonial street with its chatty Chinatown and detailed storefronts.

Robert Bateman Centre — Gallery

(Map p90; www.batemancentre.org; 470 Belleville St; adult/child $12.50/8.50; ⌚10am-6pm Sun-Wed, to 9pm Thu-Sat) Victoria's newest cultural attraction isn't just a gallery showcasing the photo-realistic works of Canada's most popular nature painter, it's also a testament to Bateman's commitment to environmental issues. Start with the five-minute intro movie, then move through a series of small exhibit areas with 160 achingly beautiful paintings and prints showing animals in nature from BC and beyond.

Parliament Buildings — Historic Building

(Map p90; www.leg.bc.ca; 501 Belleville St; ⌚tours 9am-5pm) FREE Across from the museum, this handsome confection of turrets, domes and stained glass is the province's working legislature and is open to history-loving visitors. Peek behind the facade on a colorful (and free) 30-minute tour led by costumed Victorians, then stop for lunch at the 'secret' politicians' restaurant. Return in the evening when the elegant exterior is illuminated like a Christmas tree.

Art Gallery of Greater Victoria — Gallery

(Map p89; www.aggv.bc.ca; 1040 Moss St; adult/child $13/2.50; ⌚10am-5pm Mon-Wed, Fri & Sat, to 9pm Thu, noon-5pm Sun) Head east of downtown on Fort St and follow the gallery street signs to one of Canada's best Emily Carr collections. Aside from Carr's swirling nature canvases, you'll find an ever-changing array of temporary exhibitions. Check online for events, including lectures, presentations and monthly late-night Urbanite socials, when artsy coolsters roll in to mingle. Admission is by donation on the first Tuesday of every month.

Craigdarroch Castle — Museum

(Map p89; www.thecastle.ca; 1050 Joan Cres; adult/child $13.75/5; ⌚9am-7pm) If you're in this part of town checking out the gallery, don't miss this elegant turreted mansion a few minutes' walk away. A handsome, 39-room landmark built by a 19th-century coal baron with money to burn, it's dripping with period architecture and antique-packed rooms. Climb the tower's 87 steps, checking out the stained-glass en route, for views of the snowcapped Olympic Mountains.

Parliament Buildings, Victoria
RANDY LINCKS/GETTY IMAGES ©

Victoria City Overview

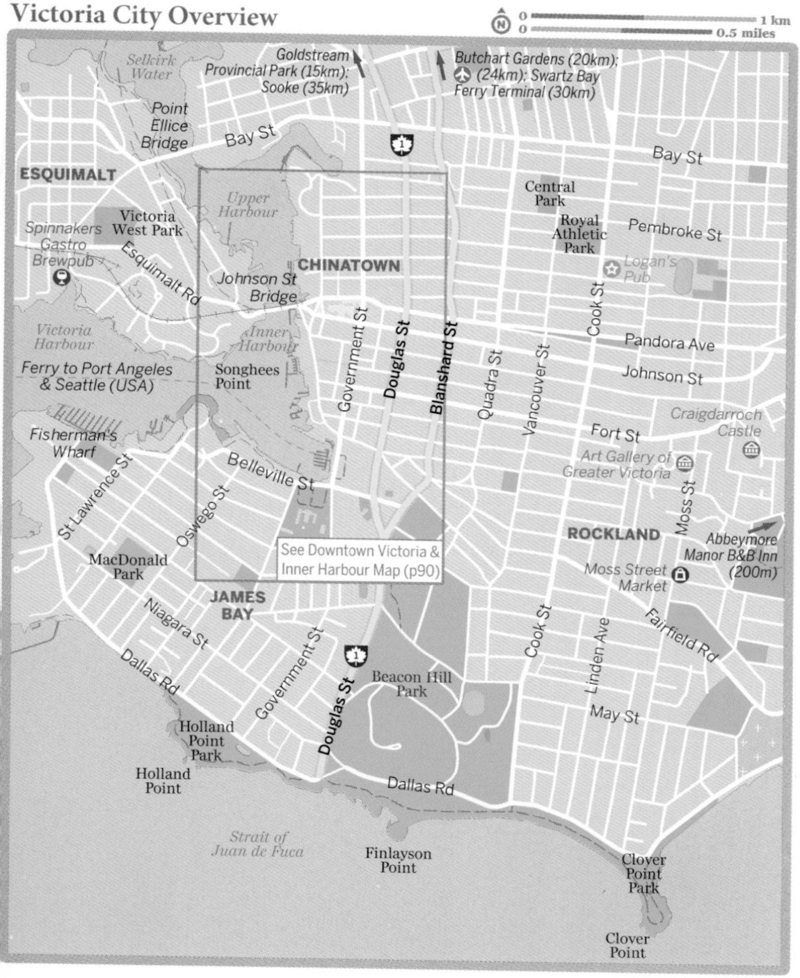

Activities

WHALE WATCHING

Prince of Whales Boat Tour

(Map p90; ☎888-383-4884, 250-383-4884; www.princeofwhales.com; 812 Wharf St; adult/child from $110/85) Long-established local operator.

Springtide Charters Boat Tour

(Map p90; ☎800-470-3474, 250-384-4444; www.springtidecharters.com; 1119 Wharf St; adult/child from $105/75) Popular local operator.

KAYAKING

Ocean River Adventures Kayaking

(Map p90; ☎800-909-4233, 250-381-4233; www.oceanriver.com; 1824 Store St; rental per 2hr $40, tours from $75; ⌚9:30am-6pm Mon-Wed & Sat, to 8pm Thu & Fri, 10am-5pm Sun) Rentals and popular three-hour harbor tours.

Downtown Victoria & Inner Harbour

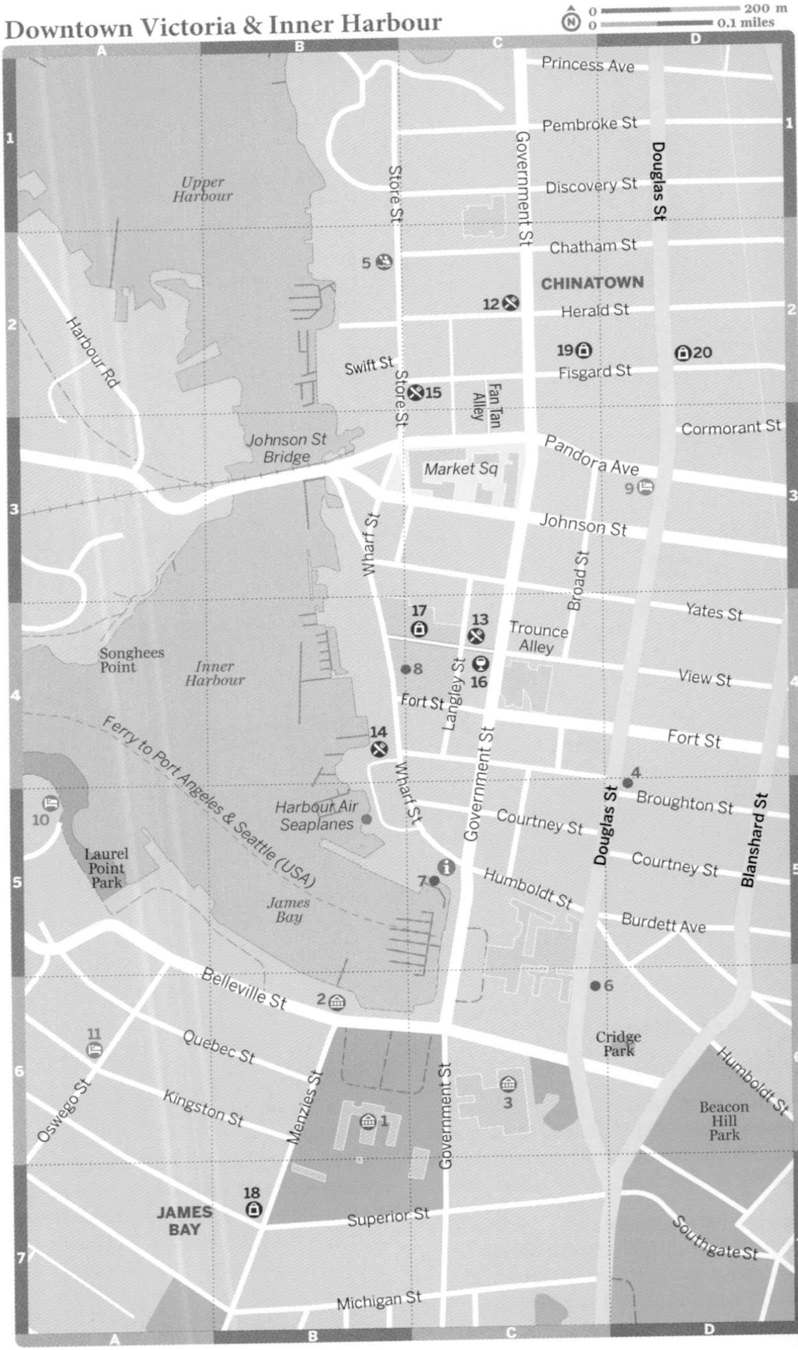

Downtown Victoria & Inner Harbour

Sights

1	Parliament Buildings	B6
2	Robert Bateman Centre	B6
3	Royal BC Museum	C6

Activities, Courses & Tours

4	Architectural Institute of BC	D5
5	Ocean River Adventures	B2
6	Pedaler	C6
7	Prince of Whales	C5
8	Springtide Charters	C4

Sleeping

9	Hotel Rialto	D3
10	Inn at Laurel Point	A5
11	Oswego Hotel	A6

Eating

12	Jam Cafe	C2
	Legislative Dining Room	(see 1)
13	ReBar	C4
14	Red Fish Blue Fish	B4
15	Ulla	C2

Drinking & Nightlife

16	Garrick's Head	C4

Shopping

17	Bastion Square Public Market	C4
18	James Bay Market	B7
19	Victoria Downtown Farmers Market	C2
20	Victoria Public Market	D2

Tours

Architectural Institute of BC — Walking Tour

(Map p90; ☎800-667-0753, ext 333, 604-683-8588; www.aibc.ca; 1001 Douglas St; tours $10; ⏰10am & 1pm Tue-Sun Jul & Aug) Six great-value, building-themed walking tours, covering angles from art deco to ecclesiastical.

Pedaler — Bicycle Tour

(Map p90; ☎778-265-7433; www.thepedaler.ca; 719 Douglas St; tours from $59; ⏰9am-6pm) Guided bike tours weave around local breweries, plus there's history-themed and coffee-and-cake tour alternatives.

Sleeping

Hotel Rialto — Hotel $$

(Map p90; ☎250-383-4157; www.hotelrialto.ca; 653 Pandora Ave; d from $179; 📶) Completely refurbished from the faded former budget hotel it once was, the Rialto is a well-located downtown option in an attractive century-old heritage building. Each of the mod-decorated rooms has a fridge, microwave and flatscreen TV and some have tubs as well as showers. The lobby's tapas lounge is popular, whether or not you're staying here.

Inn at Laurel Point — Hotel $$

(Map p90; ☎800-663-7667, 250-386-8721; www.laurelpoint.com; 680 Montreal St; d from $169; ❄@📶🏊🐾) Tucked along the Inner Harbour a short seaside stroll from the downtown action, this friendly, art-lined and ever-comfortable sleepover is all about the views across the waterfront. Spacious rooms come with private balconies for drinking in the mesmerizing sunsets. Still owned by a local family, there's a resort-like level of calm relaxation.

Oswego Hotel — Hotel $$$

(Map p90; ☎250-294-7500, 877-767-9346; www.oswegovictoria.com; 500 Oswego St; d $205; 📶🐾) Well hidden on a residential side street a short stroll from the Inner Harbour, this contemporary boutique hotel is an in-the-know favorite. Rooms come with granite floors, cedar beams and, in most units, small balconies. All have kitchens – think stainless steel – and deep baths, making them more like apartments than hotel rooms. Cleverly, the smaller studio rooms have space-saving high-end Murphy beds.

Abbeymoore Manor B&B Inn — B&B $$$

(☎888-801-1811, 250-370-1470; www.abbeymoore.com; 1470 Rockland Ave; d from $199; 📶) A romantic 1912 Arts and Crafts mansion, Abbeymoore's handsome colonial exterior hides seven antique-lined rooms furnished with Victorian knickknacks. Some units have kitchens and jetted tubs and the hearty breakfast will fuel you up

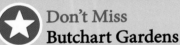

BARRETT & MACKAY/GETTY IMAGES ©

Don't Miss
Butchart Gardens

A 30-minute drive from Victoria via West Saanich Rd, the rolling farmlands of waterfront Brentwood Bay are chiefly known for **Butchart Gardens** (www.butchartgardens.com; 800 Benvenuto Ave; adult/child $30.20/10.30; ⌚9am-10pm; 🚌75), Vancouver Island's leading visitor attraction. The immaculate grounds are divided into separate gardens where there's always something in bloom. Summer is crowded, with tour buses rolling in relentlessly, but evening music performances and Saturday night fireworks in July and August make it all worthwhile. Tea fans take note: the **Dining Room Restaurant** serves a smashing afternoon tea, complete with quiches and Grand Marnier truffles; leave your diet at the door.

for a day of exploring: Craigdarroch Castle and the Art Gallery of Greater Victoria are nearby.

Eating

Red Fish Blue Fish Seafood **$**
(Map p90; www.redfish-bluefish.com; 1006 Wharf St; mains $6-20; ⌚11:30am-7pm Mon-Thu, to 8pm Fri-Sun) On the waterfront boardwalk at the foot of Broughton St, this freight-container takeout shack serves a loyal clientele who just can't get enough of its fresh-made sustainable seafood. Highlights like scallop *tacones*, wild-salmon sandwiches, tempura-battered fish and chips and chunky Pacific Rim chowder all hit the spot. Find a waterfront perch to enjoy your nosh, but watch for hovering seagull mobsters.

Jam Cafe Breakfast **$$**
(Map p90; www.jamcafevictoria.com; 542 Herald St; mains $8-16; ⌚8am-3pm) The locals won't tell you anything about this slightly off-the-beaten-path place. But that's not because they don't know about it; it's because they don't want you to add to the

lineups for the best breakfast in town. The delectable eggs Benedict varieties are ever popular, but we also recommend the amazing, and very naughty, chicken French toast.

Legislative Dining Room West Coast **$$**

(Map p90; ☎250-387-3959; www.leg.bc.ca; room 606, Parliament Bldgs, 501 Belleville St; mains $9-15; ⏰hours vary) One of Victoria's best-kept dining secrets, the Parliament Buildings has its own subsidized, old-school restaurant where both MLAs and the public can drop by for a silver-service menu of regional dishes, ranging from salmon salads to velvety steaks and a BC-only wine list. Entry is via the security desk just inside the building's main entrance; photo ID is required.

ReBar Vegetarian, Fusion **$$**

(Map p90; www.rebarmodernfood.com; 50 Bastion Sq; mains $8-16; ⏰11am-9pm Mon-Thu, to 10pm Fri, 8:30am-10pm Sat, to 8pm Sun; 🌶) A laid-back downtown fixture, ReBar mixes colorful interiors with a mostly vegetarian menu. Carnivores will be just as happy to eat here, though, with hearty savory dishes such as shrimp quesadilla, mushroom-based curries and heaping weekend brunches – the salmon-topped bagel melt is great.

Ulla West Coast **$$$**

(Map p90; ☎250-590-8795; www.ulla.ca; 509 Fisgard St; mains $24-30; ⏰5:30-10pm Tue-Sat; 🌶) Hidden at the quiet end of Chinatown's Fisgard St, this is the best restaurant in the city to dive into perfectly prepared west coast dining. In a wood-floored but contemporary room studded with local artworks and cookbooks, you'll find a seasonal menu often including BC halibut or lamb plus a bounty of organic veggies. If you're a vegetarian, the options for you are top-notch.

Drinking & Nightlife

Garrick's Head Pub

(Map p90; www.bedfordregency.com; 1140 Government St; ⏰11am-11pm Mon-Thu, till midnight Fri & Sat, till 10pm Sun) A huge overhaul has transformed this once humdrum downtown pub into Victoria's best spot for trying local-made brews. Pull up a perch at the long bar and you'll be faced with 40-plus taps serving a comprehensive menu of beers from Driftwood, Phillips, Hoyne and beyond. Once or twice a month, there are guests casks to keep things lively.

Spinnakers Gastro Brewpub Pub

(Map p89; www.spinnakers.com; 308 Catherine St; ⏰11am-10:30pm) One of Canada's first craft brewers, this wood-floored smasher

To Market, To Market

The much-anticipated **Victoria Public Market** (Map p90; www.victoriapublicmarket.com; 1701 Douglas St; ⏰9:30am-6:30pm Tue-Sat, to 5pm Sun; 🚌4) opened in 2013 with various food-focused vendors – from Silk Road Tea to Salt Spring Island Cheese – in this refurbished spot in downtown's heritage Hudson Building.

Outside the building, the **Victoria Downtown Farmers Market** (Map p90; www.victoriapublicmarket.com; 1701 Douglas St, back carriageway; ⏰11am-3pm Wed; 🚌4), which runs all year, sells locally made and farmed food.

If you want more alfresco shopping, downtown's **Bastion Square Public Market** (Map p90; www.bastionsquare.ca; Bastion Sq; ⏰from 11am Thu-Sun May-Sep) houses art-and-craft stalls all summer, while **James Bay Market** (Map p90; www.jamesbaymarket.com; 494 Superior St; ⏰9am-3pm May-Oct; 🚌27) and the large **Moss Street Market** (Map p89; www.mossstreetmarket.com; cnr Moss St & Fairfield Rd; ⏰10am-2pm May-Oct; 🚌7) offer a community-focused combo of both arts and food.

is a short hop from downtown via Harbour Ferry. Sail in for copper-colored Nut Brown Ale and hoppy Blue Bridge Double IPA and check out the daily casks to see what's on special. Save room to eat: the menu here is true gourmet gastropub grub.

Entertainment

Check the weekly freebie *Monday Magazine* to get the lowdown on local happenings.

Logan's Pub — Live Music

(Map p89; www.loganspub.com; 1821 Cook St; ⏲3pm-1am Mon-Fri, 10am-1am Sat, 10am-midnight Sun) A 10-minute walk from downtown, this no-nonsense pub looks like nothing special from the outside, but its roster of shows is a fixture of the local indie scene. Fridays and Saturdays are your best bet for performances but other nights are frequently also scheduled; check the online calendar to see what's coming up.

Information

Victoria Visitors Centre (Map p90; www.tourismvictoria.com; 812 Wharf St; ⏲8:30am-8:30pm) Busy, flyer-lined visitors center overlooking the Inner Harbour.

Getting There & Away

Air

Victoria International Airport (www.victoriaairport.com) is 26km north of the city via Hwy 17.

Harbour Air (Map p90; www.harbour-air.com) flies into the Inner Harbour from downtown Vancouver ($185, 35 minutes) throughout the day.

Boat

BC Ferries (www.bcferries.com) arrive from mainland Tsawwassen (adult/vehicle $15.50/51.25, 1½ hours) at Swartz Bay, 27km north of Victoria via Hwy 17.

Victoria Clipper (www.clippervacations.com) services arrive in the Inner Harbour from Seattle (adult/child US$88/44, three hours, up to three a day). **Black Ball Transport (www.ferrytovictoria.com)** boats also arrive here from Port Angeles (adult/child/vehicle US$17/8.50/$60.50, 1½ hours, up to four daily).

Totem poles, Duncan

CHRIS CHEADLE/GETTY IMAGES

Getting Around

To/From the Airport

AKAL Airporter (www.victoriaairporter.com) minibuses run between the airport and area hotels ($21, 30 minutes). In contrast, a taxi to downtown costs around $50, while airport-serving transit buses 83, 86 and 88 take around 35 minutes, run throughout the day and cost $2.50 – you may need to change buses at McTavish Exchange.

Cowichan Valley

A swift Hwy 1 drive northwest of Victoria, the farm-filled Cowichan Valley region is ripe for discovery, especially if you're a traveling foodie or an outdoor activity nut. Contact **Tourism Cowichan** (888-303-3337, 250-746-4636; www.tourismcowichan.com) for more information.

DUNCAN

Developed as a logging-industry railroad stop – the gabled little station now houses a museum – Duncan is the valley's main community. A useful base for regional exploration, it's known for its dozens of totem poles, which dot downtown like sentinels.

If your First Nations curiosity is piqued, head to the **Quw'utsun' Cultural & Conference Centre** (www.quwutsun.ca; 200 Cowichan Way; adult/child $13/6; 10am-4pm Mon-Sat Jun-Sep) to learn about carving and traditional salmon runs. Its on-site **Riverwalk Café** serves First Nations–inspired cuisine.

The area's chatty hub, **Duncan Garage Cafe** (www.communityfarmstore.ca; 3330 Duncan St; mains $4-9; 7:30am-6pm Mon-Sat, 9am-5pm Sun) is in a refurbished heritage building that also houses a bookshop and an organic grocery store. Libations of the boozy variety are on the menu at **Craig Street Brew Pub** (www. craigstreet.ca; 25 Craig St; mains $11-16; 11am-11pm Mon-Thu, to midnight Fri & Sat, to 10pm Sun), where comfort grub and own-brewed beer lure the locals; the pizzas are recommended.

Local Knowledge

Cowichan Valley

RECOMMENDATIONS FROM DANIEL HUDSON, CHEF/OWNER OF HUDSON'S ON FIRST, DUNCAN, BC

1 FOODIE SPECIALTIES

There are tons of farms in the valley. You name it and we produce it: chilies, cheese, honey. 'Cowichan' is from an aboriginal word meaning 'the warm land' – you can grow anything here. The valley's wineries and cider makers are a big draw. We're not the Okanagan Valley yet, with that sort of national and international recognition, but people are becoming more aware of what it's all about here in the Cowichan Valley. Merridale Estate Cidery (p96) is a good one to try.

2 ARTS AND CRAFTS

It's not just food and wine producers here – the valley also has a big arts and crafts movement, with glass blowing, painting and clothing made locally. Duncan, Chemainus and Ladysmith all have tons of galleries.

3 BEST PLACE IF YOU'RE SHORT ON TIME

Cowichan Bay – it's the valley in a nutshell, where a cheesemonger sits next to an artisan bakery, and fishing boats dock nearby. It's a Cittaslow town, meaning it's more than just slow food, but a whole movement of things produced locally and slowly in the community to improve the quality of life.

4 OTHER SIGHTS AND ACTIVITIES

You can visit the Quw'utsun' Cultural Centre in Duncan, which has a mock-up aboriginal village. The valley has lots of trails – the Trans Canada Trail goes through the area. Provincial parks have hiking and cycling. Bring a full wallet, an open mind and just explore. There's lots of stuff here you won't get anywhere else. The Taste the Cowichan website (www.tastecowichan.ca) is a good resource for everything.

Vancouver Island Booze Trail

In the Cowichan region, check out **Cherry Point Vineyards** (www.cherrypointvineyards.com; 840 Cherry Point Rd, Cobble Hill; 10am-5pm), with its lip-smacking blackberry port; **Averill Creek** (www.averillcreek.ca; 6552 North Rd, Duncan; 11am-5pm), with its patio views and lovely pinot noirs; and the smashing **Merridale Estate Cidery** (www.merridalecider.com; 1230 Merridale Rd, Cobble Hill; 10:30am-7pm), an inviting apple-cider producer that also makes brandy and has a great patio bistro.

But it's not all about the Cowichan. Further south in Saanich – and just a short drive from Victoria – organic apples are also on the taste-tripping menu at **Sea Cider** (www.seacider.ca; 2487 Mt St Michael Rd, Saanichton; 11am-4pm). While booze of a stronger hue is the approach at nearby **Victoria Spirits** (www.victoriaspirits.com; 6170 Old West Saanich Rd, Victoria; 10am-5pm Sat & Sun Apr-Sep), where the lovely Oaken Gin is recommended. Both offer tours and tastings.

For more information on wineries, cideries and distilleries throughout Vancouver Island, check www.wineislands.ca.

But the town's newest restaurant has really cranked Duncan dining up a notch. Housed in an immaculately restored former music-school building, the delightful **Hudson's on First** (www.hudsonsonfirst.ca; 163 First St; mains $16-26; 11am-2:30pm & 5-8:30pm Tue-Sun) would be a top table option in far bigger cities. Farm-to-table local produce is the approach on an ever-changing seasonal menu that fuses west coast ingredients with subtle European influences.

COWICHAN BAY

'Cow Bay' to the locals, the region's most attractive pit stop is a colorful string of wooden buildings perched over a mountain-framed ocean inlet. It's well worth an afternoon of your time, although it might take that long to find parking on a busy summer day. Arrive hungry and drop into **Hilary's Artisan Cheese** (www.hilaryscheese.com; 1737 Cowichan Bay Rd; 9am-6pm) and **True Grain Bread** (www.truegrain.ca; 1725 Cowichan Bay Rd; 8am-7pm Mon-Sat, to 5pm Sun) for the makings of a great picnic.

Nanaimo

Vancouver Island's 'second metropolis,' Nanaimo will never have the allure of tourist-magnet Victoria, but the Harbour City has undergone a quiet upgrade since the 1990s, with the emergence, especially on Commercial St and in the Old City Quarter, of some good shops and eateries, plus a slick new museum. With dedicated ferry services from the mainland, the city is also a handy hub for exploring the rest of the island.

Sights

Nanaimo Museum Museum

(www.nanaimomuseum.ca; 100 Museum Way; adult/child $2/75¢; 10am-5pm) Just off the Commercial St main drag, this excellent museum showcases the region's heritage from First Nations to colonial, maritime, sporting and beyond. Ask at the front desk about summer-only city walking tours and entry to the nearby Bastion, an 1853 wooden tower fortification.

Newcastle Island Marine Provincial Park Park

(www.newcastleisland.ca) Nanaimo's rustic outdoor gem offers 22km of hiking and biking trails, plus beaches and wildlife spotting. Traditional Coast Salish land, it was the site of shipyards and coal mines before becoming a popular summer excursion for locals in the 1930s when a tea pavilion was added. Accessed by a 10-minute ferry hop from the harbor (adult/child return $9/5), there's a seasonal eatery and regular First Nations dancing displays.

Old City Quarter Neighborhood

(www.oldcityquarter.com; cnr Fitzwilliam & Wesley Sts) A steep hike uphill from the waterfront on Bastion and Fitzwilliam Sts delivers you to a strollable heritage hood of independent stores, galleries and eateries in brightly painted old buildings. Highlights include McLeans Specialty Foods; A Wee Cupcakery; and Fibber Magees, a handsome large pub that has taken over the town's old train station.

Sleeping

Buccaneer Inn Motel $$

(250-753-1246, 877-282-6337; www.buccaneerinn.com; 1577 Stewart Ave; d/ste from $80/140;) Handy for the Departure Bay ferry terminal, this friendly, family-run motel has a gleaming white exterior that makes it hard to pass by. It's worth stopping though, as the neat-and-tidy approach is carried over into the maritime-themed rooms, many of which have kitchenettes. Splurge on a spacious suite and you'll have a fireplace, full kitchen and flatscreen TV.

Coast Bastion Hotel Hotel $$

(250-753-6601, 800-716-6199; www.coasthotels.com; 11 Bastion St; d from $157;) Downtown's best hotel has an unbeatable location overlooking the harbor, with most guests enjoying sparkling waterfront views, when it's not foggy. Rooms have been well refurbished with a lounge-modern élan in recent years, adding flatscreen TVs and, in most rooms, small fridges.

Nanaimo harbour

CHRIS CHEADLE/GETTY IMAGES ©

VANCOUVER & BRITISH COLUMBIA NANAIMO

Eating

Gabriel's Café International $

(183 Commercial St; mains $6-9; ⏲8am-7pm Mon-Fri, 9am-5pm Sat & Sun; 🌿) This perfectly located downtown hole-in-the-wall is like a static food truck. Chat with the man himself behind the counter, then tuck into made-from-scratch treats, like pulled-pork breakfast wraps or the ever-popular Thai-green-curry rice bowl. Vegetarians are well looked after; try the black-bean burger.

Modern Cafe International $$

(www.themoderncafe.ca; 221 Commercial St; mains $15-23; ⏲11am-11pm Mon-Wed, to midnight Thu-Sat, 10am-11pm Sun) This reinvented old coffee shop has cool, loungy interiors combining exposed brick and comfy booths and, for when it's sunny, a ray-warmed street-side patio. The menu has risen up a notch or two in recent years and now includes gourmet comfort food with international influences – go for the Caribbean-jerk-chicken dish. Excellent burgers are also served up.

Drinking & Entertainment

Longwood Brewpub Brewpub

(www.longwoodbrewpub.com; 5775 Turner Rd; ⏲11am-midnight) Incongruously located in a strip mall (northwest of the downtown harborfront, via the Island Hwy), this handsome stone and gabled restaurant-pub combines a surprisingly good menu with lip-smacking self-brewed beers.

Nanaimo

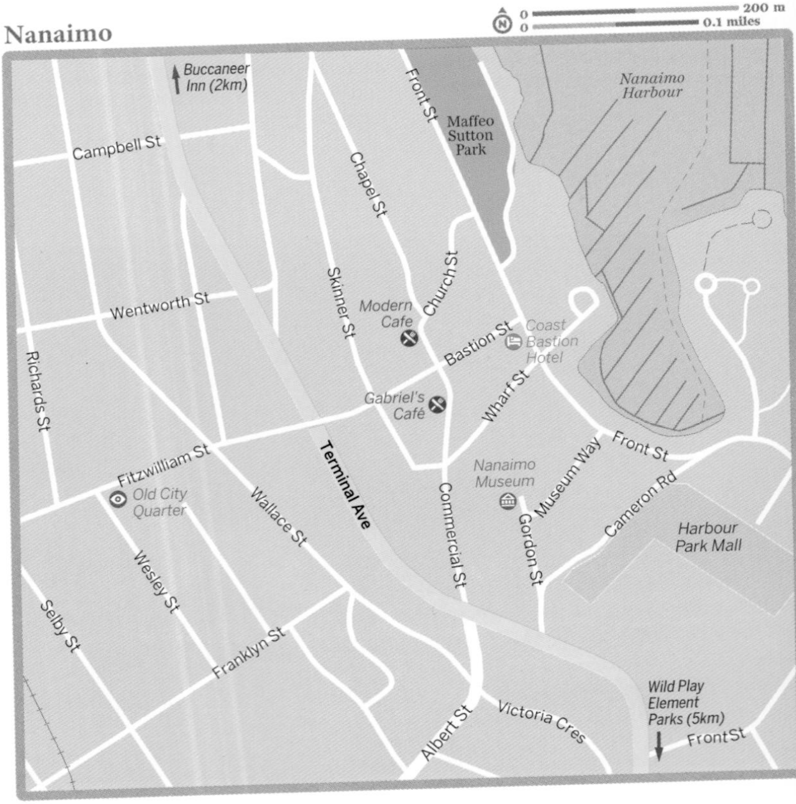

Detour: Salt Spring Island

The busiest and most developed of the Southern Gulf Islands – which float like a necklace between the mainland and Vancouver Island – Salt Spring (pop 10,500) has a reputation for palatial vacation homes, but it's also lined with artist studios and artisan food and drink producers. Well worth a visit, the center of the community is Ganges.

Locals tell you they avoid the gigantic **Saturday Market** (www.saltspringmarket.com; Centennial Park, Ganges; 8am-4pm Sat Apr-Oct) that animates the heart of Ganges; they claim to do their shopping at the smaller Tuesday and Wednesday versions. But everyone on the island seems to be here on the big day, checking out the stalls topped with goodies made, baked or grown on the island.

Drop by **Salt Spring Island Cheese** (www.saltspringcheese.com; 285 Reynolds Rd; 10am-5pm) for a wander around the idyllic farmstead, and a tasting or two in the winery-style shop. Consider some Ruckles goat cheese to go.

Art fans should hit the trail on Salt Spring by checking out gallery and studio locations via the free downloadable map at **Salt Spring Studio Tour** (www.saltspringstudiotour.com). Highlights include **Blue Horse Folk Art Gallery** (www.bluehorse.ca; 175 North View Dr; 10am-5pm Sun-Fri Mar-Dec) and **Duthie Gallery** (www.duthiegallery.com; 125 Churchill Rd, Ganges; 10am-5pm & 9-11pm Thu-Mon Jul & Aug), which stages the popular summer Night Gallery in its art-lined woodland park.

BC Ferries runs to Salt Spring from Swartz Bay (by Victoria) and Tsawwassen (near Vancouver). See www.saltspringtourism.com for more information.

Information

Nanaimo Visitors Centre (800-663-7337, 250-751-1556; www.tourismnanaimo.com; 2450 Northfield Rd; 9am-6pm) For tourist information, drop into the main visitors center or the summer-only satellite behind downtown's Nanaimo Museum.

Getting There & Away

Air

Nanaimo Airport (www.nanaimoairport.com) is 18km south of town via Hwy 1.

Boat

BC Ferries (www.bcferries.com) from Tsawwassen (passenger/vehicle $14.55/49.05, two hours) arrive at Duke Point, 14km south of Nanaimo. Services from West Vancouver's Horseshoe Bay (passenger/vehicle $15.50/51.25, 95 minutes) arrive at Departure Bay, 3km north of the city center via Hwy 1.

Parksville, Coombs & Qualicum Beach

This popular mid-island seaside region, which also includes rustic Coombs, has been a traditional destination for vacationing families for decades – hence the water parks and miniature golf attractions.

Sights

Coombs Old Country Market — Market

(www.oldcountrymarket.com; 2326 Alberni Hwy, Coombs; 9am-7pm) The mother of all pit stops, this sprawling food and crafts menagerie is stuffed with bakery and produce delectables. It attracts huge numbers of visitors on balmy summer days, when cameras are pointed at the grassy roof where a herd of goats spends the season.

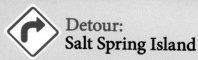

Below: Modern Cafe (p98), Nanaimo; **Right:** Tofino

World Parrot Refuge Wildlife Reserve
(www.worldparrotrefuge.org; 2116 Alberni Hwy, Coombs; adult/child $14/10; ⌚10am-4pm) Rescuing exotic birds from captivity and nursing them back to health, this excellent educational facility preaches the mantra that parrots are not pets. Pick up your earplugs at reception and stroll among the enclosures, each alive with recovering, and very noisy, birds.

Sleeping & Eating

Free Spirit Spheres Cabin $$
(☎250-757-9445; www.freespiritspheres.com; 420 Horne Lake Rd, Qualicum Beach; cabins from $145) These unique spherical tree houses enable guests to cocoon themselves in the forest canopy. Compact inside, 'Eve' is small and basic, while 'Eryn' and 'Melody' are lined with built-in cabinets.

Tofino

Transforming from resource outpost to hippie enclave and now eco resort town, Tofino is Vancouver Island's favorite outdoorsy retreat. It's not surprising that surf fans, families and city-escaping Vancouverites keep coming: packed with activities and blessed with stunning regional beaches, the funky community sits on Clayoquot Sound, where forested mounds rise from roiling, ever-dramatic waves.

Sights & Activities

Tofino Botanical Gardens Gardens
(www.tbgf.org; 1084 Pacific Rim Hwy; 3-day admission adult/child $10/free; ⌚9am-dusk) Explore what coastal temperate rainforests are all about by checking out the frog pond, forest boardwalk, native plants and educational workshops at this bird-packed rustic attraction.

Maquinna Marine Provincial Park Park

(www.bcparks.ca) One of the most popular day trips from Tofino, the highlight here is **Hot Spring Cove**. Tranquility-minded trekkers travel to the park by Zodiac boat or seaplane, watching for whales and other sea critters en route. From the boat landing, 2km of boardwalks lead to the natural hot pools.

Pacific Surf School Surfing

(www.pacificsurfschool.com; 430 Campbell St; board rental 6/24hr $15/20) Offers rentals, camps and lessons for beginners.

Surf Sister Surfing

(www.surfsister.com; 625 Campbell St; lessons $79) Introductory lessons for boys and girls, plus women-only multiday courses.

Tours

Remote Passages Kayaking

(www.remotepassages.com; 51 Wharf St; tours from $64) Gives short guided kayaking tours around Clayoquot Sound and the islands.

Jamie's Whaling Station Boat Tour

(www.jamies.com; 606 Campbell St; adult/child $99/69) Spot whales, bears and sea lions on Jamie's boat jaunts.

Sleeping

Tofino Inlet Cottages Cabin $$

(250-725-3441; www.tofinoinletcottages.com; 350 Olsen Rd; ste from $130;) Located in a pocket of tranquility just off the highway, this hidden gem is perfect for waking up to glassy-calm waterfront views. It consists of a pairing of two 1960s-built A-frame cottages, divided into two suites each, and a spacious woodsy house, which has a lovely circular hearth and is ideal for families.

Ocean Village Beach Resort Cabin $$$

(866-725-3755, 250-725-3755; www.oceanvillageresort.com; 555 Hellesen Dr;

ste from $229;) Recently renovated, this immaculate beachside resort of 53 beehive-shaped cedar cabins – hence the woodsy aroma when you step in the door – is a family favorite with a Scandinavian look. Each unit faces a shoreline just a few steps away and all have handy kitchens. No in-room TVs.

Wickaninnish Inn Hotel **$$$**
(800-333-4604, 250-725-3100; www.wickinn.com; Chesterman Beach; d from $399;) Cornering the market in luxury winter storm-watching packages, 'the Wick' is worth a stay any time of year. Embodying nature with its recycled wood furnishings, natural stone tiles and the ambience of a place grown rather than constructed, the sumptuous guest rooms have push-button gas fireplaces, two-person hot tubs and floor-to-ceiling windows. The region's most romantic sleepover.

Eating

Shelter West Coast **$$**
(www.shelterrestaurant.com; 601 Campbell St; mains $12-30; 11am-midnight) This woodsy, low-ceilinged haunt has kept expending over the years, but has never lost its welcoming locals' hangout feel. The perfect spot to grab lunch, salmon surf bowls and a patio seat are recommended. Shelter becomes an intimate dinner venue every evening, when the menu ratchets up to showcase finger-licking BC-sourced treats from seafood to gourmet burgers.

Sobo West Coast **$$**
(www.sobo.ca; 311 Neill St; mains $15-30; 11am-9pm) This local favorite started out as a still-remembered purple food truck and is now a popular sit-down eatery. The focus at Sobo – meaning Sophisticated Bohemian – is seasonal west coast ingredients prepared with international influences.

Information

Tofino Visitors Centre (250-725-3414; www.tourismtofino.com; 1426 Pacific Rim Hwy; 9am-5pm) A short drive south of town, the visitors center has detailed information on area accommodations, hiking trails and hot surf spots.

Getting There & Around

Orca Airways (www.flyorcaair.com) Flights arrive at Tofino Airport from Vancouver International Airport's South Terminal (from $174, one hour, up to five daily).

Tofino Bus (www.tofinobus.com) Local company with service to Victoria ($69) and Nanaimo ($46).

OKANAGAN VALLEY

It is hard to know which harvest is growing faster in this fertile and beautiful valley: tourists or fruit. The moniker 'Canada's Napa Valley' is oft repeated and somewhat apt. The 180km-long Okanagan Valley is home to dozens of excellent wineries, whose vines spread across the terraced hills, soaking up some of Canada's sunniest weather.

Near the center, Kelowna is one of the fastest-growing cities in Canada. It's a heady mix of culture, lakeside beauty and fun. In July and August, however, the entire valley can seem as overburdened as a grapevine right before the harvest. For many, the best time to visit is late spring and early fall, when the crowds are manageable.

Penticton

Not as frenetic as Kelowna, Penticton combines the idle pleasures of a beach resort with its own edgy vibe.

Sights

Okanagan Beach boasts about 1300m of sand, with average summer water temperatures of about 22°C (72°F). If things are jammed, there's often quieter shores at 1.5km-long **Skaha Beach**, south of the center.

Okanagan Valley

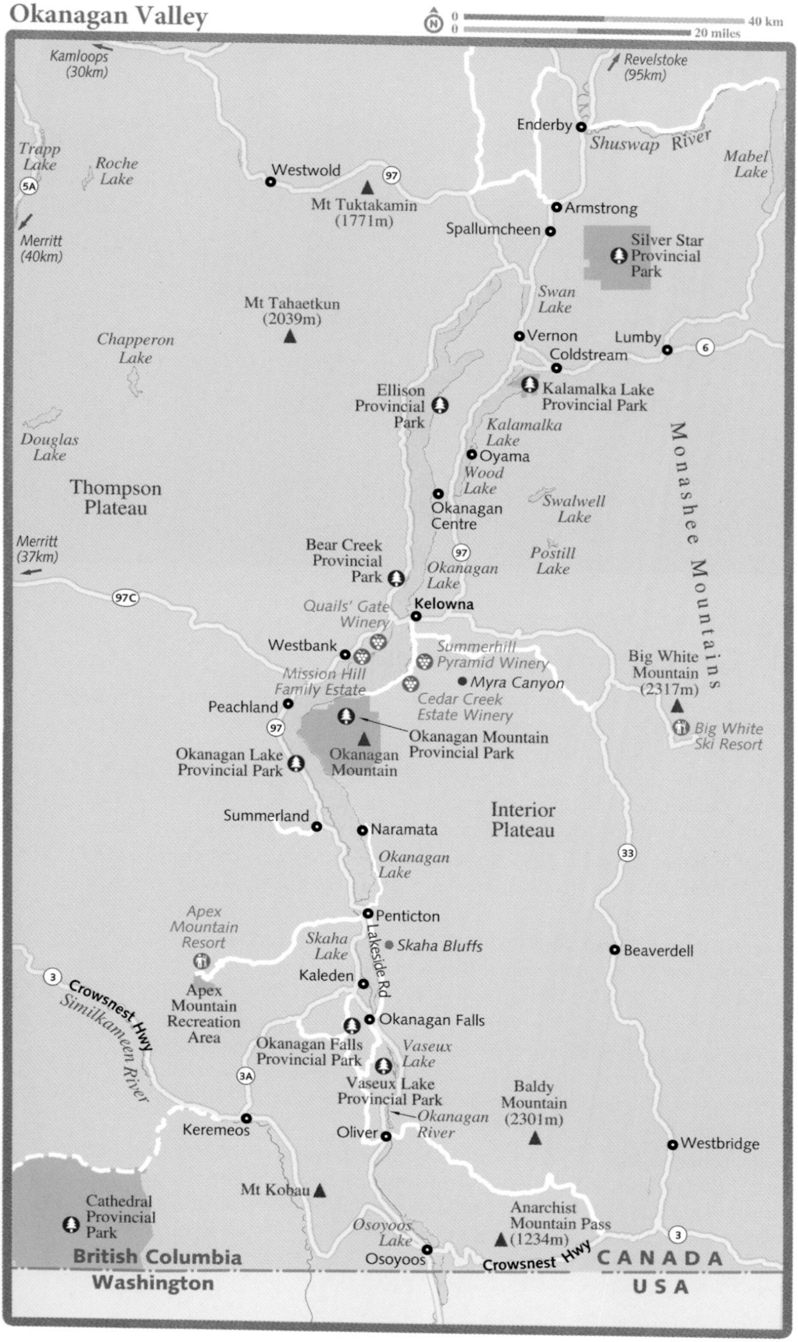
0 40 km
0 20 miles
Kamloops (30km)
Revelstoke (95km)
Enderby
Shuswap River
Mabel Lake
Trapp Lake
Roche Lake
5A
Westwold
97
Mt Tuktakamin (1771m)
Armstrong
Spallumcheen
Silver Star Provincial Park
Merritt (40km)
Swan Lake
Mt Tahaetkun (2039m)
Chapperon Lake
Vernon
Lumby
6
Coldstream
Ellison Provincial Park
Kalamalka Lake Provincial Park
Kalamalka Lake
Douglas Lake
Oyama
Wood Lake
Monashee Mountains
Thompson Plateau
Okanagan Centre
Swalwell Lake
Merritt (37km)
Bear Creek Provincial Park
Postill Lake
Okanagan Lake
97C
Quails' Gate Winery
Kelowna
Westbank
Summerhill Pyramid Winery
Big White Mountain (2317m)
Mission Hill Family Estate
Myra Canyon
Peachland
Cedar Creek Estate Winery
Okanagan Mountain Provincial Park
Big White Ski Resort
Okanagan Lake Provincial Park
Okanagan Mountain
Interior Plateau
Summerland
Naramata
Okanagan Lake
33
Penticton
Apex Mountain Resort
Skaha Lake
Lakeside Rd
Skaha Bluffs
Beaverdell
3
Crowsnest Hwy
Similkameen River
Kaleden
Apex Mountain Recreation Area
Okanagan Falls
Okanagan Falls Provincial Park
Vaseux Lake
3A
Vaseux Lake Provincial Park
Baldy Mountain (2301m)
Okanagan River
Keremeos
Oliver
Westbridge
Mt Kobau
Cathedral Provincial Park
Anarchist Mountain Pass (1234m)
Osoyoos Lake
3
Osoyoos
British Columbia
Crowsnest Hwy
CANADA
Washington
USA

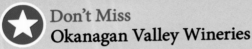

LAUGHINGMANGO/GETTY IMAGES ©

Don't Miss
Okanagan Valley Wineries

Among the dozens of options, the following (listed north to south) are recommended. Summerhill Pyramid and Cedar Creek Estate are south of Kelowna along the lake's east shore. The rest of the wineries can be reached via Hwy 97.

Two good sources of information on Okanagan Valley wines are the **BC Wine Information Centre** in Penticton's visitors center and the BC Wine Museum & VQA Wine Shop (p106) in Kelowna.

Summerhill Pyramid Winery (☎250-764-8000; www.summerhill.bc.ca; 4870 Chute Lake Rd, Kelowna; ⏲9am-7pm) On Kelowna's eastern shore, wines are aged in a huge pyramid. Noted for ice wine, it has a cafe.

Cedar Creek Estate Winery (☎250-764-8866; www.cedarcreek.bc.ca; 5445 Lakeshore Rd, Kelowna; ⏲10am-7pm) Known for excellent tours, as well as Rieslings and Ehrenfelser, a refreshing fruity white wine. The **Vineyard Terrace** (mains $12-20; ⏲11am-4pm Jun-Sep) is good for lunch.

Quails' Gate Winery (☎250-769-4451; www.quailsgate.com; 3303 Boucherie Rd, Kelowna; ⏲10am-8pm) A small winery with a huge reputation, it's known for its pinot noir, chardonnay and chenin blanc. The **Old Vines Restaurant** (mains $20-30; ⏲11:30am-9pm) is among the best.

Mission Hill Family Estate (☎250-768-7611; www.missionhillwinery.com; 1730 Mission Hill Rd, Westbank; ⏲10am-6pm) Like a Tuscan hill town, this winery's architecture wows. Go for a taste of one of the blended reds (try the Bordeaux) or the excellent Syrah. **Terrace** (mains $25-33; ⏲11am-9pm Jun-Oct) is one of the valley's finest restaurants and sources fine foods locally; book ahead.

SS Sicamous Inland Marine Museum Historic Site
(☎250-492-0405; www.sssicamous.ca; 1099 Lakeshore Dr W; adult/child $6/3.50; ⏰9am-6pm) Back when the best way to get around inland BC was by boat, the SS *Sicamous* hauled passengers and freight on Okanagan Lake from 1914 to 1936. Now restored and beached, a tour of the boat is an evocative self-guided ramble.

Activities

WATER SPORTS

The paved **Okanagan River Channel Biking & Jogging Path** follows the rather arid channel that links Okanagan Lake to Skaha Lake. But why pound the pavement when you can float?

Coyote Cruises Water Sports
(☎250-492-2115; www.coyotecruises.ca; 215 Riverside Dr; rental & shuttle $10; ⏰10am-5pm Jun-Aug) Coyote Cruises rents out inner tubes that you can float on to a midway point on the channel. It then buses you back to the start near Okanagan Lake.

MOUNTAIN BIKING & CYCLING

Freedom – The Bike Shop Bicycle Rental
(☎250-493-0686; www.freedombikeshop.com; 533 Main St; bicycle rental per day $40; ⏰9am-5:30pm Mon-Sat) Rents bikes and offers a wealth of information. Can arrange transport to/from the Kettle Valley Rail Trail.

SKIING & SNOWBOARDING

Apex Mountain Resort (☎877-777-2739, conditions 250-487-4848; www.apexresort.com; lift tickets adult/child $60/37), 37km west of Penticton off Green Mountain Rd, is one of Canada's best small ski resorts. It has more than 68 downhill runs for all ability levels, but the mountain is known for its plethora of double-black-diamond and technical runs; the drop is over 600m. It is usually quieter than nearby Big White (p107).

Eating & Drinking

Burger 55 Burgers $
(☎778-476-5529; www.burger55.com; 85 Westminster Ave E; mains $7-12; ⏰11am-8pm) Best burger in Canada? It's your own damn fault if it isn't, as you have myriad ways to customize at this tiny outlet by the creek and downtown. Six kinds of buns, eight kinds of cheese, and toppings that include roasted garlic and *pico de gallo* are just some of the options. Sides like fries are equally superb.

Dream Cafe Fusion $$
(☎250-490-9012; www.thedreamcafe.ca; 67 Front St; mains $11-20; ⏰8am-late Tue-Sun; 🌶) The heady aroma of spices envelopes your, well, head as you enter this pillow-bedecked, upscale-yet-funky bistro. Asian and Indian flavors mix on the menu, which has many veggie options. On several nights there's live acoustic music by touring pros; tables outside hum all summer long.

Information

A whole room of the **visitors center** (☎250-493-4055, 800-663-5052; www.tourismpenticton.com; 553 Railway St, cnr Hwy 97 & Eckhardt Ave W; ⏰8am-7pm; 📶) is devoted to the BC Wine Information Centre, with regional wine information, tasting and sales of over 600 varieties.

Kelowna

A kayaker paddles past scores of new tract houses on a hillside: it's an iconic image for fast-growing Kelowna, the unofficial 'capital' of the Okanagan and the sprawling center of all that's good and not-so-good with the region.

Sights

The focal point of the city's shoreline, the immaculate downtown **City Park** is home to manicured gardens, water features and **Hot Sands Beach**, where the water is a respite from the summer air.

Restaurants and pubs take advantage of the uninterrupted views of the lake and forested shore opposite. North of the marina, **Waterfront Park** has a variegated shoreline and a popular open-air stage.

Public Art Public Art

Among the many outdoor statues near the lake, look for the one of the **Ogopogo** (lakefront), the lake's mythical – and hokey – monster. More prosaic is **Bear** (Water St), a huge, lacy confection in metal. The visitors center has a good public art guide.

BC Wine Museum & VQA Wine Shop Museum

(250-868-0441; 1304 Ellis St; 10am-6pm Mon-Fri, 11am-5pm Sat & Sun) FREE In the same building as the BC Orchard Industry Museum, the knowledgeable staff at the BC Wine Museum & VQA Wine Shop can recommend tours, steer you to the best wineries for tastings and help you fill your trunk from the selection of over 600 wines on sale from 90 local wineries.

Activities

Monashee Adventure Tours Bicycle Rental/Tour

(250-762-9253; www.monasheeadventuretours.com; bicycle rental per day from $40) Offers scores of biking and hiking tours of the valley, parks, Kettle Valley Rail Trail (from $80) and wineries. Many tours are accompanied by entertaining local guides. Prices usually include a bike, lunch and shuttle to the route.

Sleeping

Abbott Villa Motel $$

(250-763-7771, 800-578-7878; www.abbottvilla.com; 1627 Abbott St; r $90-180;) Perfectly located downtown and across from City Park, this 52-room motel is as unadorned as a grapevine in winter. There is a decent outdoor pool and a hot tub. Self-cooked waffles are free for breakfast.

Royal Anne Hotel Hotel $$

(250-763-2277, 888-811-3400; www.royalannehotel.com; 348 Bernard Ave; r $90-200;) Location, location, location are the three amenities that count at this otherwise unexciting, older five-story hotel in the heart of town. Rooms have standard modern decor, fridges and huge, openable windows.

Hotel Eldorado Hotel $$$

(250-763-7500, 866-608-7500; www.hoteleldoradokelowna.com; 500 Cook Rd; r $180-400;) This historic lakeshore retreat, south of Pandosy Village, has 19 heritage rooms, where you can bask in antique-filled luxury. A modern low-key wing has 30 more rooms and six opulent waterfront suites. It's classy, artful and funky all at once.

Eating & Drinking

BC Fruit Market Market $

(250-763-8872; 816 Clement Ave; fruit from $1; 9am-5pm Mon-Sat) Like a county fair right inside the local fruit-packing cooperative, dozens upon dozens of the Okanagan's best fruits are on display and available for tasting. Prices are half that in supermarkets.

RauDZ Fusion $$

(250-868-8805; www.raudz.com; 1560 Water St; mains $12-25; 5-10pm) Noted chef Rod Butters has defined the farm-to-table movement with his casual bistro that's a temple to Okanagan produce and wine. The dining room is as airy and open as the kitchen and the seasonal menu takes global inspiration for Mediterranean-infused dishes good for sharing, as well as steaks and seafood. Suppliers include locally renowned Carmelis goat cheese.

Rotten Grape Tapas $$

(250-717-8466; www.rottengrape.com; 231 Bernard Ave; mains $10-20; 5pm-midnight Wed-Sat) Enjoy flights of local wines (over 200 by the glass) without the froufrou in the heart of town. If you utter 'tannin, the hobgoblin of pinot' at any point, be quiet and eat some of the tasty tapas inside or out.

Information

The **visitors center** (☎ **800-663-4345, 250-861-1515; www.tourismkelowna.com; 544 Harvey Ave; 🕘 8am-7pm**) is near the corner of Ellis St.

Getting There & Away

Kelowna airport (**YLW; ☎ 250-765-5125; www.kelownaairport.com**) is a long 20km north of the city center on Hwy 97.

Getting Around

To/From the Airport

Cabs cost about $36.

Big White Ski Resort

Perfect powder is the big deal at **Big White Ski Resort** (**☎ 250-765-8888, 800-663-2772, snow report 250-765-7669; www.bigwhite.com; off Hwy 33; 1-day lift pass adult/child $79/43**), located 55km east of Kelowna off Hwy 33. With a vertical drop of 777m, it features 16 lifts and 118 runs that offer excellent downhill and backcountry skiing, while deep gullies make for killer snowboarding. Because of Big White's isolation, most people stay up here. The resort includes numerous restaurants, bars, hotels, condos, rental homes and a hostel. The resort has lodging info and details of the ski-season shuttle to Kelowna.

HAIDA GWAII

Haida Gwaii, which means 'Islands of the People,' offers a magical trip for those who make the effort. Attention has long focused on the many unique species of flora and fauna to the extent that 'Canada's Galápagos' is a popular moniker. But each year it becomes more apparent that the real soul of the islands is the Haida culture itself. Long one of the most advanced and powerful First Nations, the Haida suffered terribly after Westerners arrived.

Now, however, their culture is resurgent and can be found across the islands in myriad ways beyond their iconic totem poles. Haida reverence for the environment is protecting the last stands of superb old-growth rainforests, where the spruce and cedars are some of the world's largest. Amid this sparsely populated, wild and rainy place are bald

Mortuary poles, Gwaii Haanas National Park Reserve (p109)

DON JOHNSTON/GETTY IMAGES ©

eagles, bears and much more wildlife. Offshore, sea lions, whales and orcas abound; in 2013 rare right whales and sea otters were spotted.

In 2010 the name used by Europeans since their arrival in the 18th century, Queen Charlotte Islands, was officially ditched; and the federal government moved forward with its plans to make the waters off Haida Gwaii a marine preserve. In 2013 the magificent Gwaii Haanas Legacy Pole was raised at Windy Bay, the first new pole in the protected area in 130 years.

Haida Gwaii forms a dagger-shaped archipelago of some 450 islands lying 80km west of the BC coast, and about 50km from the southern tip of Alaska. Mainland ferries dock at Skidegate Landing on Graham Island, which houses 80% of the 5000 residents. The principal town is Queen Charlotte (previously Queen Charlotte City and still known by its old QCC acronym), 7km west of Skidegate. The main road on Graham Island is Hwy 16, which is fully paved.

Sights & Activities

Haida Heritage Centre at Kay Llnagaay — Museum

(**250-559-7885; www.haidaheritagecentre.com; Hwy 16, Skidegate; adult/child $15/5; 10am-6pm Sun-Wed, to 9pm Thu-Sat**) One of the top attractions in the north is this marvelous cultural center. With exhibits on history, wildlife and culture, it would be enough reason to visit the islands just by itself. The rich traditions of the Haida are fully explored in galleries, programs and work areas, where contemporary artists create works such as the totem poles lining the shore.

Naikoon Provincial Park — Park

(**250-626-5115; www.bcparks.ca; off Hwy 16; campsites $16**) Much of the island's northeastern side is devoted to the beautiful 726-sq-km Naikoon Provincial Park, which combines sand dunes and low sphagnum bogs, surrounded by stunted and gnarled lodgepole pine, and red and yellow cedar. The **beaches** on the north coast feature strong winds, pounding surf and flotsam from across the Pacific. They can be reached via the stunning 26km-long Tow Hill Rd, east of Masset.

Sleeping

Small inns and B&Bs are mostly found on Graham Island. There are numerous choices in QCC and Masset, with many in between and along the spectacular north coast.

Premier Creek Lodging — Inn $

(**250-559-8415, 888-322-3388; www.qcislands.net/premier; 3101 3rd Ave, QCC; dm from $25, r $45-140; @ wifi**) Dating from 1910, this friendly lodge has eight beds in a hostel building out back and 12 rooms in the main

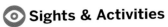

Sea lions, Haida Gwaii

STUART MCCALL/GETTY IMAGES ©

Don't Miss
Gwaii Haanas National Park Reserve, National Marine Conservation Area Reserve & Haida Heritage Site

This huge Unesco World Heritage site, with a name that's a mouthful, encompasses Moresby and 137 smaller islands at its southern end. It combines a time-capsule look at abandoned Haida villages, hot springs, amazing natural beauty and some of the continent's best kayaking.

Access to the park is by boat or plane only. A visit demands a decent amount of advance planning and usually requires several days. From May to September, you must obtain a reservation, unless you're with a tour operator.

Contact **Parks Canada** (250-559-8818; www.parkscanada.ca/gwaiihaanas; Haida Heritage Centre at Kay Llnagaay, Skidegate; 8:30am-noon & 1-4:30pm Mon-Fri) with questions. The website has links to the **essential annual trip planner**. Any visitor not on a guided tour and who has not visited the park during the previous three years must attend a free orientation at the park office. All visitors must register.

The number of daily reservations is limited: plan well in advance. There are user fees (adult/child $20/10 per night). Nightly fees are waived if you have a Parks Canada Season Excursion Pass. A few much-coveted standby spaces are made available daily: call Parks Canada.

The easiest way to get into the park is with a tour company. Parks Canada can provide you with lists of operators; tours last from one day to two weeks. Many can also set you up with **rental kayaks** (average per day/week $60/300) and gear for independent travel.

NEED TO KNOW

250-559-8818, reservations 877-559-8818; www.parkscanada.ca/gwaiihaanas

Below: Bat stars, Haida Gwaii; **Right:** Naikoon Provincial Park (p108), Haida Gwaii

(BELOW) DON JOHNSTON/GETTY IMAGES ©; (RIGHT) MICHAEL DEFREITAS/GETTY IMAGES ©

building, ranging from tiny but great-value singles to spacious rooms with views and porches.

North Beach Cabins Cabin **$$**

(☎250-557-2415; www.northbeachcabins.com; 16km marker Tow Hill Rd; cabins $85-100) Tucked into the dunes of beautiful North Beach are four cozy cabins. You're totally off the grid but, thanks to propane, you can cook, which will be about the only diversion from the fabulous views and endless sandy strolls.

Eating

Ask at the visitors centers about local Haida feasts, where you'll enjoy the best salmon and blueberries you've ever had.

Queen B's Cafe **$**

(☎250-559-4463; 3201 Wharf St, QCC; mains $3-10; ⏰9am-5pm) This funky place excels at baked goods, which emerge from the oven all day long. There are tables with water views outside and lots of local art inside.

Ocean View Restaurant Seafood **$$**

(☎250-559-8503; Sea Raven Motel, 3301 3rd Ave, QCC; mains $10-25; ⏰11am-9pm) Good fresh seafood (try the halibut) is the specialty at this casual dining room, where some tables look out to the harbor.

Information

Either download or pick up a free copy of the encyclopedic annual *Guide to Haida Gwaii* (www.guidetohaidagwaii.com).

The **QCC visitors center** (☎250-559-8316; www.qcinfo.ca; 3220 Wharf St, QCC; ⏰8:30am-9pm) is handy and can make advance excursion bookings by phone, although there's been a recent encroachment of gift items. Get a free copy of *Art Route*, a guide to more than 30 studios and galleries.

Getting There & Away

Air

The main airport for Haida Gwaii is at **Sandspit** (YZP; ☎250-559-0052) on Moresby Island. Note that reaching the airport from Graham Island is time consuming: if your flight is at 3:30pm, you need to line up at the car ferry at Skidegate Landing at 12:30pm (earlier in summer). There's also a small airport at **Masset** (YMT; ☎250-626-3995).

Ferry

The **BC Ferries** (☎250-386-3431; www.bcferries.com) service from Prince Rupert is the most popular way to reach the islands. Services ply from Prince Rupert to Skidegate Landing (adult $37 to $45, child fare 50%, car $132 to $160, six to seven hours) six times per week in summer and three times a week in winter on the *Northern Adventure*. Cabins are useful for overnight schedules (from $90).

Getting Around

Off Hwy 16, most roads are gravel or worse. **BC Ferries** (adult/child $10/5, cars from $23, 20 minutes, almost hourly 7am to 10pm) links the two main islands at Skidegate Landing and Alliford Bay.

Renting a car can be as expensive ($60 to $100 per day) as bringing one over on the ferry.

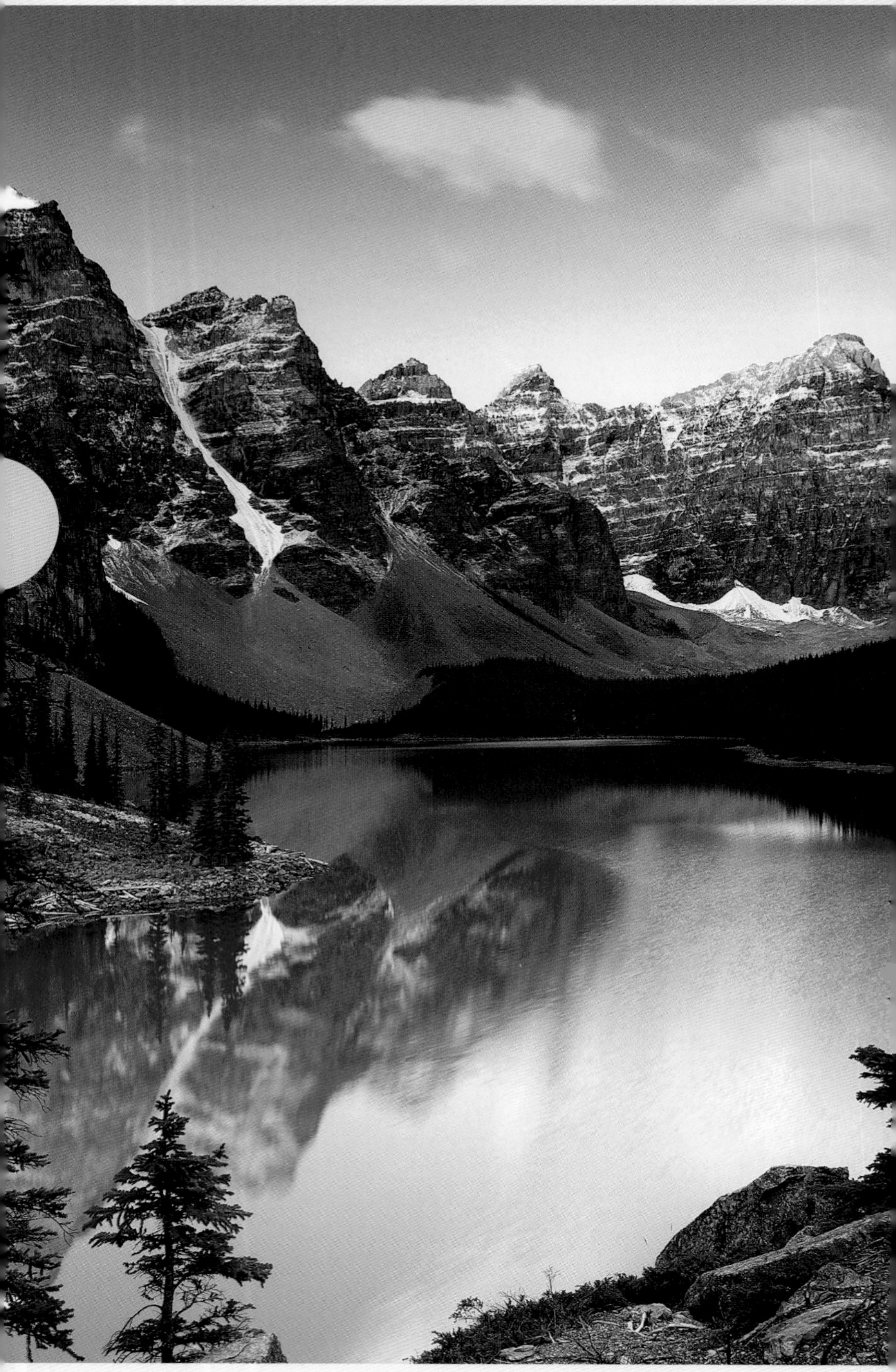

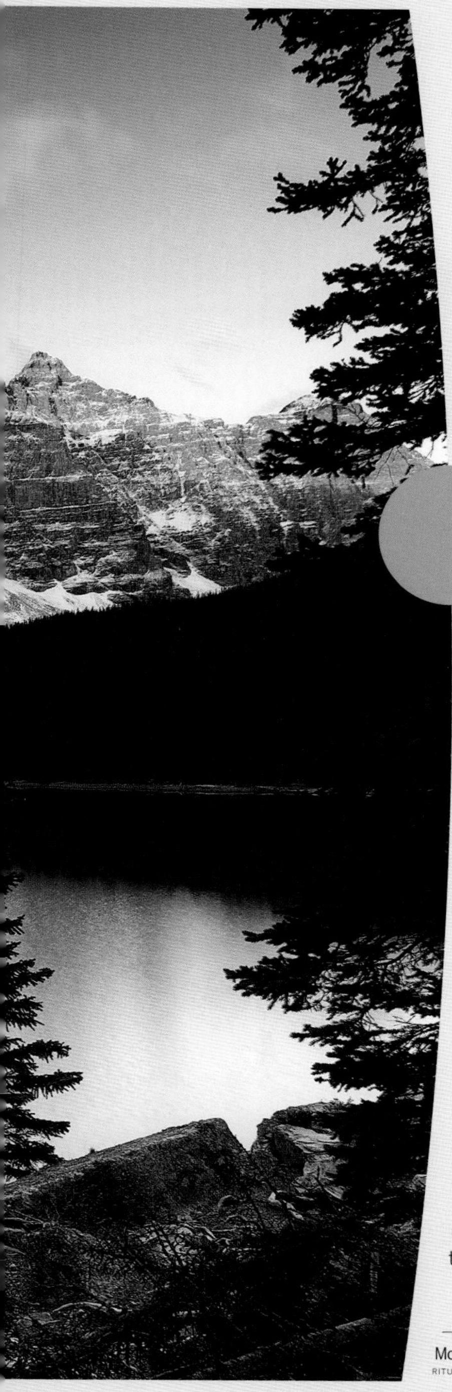

Banff & the Canadian Rockies

When dreamers from around the world imagine trips to Canada, they almost always think of the Rockies. The mammoth, white-dipped mountains looming over glassy turquoise lakes encircled by wildlife – elk, grizzlies, bighorn sheep and much more – are usually spotted only on TV nature programs. But unlike most fantasies of the perfect vacation destination, this mountain region really delivers.

Banff and Jasper National Parks are easily accessible, despite their wild and rugged terrain. Both areas offer excellent hiking for all energy levels, and both have characterful townsites that go well beyond the usual offerings for eating and entertainment. The awesomely Gothic Icefields Parkway connects the two parks for much of the way, leaving a trail of foaming waterfalls and glinting glaciers in its wake. City slickers should also check out the scenes in Calgary and Edmonton, the main Alberta access points for the Rockies region.

Moraine Lake (p129), Banff National Park

Ice-climber at Lake Louise (p127)
CORY RICHARDS/GETTY IMAGES ©

Banff & the Canadian Rockies

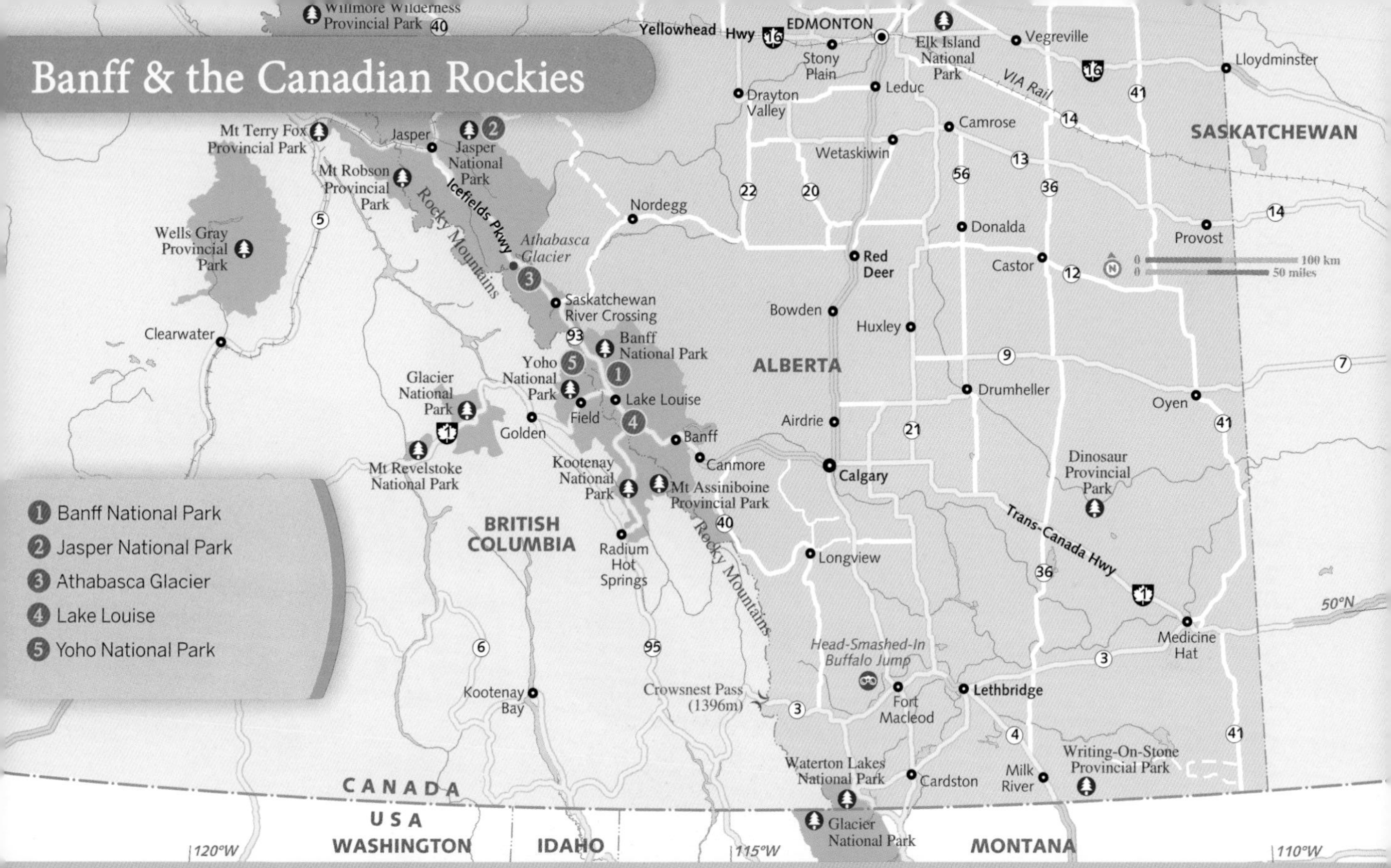

Banff National Park
Jasper National Park
Athabasca Glacier
Lake Louise
Yoho National Park
Willmore Wilderness Provincial Park
Yellowhead Hwy
EDMONTON
Stony Plain
Drayton Valley
Leduc
Elk Island National Park
Vegreville
Lloydminster
VIA Rail
Camrose
Wetaskiwin
SASKATCHEWAN
Mt Terry Fox Provincial Park
Jasper
Jasper National Park
Mt Robson Provincial Park
Icefields Pkwy
Rocky Mountains
Nordegg
Wells Gray Provincial Park
Athabasca Glacier
Donalda
Provost
Red Deer
Castor
Saskatchewan River Crossing
Clearwater
Bowden
Huxley
Banff National Park
Yoho National Park
ALBERTA
Glacier National Park
Lake Louise
Field
Golden
Drumheller
Oyen
Airdrie
Banff
Canmore
Calgary
Mt Revelstoke National Park
Kootenay National Park
Mt Assiniboine Provincial Park
Dinosaur Provincial Park
BRITISH COLUMBIA
Radium Hot Springs
Longview
Trans-Canada Hwy
50°N
Medicine Hat
Head-Smashed-In Buffalo Jump
Kootenay Bay
Crowsnest Pass (1396m)
Fort Macleod
Lethbridge
Waterton Lakes National Park
Cardston
Milk River
Writing-On-Stone Provincial Park
CANADA
USA
WASHINGTON
IDAHO
MONTANA
Glacier National Park
120°W
115°W
110°W
0 100 km
0 50 miles

Banff & the Canadian Rockies' Highlights

Banff National Park

The best way to immerse in Canada's most dramatic panoramas is on foot. You can hike fro Banff's town center (p122) and quickly be out among waterfalls, rock spires and all the whit frosted peaks reflected in teal-colored lakes that your camera can handle. Then again, the Banff Gondola (p123) can whisk you atop gorgeous Sulphur Mountain in 10 minutes. Either way, a hard day of view-gaping deserves a soak in Banff's hot springs (p123).

1

2

Jasper National Park

Jasper (p136) is a magical wilderness of clear lakes, razor-sharp mountains and critters large and small. Pick a trail – sa one around Maligne Lake (p141) or Lal Edith (p137) – and elk, moose, bear ar loon sightings are often the reward. N a hiker? Not a problem: gape-worthy wildlife spotting occurs along local roadways and from the tramway up Whistlers Mountain. Left: Grizzly bear cubs

JOHN E MARRIOTT/GETTY IMAGES ©

Athabasca Glacier

Just off the Icefields Parkway, the multitudes stop to gaze at the icy toe of this mighty glacier (p135), the most accessible of the vast Columbia Icefield. But you don't just get to look: jumbo-wheeled 'Snocoaches' crunch onto its rugged surface all day long or you can walk out yourself on a fascinating guided hike, gear supplied.

Lake Louise

Yes, there are a lot of people staring slack-jawed at Banff National Park's star attraction (p130). But who cares about the waterside claustrophobia? This shamelessly gorgeous, shimmering, true-blue-hued lake isn't about dodging other tourists. It's about viewing what should be everyone's god-given right to see. The accoutrements – alpine teahouses, grizzly bears, a grand hotel and Victoria Glacier – add to the enchantment.

Yoho National Park

The tiniest of British Columbia's Rocky Mountain national parks, dramatic Yoho (p132) contains more than its fair share of hulking peaks, glacial lakes and pretty meadows, yet it's relatively unexploited by the Banff-bound hordes. If you're a waterfall fan, you'll be able to view some of Canada's finest cascades. Bonus: Yoho is also a World Heritage Site protecting 515-million-year-old fossil beds.

Above: Takakkaw Falls (p133)

Banff & the Canadian Rockies' Best...

Vistas

Banff Gondola Takes you to the top of Sulphur Mountain for great summit views. (p123)

Big Beehive Challenging hike to an unexpected gazebo viewpoint. (p130)

Peyto Lake Idyllic platform view across the water. (p134)

Lake Louise Sightseeing Gondola True-blue water and glacier gazing. (p129)

Jasper Tramway Breathtaking mountain and glacier views. (p136)

Wildlife

Icefields Parkway Scenic drive with frequent elk, deer and bighorn sheep sightings. (p134)

Maligne Lake Spectacular lake vistas with moose and grizzly bear glimpses. (p141)

Discovery Trail Encircling Jasper, expect to catch sight of wandering elk. (p137)

Miette Hot Springs Sit in the pool while bighorn sheep hangout on the surrounding crags. (p124)

Lakes Annette & Edith Prime area for elk, white-tailed deer and soaring bald eagles. (p137)

Hiking

Lake Louise The trek past Mirror Lake to Lake Agnes Teahouse is one of the region's best. (p127)

Bow River Falls Popular waterfall trail, also leading to oddball Hoodoo rock formations. (p124)

Moraine Lake Short or day-long hikes from a magical teal-colored lake. (p129)

Old Fort Loop Short Jasper gem to the site of an old fur-trading post. (p137)

Glaciers

- **Columbia Icefield** Access point to a 30-glacier complex with large visitor center. (p134)
- **Athabasca Glacier** Adrenaline-pumping ice walks or bus trips from the glacier base. (p135)
- **Path of the Glacier Trail** Day hike to the foot of Angel Glacier. (p138)
- **Victoria Glacier** Primo views of the ice river from the Lake Louise Sightseeing Gondola. (p129)

Bighorn sheep, Jasper National Park (p136); **Above:** Columbia Icefield (p134)

Need to Know

ADVANCE PLANNING

- **One month before** For peak summer accommodation, book well ahead.
- **Two weeks before** Book tours and activities in Banff and Jasper.
- **One week before** Start wearing-in your new hiking boots.

RESOURCES

- **Banff Lake Louise Tourism** (www.banfflakelouise.com) Information, resources and activities on the region.
- **Tourism Jasper** (www.jasper.travel) Local sights and resources for visitors.
- **Parks Canada** (www.parkscanada.gc.ca) Visitor information for national parks throughout the Rockies.
- **Travel Alberta** (www.travelalberta.com) General visitor resources for the province.
- **Edmonton Tourism** (www.edmonton.com) Resources for city visitors.
- **Tourism Calgary** (www.visitcalgary.com) Visitor information for Calgary-bound tourists.

GETTING AROUND

- **Fly** Many visitors arrive via either Calgary or Edmonton International Airports, before heading on to Jasper (closer to Edmonton) or Banff (closer to Calgary).
- **Car** All major car-hire companies are available, and highways link the region's main sites: Hwy 16 runs from Edmonton to Jasper (365km); Hwy 93 (aka Icefields Parkway) from Jasper to Banff (290km); and Hwy 1 from Banff to Calgary (130km).
- **Train** VIA Rail services run from Vancouver to Jasper and Edmonton then across the country. Luxury *Rocky Mountaineer* services (www.rockymountaineer.com) run from Vancouver to Jasper, Banff and Calgary.

BE FOREWARNED

- **Winter Break** Some popular attractions, such as the Athabasca Glacier tours and Jasper Tramway, close from November to April.
- **Road Conditions** In summer the Icefields Parkway and other roads can be slow moving due to heavy tourist traffic. In winter they can close due to snow. See 511.alberta.ca for road reports.

Banff & the Canadian Rockies Itineraries

For a whirlwind Rockies tour, take a three-day jaunt from Jasper to Banff, stopping off at the Athabasca Glacier en route. Augment this on the five-day route by starting and finishing in Alberta's two biggest cities.

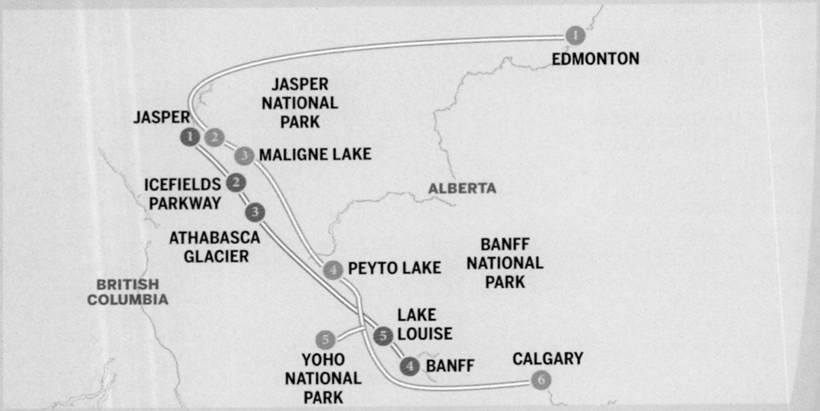

3 DAYS

JASPER TO BANFF

ROCKY MOUNTAINS HIGHLIGHTS

Start your north-to-south jaunt in ❶ **Jasper** (p136), snapping as many wildlife photos as possible in the national park: extras points for wolf and grizzly bear sightings in this region. After a sleepover in the charming, mountain-encircled town, plan for an early start the next day and hit the ❷ **Icefields Parkway** (p134) for the four-hour drive southward. There's a good chance that any wildlife you failed to spot in Jasper will be hanging around the sides of the highway here – this area is especially good for catching a longhorn sheep or three. Save some juice in your camera, though: the Columbia Icefields are also en route and you should plan to pull over at the popular ❸ **Athabasca Glacier** (p135). There's an ever-busy cafeteria across the street if it's time for lunch, but make sure you're back on the road in time to make it to ❹ **Banff** (p122) before sunset. Aim to spend a night or two here – it's bigger than Jasper.

After exploring the many top attractions in Banff National Park such as the Banff Gondola and Whyte Museum of the Canadian Rockies, don't miss taking the 45-minute drive out to picture-perfect ❺ **Lake Louise** (p130).

5 DAYS

EDMONTON TO CALGARY

THE 'C' TOUR

Use the three-day itinerary for the middle of this tour, but bookend it with visits to the region's two biggest cities – this C-shaped route is handy for flying into one airport and departing from another. Start your journey in ❶ **Edmonton** (p140), where a sleepover in town should be combined with visits to the excellent Royal Alberta Museum and the Art Gallery of Alberta. On the road early the next morning, head westward on Hwy 16.

There are places to stop en route for lunch but you should be in ❷ **Jasper** (p136) in four to five hours. Switch to the three-day itinerary here and, if time allows, add in extra visits to ❸ **Maligne Lake** (p141), 50km from Jasper; ❹ **Peyto Lake** (p134) along the Icefields Parkway; and ❺ **Yoho National Park** (p132), over the border in BC and 80km from Banff via Hwy 1.

Once you've had your fill of the Rockies – which could take a while – hop back in the car and take Hwy 1 eastward for the 90-minute drive to ❻ **Calgary** (p143). Take a break from all that driving by booking a downtown hotel and checking out the first-rate Glenbow Museum and cowboy-style footwear at Alberta Boot Co.

Maligne Lake Boathouse (p141)
MICHELE FALZONE/GETTY IMAGES ©

Discover Banff & the Canadian Rockies

At a Glance

- **Banff National Park** Dramatic mountain, glacier and azure-lake vistas.
- **BC's Rocky Mountain Parks** (p132) Spectacular views and craggy landscapes at Yoho and Kootenay.
- **Jasper National Park** (p136) Camera-hogging wildlife in a dazzling forest and peak setting.
- **Edmonton** (p140) Bustling northern city with lively arts scene.
- **Calgary** (p143) Alberta's biggest, brashest metropolis.

Banff Gondola, Sulphur Mountain

PAUL THOMPSON/GETTY IMAGES ©

BANFF & JASPER NATIONAL PARKS

While Italy has Venice and Florence, Canada has **Banff (Map p125)** and **Jasper (Map p136)**, legendary natural marvels that are as spectacular and vital as anything the ancient Romans ever built. Situated on the eastern side of the Canadian Rockies, the two bordering parks were designated Unesco World Heritage sites in 1984, along with BC's Yoho and Kootenay, for their exceptional natural beauty coupled with their manifestation of important glacial and alluvial geological processes. In contrast to some of North America's wilder parks, they both support small towns that lure between 2 to 5 million visitors each year. Despite all this, the precious balance between humans and nature continues to be delicately maintained – just.

Visiting the Parks

As you pass through this special area, you are under the ever-watchful eye of the animals that call it home. This is the place to see the Canadian Rockies' Big Five: deer, elk, moose, wolf and bear. (But only if you're lucky: they don't pose for everyone's photos.)

The one-day park entry fee (for entry to both parks) is $9.80/4.90 per adult/child; the passes are good until 4pm the following day.

Banff Town

Like the province in which it resides, Banff is something of an enigma. A resort town with souvenir shops, nightclubs and fancy restaurants is not something any national park purist would want to claim credit for.

But, looks can be misleading. First, Banff is no ordinary town. It developed not as a residential district, but as a service center for the park that surrounds it. Second, the commercialism of Banff Ave is delusory. Wander five minutes in either direction and (though you may not initially realize it) you're in wild country, a primeval food chain of bears, elk, wolves and bighorn sheep. Banff civilized? It's just a rumor.

Sights

Whyte Museum of the Canadian Rockies — Museum

(Map p126; www.whyte.org; 111 Bear St; suggested donation $5; ⏲10am-5pm) The century-old Whyte Museum is more than just a rainy-day option. There is a beautiful gallery displaying some great pieces on an ever-changing basis. The permanent collection tells the story of Banff and the hardy men and women who forged a home among the mountains.

The museum also gives out leaflets for a self-guided **Banff Culture Walk**.

Banff Gondola — Cable Car

(☎403-762-2523; Mountain Ave; adult/child $34.95/16.95; ⏲8am-9pm) In summer or winter you can summit a peak near Banff thanks to the Banff Gondola, whose four-person enclosed cars glide up to the top of Sulphur Mountain in less than 10 minutes. Named for the thermal springs that emanate from its base, this peak is a perfect viewing point and a tick-box Banff attraction.

There are a couple of restaurants on top plus an extended hike on boardwalks to Sanson Peak, an old weather station. Some people hike all the way up on a zigzagging 5.6km trail. You can travel back down on the gondola for half price and recover in the hot springs.

The gondola is 4km south of central Banff.

Banff Upper Hot Springs — Spa

(☎403-762-1515; Mountain Ave; adult/child $7.30/6.30; ⏲9am-11pm) Modern tourists use these soothing (if often crowded) hot pools, steam room and spa furnished with excellent mountain views near the Banff Gondola, 4km south of town. The water emerges from the spring at 47°C; in winter it has to be cooled to 39°C before entering the pool, but in spring the snow-melt does that job.

In addition to the pool, you can indulge in a massage or an aromatherapy wrap. Bathing suits, towels and lockers can be rented.

> ### Legacy Trail
>
> After years of planning, Parks Canada opened the long-awaited **Legacy Trail** in 2010, a paved multiuse path for cyclists, skaters and pedestrians that runs between Canmore and Banff. The 19km trail extends from Banff National Park's eastern gate 6km west of Canmore all the way to Banff town closely shadowing Hwy 1. From the park gate you can then pick up the **Canmore Trail**, which crosses the highway to reach Canmore. For those not up to cycling/walking in both directions, **Bike 'n' Hike Shuttle** (☎403-762-4453; www.bikeandhikeshuttle.com; one-way from $10) offer a handy bus service between the trailheads to get you back to your starting point.
>
> All of the trails were washed out in the June 2013 floods. Check with **Parks Canada** (www.pc.gc.ca) for current status.

Activities

CYCLING

There are lots of riding options around Banff, both on road and on selected trails. Popular routes around Banff Town include **Sundance** (7.4km round-trip) and **Spray River Loop** (12.5km); either is good for families.

Snowtips/Bactrax (Map p126; www.snowtips-bactrax.com; 225 Bear St; bicycles per

If You Like… Hot Springs

If you like soaking in Banff Upper Hot Springs, the region offers more toasty pools in which to immerse.

1 **MIETTE HOT SPRINGS**
(Map p136; www.parkscanada.gc.ca/hotsprings; Miette Rd; adult/child/family $6/5/18.50; ⌚8:30am-10:30pm) Located 61km northeast of Jasper off Hwy 16, near the park boundary, Miette's soothing waters are kept at a pleasant 39°C and are especially enjoyable when the fall snow is falling on your head and steam envelops the crowd.

2 **RADIUM HOT SPRINGS**
(Map p115; ☎250-347-9485; www.pc.gc.ca/hotsprings; off Hwy 93; adult/child $7/6; ⌚9am-11pm) Just outside the southwest corner of Kootenay National Park, the pools here are quite modern and can get very busy in summer. The water comes from the ground at 44°C, enters the first pool at 39°C and hits the final one at 29°C.

hr/day from $12/42) has a barn full of bikes to rent and will also take you on a tour to one of the many bike trails in the Banff area ($20 per hour). Ask about shuttles to trailheads.

HIKING

Hiking is Banff's tour de force and the main focus of many travelers' visits to the area. The trails are easy to find, well signposted and maintained enough to be comfortable to walk on, yet rugged enough to still get a wilderness experience.

Before you head out, check at the Banff Information Centre (p127) for trail conditions and possible closures. Keep in mind that trails are often snow-covered much later into the summer season than you might realize, and bear trail closures are a possibility, especially in berry season (June to September).

One of the best hikes from the town center is the **Bow River Falls and the Hoodoos Trail** which starts by the Bow River Bridge and tracks past the falls to the Hoodoos – weird rock spires caused by wind and water erosion. The trail plies its way around the back of Tunnel Mountain through forest and some river meadows and is 10.2km return.

Some of the best multiday hikes start at the Sunshine parking lot where skiers grab the gondola in winter. From here you can plan two- to four-day sorties up over Healy Pass and down to **Egypt Lake**, or get a bus up to Sunshine Village where you can cross the border into BC and head out across **Sunshine Meadows** and **Mount Assiniboine Provincial Park**.

SKIING & SNOWBOARDING

Sunshine Village (Map p125; www.skibanff.com; day ski passes $75) straddles the Alberta–BC border. Though slightly smaller than Lake Louise in terms of skiable terrain it gets much bigger dumpings of snow, or 'Champagne powder' as Albertans like to call it (up to 9m annually). Aficionados laud Sunshine's advanced runs and lengthy ski season, which lingers until Victoria Day weekend in late May. A high-speed gondola whisks skiers up in 17 minutes to the village, which sports Banff's only ski-in hotel, the Sunshine Mountain Lodge.

Tours

Discover Banff Tours Guided Tour
(Map p126; ☎403-760-5007; www.banfftours.com; Sundance Mall, 215 Banff Ave; tours from $54) Discover Banff has a great selection of tours to choose from: three-hour Banff Town tours, sunrise and evening wildlife tours, Columbia Icefield day trips and even a 10-hour grizzly bear tour, where if you don't see a bear you get your money back.

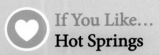

Banff National Park

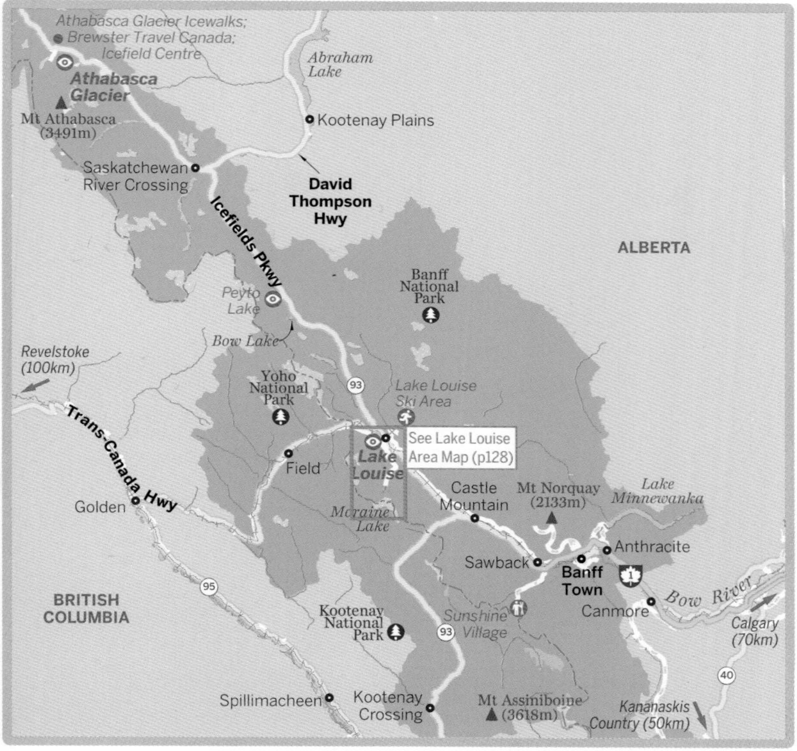

Sleeping

Banff Rocky Mountain Resort Hotel **$$**
(☎403-762-5531; www.bestofbanff.com; 1029 Banff Ave; r from $159;) Being 4km out of town at the far, far end of Banff Ave is a small price to pay for the preferential prices and excellent all-round facilities here (including a hot tub, pool, tennis courts and cafe-restaurant).

There's a free shuttle into town (hourly) or you can walk or cycle 4km along the Legacy Trail.

Banff Caribou Lodge Hotel **$$**
(☎403-762-5887; www.bestofbanff.com; 521 Banff Ave; d from $179; @) One of the posher places in the locally run Banff Lodging Co empire (who don it three-and-a-half stars), the Caribou fits the classic stereotype of a mountain lodge, with its log and stone exterior, giant lobby fireplace and general alpine coziness.

Fairmont Banff Springs Hotel **$$$**
(☎403-762-2211; www.fairmont.com/banff-springs; 405 Spray Ave; r from $412; @) Sitting at the top end of the 'lost-for-words' category comes this exquisite beauty. Imagine crossing a Scottish castle with a French chateau and then plonking it in the middle of one of the world's most spectacular (and accessible) wilderness areas.

Banff Town

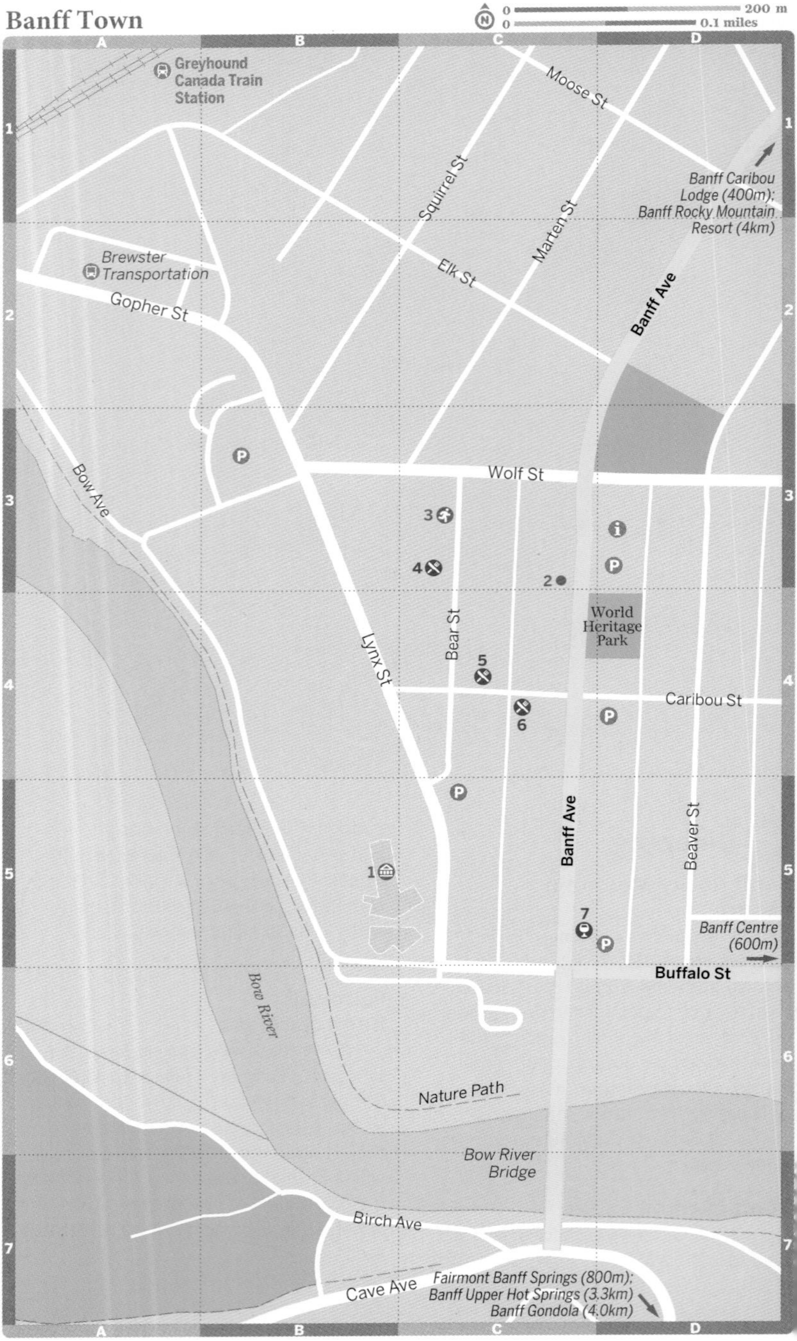

0 200 m
0 0.1 miles
Greyhound Canada Train Station
Brewster Transportation
Gopher St
Moose St
Squirrel St
Marten St
Elk St
Banff Ave
Banff Caribou Lodge (400m); Banff Rocky Mountain Resort (4km)
Wolf St
Bow Ave
Lynx St
Bear St
World Heritage Park
Caribou St
Beaver St
Banff Centre (600m)
Buffalo St
Bow River
Nature Path
Bow River Bridge
Birch Ave
Cave Ave
Fairmont Banff Springs (800m); Banff Upper Hot Springs (3.3km) Banff Gondola (4.0km)

Banff Town

Sights

Activities, Courses & Tours

Eating

Drinking & Nightlife

Eating

Coyote's Deli & Grill Fusion **$$**

(Map p126; ☎403-762-3963; www.coyotesbanff.com; 206 Caribou St; lunch mains $8-14, dinner mains $20; ⏰7:30am-10:30pm) Coyote's is best at lunchtime, when you can bunk off hiking and choose a treat from the deli and grill menu, which is inflected with a strong southwestern slant. Perch on a stool and listen to the behind-the-bar banter as you order up flatbreads, seafood cakes, quesadillas or some interesting soups (try the sweet potato and corn chowder).

Eddie Burger & Bar Burgers **$$**

(Map p126; ☎403-762-2230; www.theeddieburgerbar.ca; Caribou St; burgers $13) Avoid the stereotypes. The Eddie might appear pretentious (black leather seats and mood lighting), and its name may contain the word 'burger,' but it welcomes all types (including exhausted hikers and kids) and its gourmet meals-in-a-bun are subtler and far less greasy than your standard Albertan patty.

Bison Restaurant & Terrace Canadian, Fusion **$$$**

(Map p126; ☎403-762-5550; www.thebison.ca; 211 Bear St; mains $29-45; ⏰5pm-late) The Bison might look like it's full of trendy, well-off Calgarians dressed in expensive hiking gear, but its a two-level affair, with a rustically elegant restaurant upstairs sporting a menu saturated with meat and a cheaper, more casual terrace below, where you can procure big salads and weird starch-heavy pizzas with butternut squash and rosemary-potato toppings.

Drinking & Nightlife

Banff Ave Brewing Co Pub

(Map p126; www.banffavebrewingco.ca; 110 Banff Ave; ⏰11:30am-2am) An offshoot of the excellent Jasper Brewing Co, this brewpub opened in Banff in 2010. It's best for a drink of craft beer, brewed on the premises and infused with Saskatoon berries and the like.

Entertainment

Banff Centre Theater

(www.banffcentre.ca; 107 Tunnel Mountain Dr) A cultural center in a national park? Banff never ceases to surprise. This is the cultural hub of the Bow Valley – concerts, art exhibitions and the popular Banff Mountain Film Festival are all held here.

Information

Banff Information Centre (Map p126; www.parkscanada.gc.ca/banff; 224 Banff Ave; ⏰8am-8pm) Offices for Parks Canada.

Getting There & Away

The nearest airport is in Calgary.

All of the major car-rental companies have branches in Banff Town. During summer all the cars might be reserved in advance, so call ahead.

Getting Around

Over 20 shuttle buses a day operate year-round between Calgary International Airport and Banff. Buses are less frequent in the spring and fall. Companies include **Brewster Travel Canada (Map p126; www.brewster.ca)** and **Banff Airporter (www.banffairporter.com)**. The adult fare for both is around $54 one way.

Lake Louise

Famous for its teahouses, grizzly bears, grand hotel, skiing, Victoria Glacier, hiking and lakes (yes, plural), Lake Louise is what makes Banff National Park the phenomenon it is, an awe-inspiring

Lake Louise Area

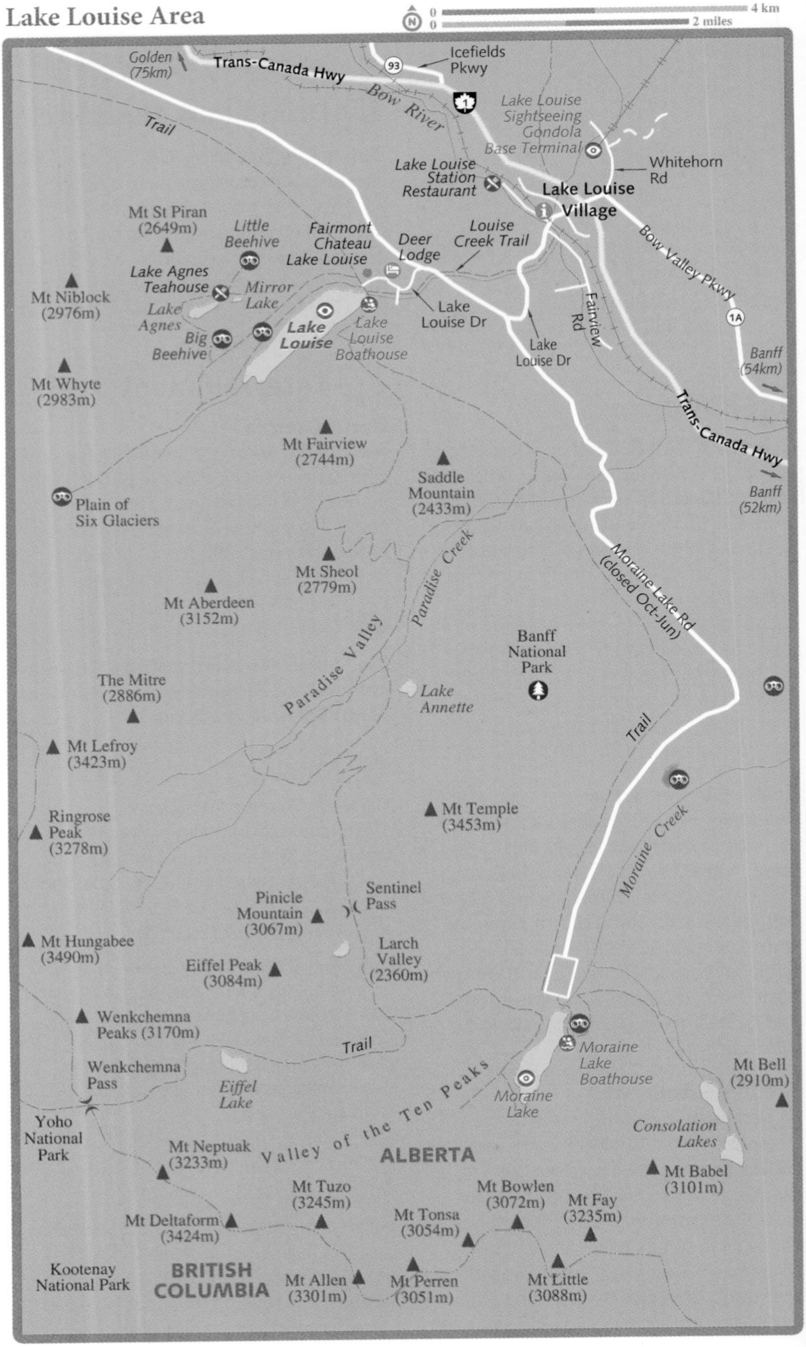
0 4 km
0 2 miles
Golden (75km)
Trans-Canada Hwy
93
Icefields Pkwy
1
Bow River
Trail
Lake Louise Sightseeing Gondola Base Terminal
Whitehorn Rd
Lake Louise Station Restaurant
Lake Louise Village
Bow Valley Pkwy
1A
Mt St Piran (2649m)
Little Beehive
Fairmont Chateau Lake Louise
Deer Lodge
Louise Creek Trail
Mt Niblock (2976m)
Lake Agnes Teahouse
Mirror Lake
Lake Agnes
Big Beehive
Lake Louise
Lake Louise Boathouse
Lake Louise Dr
Fairview Rd
Lake Louise Dr
Banff (54km)
Mt Whyte (2983m)
Trans-Canada Hwy
Mt Fairview (2744m)
Saddle Mountain (2433m)
Banff (52km)
Plain of Six Glaciers
Paradise Creek
Mt Sheol (2779m)
Moraine Lake Rd (closed Oct-Jun)
Mt Aberdeen (3152m)
Paradise Valley
Banff National Park
The Mitre (2886m)
Lake Annette
Trail
Mt Lefroy (3423m)
Mt Temple (3453m)
Ringrose Peak (3278m)
Moraine Creek
Sentinel Pass
Pinicle Mountain (3067m)
Mt Hungabee (3490m)
Larch Valley (2360m)
Eiffel Peak (3084m)
Wenkchemna Peaks (3170m)
Trail
Moraine Lake Boathouse
Wenkchemna Pass
Eiffel Lake
Valley of the Ten Peaks
Moraine Lake
Mt Bell (2910m)
Yoho National Park
Consolation Lakes
Mt Neptuak (3233m)
ALBERTA
Mt Babel (3101m)
Mt Tuzo (3245m)
Mt Bowlen (3072m)
Mt Fay (3235m)
Mt Tonsa (3054m)
Mt Deltaform (3424m)
Kootenay National Park
BRITISH COLUMBIA
Mt Allen (3301m)
Mt Perren (3051m)
Mt Little (3088m)

natural feature that is impossible to describe without resorting to shameless clichés.

The village of Lake Louise, just off Hwy 1, is little more than an outdoor shopping mall, a gas station and a handful of hotels. The object of all your yearnings is 5km away by car or an equitable distance on foot along the pleasantly wooded Louise Creek trail, if the bears aren't out on patrol (check at the visitors center).

The Bow Valley Parkway between Banff Town and Lake Louise is slightly slower, but much more scenic, than Hwy 1.

Sights

Moraine Lake Lake

The scenery will dazzle you long before you reach the spectacular deep-teal colored waters of Moraine Lake. The lake is set in the Valley of the Ten Peaks, and the narrow winding road leading to it offers views of these distant imposing summits. With little hustle or bustle and lots of beauty, many people prefer the more rugged and remote setting of Moraine Lake to Lake Louise.

There are some excellent day hikes from the lake, or rent a boat at the **Moraine Lake Boathouse** (per hr $40; 9am-4pm Jun-Oct) and paddle through the glacier-fed waters.

Moraine Lake Rd and its facilities are open from June to early October.

Lake Louise Sightseeing Gondola Cable Car

(www.lakelouisegondola.com; 1 Whitehorn Rd; round-trip adult/child $28.75/14.25, guided hikes per person $5; 9am-5pm, guided hikes 11am, 1pm & 3pm) To the east of Hwy 1, this sightseeing gondola will lever you to the top of Mt Whitehorn, where the views of the lake and Victoria Glacier are phenomenal. At the top, there's a restaurant and a Wildlife Interpretive Centre where you can partake in 45-minute **guided hikes**.

Local Knowledge

Banff National Park

RECOMMENDATIONS FROM TAMARA DYKSHOORN, LOCAL HIKING GUIDE

1 LAKE LOUISE

Once at the lake, walk along the shoreline: the trail offers 2km of flat walking. From here you have many options: hiking a full day to two high teahouses or perhaps hitting the top of Fairview Mountain. All the while, the summit of Victoria and its surrounding glacier-covered peaks are in your view.

2 SUNSHINE MEADOWS

The stunning meadows area is dotted with wildflowers and alpine lakes, and offers an opportunity to see wildlife. Take a 15-minute shuttle bus to the treeline and begin your hike – perhaps sign-up for a guided walk and you'll see even more. Trails in this special area are well maintained and have something for every hiker's ability.

3 MORAINE LAKE

Also known as the Valley of Ten Peaks, Moraine Lake is quick drive from Lake Louise. There's a short trail up the Moraine that gives great vistas of the area and there's a level walking trail along the shoreline. Because of the high elevation, the autumn colors of the Larch trees here are a big draw.

4 BANFF TOWN

There's much more to Banff than wandering the main strip. Hikers can hit Tunnel Mountain in the evening or spend a few hours hiking up Sulphur and taking the gondola down. Consider a self-guided trip through the historic cemetery: the beginnings of Banff and its stories lie here. Ask at the Whyte Museum about guided tours.

JOSH MCCULLOCH/GETTY IMAGES ©

Don't Miss
Lake Louise

Named for Queen Victoria's otherwise anonymous fourth daughter (who also lent her name to the province), Lake Louise is a place that requires multiple viewings. Aside from the standard picture-postcard shot (blue sky, even bluer lake), try visiting at six in the morning, at dusk in August, in the October rain or after a heavy winter storm.

You can rent a canoe from the **Lake Louise Boathouse** (per hr $45; 9am-4pm Jun-Oct) and go for a paddle around the lake. Don't fall overboard – the water is freezing.

Activities

HIKING

In Lake Louise beauty isn't skin-deep. The hikes behind the stunning views are just as impressive. Most of the classic walks start from Lake Louise and Moraine Lake. Some are straightforward, while others will give even the most seasoned alpinist reason to huff and puff.

From the Fairmont Chateau Lake Louise, two popular day walks head out to alpine-style teahouses perched above the lake. The shorter but slightly harder hike is the 3.4km grunt past **Mirror Lake** up to the Lake Agnes Teahouse on its eponymous body of water. After tea and scones you can trek 1.6km further and higher to the view-embellished **Big Beehive** lookout and Canada's most unexpectedly sited gazebo. Continue on this path down to the Highline Trail to link up with the **Plain of Six Glaciers**, or approach it independently from Chateau Lake Louise along the lakeshore (5.6km one-way). Either way, be sure to get close enough for ice-crunching views of the Victoria Glacier. There's another teahouse on this route that supplements its brews with thick-cut sandwiches and spirit-lifting mugs of hot chocolate with marshmallows.

SKIING & SNOWBOARDING

Lake Louise Ski Area (Map p125; www.skilouise.com; lift tickets from $75), 3km east of Lake Louise Village and 60km northwest of Banff, is marginally larger than Sunshine Village but gets less natural snow. The ample runs, containing plenty of beginner and intermediate terrain, are on four separate mountains, so it's closer to a European ski experience than anything else on offer in Canada.

Sleeping

Deer Lodge Hotel $$
(☎403-410-7417; www.crmr.com; 109 Lake Louise Dr; r from $175) Tucked demurely behind the Fairmont Chateau Lake Louise, the Deer Lodge is another historic throwback dating from the 1920s. But, although the rustic exterior and creaky corridors can't have changed much since the days of bobbed hair and F Scott Fitzgerald, the refurbished rooms are another matter, replete with new comfy beds and smart boutique-like furnishings.

Eating

Lake Agnes Teahouse Cafe $
(Lake Agnes Trail; snacks $3-6; ⏲Jun-Oct) You thought the view from Lake Louise was good? Wait till you get up to this precariously perched alpine-style teahouse that seems to hang in the clouds beside ethereal Lake Agnes and its adjacent waterfall. The small log cabin runs on gas power and is hike-in only (3.4km uphill from the Fairmont Chateau).

Lake Louise Station Restaurant Canadian $$
(mains $15-25; ⏲11:30am-9:30pm) Restaurants with a theme have to be handled so carefully – thankfully this railway-inspired eatery, at the end of Sentinel Rd, does it just right. You can either dine in the station among the discarded luggage or in one of the dining cars, which are nothing short of elegant. The food is simple yet effective. A must-stop for trainspotters.

Information

Lake Louise Visitors Centre (Samson Mall, Lake Louise village; ⏲9am-8pm) Has some good geological displays, a Parks Canada desk and a small film theater.

Getting There & Around

The easiest way to get here from Banff is by car or the Brewster Travel Canada bus (p127).

Hikers near Moraine Lake (p129), Banff National Park

Below: Marble Canyon, Kootenay National Park; **Right:** Yoho National Park
(BELOW) BEN COOPER/GETTY IMAGES ©; (RIGHT) MIKE GRANDMAISON/GETTY IMAGES ©

Kootenay National Park

Shaped like a lightning bolt, **Kootenay National Park** (Map p125; ☎250-347-9505; www.pc.gc.ca/kootenay; Hwy 93; entrance fee adult/child $10/5, campsites $22-39; ⏲camping May-Oct) is centered on a long, wide, tree-covered valley shadowed by cold, gray peaks. Encompassing 1406 sq km, Kootenay has a more moderate climate than the other Rocky Mountains parks and, in the southern regions especially, summers can be hot and dry, which is a factor in the frequent fires. It's the only national park in Canada to contain both glaciers and cacti.

The interpretive **Fireweed Trail** (500m or 2km) loops through the surrounding forest at the north end of Hwy 93. Some 7km further on, **Marble Canyon** has a pounding creek flowing through a nascent forest. Another 3km south on the main road is the easy 2km trail through forest to ochre pools known as the **Paint Pots**. Panels describe both the mining history of this rusty earth and its importance to Aboriginal people.

Learn how the park's appearance has changed over time at the **Kootenay Valley Viewpoint**, where informative panels vie with the view. Just 3km south, **Olive Lake** makes a perfect picnic or rest stop.

Yoho National Park

This dramatic **national park** (Map p125; ☎250-343-6783; www.pc.gc.ca/yoho; adult/child $10/5) is home to looming peaks, pounding waterfalls, glacial lakes and patches of pretty meadows.

Although the smallest (1310 sq km) of BC's four national parks in the Rockies, Yoho is a diamond in the (very) rough.

This wilderness is the real deal; it's some of the continent's least tarnished.

East of Field on Hwy 1 is the **Takakkaw Falls road**, open late June to early October. At 254m, Takakkaw is one of the highest waterfalls in Canada. From here **Iceline**, a 20km hiking loop, passes many glaciers and spectacular scenery.

This World Heritage Site protects the amazing Cambrian-age **fossil beds** on Mt Stephen and Mt Field. These 515-million-year-old fossils preserve the remains of marine creatures that were some of the earliest forms of life on earth. You can only get to the fossil beds by guided hikes, which are led by naturalists from the **Yoho Shale Geoscience Foundation** (☎800-343-3006; www.burgess-shale.bc.ca; tours from adult/child $120/25; ⏰Jul-Sep). Reservations are essential.

Near the south gate of the park, you can reach pretty **Wapta Falls** along a 2.4km trail. The easy walk takes about 45 minutes each way.

LAKE O'HARA

Perched high in the mountains east of Field, Lake O'Hara is worth the significant hassle involved in reaching the place, which is an encapsulation of the whole Rockies. Compact wooded hillsides, alpine meadows, snow-covered passes, mountain vistas and glaciers are all wrapped around the stunning lake.

To reach the lake, you can take the **shuttle bus** (Field; adult/child return $15/7.50; ⏰mid-Jun–Sep) from the Lake O'Hara parking lot, 15km east of Field on Hwy 1. A quota system governs bus access to the lake and limits permits for the 30 backcountry campsites.

Make **reservations** (☎250-343-6433; reservation fee $12) for the bus trip or for **camping** (a permit costs $10 per night) three months in advance. Available spots often go the first hour lines are open, from 8am mountain time. Given the popularity of Lake O'Hara, reservations are basically mandatory, unless you want to walk. However, if you don't have advance reservations, six day-use seats on the bus and three to five campsites are set aside for 'standby' users. To try to snare these, call at 8am the day before.

Icefields Parkway

Paralleling the Continental Divide for 230km between Lake Louise and Jasper Town, plain old Hwy 93 has been wisely rebranded as the Icefields Parkway (or the slightly more romantic 'Promenade des Glaciers' in French) as a means to somehow prepare people for the majesty of its surroundings. And what majesty! The highlight is undoubtedly the humungous Columbia Icefield and its numerous fanning glaciers, and this dynamic lesson in erosive geography is complemented by weeping waterfalls, aquamarine lakes, dramatic mountains and the sudden dart of a bear, an elk, or was it a moose?

Sights

Peyto Lake Lake

(Map p125) You'll have already seen the indescribable blue of Peyto Lake in a thousand publicity shots, but there's nothing like gazing at the real thing; especially since the viewing point for this lake is from a lofty vantage point several hundred feet above the water. The lake is best visited in early morning, between the time the sun first illuminates the water and the first tour bus arrives.

From the bottom of the lake parking lot, follow a paved trail for 15 minutes up a steady gradual incline to the wooden platform overlooking the lake. From here you can continue up the paved trail, keeping right along the edge of the ridge.

Columbia Icefield Outdoors

About halfway between Lake Louise Village and Jasper Town is the only accessible section of the vast Columbia Icefield, which covers an area the size of the city of Vancouver and feeds eight glaciers. This remnant of the last ice age, which is up to 350m thick in places, stretches across the plateau between Mt Columbia (3747m) and Mt Athabasca (3491m).

It's the largest icefield in the Rockies and feeds the North Saskatchewan, Columbia, Athabasca, Mackenzie and Fraser River systems with its meltwaters.

Peyto Lake, Icefields Parkway

JOHN E MARRIOTT/GETTY IMAGES ©

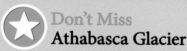

MARTIN CHILD/GETTY IMAGES ©

Don't Miss
Athabasca Glacier

The best way to experience the Columbia Icefield is to walk on it. For that you will need the help of **Athabasca Glacier Icewalks** (Map p125; 780-852-5595; www.icewalks.com; Icefield Centre; 3hr tours adult/child $70/35, 6hr tours $85/45), which supplies all the gear you'll need and a guide to show you the ropes. It offers a three-hour tour (departing 10:40am daily June to September), and a six-hour option (Sunday and Thursday) for those wanting to venture further out on the glacier.

The other far easier (and more popular) way to get on the glacier is via a 'Snocoach' ice tour offered by **Brewster Travel Canada** (Map p125; 877-423-7433; www.brewster.ca; adult/child $49.95/24.95; tours 9am-5pm May-Oct). For many people this is the defining experience of their Columbia Icefield visit. The large hybrid bus-truck grinds a track onto the ice where it stops to allow you to go for a short walk in a controlled area on the glacier. Dress warmly and wear good shoes. Tickets can be bought at the Icefield Centre or online; tours depart every 15 to 30 minutes.

NEED TO KNOW

Map p125

Be sure to stop at the **Icefield Centre** (Map p125; 780-852-6288; 9am-6pm May-Oct) FREE, where you can chat with the rangers from Parks Canada about camping options and climbing conditions; they can answer any questions you might have regarding the park.

Athabasca Glacier to Jasper Town
Scenic Highway

As you snake your way through the mountains on your way to Jasper, there are a few places worth stopping at. **Sunwapta Falls** (Map p136) and **Athabasca Falls** (Map p136), closer to Jasper, are both worth a

Jasper National Park

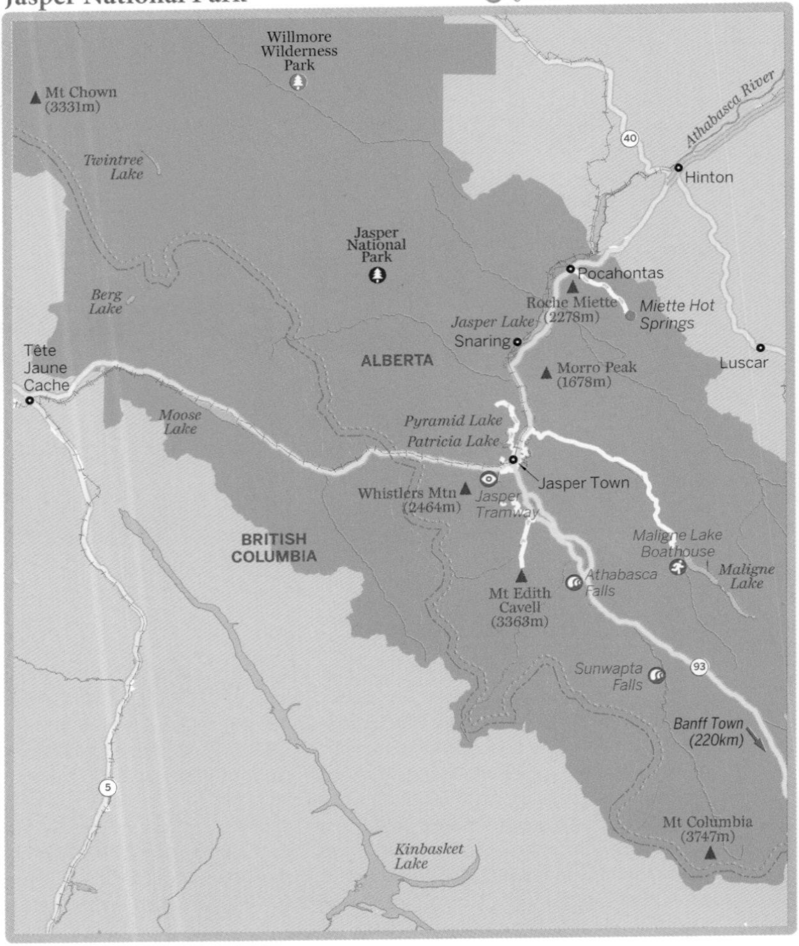

stop. The latter is the more voluminous and is at its most ferocious in the summer when it's stoked with glacial meltwater.

Jasper Town & Around

Take Banff, half the annual visitor count, increase the total land area by 40%, and multiply the number of bears, elk, moose and caribou by three. The result: Jasper, a larger, less-trammeled more wildlife-rich version of the other Rocky Mountains parks.

Most people enter Jasper Town from the south via the magnificently Gothic Icefields Parkway that meanders up from Lake Louise amid foaming waterfalls and glacier-sculpted mountains, including iconic Mt Edith Cavell, easily visible from the townsite.

Sights

Jasper Tramway Cable Car

(Map p136; ☎780-852-3093; www.jaspertram-way.com; Whistlers Mountain Rd; adult/child

$32/16; ⌚9am-8pm Apr-Oct) If the average, boring views from Jasper just aren't blowing your hair back, go for a ride up this sightseeing tramway. The vista is sure to take your breath away, with views, on a clear day, of the Columbia Icefield 75km to the south.

From the top of the tram you can take the steep 1.5km hike to the summit of Whistlers Mountain, where the outlook is even better. The tramway is about 7km south of Jasper Town along Whistlers Mountain Rd, off the Icefields Parkway.

Lakes Annette & Edith Lake

On the opposite side of the highway to the town, Lakes Annette and Edith are popular for water activities in the summer and skating in the winter. If you're brave and it's very hot, Annette is good for a quick summer dip – just remember the water was in a glacier not too long ago! Edith is more frequented by kayakers and boaters.

Activities

CYCLING

Jasper is way better than Banff for single-track mountain biking; in fact, it's one of the best places in Canada for the sport. Many routes are within striking distance of the townsite.

Vicious Cycle **(Map p138; ☎780-852-1111; www.viciouscyclecanada.com; 630 Connaught Dr; per day from $32; ⌚9am-6pm)** can sort out bike rentals and offer additional trail tips.

HIKING

Even when judged against other Canadian national parks, Jasper's trail network is mighty, and with comparatively fewer people than its sister park to the south, you've a better chance of seeing more wildlife and fewer humans.

Initiate yourself on the interpretative **Discovery Trail**, an 8km easy hike that encircles the townsite and highlights its natural, historical and railway heritage.

Other short trails include the 3.2km **Mary Schäffer Loop** by Maligne Lake, named for one of the earliest European visitors to the area; the **Old Fort Loop** (3.5km) to the

Local Knowledge

Jasper National Park

RECOMMENDATIONS FROM WES BRADFORD, RETIRED PARKS CANADA WARDEN AND JASPER WILDLIFE SPECIALIST

1 **JASPER TRAMWAY**
The Tramway takes you up Whistlers Mountain for excellent views of the Athabasca and Miette river valleys. Mountain goats, hoary marmots and golden-mantled ground squirrels are observed on the slopes near the lower trail. Hiking along the upper ridge and onto the backside of the mountain provides opportunities to see grizzly bears, elk and mule deer. Be equipped: sudden weather changes are common.

2 **MIETTE HOT SPRINGS**
The road to the hot springs climbs out of the Athabasca Valley and then descends steeply into the Riddle River Valley – watch for golden eagles soaring above the cliffs. At the hot springs, where you can enjoy a soothing soak in these sulphur-rich hot pools, bighorn sheep are often observed on the slopes above. Black bear, red fox and mule deer are common in this area.

3 **MALIGNE LAKE**
Wildlife-viewing along the road to the lake in spring and fall is superb, with black bears, bighorn sheep, mule deer, moose, and osprey common. The Maligne River is also an excellent place to test your fly-fishing (with no bait) skills against rainbow trout during August and September.

4 **JASPER TOWN**
Take an evening or early morning walk on the Discovery Trail that transects Jasper Town to observe elk, mule deer, coyotes, ground squirrels and abundant birdlife. Watch for black bears in spring on the south-facing slopes to the north where they're often searching for the first green grass and dandelions.

Jasper Town

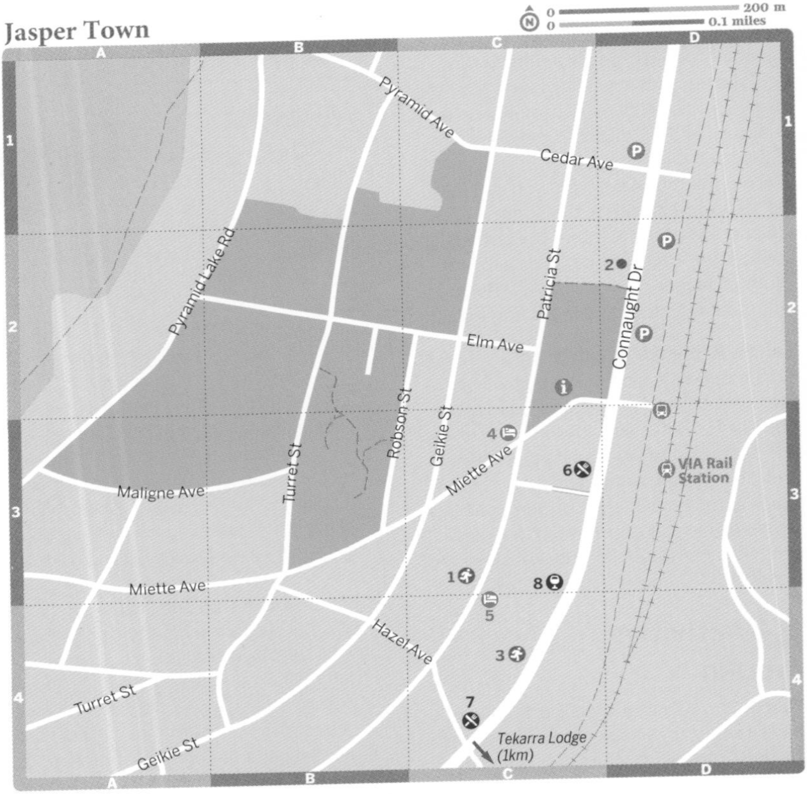

Jasper Town

Activities, Courses & Tours

1	Maligne Rafting Adventures	C3
	Maligne Tours	(see 1)
2	SunDog Tour Company	D2
3	Vicious Cycle	C4

Sleeping

4	Athabasca Hotel	C3
5	Park Place Inn	C4

Eating

6	Other Paw	C3
7	Villa Caruso	C4

Drinking & Nightlife

8	Jasper Brewing Co	C3

site of an old fur-trading post; and the 9km **Mina and Riley Lakes Loop** that leads out directly from the townsite.

Further away and slightly harder is the famous 9.1km **Path of the Glacier Trail** below the impressive face of Mt Edith Cavell, which takes you to the foot of the Angel Glacier through the flower-scattered Cavell meadows.

WHITE-WATER RAFTING

Maligne Rafting Adventures Rafting

(Map p138; ☎780-852-3370; www.raftjasper.com; 616 Patricia St; trips from $59) Everything from float trips to grade II and III adventures, plus overnight trips.

Tours

SunDog Tour Company Guided Tour

(Map p138; ☎780-852-4056, 888-786-3641; www.sundogtours.com; Connaught Dr) SunDog Tour Company is one of many tour companies and booking centers in Jasper. They run a whole host of tours, including trips to the icefields, train rides, boat rides, wildlife viewing, rafting, horseback riding and more.

Sleeping

Athabasca Hotel Hotel $$
(Map p138; ☎780-852-3386; www.athabascahotel.com; 510 Patricia St; r without/with bathroom $99/175; @ 🛜) If you can take the stuffed moose heads, noisy downstairs bar-nightclub and service that is sometimes as fickle as the mountain weather, you'll have no problems at the Athabasca (or Atha-B, as it's known). Centrally located with an attached restaurant and small, but comfortable, rooms (many with shared bathroom) it's been around since 1929 and is the best bargain in town.

Park Place Inn Boutique Hotel $$$
(Map p138; ☎780-852-9970; www.parkplaceinn.com; 623 Patricia St; r from $229; @) Giving nothing away behind its rather ordinary exterior among a parade of downtown shops, the Park Place is a head-turner as soon as you ascend the stairs to its plush open lobby. The 14 self-proclaimed heritage rooms are well deserving of their superior status, with marble surfaces, fine local art, claw-foot baths and a general air of refinement and luxury.

Tekarra Lodge Hotel $$$
(☎780-852-3058; www.tekarralodge.com; Hwy 93A; d from $219; ⏲May-Oct) The most atmospheric cabins in the park are set next to the Athabasca River amid tall trees and splendid tranquility. Hardwood floors, wood-paneled walls plus fireplaces and kitchenettes inspire coziness. It's only 1km from the townsite, but has a distinct backcountry feel.

Eating

Other Paw Cafe, Bakery $
(Map p138; ☎780-852-2253; 610 Connaught Dr; snacks $2-6; ⏲7am-6pm) An offshoot of The Bear's Paw, a larger cafe around the corner, The Other Paw offers the same insanely addictive mix of breads, pastries, muffins and coffee, but it stays open longer, plus it's right opposite the train station.

Mountain bikers, Jasper National Park

Villa Caruso Steakhouse **$$$**
(Map p138; ☎780-852-3920; 640 Connaught Dr; mains $22-36; ⏰11am-11:30pm; 🥕) Carnivore, pescatarian and vegetarian needs are all catered for here. Plush wood trimmings and great views are the perfect appetizer for a fine meal out.

Drinking & Nightlife

Jasper Brewing Co Brewery, Pub
(Map p138; ☎780-852-4111; www.jasperbrewingco.ca; 624 Connaught Dr; ⏰11:30am-1am) Open since 2005, this brewpub, the first of its type in a Canadian national park, uses glacial water to make its fine ales, including the signature Rockhopper IPA or – slightly more adventurous – the Rocket Ridge Raspberry Ale. It's a sit-down affair, with TVs and a good food menu.

Information

Jasper Information Centre (Map p138; ☎780-852-6176; www.parkscanada.gc.ca/jasper; 500 Connaught Dr; ⏰8am-7pm) Informative office in historic 'parkitecture' building.

Getting There & Around

Bus

The **bus station** (Map p138; www.greyhound.ca; 607 Connaught Dr) is at the train station.

Car

International car-rental agencies have offices in Jasper Town.

Train

VIA Rail (www.viarail.ca) offers tri-weekly train services west to Vancouver ($125, 20 hours) and east to Toronto ($340, 62 hours). In addition, there is a tri-weekly service to Prince Rupert, BC ($102, 32 hours). Call or check at the **train station** (Map p138; 607 Connaught Dr) for exact schedule and fare details.

EDMONTON

Modern, spread-out and frigidly cold for much of the year, Alberta's second-largest city and capital is a demure government town that you're more likely to read about in the business pages than the travel supplements.

Most non-Albertans pass through on their way to somewhere else – usually

West Edmonton Mall, Edmonton

MARK NEWMAN/GETTY IMAGES ©

Detour: Maligne Lake

Almost 50km from Jasper at the end of the road that bears its name, 22km-long **Maligne Lake** is the recipient of a lot of hype. It is billed as one of the most beautiful lakes within the park and there's no denying its aesthetics: the baby-blue water and a craning circle of rocky, photogenic peaks are feasts for the eyes.

Although the north end of the lake is heavy with the summer tour bus brigade, most of the rest of the shoreline is accessible only by foot or boat – hence it's quieter. Numerous campgrounds are available lakeside and are ideal for adventurous kayakers and backcountry hikers. Moose and grizzly bears are also sometimes seen here.

The **Maligne Lake Boathouse** (Map p136; ☎780-852-3370; boats per hr/day $30/90) rents canoes for a paddle around the lake. Not many people paddle all the way to Spirit Island – the lake's most classic view; it would take you all day. If you are really keen to see it, **Maligne Tours** (Map p138; ☎780-852-3370; www.malignelake.com; 616 Patricia St; adult/child $59/35; ⏲10am-5pm May-Oct) will zip you out there on its 1½-hour boat tours to the island.

Jasper National Park, which lies four hours to the west, or, for a handful of visitors, the overhyped West Edmonton Mall, the largest mall in North America. If you're searching for the soul of the city, head south of the river to the university district and happy-go-lucky Whyte Avenue, home to small theaters, dive diners and a spirited Friday night mood.

Sights & Activities

Royal Alberta Museum — Museum

(☎780-453-9100; www.royalalbertamuseum.ca; 12845 102nd Ave; adult/child $11/5; ⏲9am-5pm) Since getting its 'royal' prefix in 2005 when Queen Liz 2 dropped by, Edmonton's leading museum has successfully received funding – a cool $340 million – for a new downtown home which should be complete by 2015. For the time being, you can call in to these longstanding digs, on a bluff overlooking the river valley 2km west of downtown.

The museum is known for its enormous collection of insects (the world's largest) and a lauded display of Alberta's aboriginal culture.

Art Gallery of Alberta — Gallery

(☎780-422-6223; www.youraga.ca; 2 Sir Winston Churchill Sq; adult/child $12.50/8.50; ⏲11am-5pm Tue-Sun, to 9pm Wed) With the opening of this maverick art gallery in 2010, Edmonton at last gained a modern signature building to counter the ubiquitous boxy skyscrapers. Looking like a giant glass-and-metal space helmet, the futuristic structure in Churchill Sq is an exhibit in its own right. Its collection comprises 6000 pieces of historical and contemporary art, many of which have a strong Canadian bias, including a couple of works by BC's master of green, Emily Carr.

West Edmonton Mall — Shopping Mall

(www.westedmontonmall.com; 170th St; ⏲10am-9pm Mon-Fri, to 6pm Sat, noon-6pm Sun; 👪) Kitsch lovers who can't afford the trip to Vegas will have a field day in West Edmonton Mall, while those less enamored by plastic plants and phony re-creations of 15th-century galleons will hate it.

Not content to simply be a shopping mall, Edmonton's urban behemoth has the world's largest waterslides, an equipped indoor wave pool, a full-size amusement park, a skating rink, two mini-golf courses, a fake reef with real seals swimming around, a petting zoo, a hotel and 800 stores thrown in as a bonus.

Sleeping

Metterra Hotel on Whyte Boutique Hotel **$$**
(780-465-8150; www.metterra.com; 10454 Whyte Ave; r from $150; @) If you can wade through the uncreative hotel brochure blurb ('urban oasis,' 'contemporary decor,' 'traditional hospitality'), you'll find that the Met is actually a decent place to stay and a fitting reflection of the happening entertainment district (Old Strathcona) in which it sits. The modern, luxurious interior is accented with Indonesian artifacts hinting at the owner's secret love for all things Eastern.

Matrix Boutique Hotel **$$**
(780-429-2861; www.matrixedmonton.com; 10001 107th St; r from $150; @) One of a triumvirate of Edmonton boutique hotels, the Matrix claims to serve the 'sophisticated traveler,' and largely succeeds, with cool minimalist architecture punctuated with woody color accents and plenty of handy modern gadgets. In keeping with its boutique image, there's free wine and cheese every evening at 5:30pm.

Eating

DOWNTOWN & WEST END

Duchess Bake Shop Bakery, Cafe **$**
(780-488-4999; www.duchessbakeshop.com; 10720 124th St; baked goods from $1.50; 9am-8pm Tue-Fri, 10am-6pm Sat, to 5pm Sun) Duchess is what you call a destination cafe/bakery. You'd cross town to eat here – on foot in the snow if necessary. It possesses a detectable French flavour in both taste and decor: the croissants and cakes are buttery, and the furniture is all marble tables and Louis XV–style chairs. Arrive early, before the queuing locals have stripped the cases bare.

OLD STRATHCONA & GARNEAU

Da-De-O Cajun **$$**
(780-433-0930; www.dadeo.ca; 10548A Whyte Ave; mains $10-16; 11:30am-11pm Mon, Tue & Thu-Sat, noon-10pm Sun) Wave goodbye to cloth serviettes and serious waitstaff and say hello to retro jukeboxes, art-deco lighting and jazz etchings on the wall. This dive diner serving Cajun food could well be Edmonton's best eating establishment. The key lies in the food – an unexpected summoning up of the Big Easy in the frozen north.

Drinking & Nightlife

Black Dog Freehouse Pub
(780-439-1089; www.blackdog.ca; 10425 Whyte Ave; 2pm-2am) Insanely popular with all types, the Black Dog is essentially a pub with a couple of hidden extras: a rooftop patio, known as the 'wooftop patio,' with heaters (naturally: this is Alberta), a traditional ground-floor bar (normally packed cheek to jowl on weekday nights), and a basement that features live music, DJs and occasional parties. The sum of the three parts has become a rollicking Edmonton institution.

Information

Edmonton Tourism (9797 Jasper Ave; 8am-5pm) Friendly place with tons of flyers and brochures.

Getting There & Away

Air

Edmonton International Airport (YEG; www.flyeia.com) is about 30km south of the city along the Calgary Trail, about a 45-minute drive from downtown.

Train

The small **VIA Rail station** (www.viarail.ca; 12360 121st St) is rather inconveniently situated 5km northwest of the city center near Edmonton City Centre Airport.

Getting Around

To/From the Airport

Sky Shuttle Airport Service (www.edmontonskyshuttle.com; adult/child $18/10) runs three different routes that service hotels in most areas of town, including downtown and the Strathcona area. The office is by carousel 12. Journey time is approximately 45 minutes.

Cab fare from the airport to downtown is about $50.

Public Transportation

City buses and a 16-stop Light Rail Transit (LRT) system cover most of the city. The fare is $3.20. Check out the excellent transit planning resources at www.edmonton.ca.

CALGARY

Calgary, to most non-Calagarians, is Canada in a Stetson with a self-confident American swagger and a seemingly insatiable thirst for business, especially if it involves oil. But like most stereotypes, the truth is more complex. Shrugging off its image as the city other Canadians love to hate, and standing strong despite serious flooding that caused havoc in June 2013, Alberta's largest metropolis continues to stride cool-headed towards the future with a thick skin and clear sense of its own destiny. The famous July Stampede is subtitled, with typical Calgarian immodesty, 'the greatest outdoor show on earth.'

Sights

Glenbow Museum Museum

(☎403-777-5506; www.glenbow.org; 130 9th Ave SE; adult/child $14/9; ⏲9am-5pm Fri-Wed, to 9pm Thu) For a town with such a short history, Calgary does a fine job telling it at the commendable Glenbow Museum, which traces the legacy of Calgary and Alberta from pre- to post-oil. Contemporary art exhibitions and story-worthy artifacts dating back centuries fill its halls and galleries.

Sleeping

Hotel Alma Boutique Hotel $$

(☎403-220-3203; www.hotelalma.ca; 169 University Gate NW; r from $129, apt $180; 📶) Some cruel critics claim Calgary lacks *alma* (soul), and although this fashionable boutique establishment in – of all places – Calgary's university campus can't really be described as soulful, it *is* funky and arty. Supermodern rooms are either one- or two-bedroom apartments or 'Euro-style' rooms, which in Alberta means 'small,' although small by Alberta standards isn't that small.

The university is 6km northeast of downtown, but easily accessible on the C-train.

Cowboy at the Calgary Stampede (p44)

Calgary

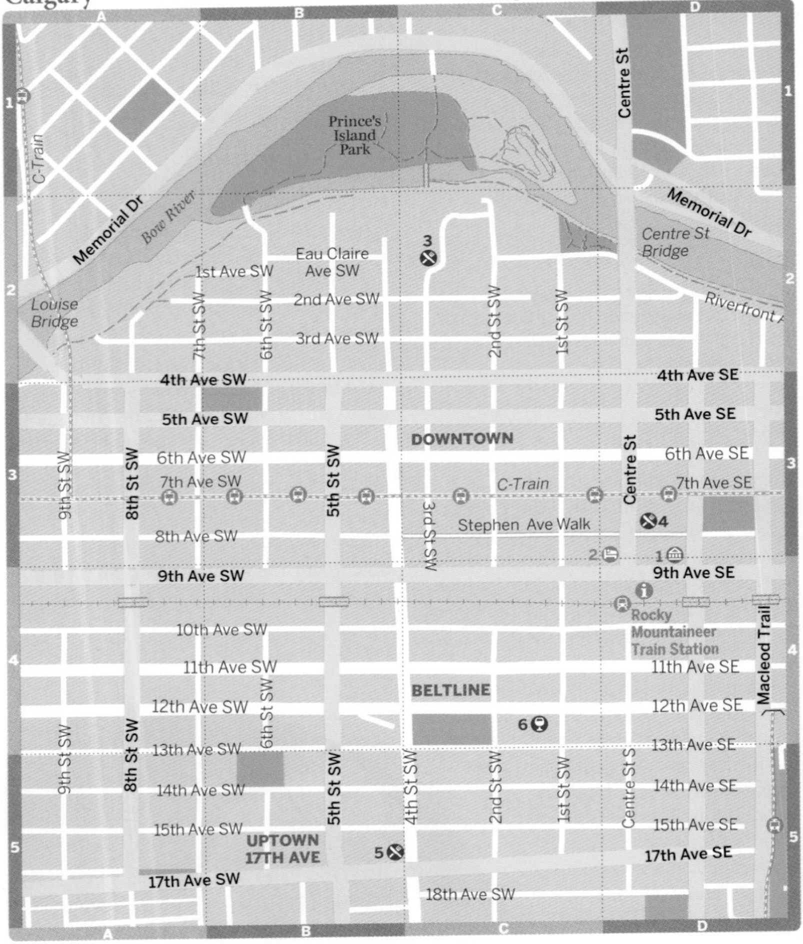

Calgary

Sights
1 Glenbow Museum D3

Sleeping
2 Hotel Le Germain D3

Eating
3 1886 Buffalo Cafe C2
4 Catch D3
5 Model Milk B5

Drinking & Nightlife
6 Hop In Brew C4

Hotel Le Germain Boutique Hotel **$$$**
(403-264-8990; www.germaincalgary.com; 899 Centre St SW; d from $329;) At last, a posh boutique hotel to counteract the bland assortment of franchise inns that service downtown Calgary. Germain is actually a member of a franchise, albeit a small French-Canadian one, but the style (check out the huge glass wall in reception) verges on opulent, while the 24-hour gym, in-room massage, compli-

Barnes & Noble Booksellers #1913
1991 Sproul Rd Suite 34
Broomall, PA 19008
610-353-3255

STR:1913 REG:004 TRN:1649 CSHR:Jane L

Lonely Planet Discover Canada
9781742205625 T1
(1 @ 24.99) 24.99

Subtotal 24.99
Sales Tax T1 (6.000%) 1.50
TOTAL 26.49
MASTERCARD 26.49
Card#: XXXXXXXXXXXX8418
Expdate: XX/XX
Auth: 06478Z
Entry Method: Chip Read

Application Label: CAPITAL ONE
AID: a0000000041010
TVR: 0000008000
TSI: e800

A MEMBER WOULD HAVE SAVED 2.50

Thanks for shopping at
Barnes & Noble

101.41B 08/16/2016 04:05PM

CUSTOMER COPY

days or without receipt or (ii) for product not carried by Barnes & Noble or Barnes & Noble.com.

Policy on receipt may appear in two sections.

Return Policy

With a sales receipt or Barnes & Noble.com packing slip, a full refund in the original form of payment will be issued from any Barnes & Noble Booksellers store for returns of undamaged NOOKs, new and unread books, and unopened and undamaged music CDs, DVDs, vinyl records, toys/games and audio books made within 14 days of purchase from a Barnes & Noble Booksellers store or Barnes & Noble.com with the below exceptions:

A store credit for the purchase price will be issued (i) for purchases made by check less than 7 days prior to the date of return, (ii) when a gift receipt is presented within 60 days of purchase, (iii) for textbooks, (iv) when the original tender is PayPal, or (v) for products purchased at Barnes & Noble College bookstores that are listed for sale in the Barnes & Noble Booksellers inventory management system.

Opened music CDs, DVDs, vinyl records, audio books may not be returned, and can be exchanged only for the same title and only if defective. NOOKs purchased from other retailers or sellers are returnable only to the retailer or seller from which they are purchased, pursuant to such retailer's or seller's return policy. Magazines, newspapers, eBooks, digital downloads, and used books are not returnable or exchangeable. Defective NOOKs may be exchanged at the store in accordance with the applicable warranty.

Returns or exchanges will not be permitted (i) after 14 days or without receipt or (ii) for product not carried by Barnes & Noble or Barnes & Noble.com.

Policy on receipt may appear in two sections.

Return Policy

With a sales receipt or Barnes & Noble.com packing slip, a full refund in the original form of payment will be issued from any Barnes & Noble Booksellers store for returns of undamaged NOOKs, new and unread books, and unopened and undamaged music CDs, DVDs, vinyl records, toys/games and audio books made within 14 days of purchase from a Barnes & Noble Booksellers store or Barnes & Noble.com with the below exceptions:

mentary newspapers and funky lounge add luxury touches.

Eating

1886 Buffalo Cafe
Breakfast $

(187 Barclay Pde SW; 6am-3pm Mon-Fri, from 7am Sat & Sun) A salt-of-the-earth diner in the high-rise-dominated city center that the realty lords forgot to knock down, this wooden shack construction is famous for its brunches fortified by huevos rancheros.

Catch
Seafood $$

(403-206-0000; www.catchrestaurant.ca; 100 8th Ave SW; mains $17-27; 11:30am-2pm Mon-Fri & 5pm-10pm Mon-Sat) The problem for any saltwater fish restaurant in landlocked Calgary is that, if you're calling it fresh, it can't be local. Overcoming the conundrum, Catch, situated in an old bank building on Stephen Ave Walk, flies its 'fresh catch' in daily from both coasts (BC and the Maritimes).

Model Milk
Canadian $$$

(403-265-7343; www.modelmilk.ca; 108 17th Ave SW; mains $19-32; 5pm-1am) Model Milk has a revolving menu that changes before the ink's even dry, so it's impossible to predict what you'll get to eat at the former dairy turned hip restaurant. Grits and prawns with a fried egg on top was heading the 'starter' line-up at last visit.

Drinking & Nightlife

Hop In Brew
Pub

(403-266-2595; 213 12th Ave SW; 4pm-late) An old Craftsman-style house clinging on for dear life amid the spanking new condos of the Victoria Park district, the Hop still gets hopping on a good night, with great tunes, a grungy atmosphere and plenty of beers on tap.

Shopping

Alberta Boot Co
Shoes

(403-263-4605; www.albertaboot.com; 50 50th Ave SE; boots $235-1700; 9am-6pm Mon-Sat) Visit the factory and store run by the province's only Western boot manufacturer and pick up a pair of your choice made from kangaroo, ostrich, python, rattlesnake, lizard, alligator or boring old cowhide.

Information

Tourism Calgary **(www.tourismcalgary.com; 101 9th Ave SW; 8am-5pm)** Operates a visitors center in the base of the Calgary Tower. The staff will help you find accommodations.

Getting There & Away

Air

Calgary International Airport **(YYC; www.calgaryairport.com)** is about 15km northeast of the center off Barlow Trail, a 25-minute drive away.

Bus

Canmore and Banff ($54, 2¼ hours, eight daily) are served by the legendary **Brewster Travel Canada** **(www.brewster.ca)**.

Brewster buses pick up at various downtown hotels. Inquire when booking.

Train

Inexplicably, Calgary welcomes no passenger trains (which bypass the city in favor of Edmonton and Jasper). Rocky Mountaineer Railtours runs expensive cruise ship–like rail excursions here (two-day tours per person from $1000).

Getting Around

To/From the Airport

Sundog Tours **(403-291-9617; www.sundogtours.com; one-way adult/child $15/8)** runs every half-hour from around 8:30am to 9:45pm between all the major downtown hotels and the airport.

A taxi to the airport costs about $35 from downtown.

Car & Motorcycle

Parking in downtown Calgary is an expensive nightmare – a policy designed to push people to use public transportation. Private lots charge about $20 per day.

Public Transportation

Calgary Transit **(www.calgarytransit.com)** is efficient and clean. You can choose from the Light Rapid Transit (LRT) rail system, aka the C-Train, and ordinary buses. One fare ($3) entitles you to transfer to other buses or C-Trains.

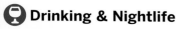

Toronto, Niagara Falls & Ontario

When it comes to culture, cuisine and sophistication, Ontario is on top of its game. When you're here, you can't help but feel a palpable connection with the rest of the planet. Forget ice fishing, conifers and bears for a minute – this is global Canada; big-city Canada; sexy, progressive, urbane Canada.

Toronto, Canada's largest city, is a blazing metropolis overflowing with multicultural arts, entertainment and eating opportunities. Ottawa, Canada's capital, is no longer a steadfast political filing cabinet: contemporary Ottawa is as hip as you want it to be. Not far from the madding crowds, low-key agricultural towns and historic settlements define Ontario's country civility. And if you're into wildlife, excellent national parks abound. From north to south you'll find more than enough boreal forests, undulating hills and vineyards to keep you feeling green.

Algonquin Provincial Park (p197)
GARRY BLACK/GETTY IMAGES ©

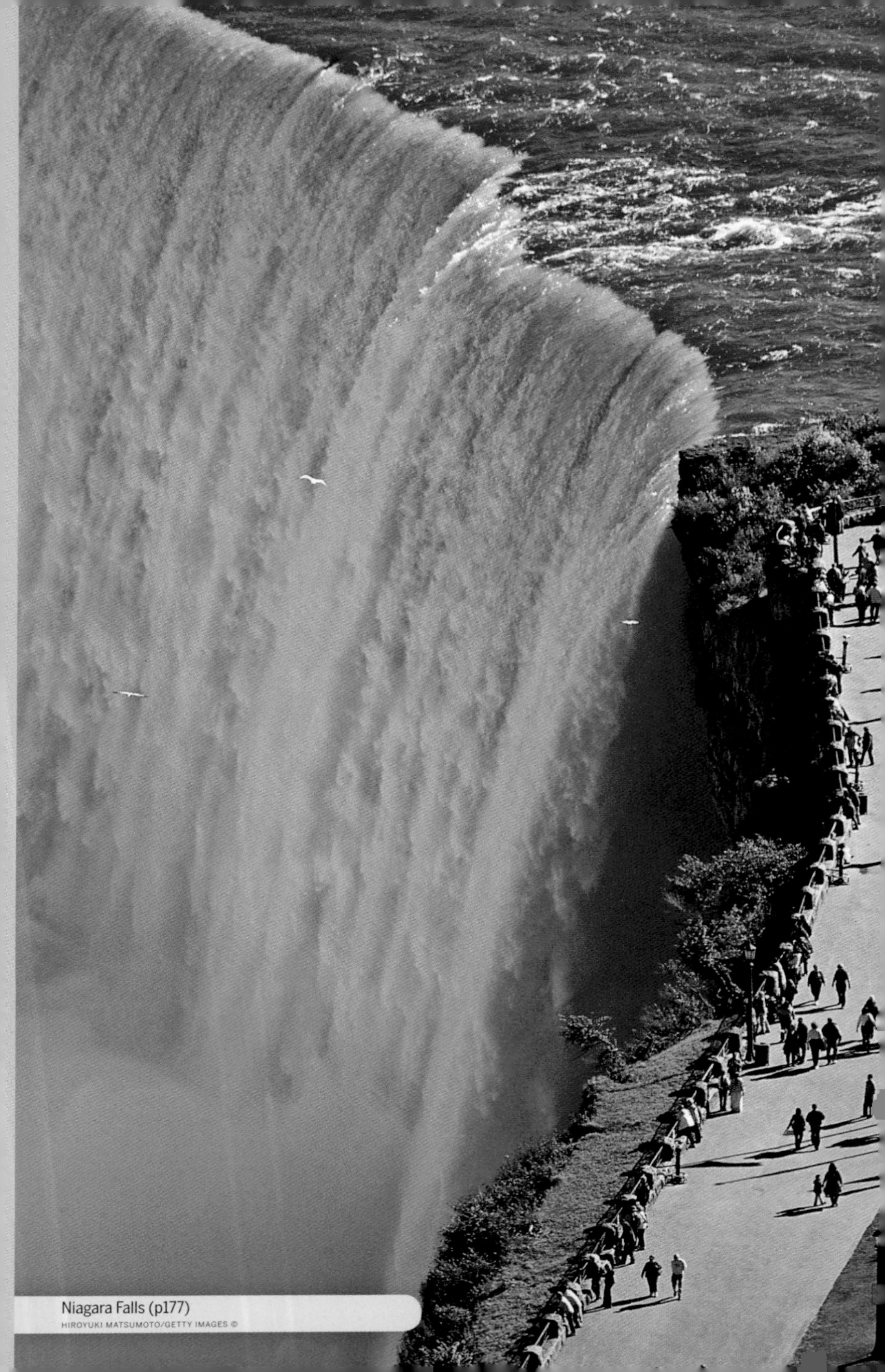

Niagara Falls (p177)

Toronto, Niagara Falls & Ontario

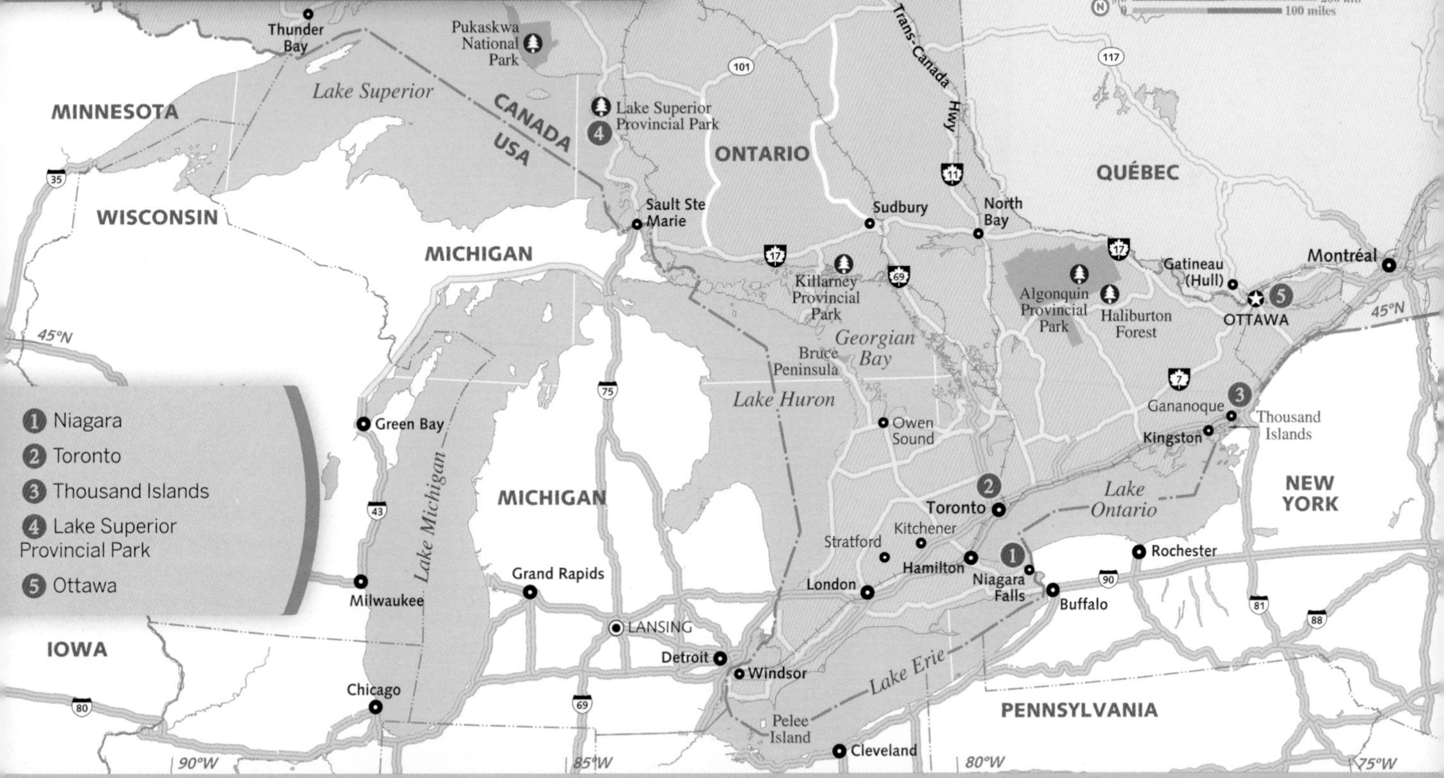

Toronto, Niagara Falls & Ontario's Highlights

Niagara

Of course there's the falls (p177), one of the world's most famous torrents, to ogle. But the Niagara region also struts its pretty stuff with leafy trails and slowpoke backroads to cycle; wooded gorges and nature-reserve paths to hike; and a lush, vineyard-striped landscape to explore. Indulge in the local wine, and don't forget to see who's treading the boards at the popular Shaw Festival (p175). Below: Niagara Peninsula (p184)

1

2

Toronto

A hyperactive stew of cultures and neighborhoods, Toronto (p156) strikes you with sheer urban awe. Will you hav dinner in Chinatown or Greektown? De signer shoes from Bloor-Yorkville are a cessorized with tattoos in Queen Wes Mod art galleries, theater par excellen and hockey mania add to the megalopolis, and it's all viewable atop the CN Tower (p160), the Western Hemisphere highest structure. Left: CN Tower

JA. KRAULIS/GETTY IMAGES ©

Thousand Islands

3

'he Thousand Islands Parkway (p185) olls along a pastoral strip by the St .awrence River, where a fog-cloaked :onstellation of 1800 islands floats. 'he road offers picture-perfect 'istas and dreamy picnic areas, as vell as dainty Victorian towns such ıs Gananoque (p185). Pull over to ;pend the night at an inn or take a ›oat ride through the isles, many of vhich hold rambling old mansions ınd castles.

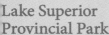

4

Lake Superior Provincial Park

It might not have sky-high mountains or whale sightings like its counterparts east and west, but Lake Superior Provincial Park (p202) offers a landscape every bit as dramatic. Wispy, beard-like fog and shivering arctic trees give it a distinctly primeval flavor. Shore-clasping drives and day hikes reward with isolated beaches, tumbling waterfalls and mysterious, red-ochre pictographs.

5

Ottawa

With its French flavors, world-class museums and bustling ByWard Market (p197), Canada's capital is cooler than you think. Its gastronomic fare rivals that of Toronto and Montréal, but it's more accessible: neighborhoods are walkable and prices fit all budgets. Districts like the Glebe ratchet up the cool-cat factor with quirky shops and cafes. Time for just one museum? Make it the Canadian Museum of Civilization (p190). Above: Canadian Museum of Civilization

Toronto, Niagara Falls & Ontario's Best...

Dining

- **Lee** Artisan selection of east-meets-west Asian delights in Toronto. (p170)
- **Beckta Dining & Wine** Ottawa's hottest table draws foodies galore. (p196)
- **ND Sushi** Unassuming Toronto spot offering authentic Japanese fare. (p170)
- **Fraser Cafe** The place to be for brunch in Ottawa. (p196)
- **Union** French and Italian fusion for hipsters in Toronto. (p172)

Art

- **National Gallery of Canada** Ottawa's sprawling trove with Rembrandts, Warhols, and Canadian and Inuit art. (p192)
- **Art Gallery of Ontario** From rare Québecois religious statuary to the Henry Moore sculpture pavilion. (p158)
- **Owen Sound** Fifty-plus studios pepper the region around this thriving artists' colony. (p199)
- **401 Richmond** A rambling old lithographer's warehouse bursting with mod galleries. (p158)

Uncommon Museums

- **Bata Shoe Museum** Polar boots, crushing clogs and Elton John's bedazzlers rest among the soles. (p161)
- **Hockey Hall of Fame** Skate against Gretzky and hoist the Stanley Cup (virtually, of course). (p157)
- **Daredevil Gallery** Cautionary tales of what happens when you go over Niagara Falls in a barrel. (p180)
- **Canadian War Museum** Explores human conflict in an admirably nonheroic way. (p187)

Scenic Parks

- **Lake Superior Provincial Park** Shore-clasping drives and hikes to mysterious pictographs. (p202)
- **Pukaskwa National Park** Wildlife-rich hinterland with only 4km of road. (p203)
- **Algonquin Provincial Park** Moose and wolves, and sapphire lakes primed for paddlers. (p197)
- **Fathom Five National Marine Park** Lightstations, shipwrecks and eerie, wave-bashed rock formations. (p201)

t: Moose, Algonquin Provincial Park (p197); **ove:** Canadian War Museum (p187), Ottawa

(LEFT) BOB GURR/GETTY IMAGES ©; (ABOVE) ALAN MARSH/GETTY IMAGES ©

Need to Know

ADVANCE PLANNING

- **One month before** Book accommodation for summer stays.
- **Two weeks before** Book theater tickets in Toronto, and cycling and paddling excursions in Niagara and other parks.
- **One week before** Make dinner reservations at trendy restaurants.

RESOURCES

- **Ontario Tourism** (www.ontariotravel.net) Includes activity and accommodation information.
- **Tourism Toronto** (www.seetorontonow.com) Theater listings and accommodation bookings for Canada's biggest city.
- **Niagara Falls Tourism** (www.niagarafallstourism.com) Everything about the waterfall and its carnival attractions.
- **Ontario Parks** (www.ontarioparks.com) The low-down for visiting the province's 104 parks.
- **Wine Council of Ontario** (www.winesofontario.ca) Information on wines, vineyards and boozy festivals.

GETTING AROUND

- **Fly** Many visitors arrive via Toronto's Lester B Pearson International Airport, Canada's busiest. Small Billy Bishop Toronto City Airport is home to regional airlines. Flights to and from Ottawa often land at this downtown facility.
- **Car** Extensive highway system links most towns, with all major hire-car companies readily available. Surprisingly, no major highway shoots directly between Toronto and Ottawa. The speediest option is to take Hwy 401 from Toronto to Prescott, and use Hwy 416 to complete the L-shaped, 440km journey.
- **Train** From Toronto, VIA Rail runs three times per week to Vancouver via Jasper, and several times daily to Montréal. There's Amtrak service to/from New York City.

BE FOREWARNED

- **Toronto traffic** Roads around Toronto are wildly congested, as is the public transit system. Infrastructure fixes are in the works, but in the interim you'll need patience to get around. See www.bigmove.ca for construction updates.

Toronto, Niagara Falls & Ontario Itineraries

It sure is handy that Toronto sits a mere 140km from Niagara's vineyards and pounding falls. Helpful, too, that Ottawa is a straight shot northeast via pretty islands prime for pit stops.

3 DAYS — TORONTO TO NIAGARA ALL THINGS BIG

Prime yourself for high times in the neighborhoods of multicultural ❶**Toronto** (p156). Take a rocket ride up the CN Tower – the brave can walk around the open-air circumference. Have lunch at St Lawrence Market – perhaps a peameal bacon sandwich – then head up to Bloor-Yorkville to splash some cash in the shops. Compensate by having a thrifty dumpling dinner in Chinatown.

On day two check out the amazing Royal Ontario Museum, Hockey Hall of Fame or Art Gallery of Ontario – then take a long lunch in Baldwin Village. Afterward, ride the ferry to the ❷**Toronto Islands** (p170); hire a bike and wheel away the afternoon. Back on the mainland, relax with a pint at a downtown pub.

On day three, bow down before the power and grace of ❸**Niagara Falls** (p177). Don a raincoat and board the Hornblower to get up close to the thundering cascade, then trundle up the pretty, picnic-grove-studded Niagara Parkway. By now you've noticed signposts for more than a few wineries. Pick one to stop at, sip a riesling or cabernet squeezed from the vines, and toast your three-day jaunt.

5 DAYS

TORONTO TO OTTAWA
ONTARIO'S MAIN VEIN

Start in ❶ **Toronto** (p156), and wallow in the wealth of architecture, museums, restaurants and nightclubs. Consider a day trip to Niagara.

Pastoral ❷ **Prince Edward County** (p186) makes a fine pit stop, especially for foodies. The hilly island, attached by bridges to the mainland, is a budding region for new wineries and rustic gourmet restaurants.

Next up: more islands. The misty, mansion-covered ❸ **Thousand Islands** (p185) dot the St Lawrence River. Victorian ❹ **Gananoque** (p185), where you can take boat rides into the archipelago and see castle turrets poking through the prevailing fog, makes a good break. Pull up the covers in one of the town's romantic inns.

Then it's on to ❺ **Ottawa** (p187), Canada's capital, for a day or two. Start at Parliament Hill for Kodak moments with the Peace Tower, swap copper towers for shimmering glass spires at the National Gallery of Canada, then pause for lunch at the ByWard Market where vendors hawk fresh farm produce and kitschy souvenirs. Don't forget to see the gorgeous Canadian Museum of Civilization. Take in the awesome architecture and the skyline.

Parliament Hill (p189), Ottawa
OLEKSIY MAKSYMENKO/GETTY IMAGES ©

Discover Toronto, Niagara Falls & Ontario

At a Glance

- **Toronto** Canada's biggest, busiest and, many say, best city for eating and shopping.
- **Niagara Falls** (p177) World-famous wonder of water surrounded by wine country.
- **Thousand Islands** (p185) Hushed, windswept isles and 19th-century mansions.
- **Ottawa** (p187) Canada's museum-rich capital.
- **Bruce Peninsula** (p198) Shorescapes for hikers and artists.

Distillery District (p158), Toronto

KLAUS LANG/GETTY IMAGES ©

TORONTO

Welcome to Toronto, the most multiculturally diverse city *on the planet:* over 140 languages are spoken. The flavors, aromas, sights and sounds of almost every nation converge peacefully in the streets of Toronto's many neighborhoods: microcosms of culture thriving in a somewhat hazy 'bigger picture' that proud locals defend regardless. You're likely to feel accepted here: it's estimated that over half of Toronto's residents were born outside Canada, and despite its complex make-up, Torontonians generally get along.

When the weather is fine, Toronto is a blast: a vibrant, big-time city abuzz with activity: some of the world's finest restaurants, happening bars, clubs and eclectic festivals are found here. At the height of summer, humid downtown neighborhoods become an endless convergence of patios bursting at the seams: alfresco is the way to drink and dine. Locals lap up every last drop of sunshine, beer or martini while they can.

Sights

Most tourist sights hug the Harbourfront, Entertainment and Financial Districts at the southern end of downtown. South of the lakeshore, locals retreat to the Toronto Islands for solace and the hands-down best views of Toronto's gargantuan skyline – well worth the half-day round trip. Back on the mainland, east of Yonge St and west of the Don Valley Parkway, the former Old York area is home to some of Toronto's oldest and most well-preserved neighborhoods. Many argue that west is best: The Annex, Kensington Market and Queen West are all here.

HARBOURFRONT

Harbourfront Centre Landmark

Map p162; ☎416-973-4000; www.harbourfront-centre.com; York Quay, 235 Queens Quay W; ⊙box office 1-6pm Tue-Sat, to 8pm show nights; 🚊509, 510) The 4-hectare not-for-profit Harbourfront Centre exists to educate and entertain Toronto's diverse community, through a kaleidoscope of performances and events held in its numerous stages and halls. Many are kid-focused, some are free. There's also a lakeside ice-skating rink where you can slice up the winter ice. Don't miss the free galleries, including the **Photo Passage** and the functioning **Craft Studio**.

Delicately strung along the western harborfront, the **Toronto Music Garden** was designed in collaboration with cellist Yo-Yo Ma. It expresses Bach's Suite No 1 for Unaccompanied Cello through landscape, with an arc-shaped grove of conifers, a swirling path through a wildflower meadow and a grass-stepped amphitheater where free concerts are held.

Canada Square (Map p162) and **Ontario Square** (Map p162), two vast new public spaces, opened in June 2013.

Power Plant Gallery Art Gallery

Map p162; ☎416-973-4949; www.thepowerplant.org; ⊙10am-6pm Tue, Wed & Sun, to 8pm Thu-Sat) FREE Easily recognized by its painted smokestack, the Power Plant Gallery is at the Harbourfront Centre and is just that – a former power plant transformed into Toronto's premier gallery of contemporary Canadian art. Best of all, it's free and exhibitions change regularly.

Steam Whistle Brewing Brewery

Map p162; www.steamwhistle.ca; 255 Bremner Blvd; 45min tour $10; ⊙noon-6pm Mon-Thu, 11am-6pm Fri & Sat, to 5pm Sun; Ⓢ Union, 🚊509, 510) 🌿 'Do one thing really, really well,' is the motto of Steam Whistle Brewing, a microbrewery that makes only a crisp European-style pilsner. Bubbling away in a 1929 train depot, Steam Whistle continually works on being environmentally friendly, in part by using renewable energy, steam heating, all-natural (and often local) ingredients, and using supercool ginger ale bottles that can be reused up to 40 times. Tours depart half-hourly from 1pm to 5pm and include tastings.

Ripley's Aquarium of Canada Aquarium

(Map p162; ☎416-360-7831; www.ripleysaquariumofcanada.com; 288 Bremner Blvd; adult/child $30/20; ⊙9am-9pm) Although almost-but-not-quite open at time of writing, Ripley's Aquarium of Canada is earmarked to be Toronto's hottest new attraction for young and old. Expect over 15,000 aquatic animals, 5.7 million litres of water in the combined tanks, as well as sleepovers, touch tanks and educational dive presentations.

FINANCIAL DISTRICT

Hockey Hall of Fame Museum

(Map p162; ☎416-360-7765; www.hhof.com; Brookfield Pl, 30 Yonge St; adult/child $17.50/11; ⊙9:30am-6pm; Ⓢ Union) Inside an ornate rococo gray stone Bank of Montréal building (c 1885), the Hockey Hall of Fame is a Canadian institution. Even those unfamiliar with the superfast ultraviolent sport are likely to be impressed by this, the largest collection of hockey memorabilia in the world. Check out the collection of *Texas Chainsaw Massacre*–esque goalkeeping masks or go head to head with the great Wayne Gretzky, virtual reality style.

Cloud Gardens Conservatory Gardens

(Map p162; ☎416-392-7288; 14 Temperance St; ⊙10am-2:30pm Mon-Fri; Ⓢ Queen) FREE An unexpected sanctuary with its own waterfall, the steamy Cloud Gardens Conservatory is crowded with enormous jungle leaves, vines and palms. Information plaques answer the question 'What Are Rainforests?.' It's a great place to warm up during winter, but avoid the area after dark – the adjacent park attracts some shady characters.

TD Gallery of Inuit Art Museum

(Map p162; ☎416-982-8473; www.td.com/inuitart/gallery/inuit-gallery; ground fl & mezzanine, TD Centre, 79 Wellington St W; ⌚8am-6pm Mon-Fri, 10am-4pm Sat & Sun; **S** St Andrew) FREE A quiet pause in the bustle of the Financial District, the Toronto Dominion (TD) Gallery of Inuit Art provides an exceptional insight into Inuit culture. Inside the Toronto Dominion Centre, a succession of glass cases displays otter, bear, eagles and carved Inuit figures in day-to-day scenes.

OLD YORK

Distillery District Landmark

(Map p159; ☎416-364-1177; www.thedistillerydistrict.com; 9 Trinity St; ⌚10am-7pm Mon-Wed, to 8pm Thu-Sat, 11am-5pm Sun; 🚋503, 504) Centered around the 1832 Gooderham and Worts distillery – once the British Empire's largest – the 5-hectare Distillery District is one of Toronto's best downtown attractions. Its Victorian industrial warehouses have been converted into soaring galleries, artists studios, design boutiques, cafes and eateries. The Young Centre for Performing Arts and the Mill Street Brewery are also here.

ENTERTAINMENT DISTRICT & KING STREET WEST

401 Richmond Gallery

(Map p166; www.401richmond.net; 401 Richmond St W; ⌚9am-7pm Mon-Fri, to 6pm Sat; 🚋510) FREE Inside an early-20th-century lithographer's warehouse, restored in 1994, this 18,500-meter-sq New York-style artist collective hums with the creative vibes of 130 diverse contemporary galleries showcasing works in almost any artistic medium you can think of. Grab a snack and a latte at the ground-floor cafe and enjoy it on the expansive roof garden: a little-known oasis in the summer.

Canadian Broadcasting Centre Museum

(CBC; Map p162; ☎416-205-5574; www.cbc.ca/museum; 250 Front St W; ⌚9am-5pm Mon-Fri; **S** Union, 🚋504) FREE Toronto's enormous Canadian Broadcasting Centre is the headquarters for English-language radio and TV across Canada. You can peek at the radio newsrooms anytime or attend a concert in the world-class Glenn Gould Studio. Be sure to check out the **CBC Museum** with its fantastic collection of antique microphones and broadcasting memorabilia. Next door, the **Graham Spry Theatre** screens ever-changing CBC programming. Best of all, it's free!

DOWNTOWN YONGE

Elgin & Winter Garden Theatre Theater

(Map p166; ☎416-314-2901; www.heritagetrust.on.ca/ewg; 189 Yonge St; tours adult/concession $12/10; **S** Queen) A restored masterpiece, the Elgin & Winter Garden Theatre is the world's last operating double-decker theater. Celebrating its centennial in 2013, the Winter Garden was built as the flagship for a vaudeville chain that never really took off, while the downstairs Elgin was converted into a movie house in the 1920s. Fascinating tours run Thursdays at 5pm and Saturdays at 11am.

City Hall Historic Building

(Map p166; ☎416-392-2489, 311; www.toronto.ca; 100 Queen St W; ⌚8:30am-4:30pm Mon-Fri; **S** Queen) FREE Much-maligned City Hall was Toronto's bold leap of faith into architectural modernity. Its twin clamshell towers, central 'flying-saucer,' ramps and mosaics were completed in 1965 to Finnish architect Viljo Revell's award-winning design. An irritable Frank Lloyd Wright called it a 'headmarker for a grave'; in a macabre twist, Revell died before construction was finished. Collect a self-guided tour pamphlet at the info desk.

Out front is **Nathan Phillips Square**, a meeting place for skaters, demonstrators and office workers on their lunch breaks. In summer, look for the Fresh Wednesdays farmers market, free concerts and special events. The fountain pool becomes a fun-filled ice-skating rink in winter.

CHINATOWN & BALDWIN VILLAGE

Art Gallery of Ontario Gallery

(AGO; Map p166; ☎877-225-4246, 416-979-6648; www.ago.net; 317 Dundas St W; adult/concession $19.50/11, admission free 6-8:30pm

Toronto City Overview

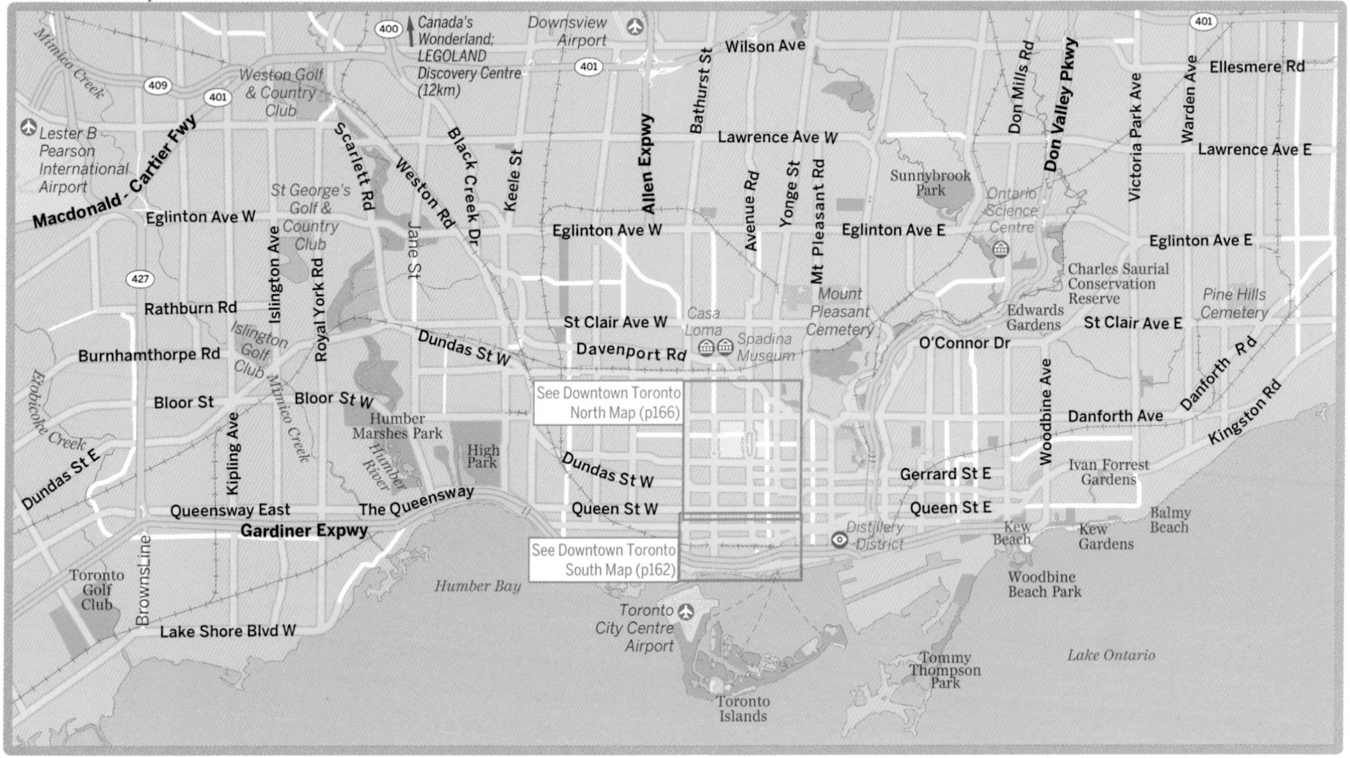

0 5 km
0 2.5 miles
Canada's Wonderland; LEGOLAND Discovery Centre (12km)
Downsview Airport
Lester B Pearson International Airport
Weston Golf & Country Club
St George's Golf & Country Club
Islington Golf Club
Toronto Golf Club
Humber Marshes Park
High Park
Humber River
Mimico Creek
Etobicoke Creek
Humber Bay
Casa Loma
Spadina Museum
Mount Pleasant Cemetery
Sunnybrook Park
Ontario Science Centre
Charles Saurial Conservation Reserve
Edwards Gardens
Pine Hills Cemetery
Ivan Forrest Gardens
Kew Beach
Kew Gardens
Balmy Beach
Woodbine Beach Park
Distillery District
Tommy Thompson Park
Toronto Islands
Toronto City Centre Airport
Lake Ontario
See Downtown Toronto North Map (p166)
See Downtown Toronto South Map (p162)
Macdonald - Cartier Fwy
Eglinton Ave W
Rathburn Rd
Burnhamthorpe Rd
Bloor St
Dundas St E
Kipling Ave
Islington Ave
Royal York Rd
Scarlett Rd
Weston Rd
Black Creek Dr
Jane St
Keele St
Allen Expwy
Bathurst St
Wilson Ave
Lawrence Ave W
Avenue Rd
Yonge St
Mt Pleasant Rd
Eglinton Ave E
St Clair Ave W
Davenport Rd
Dundas St W
Bloor St W
Queensway East
Gardiner Expwy
The Queensway
Queen St W
BrownsLine
Lake Shore Blvd W
Don Mills Rd
Don Valley Pkwy
Victoria Park Ave
Warden Ave
Ellesmere Rd
Lawrence Ave E
O'Connor Dr
St Clair Ave E
Woodbine Ave
Danforth Ave
Danforth Rd
Kingston Rd
Gerrard St E
Queen St E
400
401
409
427

CHRIS CHEADLE/GETTY IMAGES ©

Don't Miss
CN Tower

Toronto's iconic CN Tower, a marvel of 1970s engineering, looks like a giant concrete hypodermic needle. Its function as a communications tower takes a backseat to relieving tourists of as much cash possible: riding those glass elevators up the highest freestanding structure in the world (553m) is one of those things in life you just *have* to do. If not, you're bound to catch a glimpse of the tower at night, when the entire structure puts on a brilliant free light show year-round. Try the intersection of McCaul St and Queen St W, due north of the tower, for best vantage.

On a clear day, the views from the top are astounding; if it's hazy (often) you won't see a thing. Queues for the elevator can be up to two hours long in each direction. Buying tickets online saves 15%. There's an obligatory revolving restaurant (called 360°): it's expensive, but the elevator price is waived for diners. Cashed-up daredevils (13 years+) can now opt for the EdgeWalk, a 20-minute outdoor walk around the unbounded perimeter of the main pod (356m). Not for the fainthearted.

NEED TO KNOW

La Tour CN; Map p162; ☎416-868-6937; www.cntower.ca; 301 Front St W; Tower Experience adult/child $32/24, Skypod +$12; Edgewalk $175; ⏰9am-10pm Sun-Thu, to 11pm Fri & Sat; Ⓢ Union

Wed; ⏰10am-5:30pm Tue & Thu-Sun, to 8:30pm Wed; 🚋505) The AGO houses art collections both excellent and extensive (bring your stamina). Renovations of the facade, designed by the great Frank Gehry and completed in 2008, fail to impress at street level: perhaps because of a drab downtown location. Fortunately, everything changes once you step inside. Highlights of the permanent collection nclude rare Québecois religious statuary, First Nations and Inuit carvings, stunningly presented works by Canadian greats, the Group of Seven, the Henry Moore sculpture pavilion and a restored Georgian house, The Grange.

BLOOR-YORKVILLE

Royal Ontario Museum — Museum

(ROM; Map p166; ☎416-586-8000; www.rom.on.ca; 100 Queen's Park; adult/child $15/12, special exhibit surcharges apply; ⏲10am-5:30pm Sat-Thu, to 8:30pm Fri; S Museum) Celebrating its centennial in 2014, the multidisciplinary ROM is Canada's biggest natural history museum and one of the largest museums in North America.

Inside, the permanent collection features over 6 million specimens and artifacts, divided between two main galleries: the Natural History Galleries (all on the 2nd floor) and the World Culture Galleries (on floors 1, 3 and 4). The Chinese temple sculptures, Gallery of Korean Art and costumes and textile collections are some of the best in the world. Kids rush to the dinosaur rooms, Egyptian mummies and Jamaican bat-cave replica. The cedar crest poles carved by First Nations tribes in British Columbia are wonderful.

Bata Shoe Museum — Museum

(Map p166; ☎416-979-7799; www.batashoemuseum.ca; 327 Bloor St W; adult/child $14/5, admission free 5-8pm Thu; ⏲10am-5pm Tue, Wed, Fri & Sat, to 8pm Thu, noon-5pm Sun; S St George) It's important in life to be well shod, a stance the Bata Shoe Museum takes seriously. Impressively designed by architect Raymond Moriyama to resemble a stylized shoebox, the museum displays 10,000 'pedi-artifacts' from around the globe. Peruse 19th-century French chestnut-crushing clogs, Canadian Aboriginal polar boots or famous modern pairs worn by Elton John, Indira Gandhi and Pablo Picasso. Come along for something truly different!

UNIVERSITY OF TORONTO & THE ANNEX

Casa Loma — Historic Building

(Map p159; ☎416-923-1171; www.casaloma.org; 1 Austin Tce; adult/child $18/10; ⏲9:30am-5pm, last entry 4pm; 🚌127, stop Davenport & Spadina, S Dupont) Toronto's only castle may have never housed royalty, but it certainly has grandeur, lording over The Annex on a cliff that was once the shoreline of the glacial Lake Iroquois, from which Lake Ontario derived. Climb the 27m **Baldwin Steps** up the slope from Spadina Ave, north of Davenport Rd.

The 98-room mansion – an architectural orgasm of castellations, chimneys, flagpoles, turrets and Rapunzel balconies – was built between 1911 and 1914 for Sir Henry Pellat, a wealthy

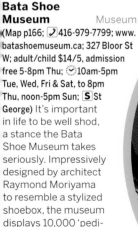

Royal Ontario Museum, designed by architect Daniel Libeskind

GRANT FAINT/GETTY IMAGES ©

Downtown Toronto South

0 500 m
0 0.25 miles

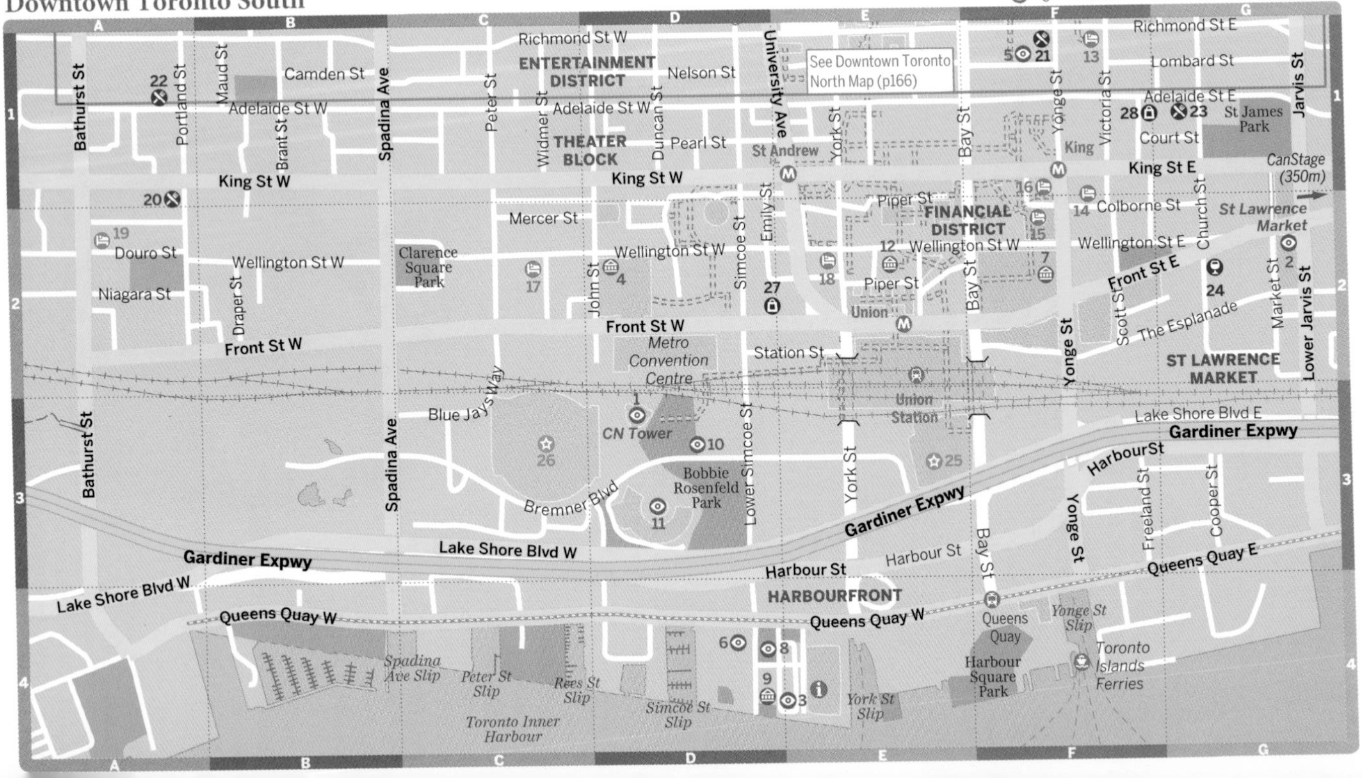

Downtown Toronto South

Don't Miss Sights
1 CN Tower D3
2 St Lawrence Market G2

Sights
3 Canada Square E4
4 Canadian Broadcasting Centre D2
5 Cloud Gardens Conservatory F1
6 Harbourfront Centre D4
7 Hockey Hall of Fame F2
8 Ontario Square D4
9 Power Plant Gallery D4
10 Ripley's Aquarium of Canada D3
11 Steam Whistle Brewing D3
12 TD Gallery of Inuit Art E2

Sleeping
13 Cambridge Suites F1
14 Cosmopolitan F1
15 Hotel Victoria F2
16 One King West F1
17 Residence Inn Toronto Downtown C2
18 Strathcona Hotel E2
19 Thompson Toronto A2

Eating
20 Lee A1
21 Richmond Station F1
22 Sadie's Diner A1
23 Terroni G1
Thompson Diner .... (see 19)

Drinking & Nightlife
24 C'est What G2

Entertainment
25 Air Canada Centre E3
26 Rogers Centre C3

Shopping
27 Bay of Spirits Gallery D2
28 Open Air Books & Maps F1

financier who made bags of cash from his contract to provide Toronto with electricity. A variety of themed guided tours are available.

Spadina Museum Museum
(Map p159; 416-392-6910; www.toronto.ca/culture/spadina; 285 Spadina Rd; tours adult/child $8/5, grounds admission free; noon-4pm Tue-Sun; S Dupont) Atop the Baldwin Steps, this gracious home and its Victorian-Edwardian gardens were built in 1866 as a country estate for financier James Austin and his family. Donated to the city in 1978, it became a museum in 1984 and was recently painstakingly transformed to evoke the heady age of the roaring 1920s and '30s: highly recommended.

QUEEN WEST & TRINITY BELLWOODS

Although Queen West isn't home to any significant attractions, a trip to Toronto's best known 'hood is a must. Any self-respecting 20-to-40-something with an interest in popular culture will want to make this hip strip their first port of call.

To do Queen St justice, make a day of it: start at the corner of Yonge St and head west, although nothing really happens until the Osgoode subway station at the intersection of Queen St W and University Ave. The Queen West district begins here and continues for about 1.5km to Bathurst St. The first few blocks over to Spadina are a wonderful mix of mainstream retailers, bars and an eclectic bunch of boutiques, but it's really from Spadina to Bathurst where the wild things are. Infinitely more grungy, here you'll find all manner of cheap and delicious eats slotted between fabric, furniture, art and music stores. There's plenty of cafes and bars in which to glean inspiration and lose track of time.

Tours

City Sightseeing Toronto Bus Tour
(416-410-0536; www.citysightseeingtoronto.com; adult/child $35/20) Hop-on, hop-off sightseeing tours on an open-top double-decker London bus, around a 24-stop city loop. Tickets are valid for 72 hours: good value if you plan to use the bus over three days and a great way to get oriented.

Chariots of Fire Bus Tour
(905-877-0855; www.chariots-of-fire.com; 33 Yonge St; day tours $60) Low-cost day tours from Toronto to Niagara Falls including a *Maid of the Mist* boat ride and free time at Niagara-on-the-Lake. These guys are highly organized and comfortably present

the best of the Falls, from Toronto, for those who only have a day to experience it all. Highly recommended.

Heritage Toronto Walking Tour
(416-338-3886; www.heritagetoronto.org; 3F, 157 King St E; donations encouraged; Apr-Oct) A diverse offering of fascinating historical, cultural and nature walks and bike and bus (TTC) tours led by museum experts and neighborhood historical society members. Tours generally last one to three hours.

Sleeping

It's essential to book in advance for stays from mid-May to late September.

Plenty of B&Bs can be found through the agencies below.

Bed & Breakfast Homes of Toronto Accommodations Service
(416-363-6362; www.bbcanada.com/associations/toronto2) Anything from modest family homes to deluxe suites.

Downtown Toronto Association of Bed and Breakfast Guest Houses Accommodations Service
(647-654-2959; www.bnbinfo.com) Rooms in various neighborhoods, mostly in renovated Victorian houses.

Toronto Bed & Breakfast Reservation Service Accommodations Service
(705-738-9449, 877-922-6522; www.torontobandb.com) The oldest agency in town with a dozen central listings.

FINANCIAL DISTRICT

Hotel Victoria Boutique Hotel **$$**
(Map p162; 416-363-1666, 800-363-8228; www.hotelvictoria-toronto.com; 56 Yonge St; d from $159; S King) The early-20th-century Hotel Victoria retains a charming period lobby. Guest rooms are on the smaller side but have been simply and sylishly refurbished and have free wi-fi. Bathrooms have great tubs but ladies might be disappointed by the lack of vanity space.

Toronto for Children

Toronto is a kid-friendly city: there's plenty of things to see and do when traveling with little ones in tow.

The Harbourfront Centre (p157) produces ongoing events through HarbourKIDS.

Inquisitive minds will love the CN Tower (p160), **Ontario Science Centre** (Map p159; 416-696-1000; www.ontariosciencecentre.ca; 770 Don Mills Rd; Science Centre adult/child $22/13, Omnimax $13/9, combined ticket $28/19; 10am-4pm Mon-Fri, to 7pm Sat & Sun; 34 (from Eglinton TTC), 25 (from Pape TTC)), Royal Ontario Museum (p161) and **LEGOLAND Discovery Centre** (855-356-2150; www.legolanddiscoverycentre.ca/toronto; 1 Bass Pro Mills Dr, Vaughan; adult/child $22/18; 10am-9pm Mon-Sat, 11am-7pm Sun; S Yorkdale).

The environmental custodians and animal doctors of the next generation will want you to take them to Ripley's Aquarium of Canada (p157).

If they've got ants in their pants, they won't have after a trip to **Canada's Wonderland** (905-832-8131; www.canadaswonderland.com; 9580 Jane St, Vaughan; day pass adult/child $59/35; 10am-10pm Jun-Aug, Sat & Sun only May & Sep; S York Mills).

A handy online resource for parents is www.helpwevegotkids.com, which lists everything child-related in Toronto, including babysitters and day-care options.

RICHARD I'ANSON/GETTY IMAGES ©

Don't Miss
St Lawrence Market

Old York's sensational St Lawrence Market has been a neighborhood meeting place for over two centuries. The restored, high-trussed 1845 **South Market** houses more than 50 specialty food stalls: cheese vendors, fishmongers, butchers, bakers and pasta makers. Inside the old council chambers upstairs, the **Market Gallery** (416-392-0572; www.toronto.ca/culture/the_market_gallery; 10am-4pm Tue-Fri, 9am-4pm Sat) FREE has rotating displays of paintings, photographs, documents and historical relics.

On the opposite side of Front St, the North Market hosts a Saturday farmers market and a fantastic Sunday antique market – get in early for the best stuff. In 2010 the winners of a design competition to transform the North Market building were announced, but there's no sign of construction yet. A few steps further north, the glorious St Lawrence Hall (1849) is topped by a mansard roof and a copper-clad clock tower that can be seen for blocks.

NEED TO KNOW

Map p162; 416-392-7129; www.stlawrencemarket.com; 92-95 Front St E; 8am-6pm Tue-Thu, to 7pm Fri, 5am-5pm Sat; 503, 504

Strathcona Hotel Hotel $$
(Map p162; 416-363-3321, 800-268-8304; www.thestrathconahotel.com; 60 York St; d from $125; S Union) This downtown hotel features compact, renovated rooms with decent bathrooms. The downstairs pub and cafe are convenient. Despite the lack of on-site parking, its proximity to Union Station is ideal, although some will find the long-term construction projects there an annoyance.

One King West Hotel $$
(Map p162; 416-548-8100; www.onekingwest.com; 1 King St W; d from $209; S King)

Downtown Toronto North

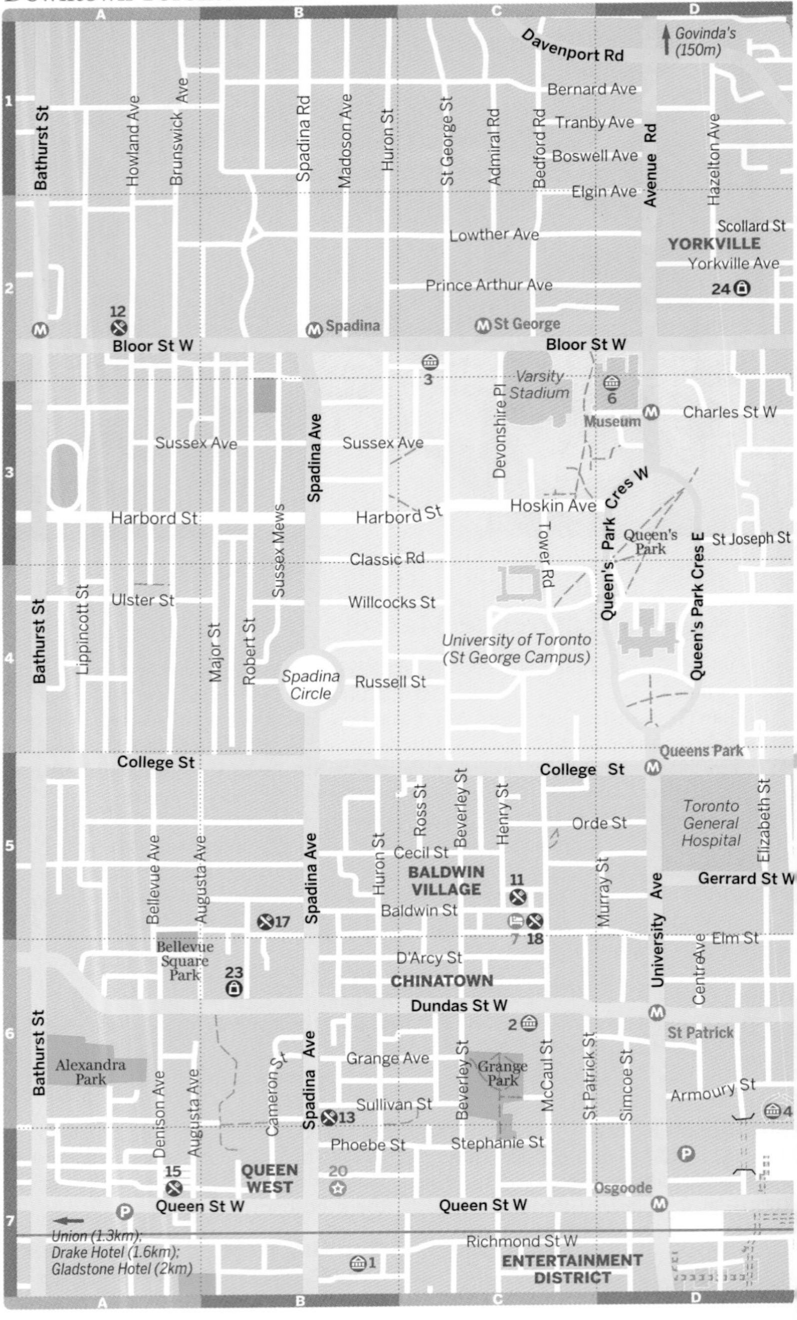
A
B
C
D
1
2
3
4
5
6
7
Davenport Rd
Govinda's (150m)
Bernard Ave
Tranby Ave
Boswell Ave
Elgin Ave
Bathurst St
Howland Ave
Brunswick Ave
Spadina Rd
Madoson Ave
Huron St
St George St
Admiral Rd
Bedford Rd
Avenue Rd
Hazelton Ave
Lowther Ave
Scollard St
YORKVILLE
Yorkville Ave
Prince Arthur Ave
24
12
Spadina
St George
Bloor St W
Bloor St W
3
Varsity Stadium
6
Devonshire Pl
Museum
Charles St W
Sussex Ave
Sussex Ave
Spadina Ave
Queen's Park Cres W
Harbord St
Harbord St
Hoskin Ave
Sussex Mews
Queen's Park
St Joseph St
Classic Rd
Tower Rd
Lippincott St
Ulster St
Willcocks St
Queen's Park Cres E
Major St
Robert St
University of Toronto (St George Campus)
Spadina Circle
Russell St
Queens Park
College St
College St
Ross St
Beverley St
Henry St
Orde St
Toronto General Hospital
Elizabeth St
Cecil St
Huron St
Bellevue Ave
Augusta Ave
BALDWIN VILLAGE
11
Murray St
University Ave
Gerrard St W
17
Baldwin St
7
18
Elm St
Bellevue Square Park
23
D'Arcy St
CHINATOWN
Centre Ave
Dundas St W
2
St Patrick
Alexandra Park
Grange Ave
Cameron St
Grange Park
McCaul St
St Patrick St
Simcoe St
Armoury St
Denison Ave
Sullivan St
13
4
Phoebe St
Stephanie St
15
QUEEN WEST
20
Osgoode
Queen St W
Queen St W
Union (1.3km); Drake Hotel (1.6km); Gladstone Hotel (2km)
Richmond St W
1
ENTERTAINMENT DISTRICT

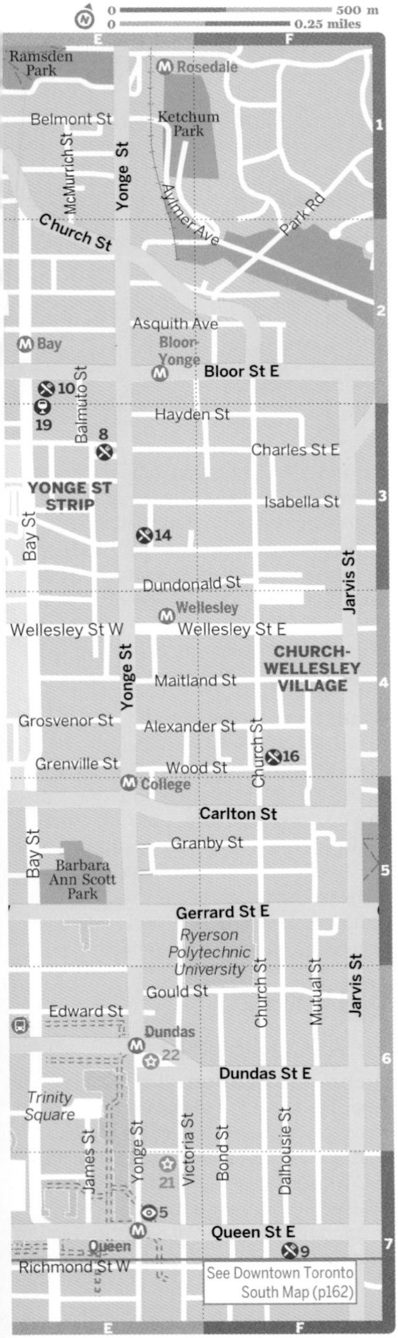

One of our favorite buildings in the Toronto skyline, the sleek One King West tower soars above the historic former head office for the Toronto Dominion bank with an effortless synergy. Studio and one-bedroom apartments are large, stylish and in a prime downtown location with subway and streetcars at your door.

OLD YORK

Cosmopolitan — Boutique Hotel $$

(Map p162; ☎416-350-2000; www.cosmotoronto.com; 8 Colborne St; ste from $209; 🚭❄📶; Ⓢ King) This compact hotel is sleek and quiet, with only five rooms per floor. Entry level Zen suites are on the small side. Lotus and Tranquility suites are significantly larger, have kitchens and some have lake views. All have balconies.

ENTERTAINMENT DISTRICT & KING STREET WEST

Residence Inn Toronto Downtown — Hotel $$

(Map p162; ☎416-581-1800; www.marriott.com; 255 Wellington St W; ste from $209; 🚭❄📶🏊🐾; 🚌504, 508) Perfect for longer stays or traveling with kids, this modern business/tourist hotel is in a prime location and has a variety of comfortable, functional room types, up to two-bedroom suites. All have fully equipped kitchens, pleasant decor and lots of light. The included full breakfast buffet makes for excellent value.

Thompson Toronto — Hotel $$

(Map p162; ☎416-640-7778; www.thompsonhotels.com/toronto; 550 Wellington St W; d from $229; ❄📶🏊🐾; 🚌504, 508) We love Thompson Toronto – it's just so LA. Funky, sharp rooms will be favored by those with a penchant for design, the rooftop bar, patio and pool are easily Toronto's finest and the two on-site dining options, Thompson Diner and Scarpetta, independently deserve mention. Combine all this with a brilliant location and exceptional service and you've got something that's worth splurging on, but don't bring grandma (check the website to see what the fuss is about).

Downtown Toronto North

Sights

1	401 Richmond	B7
2	Art Gallery of Ontario	C6
3	Bata Shoe Museum	C2
4	City Hall	D6
5	Elgin & Winter Garden Theatre	E7
6	Royal Ontario Museum	D3

Sleeping

7	Baldwin Village Inn	C5

Eating

8	7 West Café	E3
9	B Espresso Bar	F7
10	Bloor Street Diner	E2
11	Cafe la Gaffe	C5
12	Country Style	A2
13	Dark Horse Espresso	B6
14	Fire on the East Side	E3
15	Grasslands	A7
16	Hair of the Dog	F4
17	Moonbean Coffee Company	B5
18	ND Sushi	C5

Drinking & Nightlife

19	Panorama	E3

Entertainment

20	Horseshoe Tavern	B7
21	Massey Hall	E7
22	TO Tix	E6

Shopping

23	Courage My Love	B6
24	Guild Shop	D2

DOWNTOWN YONGE

Baldwin Village Inn B&B **$**

(Map p166; ☎416-591-5359; www.baldwininn.com; 9 Baldwin St; d incl breakfast with shared bathroom $90-110; ; 505, 506) Technically in the pretty enclave of Baldwin Village, just a few blocks from the Art Gallery of Ontario, this yellow-painted B&B faces a leafy street filled with cheap eateries and cafes. The front courtyard is perfect for lounging about and watching the people.

Cambridge Suites Hotel **$$**

(Map p162; ☎416-368-1990; www.cambridgesuitestoronto.com; 15 Richmond St E; ste from $175; ; S Queen) An excellent midrange choice, this all-suite hotel has spacious, good-looking rooms with separate living and kitchen facilities. Cityscape suites are on upper floors, are more luxuriously appointed and include continental breakfast in the restaurant. Three impressive penthouses are available.

QUEEN WEST & TRINITY BELLWOODS

Drake Hotel Boutique Hotel **$$**

(☎416-531-5042; www.thedrakehotel.ca; 1150 Queen St W; d/ste from $169/319; ; 501) While other hotels have rooms, the Drake has 'crash pads, dens, salons' and a rockin' little suite, beckoning bohemians, artists and indie musicians with a little cash to burn. The crash pads are tiny yet ineffably stylish and functional. In fact, all the rooms are on the small side, but are impeccably furnished with a sense of fun and good design. The attached bar and bandroom is one of Toronto's finest venues for live music, and in summer, the Sky Yard rooftop patio goes off to DJ beats and icy buckets of Coronas.

Gladstone Hotel Boutique Hotel **$$**

(☎416-531-4635; www.gladstonehotel.com; 1214 Queen St W; d/ste from $199/375; ; 501) The 37 artist-designed rooms at this trendsetting hotel could have leapt straight from a Taschen design book. Pick a room theme from the awesome website, then when you arrive, take the hand-cranked birdcage elevator to your arty boudoir on the 3rd and 4th floors.

Eating

FINANCIAL DISTRICT

Richmond Station International **$$**

(Map p162; ☎647-748-1444; www.richmondstation.ca; 1 Richmond St W; mains $20-29; ⊙11:30am-10:30pm Mon-Fri, 5:30pm-10:30pm Sat; S Queen) Reservations are strongly advised at this busy and uncomplicated restaurant, brainchild of celebrity Top Chef Canada winner, Carl Heinrich. Dishes are 'ingredient focused and technique driven.' We loved the chunky lobster cocktail and buttery mushroom fettuccine. The eclectic menu is simple but gratifying, priced right and complemented by a well-paired wine list and daily chalkboard specials. Highly recommended.

Terroni Italian **$$**
(Map p162; ☎416-203-3093; 57 Adelaide St E; mains $8-18; ⏰9am-10pm Mon-Wed, to 11pm Thu-Sat; S King) The Adelaide St branch of this popular Italian eatery (there are two others, and one in LA) occupies a former courthouse with high vaulted ceilings and labyrinthine dining areas. It's open, funky and, despite the size, generally packed. Reasonably priced wood-fired pizzas, rich pastas and fresh panini would make the Godfather proud.

ENTERTAINMENT DISTRICT & KING STREET WEST

Thompson Diner Diner **$**
(Map p162; ☎416-601-3533; www.thompsondiner.com; 550 Wellington St W; breakfast from $10, mains from $11.75; ⏰24hr; 🚊504, 511) The casual dining option at the sexy Thompson hotel is open 24 hours (breakfast served 5am to 11am). Whatever time of day, there's likely good peoplewatching to be had: this is nightclub territory, remember. Comfort food is a sure thing, and the decor a classy modern twist on the classic diner theme. Will it be peameal eggs Benedict or buttermilk fried chicken with cheddar mash for breakfast?

Vegetarian Havens

Meat-free restaurants in food-obsessed Toronto run the gamut from gourmet to passe. We like the following:

Govinda's (☎888-218-1040; www.govindas.ca; 243 Avenue Rd; by donation; ⏰noon-3pm & 6-8pm Mon-Sat; 🌿; S Rosedale)

Grasslands (Map p166; ☎416-504-5127; www.grasslands.to; 478 Queen St W; dishes $9-19; ⏰5:30-10pm Wed-Sun; 🌿; 🚊501)

Sadie's Diner (Map p162; www.sadiesdiner.com; 504 Adelaide St W; mains $9-13; ⏰7:30am-10pm Mon-Fri, 9am-10pm Sat & Sun; 🌿; 🚊504, 511)

Toronto marina

TONY TREMBLAY/GETTY IMAGES ©

Detour: Toronto Islands

Once upon a time there were no Toronto Islands, just an immense sandbar stretching 9km into the lake. On April 13, 1858, a hurricane blasted through the sandbar and created the gap now known as the Eastern Channel. Toronto's jewel-like islands were born – nearly two-dozen isles covering 240 hectares and home to close-knit, 800-strong communities on **Algonquin Island** and **Ward's Island**. The islands are only accessible by ferry (15 minutes, adult/child $7/3.50).

From April to September, **Toronto Islands Ferries** (Map p162; ☎416-392-8193; www.city.toronto.on.ca/parks/island/ferry.htm; adult/child/concession $6/2.50/3.50) runs ferries every 15 to 30 minutes from 8am to 11pm. The journey (to either Ward's Island or Hanlan's Point) only takes 15 minutes, but queues can be long on weekends and holidays. From October to March, ferries run on a reduced schedule. The Toronto Islands Ferry Terminal is at the foot of Bay St, off Queens Quay.

Lee Asian $$$

(Map p162; ☎416-504-7867; www.susur.com/lee; 601 King St W; plates $7-35; 🕔5:30-10:30pm Mon-Wed, to 11:30pm Thu-Sat; 🚋504, 508) Truly a feast for the senses, dinner at acclaimed *cuisinier* Susur Lee's self-titled flagship restaurant is an experience best shared. Slick servers assist in navigating the artisan selection of east-meets-west Asian delights: you really want to get the pairings right. It's impossible to adequately convey the wonderful dance of flavors, textures and aromas one experiences in the signature Singaporean slaw, with… how many?? ingredients!

CHINATOWN & BALDWIN VILLAGE

ND Sushi Japanese $$

(Map p166; ☎416-551-6362; www.ndsushiandgrill.com; 3 Baldwin St; mains $15-22; 🕔11:30am-3pm Mon-Fri & 5-10pm Mon-Sat; 🚋505, 506) From its pole position at the beginning of Baldwin St, this unassuming *shokudō* prepares favorite Japanese treats like gyoza, tempura and mouthwatering sashimi with authenticity. Its specialty is sushi, including a variety of not-so-traditional Western *maki* rolls: the spicy rainbow roll

Kensington Market

is divine. You could pay a whole lot more for Japanese food of this caliber.

Cafe la Gaffe Cafe $$

(Map p166; ☎416-596-2397; www.cafelagaffe.com; 24 Baldwin St; mains $7-25; ⏰noon-11pm Mon-Fri, 11am-11pm Sat & Sun; 🚋505, 506) Stripy cotton tablecloths and fresh-cut flowers adorn the tables in this little cafe. There's a street patio and a leafy garden patio where you can dine on market salads, a filet mignon sandwich or the hand-tossed pizzas. A small-print wine list offers an extensive selection.

CHURCH-WELLESLEY VILLAGE

Hair of the Dog Pub $

(Map p166; ☎416-964-2708; www.hairofdogpub.com; 425 Church St; share plates from $8, mains from $13; ⏰11:30am-late Mon-Fri, 10:30am-late Sat & Sun; S College) At its best in the warmer months when two levels of shaded patios spring to life with a mixed gay/straight crowd, this chilled puppy is delightfully less mainstream than its Village neighbors a few blocks north. Equally listable as a 'Drinking' venue, the food stands on its own: sharing plates and salads are great.

Fire on the East Side Fusion $$

(Map p166; ☎416-960-3473; www.fireontheeastside.ca; 6 Gloucester St; mains $10-25; ⏰11:30am-10:30pm Mon-Fri, 10am-10:30pm Sat & Sun; S Wellesley) Best for brunch, with a feisty selection of 'East Side Bennies' and morning after cocktails, this neighborhood fave also serves dinner from 4pm with a modest selection of well-prepared modern American and European dishes. It was once known for its haywire variations on Caribbean and Cajun themes, but after some kitchen changes only the buttermilk biscuits and fried chicken have echoes of the deep South.

BLOOR-YORKVILLE

7 West Café Cafe $$

(Map p166; ☎416-928-9041; www.7westcafe.com; 7 Charles St W; mains $10.95-17.95; ⏰24hr; S Bloor-Yonge) Three floors of moody lighting, textured jade paint, framed nudes, wooden church pews and jaunty ceiling angels set the scene for a dazzling selection of pizzas, pastas and sandwiches, and 24-hour breakfasts. Make like a vampire sipping blood-red wine (by the glass or bottle) as the moon dapples shadows across the street. Cool.

Kensington Market & Little Italy

Tattered around the edges, elegantly wasted Kensington Market is multicultural Toronto at its most authentic. It's not a constrained market as much as a working residential neighborhood. Eating here is a cheap and cheery trip around the flavors and aromas of the world. Shopping too is a blast, with the biggest and best proliferation of vintage and secondhand clothing, books and bric-a-brac in the city. On weekends, it can feel like a small festival, especially on Pedestrian Sundays, when bi-pods rule.

To get here, take the College streetcar to Spadina Ave or Augusta Ave and follow the activity. Augusta Ave between College and Dundas, is the main strip, but the little stretch of Nassau St between Augusta and Bellevue has some wonderful cafes and can be a welcome oasis from the crowds.

Further along College St, Little Italy is what you expect – a tasty slice of the homeland. There's a long-established strip of outdoor cafes, bars and stylish restaurants that frequently change hands – affluent clientele are notoriously fickle. The further west you go on College, the more traditional things become, with aromatic bakeries, sidewalk gelaterias and rootsy ristoranti.

Gay & Lesbian Toronto

To say Toronto is GLBT-friendly is an understatement. That it embraces diversity more fully than most other centers of its size, is closer to the mark. In 2003 Toronto became the first city in North America to legalize same-sex marriage.

Toronto's LGBT (yup, the acronym swings both ways!) Pride Festival is one of the largest in the world. On Parade day, the streets around Church and Wellesley swell with over a million happy homosexuals and their friends and families. At other times of the year, the Church St strip of the Village draws everyone from biker bears and lipstick lesbians to its modest smattering of sunny patios, pubs, cafes and restaurants for much promenading and people-watching.

Other gay-friendly neighborhoods include the Annex, Kensington, Queen West and Cabbagetown.

Look for the *Xtra!* weekly free press – you'll find it everywhere in the Village.

Bloor Street Diner International **$$**
(Map p166; ☎416-928-3105; www.bloorstreet-diner.com; Manulife Centre, 55 Bloor St W; mains $10.50-26, brunch $25.95; ⏰noon-1am; S Bloor-Yonge) Deceptively named, the swanky Bloor Street Diner has been a Toronto favorite for over 30 years, loved for its Parisian-style patio, distinguished wine list and impressive Sunday brunch buffet with chocolate fountain. Hit the cafe section in the mall out front for speedy take-out sandwiches.

UNIVERSITY OF TORONTO & THE ANNEX

Country Style Hungarian **$$**
(Map p166; ☎416-536-5966; 450 Bloor St W; schnitzel from $18; ⏰11am-10pm; S Bathurst) This delightful Hungarian diner with its red and white checkered tablecloths and friendly family staff hasn't changed a bit in at least a generation. The variety of enormous breaded schnitzels, cooked to crunchy perfection, are the best in town, and the cucumber salad is a treat.

QUEEN WEST & TRINITY BELLWOODS

Union Fusion **$$$**
(☎416-850-0093; www.union72.ca; 72 Ossington Ave; mains $18-34; ⏰6-10pm Mon & Tue, noon-3pm & 6-11pm Wed-Sun; 🚋501) This dandy little hipster kitchen serves a delicious fusion of French and Italian inspired dishes which it touts as 'simple done right,' although the menu feels more convoluted than simple. Fortunately, the food, decor and service are masterfully executed: steak, chicken, ribs and fish are staples. There's a delightful little patio out back.

Drinking & Nightlife

Taps start flowing around midday and last call hovers between 1am and 2am.

Mill Street Brewery Brewery
(☎416-681-0338; www.millstreetbrewery.com; 55 Mill St, Bldg 63, Distillery District; ⏰11:30am-midnight; 🚋503, 504) With 13 specialty beers brewed on-site in the atmospheric Distillery District (p158), these guys are a leading light in local microbrewing. Order a sample platter so you can taste all the award-winning brews, including the Tankhouse Pale Ale, Stock Ale and Organic Lager. On a sunny afternoon, the courtyard is the place to be.

Panorama Bar
(Map p166; ☎416-967-0000; www.panoram-alounge.com; 51st fl, Manulife Centre, 55 Bloor St W; ⏰5pm-late; 🚋Bay) Swanky and priced to match, come to the city's highest licensed patio for arguably Toronto's best views

outside the CN Tower. It's in the Manulife Centre building and unlike the tower, there's no admission fee, though you'll be scoffed at if you don't drop some cash on a martini or a meal.

C'est What Pub

(Map p162; ☎416-867-9499; www.cestwhat.com; 67 Front St E; ⏰11:30am-1am; 🚋503, 504) Over 30 whiskeys and six dozen Canadian microbrews (mostly from Ontario) are on hand at this underground pub. An in-house brewmaster tightly edits the all-natural, preservative-free beers on tap and good bar food which makes the most of fresh produce from St Lawrence Market next door.

Entertainment

For the latest club, alt-culture and live-music listings, look for Toronto's free street press in venues, by subway entrances or online: *Now* (www.nowmagazine.com), *The Grid* (www.thegridto.com) and *Xtra!* (www.xtra.ca) for LGBT readers.

TO Tix (Map p166; www.totix.ca; Yonge & Dundas Sq, 5 Dundas St E; ⏰noon-6:30pm Tue-Sat) sells half-price and discount same-day 'rush' tickets.

Best Coffee Shops?

Too early for beer? Sidestep the coffee chains for some *real* barista action:

Dark Horse Espresso (Map p166; ☎416-979-1200; www.darkhorseespresso.com; 215 Spadina Ave; ⏰7am-7pm Mon-Fri, from 8am Sat & Sun; 🚋510) Fashion District/Chinatown.

B Espresso Bar (Map p166; ☎416-866-2111; bespressobar.com; 111 Queen St E; ⏰7:30am-5pm Mon-Fri; 🚋501) Financial District/Corktown.

Moonbean Coffee Company (Map p166; ☎416-595-0327; www.moonbeamcoffee.com; 30 St Andrews St; ⏰7am-9pm; 🚋510) Kensington Market.

Mill Street Brewery

LIVE MUSIC

Horseshoe Tavern
Live Music

(Map p166; ☎416-598-4753; www.horseshoetavern.com; 370 Queen St W; ⏰noon-2am; 🚋501, 510) Well past its 65th birthday, the legendary Horseshoe still plays a crucial role in the development of local indie rock. This place just oozes a history of good times and classic performances. Come for a beer and check it out.

Massey Hall
Concert Venue

(Map p166; ☎416-872-4255; www.masseyhall.com; 178 Victoria St; ⏰box office from noon on show days; S Queen) Few venues have hosted as diverse a range of performances as Massey Hall, with its over 120 years in the business. Extensive back-of-house renovations are slated to bring the 2500-seat space into the next generation, while retaining its period charm.

THEATER

CanStage
Theater

(Canadian Stage Company; ☎416-368-3110; www.canstage.com; 26 Berkeley St; ⏰box office 10am-6pm Mon-Sat, to 8pm show days; 🚋503, 504) Contemporary CanStage produces top-rated Canadian and international plays by the likes of David Mamet and Tony Kushner from its own Berkeley Street Theatre, and the wonderfully accessible (pay-what-you-can) midsummer productions of 'Shakespeare in the Park,' under the stars in High Park: bring a blanket and show up early.

SPORTS

Toronto Blue Jays
Spectator Sports

(☎416-341-1234; bluejays.com; ⏰Apr-Sep) Toronto's Major League Baseball (MLB) team plays at the **Rogers Centre** **(Map p162; ☎416-341-2770; www.rogerscentre.com; 1 Blue Jays Way; S Union)**. Buy tickets through Ticketmaster or at the Rogers Centre box office near Gate 9. The cheapest seats are way up above the field.

Toronto Maple Leafs
Spectator Sports

(☎416-815-5982; www.mapleleafs.com; ⏰Oct-Apr) The 13-time Stanley Cup–winning Toronto Maple Leafs slap the puck around the **Air Canada Centre** **(ACC; Map p162; ☎416-815-5500; www.theaircanadacentre.com; 40 Bay St; S Union)** in the National Hockey League (NHL). Every game sells out, but a limited number of same-day tickets go on

Rogers Centre, home to the Toronto Blue Jays

KLAUS LANG/GETTY IMAGES ©

sale through Ticketmaster at 10am and at the Air Canada Centre ticket window from 5pm.

Shopping

Bay of Spirits Gallery Souvenirs

(Map p162; ☎416-971-5190; www.bayofspirits.com; 156 Front St W; ⏰10am-6pm Mon-Sat; S Union) The works of Norval Morrisseau – the first indigenous artist to have a solo exhibit at the National Gallery of Canada – are proudly on display in this atmospheric space, which carries aboriginal art from across Canada. Look for the Pacific West Coast totem poles (from miniature to over 4m tall), Inuit carvings and Inukshuk figurines.

Guild Shop Souvenirs

(Map p166; ☎416-921-1721; www.theguildshop.ca; 118 Cumberland St; ⏰10am-6pm Mon-Wed & Sat, to 7pm Thu & Fri, noon-5pm Sun; S Bay) The **Ontario Crafts Council (www.craft.on.ca)** has been promoting artisans for over 70 years. Ceramics, jewelry, glassworks, prints and carvings make up most of the displays, but you could also catch a special exhibition of Pangnirtung weaving or Cape Dorset graphics. Staff are knowledgeable about First Nations art.

Courage My Love Clothing

(Map p166; ☎416-979-1992; 14 Kensington Ave; ⏰11:30am-6pm Mon-Sat, 1-6pm Sun; 🚋505, 510) Vintage clothing stores have been around Kensington Market for decades, but Courage My Love amazes fashion mavens with its secondhand slip dresses, retro pants and white dress-shirts in a cornucopia of styles. The beads, buttons, leather goods and silver jewelry are handpicked.

Open Air Books & Maps Books

(Map p162; ☎416-363-0719; www.openairbooksandmaps.com; 25 Toronto St; ⏰10am-5:30pm Mon-Sat; S King) Ramshackle basement full of travel guides and maps plus books on nature, camping, history and outdoor activities.

If You Like... Theater

If CanStage draws your applause, check out what's playing at the big theater festivals near Toronto.

Stratford Festival (☎800-567-1600, 519-273-1600; www.stratfordfestival.ca) Canada's Stratford is a lot like William Shakespeare's birthplace in England, primped to country-garden, swan-rivered perfection. And every April to November, theater buffs flock in to see internationally acclaimed productions of the Bard's (and others') works staged in four local venues. Stratford is 150km west of Toronto.

Shaw Festival (☎905-468-2172, 800-511-7429; www.shawfest.com; 10 Queens Pde, Niagara-on-the-Lake; ⏰box office 10am-8pm) In pretty, touristy Niagara-on-the-Lake, 135km south of Toronto, the much-esteemed Shaw Fest lures global audiences from April through October. Aside from an opening Shaw showstopper, the season offers a variety of works from Victorian drama to contemporary plays, musicals and classics from Wilde, Woolf and Coward.

Information

Tourist Information

Tourism Toronto (Map p162; ☎416-203-2500, 800-499-2514; www.seetorontonow.com; 207 Queens Quay W; ⏰8:30am-6pm Mon-Fri; S Union) Contact one of the telephone agents; after hours use the automated touch-tone information menu.

Getting There & Away

Air

Most Canadian airlines and international carriers arrive at Canada's busiest airport, **Lester B Pearson International Airport** (YYZ; Map p159; www.torontopearson.com), 27km northwest of downtown Toronto.

Billy Bishop Toronto City Airport (Map p159), on a small island just off the lakeshore, is the proud home of Porter Airlines with competitive

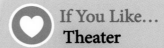

Below: Niagara Falls; **Right:** Whirlpool Aero Car (p179), Niagara Falls
(BELOW) PETER MINTZ/DESIGN PICS/GETTY IMAGES ©; (RIGHT) HENRY GEORGI/GETTY IMAGES ©

fares to a wide range of destinations within Eastern Canada and the USA. Air Canada also has services to Montréal from here.

Bus

Long-distance buses operate from the art deco **Metro Toronto Coach Terminal** (**Map p166; ☎416-393-4636; 610 Bay St; S Dundas**).

Parkbus (**www.parkbus.ca**) offers limited seasonal departures to the Bruce Peninsula, Algonquin and Killarney Provincial Parks and plans to expand its range and frequency of service: check the website for latest details.

Train

Grand **Union Station** (**☎416-869-3000; www.viarail.com; 140 Bay St**) downtown is Toronto's main rail hub, with currency exchange booths and Traveller's Aid Society help desks. The station is under renovation until 2016.

Getting Around

To/From the Airport

Airport Express (**☎800-387-6787; www.torontoairportexpress.com**) operates an express bus (one-way adult/child $28/free) connecting Pearson International Airport with the Metro Toronto Coach Terminal and a few downtown hotels. Buses depart every 20 to 30 minutes from 6am to midnight. Services are frequently late: allow 1½ hours for the journey.

The cheapest (and at times, quickest) way to get to the airport is on the TTC ($3) but it's a pain with heavy luggage: many stairs. Catch the subway to Kipling station (you may need to change lines at Bloor/Yonge) then connect with the 192 Airport Rocket Express bus. From the airport, the bus departs Terminals 1, 2 and 3 every 20 minutes from 5:30am to 2am. Allow *at least* an hour for the journey.

Taxis from Pearson Airport to the city take anywhere from 40 to 70 minutes, depending on traffic. The Greater Toronto Airports Authority

(GTAA) regulates fares by drop-off zone: it's $60 to downtown.

At time of writing a long overdue rail link from Pearson Airport to Union station called the Union Pearson Express has commenced, slated for completion in 2015. It's estimated that travel times will be slashed to just 25 minutes. For details, stay tuned to www.bigmove.ca.

Public Transportation

Rides anywhere on the Toronto Transit Corporation (TTC) network of trains, streetcars and buses cost adult/child $3/0.75. Day passes ($10.75) are good value if you plan on making three rides and are excellent value on weekends, when up to two adults and two children can use one pass.

Exact change is required for streetcars and buses.

Subway lines operate regular service from around 6am (9am Sunday) until 1:30am daily. The two main lines are crosstown Bloor–Danforth line, and the U-shaped Yonge–University–Spadina line.

Streetcars are notoriously slow during rush hours, stopping frequently.

NIAGARA FALLS

Niagara is not the tallest of waterfalls (it ranks a lowly 50th) but in terms of sheer volume, there's nothing like it – more than a million bathtubs of water plummet downward every second. By day or night, regardless of season, the falls never fail to awe: 12 million visitors annually can't be wrong. Even in winter, when the flow is partially hidden and the edges freeze solid, the extravaganza is undiminished. Very occasionally the falls stop altogether.

Otherwise, Niagara might not be what you expect: the town feels like a tacky outdated amusement park. It has been a saucy honeymoon destination ever since Napoléon's brother brought his bride here – tags like 'For newlyweds and nearly deads' and 'Viagra Falls' are apt. A crass morass of casinos, sleazy motels, tourist traps and strip joints line Clifton Hill and Lundy's Lane – a little Las Vegas! Love it or loathe it, there's nowhere quite like it.

Niagara Falls

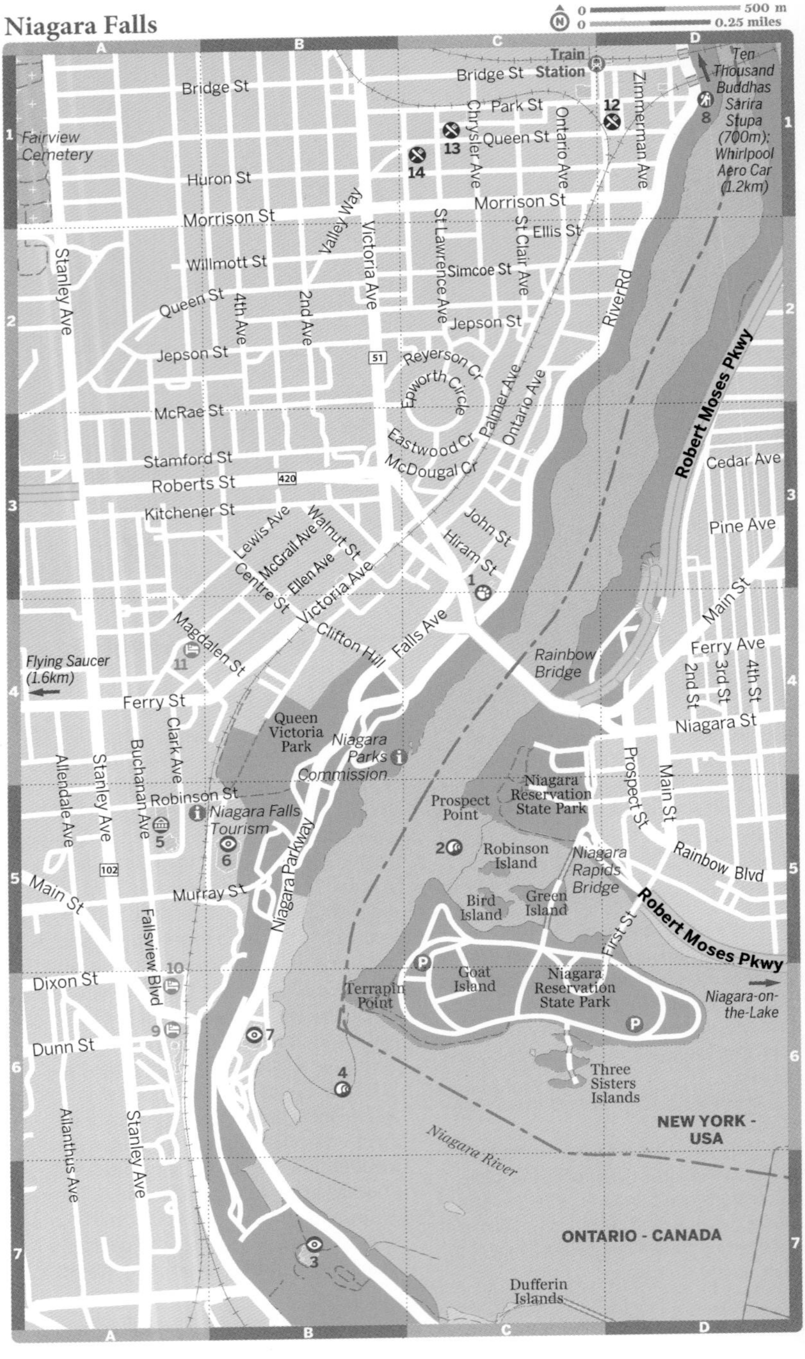

Niagara Falls

Sights

1 Bird Kingdom C4
2 Bridal Veil Falls (American Falls) C5
3 Floral Showhouse B7
4 Horseshoe Falls B6
5 IMAX Theatre & Daredevil Gallery A5
6 Skylon Tower B5
7 Table Rock B6

Activities, Courses & Tours

Journey Behind the Falls .... (see 7)
Niagara's Fury .... (see 7)
8 White Water Walk D1

Sleeping

9 Embassy Suites A6
10 Oakes Hotel A6
11 Sterling Inn & Spa A4

Eating

12 Edwin's D1
13 Paris Crepes Cafe C1
14 Taps on Queen Brewhouse & Grill C1

Sights & Activities

THE FALLS

Niagara Falls forms a natural rift between Ontario and New York State. On the US side, **Bridal Veil Falls** (aka the American Falls) crashes onto mammoth fallen rocks. On the Canadian side, the grander, more powerful **Horseshoe Falls** plunges into the cloudy **Maid of the Mist Pool**. The prime falls-watching spot is **Table Rock**, poised just meters from the drop – arrive early to beat the crowds.

Tickets for the Falls attractions listed below can be purchased separately, but the online 30% discounted **Niagara Falls Adventure Pass** (www.niagaraparks.com) is better value. It includes admission to Hornblower Niagara Cruises, Journey Behind the Falls, White Water Walk, Niagara's Fury and two days transportation on the WEGO bus system. Passes are also available from the Niagara Parks Commission at Table Rock Information Centre and most attractions.

Hornblower Niagara Cruises Boat Tour

(www.niagaracruises.com; 5920 River Rd; adult/child $20/12.25; 9am-7:45pm Jun-Aug, to 4:45pm Apr, May, Sep & Oct) Hornblower is the new boat company in town, taking over from the age-old Maid of the Mist (which still runs on the American side of the falls). Hornblower's 700-person catamarans sail up close to Bridal Veil Falls and Horseshoe Falls, among other thundering cascades. Departures are every 15 minutes, weather permitting. Sunrise and evening fireworks cruises are being added to the schedule, so check for updates.

White Water Walk Walking

(905-374-1221; 4330 Niagara Pkwy; adult/child $10.95/7; 9am-7:30pm) At the northern end of town, next to Whirlpool Bridge, the White Water Walk is another way to get up close and personal, this time via an elevator down to a 325m boardwalk suspended above the rampaging torrents, just downstream from the falls.

Whirlpool Aero Car Gondola

(905-354-5711; 3850 Niagara Pkwy; adult/child $13.50/8.50; 9am-8pm Mar-Nov) Dangling above the Niagara River, 4.5km north of Horseshoe Falls, the Whirlpool Aero Car was designed by Spanish engineer Leonardo Torres Quevedo and has been operating since 1916 (but don't worry – it's still in good shape). The gondola travels 550m between two outcrops above a deadly whirlpool created by the falls – count the logs and tires spinning in the eddies below.

Niagara's Fury Simulator

(905-358-3268; 6650 Niagara Pkwy; adult/child $13.50/8.80; every 30min 10:30am-4pm) On the upper level of Table Rock, the Falls' latest Universal Studios–style attraction takes you into an interactive 360-degree cinema-simulation of how the falls were created. Expect lots of high-tech tricks to suspend disbelief, including plenty of water, snow and a rapid drop in temperature.

The Bruce Trail

For 800km the **Bruce Trail** (www.brucetrail.org) winds along the top of the Niagara Escarpment, from the Niagara Peninsula to the Bruce Peninsula. This wide, well-maintained path is excellent for hiking during summer months, while those armed with cross-country skis take it through its winter paces. Opened in 1967, it's the oldest hiking trail in Canada and the longest in Ontario. The trail winds through public and private land, as well as roadways. Wander past wineries, farmlands and forests and marvel at Georgian Bay's shimmering azure from the escarpment's white cliffs. Day hikes along the trail are an appealing way to spend a sunny afternoon. A multitude of campgrounds en route have budget accommodations for those on longer trips and trail towns offer B&Bs galore. There are numerous access points in the Niagara area.

Journey Behind the Falls Walking Tour

(☎905-354-1551; 6650 Niagara Pkwy; adult/child Apr-Dec $15.95/10.95, Dec-Apr $11.25/6.95; ⏲9am-10pm) From Table Rock Information Centre you can don a very un-sexy plastic poncho and traverse rock-cut tunnels halfway down the cliff – as close as you can get to the falls without getting in a barrel. It's open year-round, but be prepared to queue.

CLIFTON HILL

Clifton Hill is a street name, but refers to a broader area near the Falls occupied by a sensory bombardment of artificial enticements. You name it – House of Frankenstein, Madame Tussaud's Wax Museum, Castle Dracula – they're all here. In most cases, paying the admission will leave you feeling like a sucker.

IMAX Theatre & Daredevil Gallery Museum

(☎905-358-3611; imaxniagara.com; 6170 Fallsview Blvd; Daredevil Gallery adult/child $8/6.50, movie prices vary; ⏲9am-9pm) The most engaging thing around here is the Daredevil Gallery attached to IMAX Niagara (which screens blockbusters and films about the falls; combo tickets are available). Scratch your head in amazement at the battered collection of barrels and padded bubbles in which people have ridden over the falls (not all of them successfully). There's also a history of falls 'funambulism' (tightrope walking) here.

Bird Kingdom Zoo

(☎905-356-8888, 866-994-0090; www.birdkingdom.ca; 5651 River Rd; adult/child $17/12; ⏲9am-6:30pm) The jungly Bird Kingdom claims to be the world's largest indoor aviary, with 400 species of free-flying tropical birds from around the globe. You can also buddy-up with a boa constrictor in the Reptile Encounter Zone.

Skylon Tower Viewpoint

(☎905-356-2651; www.skylon.com; 5200 Robinson St; adult/child $13/8; ⏲8am-10pm) The Skylon Tower is an ugly 158m spire with yellow elevators crawling like bugs up the exterior. The views from the indoor and outdoor observation decks are eye-poppers. There's also a revolving restaurant.

AROUND NIAGARA FALLS

The slow-roaming, leafy Niagara Pkwy meanders for 56km along the Niagara River, from Niagara-on-the-Lake past the Falls all the way to Fort Erie. Along the way you'll find parks, picnic areas and viewpoints. The idyllic 3m-wide **Niagara River Recreation Trail** (www.niagaraparks.com/nature/rectrailarea.php) for cycling, jogging or walking runs parallel to the parkway. The trail can easily be divided into four chunks, each of which takes around two hours to pedal.

Floral Showhouse Gardens

(905-354-1721; www.niagaraparks.com; 7145 Niagara Pkwy; adult/child $5/3.75; 9:30am-8pm) Around 1km south of Horseshoe Falls, the showhouse offers year-round floral displays and some warm respite on a chilly day. Opposite, lodged on rocks in the rapids, the **Old Scow** is a rusty steel barge that's been waiting to be washed over the falls since 1918 – a teetering symbol of Western imperialism, perhaps?

Ten Thousand Buddhas Sarira Stupa Temple

(905-371-2678; 4303 River Rd; 9am-5pm, main temple Sat & Sun only) If the tourist bustle is messing with your yang, find some tranquility at this out-of-context Buddhist temple. The modern building of Western construction is ultra-tacky. Visitors are welcome to wander the complex and view the various sculptures, bells and artworks.

Niagara Glen Nature Reserve Park

(905-371-0254; www.niagaraparks.com; Niagara Pkwy; dawn-dusk) About 8km north of the falls is this exceptional reserve, where you can get a sense of what the area was like pre-Europeans. There are 4km of walking trails winding down into a gorge, past huge boulders, cold caves, wildflowers and woods. The Niagara Parks Commission offers **guided nature walks** daily during the summer season for a nominal fee.

Botanical Gardens and Butterfly Conservatory Gardens

(905-356-8119; www.niagaraparks.com; 2565 Niagara Pkwy; Butterfly Conservatory adult/child $12.95/8.25, gardens free; 10am-4pm Mon-Fri, to 5pm Sat & Sun) Entry to the 40 hectares of **Botanical Gardens** is free, but you'll need tp pay to enter the **Butterfly Conservatory**, with its more than 50 species of butterflies (some as big as birds) flitting around 130 species of flowers and plants.

Sleeping

Prices spike sharply in summer, on weekends and during holidays. Check B&B availability online at www.bbniagarafalls.com. Cheap motels line Lundy's Lane.

Oakes Hotel Hotel $$

(905-356-4514, 877-843-6253; www.oakeshotel.com; 6546 Fallsview Blvd; d $99-159;) A jaunty silver spire next to the Fallsview Casino, the Oakes has front-row-center views of the great cascades. Not all rooms have falls views; try for a terrace room if you can: you'll likely pay extra. Some rooms have Jacuzzis and fireplaces. If you're on a budget, ask about the cheaper drive-up motel rooms, from $69.

Wildlife at Butterfly Conservatory
YONG BAI/GETTY IMAGES ©

Sterling Inn & Spa
Boutique Hotel $$

(☎289-292-0000; www.sterlingniagara.com; 5195 Magdalen St; r from $125) The stylish rooms of this affordable boutique hotel (with either a Jacuzzi or steam shower) beckon you relax and unwind with someone special, even if that is yourself. Quality furnishings, amenities and breakfast in bed baskets are the kind of touches to expect. Note that it is a low-rise property a little distance from the Falls: no views.

Embassy Suites
Hotel $$

(☎800-420-6980; www.embassysuitesniagara.com/; 6700 Fallsview Blvd; ste from $145) This mammoth all-suite hotel has a great position that feels like you're almost on top of the Canadian falls. For that reason, its generic rooms get a lot of use. That said, they're spacious and a variety of suite types are available: most have great views. Breakfast and a welcome drink are included.

Eating

The old downtown section is seeing a lot of new restaurants crop up and is worth exploring. For cuisine a cut above, you're better off heading up the road to Niagara-on-the-Lake.

Edwin's
Fusion $

(☎289-990-7305; www.edwinsrestaurant.com; 4616 Erie Ave; mains $2.50-6.50; ⏰11:30am-11pm) Born in Jamaica and trained in England, the illustrious Edwin blends Caribbean and Mediterranean cuisine at this little spot near the train station. Jerk chicken, fried plantains, curried goat and salmon salad are all on offer, as is a weekend breakfast buffet ($6.99).

Flying Saucer
Fast Food $

(☎905-356-4453; www.flyingsaucerrestaurant.com; 6768 Lundy's Lane; mains $8-27; ⏰6am-10pm) For extraterrestrial fast food, you can't go past this iconic diner on the Lundy's Lane motel strip. Famous $1.99 early bird breakfasts are served from 6am to 10am (eggs, fries and toast) with the purchase of a beverage. Heftier meals in the way of steaks, seafood, fajitas, burgers and hot dogs are also onboard. Take-out is in the saucer to the left.

Clifton Hill (p180), Niagara Falls

GARRY BLACK/GETTY IMAGES ©

Taps on Queen Brewhouse & Grill International **$$**
(www.tapsbeer.com; 4680 Queen St; mains $9-14; noon-10pm Mon, Tue & Sun, to midnight Wed-Sat) Does a mix of stuff, from shepherd's pie to ancient grains curry (quinoa, couscous, adzuki beans, mung beans and veggies). All dishes are, naturally, best when paired with one of the brewery's tasty beers.

Paris Crepes Cafe French **$$**
(289-296-4218; www.pariscrepescafe.com; 4613 Queen St; mains $12-30; 10am-10pm Mon-Fri, from 9am Sat & Sun) In the revitalized area of Queen St you'll find this quaint creperie, a very long way from the streets of Paris: you can't miss the dark red building. Sweet and savory crepe sensations are served among other continental delights from the wonderfully authentic Parisian menu.

Information

Niagara Falls Tourism (905-356-6061, 800-563-2557; www.niagarafallstourism.com; 5400 Robinson St; 8am-5pm Mon-Fri, 10am-4pm Sat & Sun) Everything you need to know about Niagara, served with a smile.

Niagara Parks Commission (877-642-7275, 905-371-0254; www.niagaraparks.com; 9am-11pm Jun-Aug) The Falls' governing body, with information desks at Maid of the Mist Plaza and Table Rock Information Centre.

Getting There & Away

Car

From Toronto, the Gardiner Expressway runs west into Queen Elizabeth Way (QEW) to Niagara Falls.

Train

Rail services from **Niagara Falls Train Station** (888-842-7245; www.viarail.ca; 4267 Bridge St) to Toronto were suspended in recent years, with the exception of a weekend summer service operated by GO Transit.

Local Knowledge

Niagara Falls

RECOMMENDATIONS FROM DARLENE ERSKINE, SUPERVISOR AT TABLE ROCK WELCOME CENTRE AND LIFELONG NIAGARA AREA RESIDENT

1 QUICK THRILLS

If you're short on time, focus on three things. First, head to Table Rock Welcome Centre for a view of the falls right at their brink. At Table Rock you also can experience the 'Fury,' a film and simulation of how the falls were formed, where you feel the ground shake and temperature drop 20°. 'The Journey Behind the Falls' is also here, where you walk right beside the waterfall with just a fence and 6ft to 8ft (2m to 3m) between you and the flow. It's exhilarating.

2 CATCHING A RAINBOW

The most panoramic view of the falls is from Table Rock's upper deck. The best time to see rainbows is in the afternoon, around 3pm.

3 NIAGARA PARKWAY

Winston Churchill called the Niagara Parkway 'the prettiest Sunday afternoon drive in the world.' Heritage sites pop up all along the 56km road. It's a must-do.

4 FLORAL SHOWHOUSE

Table Rock gets 8 million visitors per year. For a respite from the hustle and bustle, head to the Floral Showhouse to wander through the exquisite indoor displays of tropical plants. It's free, and an easy 10-minute walk down the road.

5 FREE ACTIVITIES

Niagara Parks has a fireworks show on Friday, Sunday and holiday nights at 10pm in summer. The Botanical Gardens at the park's north end are gorgeous and a good place to escape the crowds. And the plaza where the boats dock is always alive with free music and buskers.

Detour: Niagara Peninsula Wine Country

The Niagara Peninsula adheres to the 43rd parallel: a similar latitude to northern California and further south than Bordeaux, France. A primo vino location, the mineral-rich soils and moderate microclimate are the perfect recipe for viticulture success.

There are two main areas to focus on: west of St Catharines around Vineland, and north of the Queen Elizabeth Way (QEW) around Niagara-on-the-Lake. For more info, check out www.winesofontario.ca.

Some of our favorites (in order, coming from Toronto):

Peninsula Ridge Estates Winery (905-563-0900; peninsularidge.com; 5600 King St W, Beamsville; tours $5; 10am-5pm, tours 11:30am Jun-Nov) Unmissable on a hilltop and very photogenic. The lofty timber tasting room, restaurant and hilltop setting are magic.

Vineland Estates Winery (905-562-7088, 888-846-3526; www.vineland.com; 3620 Moyer Rd, Vineland; tastings $3, tours $6; 10am-6pm) Turn right at Cherry Ave, about 10km further down the road, go up the hill, then turn left onto Moyer Rd for the stone buildings of this winery, the elder statesman of Niagara viticulture. Almost all the wines here are excellent.

Wayne Gretzky Estate (www.gretzkyestateswines.com; 3751 King St, Vineland; 10am-8pm Mon-Sat, 11am-6pm Sun) Backtrack up to King St, to the intersection of King and Cherry where you'll find the beloved hockey star's winery.

Sunnybrook Farm Estate Winery (905-468-1122; www.sunnybrookfarmwinery.com; 1425 Lakeshore Rd, Niagara-on-the-Lake; tastings $1-3; 10am-6pm) Closer to Niagara-on-the-Lake this winery specializes in unique Niagara fruit and berry wines, and brews a mean 'hard' cider. It's only a little place, so tour buses usually don't stop here.

Getting Around

Bicycle

The Niagara region is perfect for biking. The excellent **Zoom Leisure Bicycle Rentals** (866-811-6993; www.zoomleisure.com; 431 Mississauga St, Niagara-on-the-Lake) also has offices in Niagara Falls and on the Niagara Parkway, and they'll deliver to anywhere in the Niagara region. Great bike tours are also available.

Car & Motorcycle

Driving and parking around the center is an expensive headache. Park way out and walk, or follow the parking district signs and stash the car for the day (around $6 per 30 minutes, or $15 per day). The huge Rapidsview parking lot (also the WEGO depot) is 3km south of the Falls off River Rd.

Public Transportation

Cranking up and down the steep 50m slope between the falls and Fallsview Blvd is a quaint **Incline Railway** (www.niagaraparks.com; 6635 Niagara Pkwy; one way $2.50/day pass $6).

Formerly the seasonal Niagara Parks People Mover, **WEGO** (www.niagaraparks.com/wego; day pass adult/child $7/4) is an economical and efficient year-round transit system, geared for tourists. There are three lines: red, green and blue; between them, they've got all the major sights and accommodations covered.

Walking

Put on your sneakers and get t'steppin' – walking is the way to go! You'll only need wheels to visit outlying sights along the Niagara Pkwy or if you're staying on Lundy's Lane.

THOUSAND ISLANDS & AROUND

The 'Thousand Islands' are a constellation of over 1800 rugged islands dotting the St Lawrence River from Kingston to Brockville. The lush archipelago offers loose tufts of fog, showers of trillium petals, quaking tide pools and opulent 19th-century summer mansions, whose turrets pierce the prevailing mist.

The narrow, slow-paced **Thousand Islands Parkway** dips south of Hwy 401 between Gananoque and Elizabethtown, running along the river for 35km before rejoining the highway. The scenic journey winds along the pastoral strip of shoreline offering picture-perfect vistas and dreamy picnic areas. The **Bikeway** bicycle path extends the full length of the parkway.

In Mallorytown, the **Thousand Islands National Park** (☎613-923-5261; www.pc.gc.ca/pn-np/on/lawren/index.aspx; 2 County Rd 5, Mallorytown) preserves a gentle green archipelago, consisting of over 20 islands scattered between Kingston and Brockville. A walking trail and interpretive center allow visitors to learn more about the lush terrain and resident wildlife.

Gananoque

Little Gananoque (gan-an-*awk*-way) is the perfect place to rest your eyes after a long day of squinting at the furry green islands on the misty St Lawrence River. The dainty Victorian town, deep in the heart of the Thousand Islands region, teems with cruise-hungry tourists during summer and early fall. In spring and late fall, it's quiet as a mouse.

Sights & Activities

Boldt Castle Castle

(☎315-482-9724; www.boldtcastle.com; 1 Tennis Island Rd, Alexandria Bay, NY, USA; adult/child $10/6; ⏰10am-5pm) This is technically in the USA, though only 36km from Gananoque, so you'll need your passport to visit this lavish turn-of-the-century island castle in the middle of the St Lawrence River. It was built by George C. Boldt, original proprietor of New York's famous Waldorf Astoria Hotel. The castle is accessible by road, off the Thousand

Marina at Gananoque

BARRETT&MACKAY/GETTY IMAGES ©

If You Like… Island Hopping

If you like the Thousand Islands region, glide over to these destinations to further your explorations.

1 **PRINCE EDWARD COUNTY**
(www.pecchamber.com) An emerging foodie hot spot, Prince Edward County's undulating pastoral hills are extremely photogenic, as are the myriad water views. New wineries and rustic gourmet restaurants pop up every season. The Taste Trail (www.tastetrail.ca) provides a flavorful self-guided way to explore the island, which is 75km east of Kingston. A bridge connects the island from Belleville on the mainland.

2 **WOLFE ISLAND**
(www.wolfeisland.com) It's the largest in the Thousand Islands chain, offshore from Kingston and linked via a free, hourly car ferry. The cool, 25-minute trip affords views of the city and various other isles. Wolfe itself is home to 86 wind turbines, cycle-friendly farmland and the General Wolfe Hotel. Kingston's ferry terminal is at the intersection of Ontario and Barrack Sts.

Islands Pkwy: it's linked by bridge. Many Thousand Island cruise tours also stop here.

Skydeck Viewpoint
(☎613-659-2335; www.1000islandsskydeck.com; Hill Island; adult/child $10/6; ⏲9am-dusk Apr-Oct) In Ivylea, 22km from Gananoque, a series of soaring bridges link Ontario to New York State over several islands. Halfway across, you'll find the Skydeck, a 125m-high observation tower offering some fantastic views of the archipelago from three different balconies.

Gananoque Boat Line Cruise
(☎888-717-4837; www.ganboatline.com; 6 Water St; tour prices vary; ⏲May-Oct) Several trip options including a stopover at Boldt Castle make this a popular choice for cruising the Thousand Islands. The castle is technically in the USA, so be sure you have your passport if you are planning to visit. A variety of sailings are available; check the website for details.

1000 Islands Kayaking Kayaking
(☎613-329-6265; www.1000islandskayaking.com; 110 Kate St; rentals from $35, tours from $85) If you're feeling energetic, paddling is a great way to tour the islands. Choose from a multitude of packages including courses, excellent half-day and overnight trips.

Sleeping & Eating

Gananoque sports an abundance of memorable accommodations including several upmarket and architecturally eye-catching inns.

Victoria Rose Inn Inn $$
(☎613-382-3368, 888-246-2893; www.victoriaroseinn.com; 279 King St W; d incl breakfast from $165; ⊖❄📶) A monument to Victorian splendor, this former mayoral residence has been refurbished to its original elegance. A glassed-in porch overlooks manicured terraced gardens. Guest rooms are spacious, comfortable and elegantly furnished in a neutral, classic style. Personal touches such as champagne and flowers can be ordered in advance. Lovely.

Maple Leaf Restaurant European $$
(Czech Schnitzel House; ☎613-382-7666; www.mapleleafrestaurant.ca; 65 King St E; mains $9-20; ⏲11am-9:30pm Tue-Sat, from 10am Sun) As Canadian an old-school family diner as the Maple Leaf can be, the name belies the real European gems found inside: golden breaded schnitzel, goulash, borscht and beer. There's a little patio out back, in summer.

Ivy Restaurant Modern Canadian $$$
(☎613-659-2486; www.ivylea.ca; 61 Shipman's Lane, Lansdowne; mains $14-34; ⏲noon-3pm & 5-9pm Wed-Sat, 10:30am-2pm Sun) The beautifully refurbished restaurant belonging to the opulent Ivy Lea Marina and Club is open to the public. It's in a charming wa-

terfront spot about 15 minutes' drive from Gananoque. Casual patio lunches and Sunday brunches are the more affordable way to enjoy the stunning environment but evening fine dining is available. Otherwise, just stop by for a look and a lick: there's an incredible ice-cream booth out front.

Information

Visitor Services Centre (800-561-1595, 613-382-3250; www.1000islandsgananoque.com; 10 King St E; 10am-7pm Mon-Fri, to 8pm Sat, to 5pm Sun) The delightful staff at this immaculate visitors center are a font of information for all things Thousand Islands and beyond.

Getting There & Away

It's a short detour off Hwy 401 about 35km east of Kingston.

OTTAWA

Descriptions of Ottawa read like an appealing dating profile: dynamic, gregarious, bilingual, likes kids and long walks on the river. In person, the attractive capital fits the bill.

Canada's gargantuan Gothic Parliament buildings regally anchor the downtown core, an inspiring jumble of pulsing districts at the confluence of three rivers. In the distance, the rolling Gatineau hills tenderly hug the cloudless valley. Ottawa has a wonderful conglomeration of world-class museums, from the smooth, undulating walls of the Museum of Civilization to the haunting arches of the Museum of Nature; all are architecturally inspiring homes to a variety of intriguing collections.

Parliament Hill (p189)

DENNIS MACDONALD/GETTY IMAGES ©

Sights

Most of Ottawa's numerous world-class museums are within walking distance of each other. A number of museums offer free general admissions on Thursday evenings.

Canadian War Museum Museum

(800-555-5621; www.warmuseum.ca; 1 Vimy Pl; adult/child $13/8; 9:30am-6pm Fri-Wed, to 8pm Thu) Fascinating displays twist through the labyrinthine interior of this sculpture-like, modern museum, tracing Canada's military history with the nation's most comprehensive collection of war-related artifacts. Many of the touching and thought-provoking exhibits are larger than life, including a replica of a WWI trench. Take a look at the facade in the evening, if you can: flickering lights pulse on and off spelling 'Lest We Forget' and 'CWM' in both English and French morse code.

Ottawa

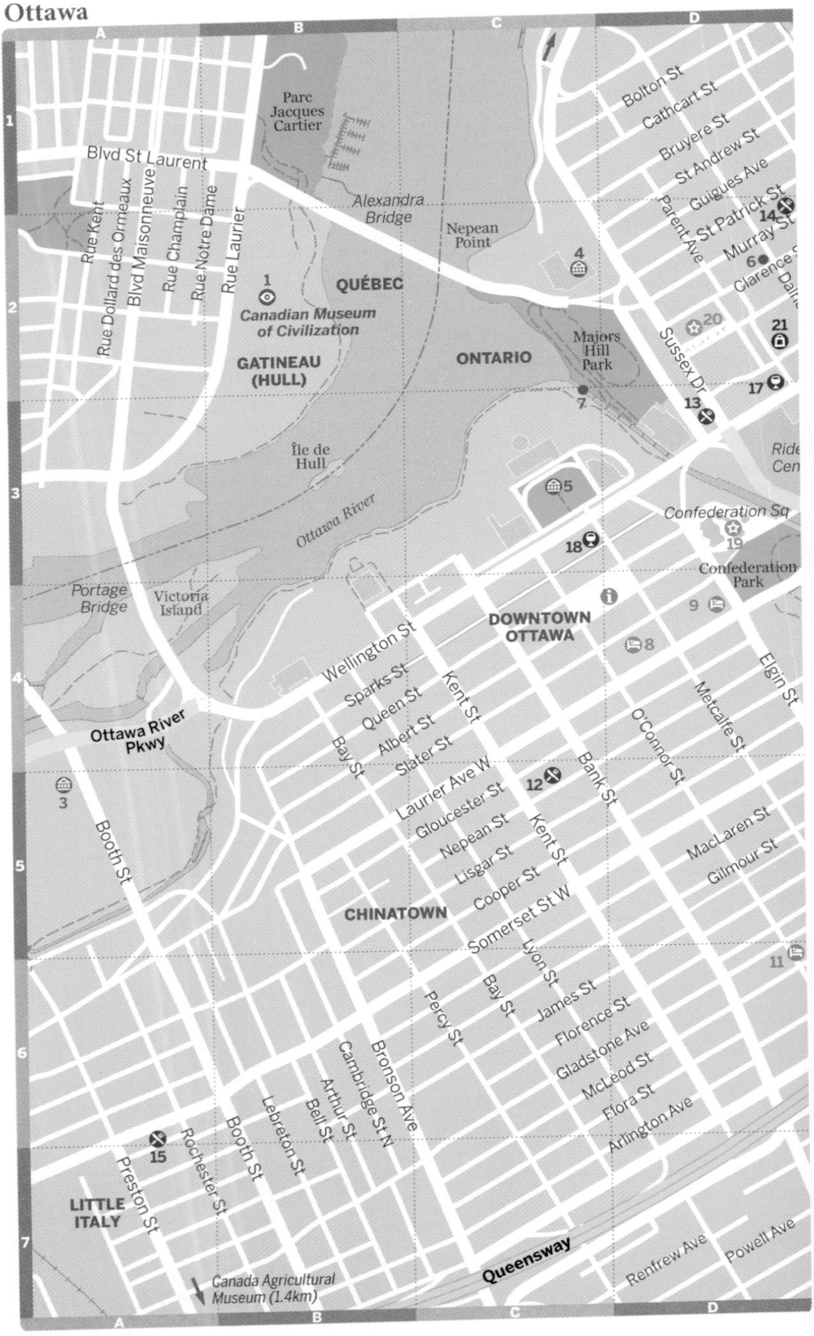

Parc Jacques Cartier
Blvd St Laurent
Alexandra Bridge
Nepean Point
Rue Kent
Rue Dollard des Ormeaux
Blvd Maisonneuve
Rue Champlain
Rue Notre Dame
Rue Laurier
1
Canadian Museum of Civilization
QUÉBEC
GATINEAU (HULL)
ONTARIO
Majors Hill Park
4
5
7
Île de Hull
Ottawa River
Portage Bridge
Victoria Island
Ottawa River Pkwy
3
Booth St
Bolton St
Cathcart St
Bruyere St
St Andrew St
Guigues Ave
St Patrick St
Murray St
Parent Ave
Clarence St
Sussex Dr
14
6
20
21
17
13
Confederation Sq
19
Confederation Park
18
9
8
11
12
15
DOWNTOWN OTTAWA
Wellington St
Sparks St
Queen St
Albert St
Slater St
Bay St
Kent St
Laurier Ave W
Gloucester St
Nepean St
Lisgar St
Cooper St
Somerset St W
Bank St
O'Connor St
Metcalfe St
Elgin St
MacLaren St
Gilmour St
CHINATOWN
Lyon St
Percy St
James St
Florence St
Gladstone Ave
McLeod St
Flora St
Arlington Ave
Bronson Ave
Cambridge St N
Arthur St
Bell St
Lebreton St
Rochester St
Preston St
LITTLE ITALY
Queensway
Renfrew Ave
Powell Ave
Canada Agricultural Museum (1.4km)
A
B
C
D
1
2
3
4
5
6
7

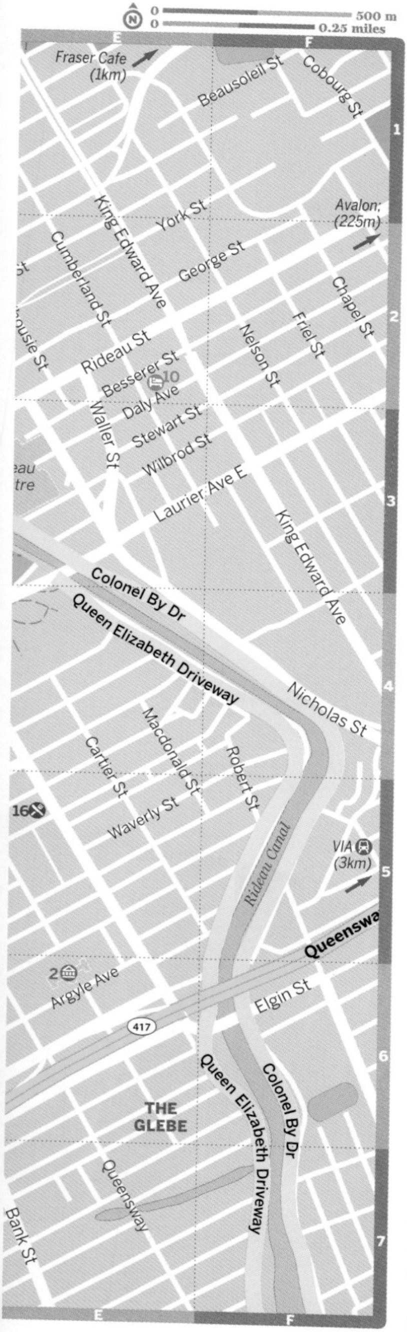

Ottawa

Don't Miss Sights
1 Canadian Museum of Civilization B2

Sights
2 Canadian Museum of Nature E6
3 Canadian War Museum A5
4 National Gallery of Canada C2
5 Parliament Hill C3

Activities, Courses & Tours
6 Haunted Walk D2
7 Paul's Boat Lines C3

Sleeping
8 Arc D4
9 Lord Elgin Hotel D4
10 Swiss Hotel E2
11 Victoria Park Suites D6

Eating
12 Beckta Dining & Wine C5
13 Brasserie Métropolitain D3
14 Chez Lucien D2
15 Hung Sum A6
16 Town E5

Drinking & Nightlife
17 Highlander Pub D2
18 Parliament Pub C3

Entertainment
19 National Arts Centre D3
20 Zaphod Beeblebrox D2

Shopping
21 ByWard Market D2

Parliament Hill Historic Building

(**613-996-0896; www.parl.gc.ca/Visitors; 111 Wellington St; 9am-5pm**) Vast, yawning archways, copper-topped turrets and Gothic revival gargoyles dominate the facade of the stunning lime and sandstone Parliament buildings. The main building, known as the Centre Block, supports the iconic **Peace Tower**, the highest structure in the city. Completed in 1865, Canada's nexus of political activity welcomes visitors year-round. You can download informative PDFs of self-guided walking tours from www.canadascapital.gc.ca, but we recommended the free 45-minute guided tours. From May to September a limited number of tickets are distributed from the Hill Centre, across the street. In other months, head to the main visitor entrance beneath the Peace Tower.

Question Time in the House of Commons occurs every afternoon and

Don't Miss
Canadian Museum of Civilization

This high-tech, must-see institution is Canada's national museum of history. Telling the story of Canada through a range of spectacular exhibits, it's an objective recounting of the nation's timeline from the perspectives of its Aboriginal peoples, its colonial beginnings and the rich multicultural diversity of Canada today.

819-776-7000

www.civilization.ca

100 Laurier St, Gatineau

adult/child $13/8

9am-6pm Fri-Wed, to 8pm Thu

Grand Hall & First Peoples Hall

The Grand Hall and First Peoples Hall are the star attractions, located on Level 1. Glass-walled Grand Hall focuses on Pacific Coast cultures, with displays of traditional homes, hulking totem poles and the original plaster pattern for Spirit of Haida Gwaii by renowned artist Bill Reid.

The First Peoples Hall displays ceremonial and everyday objects from aboriginal cultures throughout Canada. Videos and dioramas explain ancient interpretations of myths. Other exhibits reveal the achievements of contemporary aboriginal artists, athletes, writers, soldiers and political leaders.

Children's Museum & Other Exhibits

The Children's Museum, on Level 2, is based around a theme of 'the Great Adventure,' with more than 30 global exhibits. Kids can walk through Bedouin and Balinese homes, decode hieroglyphics in an Egyptian pyramid and trade with vendors in a North African bazaar. Free, drop-in art workshops take place most days in the Studio.

Levels 3 and 4 explore Canadian history from AD 1000 to 2000. This part of the museum is undergoing renovation through 2017, and various exhibits will be revamped.

Other Things to Know

Outside, note how the building's striking stone exterior has been sculpted into smooth ripples to honor the aboriginal belief that evil dwells in angled nooks. Download the museum's free mobile app/audio guide to enhance your visit. The museum is free on Thursday evenings from 4pm to 8pm. If you also plan to visit the Canadian War Museum, a discounted combination ticket is available. The Museum of Civilization is actually located across the river from Ottawa in Hull, Québec.

Local Knowledge

Canadian Museum of Civilization

RECOMMENDATIONS FROM MARK O'NEILL, PRESIDENT AND CEO

1 TAKE IN THE ARCHITECTURE

The building is internationally recognized for its beauty. The sinuous design gives the impression of a traditional Haida mask. As you approach you're entering through the mask into the main lobby. The architect, Douglas Cardinal, also was the concept designer behind the Smithsonian's National Museum of the American Indian in Washington, DC.

2 MARVEL OVER THE GRAND HALL

The Grand Hall introduces the history, cultures and beliefs of the First Peoples of Canada's Pacific Coast. With its curving, six-storey window wall, the world's largest indoor collection of totem poles, and its unrivalled view of Parliament Hill across the Ottawa River, the Grand Hall is one of the country's most impressive indoor public spaces and the museum's architectural centerpiece.

3 BE A KID AGAIN

The Children's Museum lets kids travel the world by exploring other cultures through exhibitions, props, costumes and hands-on artifacts, including a wonderful assortment of toys and games.

4 ENJOY AN IMAX MOVIE

Our IMAX Theatre was the world's first to combine an IMAX screen and dome. It's now the only one in North America presenting 3D films on the screen and 2D films on the dome. It's quite an immersive viewing experience.

5 RELAX

For a quiet place to relax, head to the end of the Grand Hall. There's a semicircular gallery with comfortable seats and lovely river views. And look up to discover the *Morning Star,* a masterwork of Dene Suline artist Alex Janvier.

Below: Great Hall, National Gallery of Canada; **Right:** Ice skaters on Rideau Canal

(BELOW) ROBERT CHIASSON/GETTY IMAGES ©; (RIGHT) CHERYL FORBES/GETTY IMAGES ©

at 11am on Fridays, when parliament is in session. Visitors are welcomed to watch the antics on a first-come, first-served basis. Expect security checks. At 10am daily in summer, see the colorful changing of the guard on the front lawns, and at night enjoy the free bilingual sound-and-light show on Parliament Hill.

National Gallery of Canada

Museum

(800-319-2787, 613-990-1985; www.gallery.ca; 380 Sussex Dr; adult/child $12/6; 10am-5pm Fri-Wed, to 8pm Thu) The National Gallery is a work of art in itself: its striking ensemble of pink granite and glass spires echo the ornate copper-topped towers of nearby Parliament. Inside, vaulted galleries exhibit predominantly Canadian art, classic and contemporary, including an impressive collection of Inuit works. It's the largest such collection in the world, although additional galleries of European and American treasures include several recognizable names and masterpieces.

Deep within the gallery's interior you'll find two smooth courtyards and the remarkable **Rideau Street Convent Chapel**. Built in 1888, this stunning wooden chapel was saved

Museums Passport

Capitalize on Ottawa's cache of fantastic museums with the **Museums Passport** (www.museumspassport.ca; adult/family $45/99), a discount card that grants carriers admission to eight of the city's best museums. Additional perks include 20% discounts on performances at the National Arts Centre (p197). The card can be purchased at any of the participating museums and is valid for use within seven days.

from demolition and restored piece-by-piece within the main building – quite extraordinary.

Canadian Museum of Nature Museum

(☎613-566-4700; www.nature.ca; 240 McLeod St; adult/child $12/10; ⏰9am-6pm Sat-Wed, to 8pm Thu & Fri; 🚌route 5, 6, 14, stop McLeod St) Sparkling after a massive renovation, this vast museum pokes its Gothic head just above the skyline, south of downtown. It houses an impressive collection of fossils, the full skeleton of a blue whale and an excellent stock of dinosaurs from Alberta. Everyone loves the realistic mammal and bird dioramas depicting Canadian wildlife. The taxidermic creatures are so lifelike, you'll be glad they're behind a sheet of glass.

Activities

The **Rideau Canal**, Ottawa's most famous outdoor attraction, doubles as the largest **ice-skating rink** in the world. The 7.8km of groomed ice is roughly the size of 90 Olympic-sized hockey rinks. Rest stops and changing stations are sprinkled throughout, but, more importantly, take note of the wooden kiosks dispensing scrumptious slabs of fried dough called beavertails. The three **skate and sled rental stations** are located at the steps of the National Arts Centre, Dow's Lake and 5th Ave.

Tours

The Capital Information Kiosk (p198) offers several handy brochures for self-guided walking tours.

Ottawa Walking Tours Walking Tour

(☎613-799-1774; www.ottawawalkingtours.com; tours $15) These informative and fun tours with professional guides depart in front of the Capital Infocentre. Cash only.

Haunted Walk Walking Tour

(☎613-232-0344; www.hauntedwalk.com; 73 Clarence St; walks $14-17) Has several

Ottawa for Children

Nope, the **Canada Agricultural Museum** (**613-991-3044; www.agriculture.technomuses.ca/; 930 Carling Ave at Prince of Wales Dr; adult/child $10/7; 9am-5pm Mar-Oct**) isn't about the history of the pitchfork – it's a fascinating experimental farm. This government-owned property includes over 500 hectares of gardens and ranches. Kids will love the livestock as they hoot and snort around the barn. Affable farmhands will let the tots help out during feeding time. Guided tours lead visitors to an observatory, a tropical greenhouse and an arboretum. The rolling farmland is the perfect place for a scenic summer picnic, and in winter the grounds become a prime tobogganing locale. Otherwise, most of Ottawa's museums have been designed with families in mind; several have entire wings devoted to child's play, like the Canadian Museum of Nature (p193), the **Canada Science & Technology Museum** (**613-991-3044; www.sciencetech.technomuses.ca; 1867 St Laurent Blvd; adult/child $12/8; 9:30am-5pm**) and the Canadian Museum of Civilization (p190).

ghoulish walking tours including visits to the old county jail. A new 'Naughty Ottawa' pub crawl is also available for those who want to get their beer on.

Paul's Boat Lines Boat Tour
(**613-255-6781; www.paulsboatcruises.com; Ottawa Locks or Rideau Canal Dock; cruises from adult/child $20/12; May-Oct**) Scenic cruises offer picture-perfect moments.

Sleeping

Locals call downtown 'Centretown.' To its east, the Sandy Hill district with its cache of stately heritage homes and international embassies has a number of pleasant B&Bs, boutique hotels and, closer to ByWard Market, hostels. All are within a healthy walking distance from downtown.

CENTRETOWN

Lord Elgin Hotel Hotel $$
(**613-235-3333; www.lordelginhotel.ca; 100 Elgin St; d from $169;**) In one of Ottawa's finest locations, the stately Lord Elgin was built in 1941 in a similar, but less grandiose style to the Fairmont Royal York. Its large, bright rooms are comfortably furnished and were recently refurbished with large flatscreen TVs. Many feature wonderful views over Confederation Park.

Victoria Park Suites Hotel $$
(**800-465-7275; www.victoriapark.com; 377 O'Connor St; d from $139**) A delightful position in a leafy downtown backstreet, bright, airy rooms with kitchenettes and plush, comfortable beds make this property an excellent choice for travelers with a limited budget. Complimentary deluxe continental breakfast, on-site gym and a fantastic rooftop courtyard with great views are all bonuses.

Arc Boutique Hotel $$
(**613-238-2888; www.arcthehotel.com; 140 Slater St; d from $129; @**) Arc is a savvy boutique hotel with 112 minimal-yet-elegant rooms in a great location; call it low-key, muted and restfully hip. This mellow adult atmosphere continues through the quiet bar and trendy restaurant.

BYWARD MARKET & SANDY HILL

Avalon B&B $
(**613-789-3443; www.avalonbedandbreakfast.com; 539 Besserer St; d $85-125;**) A refreshing departure from the usual antique-laden B&Bs, Avalon, on a lovely street near the Rideau Canal, has a tasteful

blend of modern furnishings. Enormous healthy breakfasts are the norm. Each of the four stylish rooms has en suite bathroom.

Swiss Hotel Boutique Hotel **$$**
(613-237-0335; www.swisshotel.ca; 89 Daly Ave; r incl breakfast from $128;) Reduced rates are available for extended stays, making this beautiful boutique hotel a wonderful place to call your Ottawa home. The old stone guesthouse has 22 stylish rooms, all a little different but each with iPads, free wi-fi and plush bedding. The optional Swiss buffet breakfast features delicious imported coffees, muesli, cheese and much, much more.

Eating

CENTRETOWN & CHINATOWN

Hung Sum Dim Sum **$**
(613-238-8828; 870 Somerset St; dishes $2-9; 11am-8pm Mon-Sun) Traditional Cantonese dim sum is served all day in this wonderfully plain and nontraditional little restaurant. All dishes are prepared and served fresh, unlike the pick-from-the-trolley joints you might be familiar with.

Savor Ottawa

Check out www.savourottawa.ca for details about the burgeoning local initiative that strives to match regional restaurants with the area's farmers.

Best eaten with friends, this is one of the tastiest, best-value and fun-to-eat meals you'll find in Ottawa.

Town Modern Canadian **$$**
(613-695-8696; www.townlovesyou.ca; 296 Elgin St; mains $13-34; 11:30am-2pm Wed-Fri & 5-10pm Tue-Sun) Slick, smart and ineffably cool, this joint is always packed: arty-farty hipsters bump elbows with wealthy coiffured housewives. Anyone around who knows about food knows the food here is good: real good. Town's clever young owners have pulled together the right mix of style, location, marketing and an exceptionally executed menu that everyone is talking about.

Canadian Museum of Nature (p193)

KLAUS LANG/GETTY IMAGES ©

Brasserie Métropolitain French **$$**
(☎613-562-1160; www.metropolitainbrasserie.com; 700 Sussex Dr; mains $11-38; ⏲8am-midnight) This trendy hot spot puts a modern spin on the typical brasserie with a swirling zinc countertop, flamboyant fixtures and the subtle oompah-pah from a distant accordion: you'll feel like you're dining on the set of *Moulin Rouge*. 'Hill Hour' (4pm to 7pm on weekdays) buzzes with the spirited chatter of hot-blooded pollys as they down cheap drinks and *plats du jour*.

Beckta Dining & Wine Fusion **$$$**
(☎613-238-7063; www.beckta.com; 226 Nepean St; mains $28-39; ⏲5:30-10pm) Book in advance for the hottest table in town, if not one of the hottest in the country. Beckta offers an upmarket dining experience with an original spin on regional cuisine. The inspired five-course tasting menu ($85) is the collective brainchild of chef and sommelier and a great way to experience the bigger picture at work here. Serious foodies won't fail to get a table.

BYWARD MARKET & SANDY HILL

Fraser Cafe Cafe **$$**
(☎613-749-1444; www.frasercafe.ca; 7 Springfield Rd; brunch items $9-15, mains $12-29; ⏲11:30am-2pm Tue-Fri, 10am-2pm Sat & Sun & 5:30-10pm Tue-Sun) It's worth taking a little trek over to this smart cafe/restaurant across the canal, just east of Sandy Hill, especially if you're in the mood for brunch (weekends only). Healthy, tasty, creative meals are prepared from the freshest ingredients. The atmosphere is lively and casual and the service, despite the bustle, is excellent. Reservations recommended.

Chez Lucien French **$$**
(☎613-241-3533; 137 Murray St; mains $6-16; ⏲11am-2am) Exposed burgundy brick, classics playing on the free jukebox, butter-soaked escargot to shuck down – all makes wonderful sense at Chez Lucien, one of Ottawa's favorite places to kick back in style.

Drinking & Nightlife

Highlander Pub Pub
(☎613-562-5678; www.thehighlanderpub.com; 115 Rideau St; ⏲11am-1am) Kilted servers, 17 taps and 200 single malt scotches all add to the wonderful Scottish appeal of this ByWard Market area pub. The food is good, too!

Parliament Pub Pub
(☎613-563-0636; www.parliamentpub.com; 101 Sparks St; ⏲noon-2am Mon-Sat, to 9pm Sun) There's no better place to down a quiet beer while contemplating the history of this fine city than from this summer patio directly opposite Parliament Hill.

ByWard Market
KLAUS LANG/GETTY IMAGES ©

Detour: Algonquin Provincial Park

About 300km west of Ottawa, Ontario's oldest and largest park is a sight for sore eyes, with 7800 sq km of thick pine forests, jagged cliffs, trickling crystal streams, mossy bogs and thousands (thousands!) of lakes. An easily accessible outdoor gem, this rugged expanse is a must-see for canoeists and hikers.

Algonquin is famous for its wildlife-watching and scenic lookouts. During spring, you're almost certain to see moose along Hwy 60, as they escape the pesky black flies to lick the leftover salt from winter de-icing. Other creatures you may encounter include deer, beaver, otter, mink and many bird species.

Algonquin is a nature preserve, which means that most noncamping accommodations are outside the park boundaries. Consider basing yourself in Huntsville or Bracebridge (43km and 73km from the West Gate, respectively) or Whitney, just outside the East Gate, if you plan on day-tripping to the park.

Algonquin Provincial Park is accessible year-round. Drivers can pass through the park along Hwy 60; you must pay the day-use fee to stop and look around ($16 per vehicle).

Check www.algonquinpark.on.ca for further information on lodgings, outfitters and guided tours.

Entertainment

Express (www.ottawaxpress.ca) is the city's free entertainment weekly, also found around town in cafes, bars and bookshops.

LIVE MUSIC

Zaphod Beeblebrox Live Music
(613-562-1010; www.zaphods.ca; 27 York St; 5pm-1am) 'Zaphod Beeblebrox' means 'kick-ass live music venue' in an otherwise undecipherable alien tongue. Grab a Gargleblaster cocktail, and let the trippy beats take you on a ride to the edge of the universe. Well, maybe.

THEATER

National Arts Centre Theater
(NAC; 613-755-1111; www.nac-cna.ca; 53 Elgin St) The capital's premier performing arts complex delivers opera, drama, and performances from the symphony orchestra. The modish complex stretches along the Rideau Canal in Confederation Sq.

SPORTS

Ottawa is a hard-core hockey town. It's worth getting tickets to a game even if you're not into hockey: the ballistic fans put on a show of their own. The NHL's Ottawa Senators play at the **ScotiaBank Place** (613-599-0100; www.senators.com; Palladium Dr, Kanata) in the city's west end.

Shopping

The **ByWard Market** (613-562-3325; www.byward-market.com), at the corner of George St and ByWard St, is the best place in town for one-stop shopping. Vendors cluster around the old maroon-brick market building, erected in the 1840s. Outdoor merchants operate booths from 6am to 6pm year-round (although the winter weather drastically reduces the number of businesses). In summer, over 175 stalls fill the streets, selling fresh produce from local farms, flowers, seafood, cheese, baked goods and kitschy souvenirs. Dalhousie St, a block east of the market, has been rising in popularity with a smattering of hipster boutiques and fashion houses.

The Glebe, a colorful neighborhood just south of the Queensway, bustles with quirky antique shops and charismatic cafes. Most of the action crowds along Bank St.

Information

The **Ottawa Tourism** (**www.ottawatourism.ca**) website offers a comprehensive glance at the nation's capital and can assist with planning itineraries and booking accommodations.

Capital Information Kiosk (**613-239-5000, 800-465-1867; www.canadascapital.gc.ca; World Exchange Plaza, 111 Albert St; 9am-6pm;**) The hub of information for all things Ottawa.

Getting There & Away

Air

The state-of-the-art **Ottawa MacDonald-Cartier International Airport** (YOW; **613-248-2000; www.ottawa-airport.ca; 1000 Airport Rd**) is 15km south of the city and is very small.

Train

The **VIA Rail Station** (**888-842-7245; 200 Tremblay Rd**) is 7km southeast of downtown, near the Riverside Dr exit of Hwy 417. VIA Rail operates trains to Toronto ($99, 4¼ hours, seven daily) and Montréal ($50, 1¾ hours, seven daily).

Getting Around

To/From the Airport

The cheapest way to get to the airport is by city bus. Take bus 97 from the corner of Slater and Albert Sts, west of Bronson Ave (make sure you are heading in the 'South Keys & Airport' direction). The ride takes 30 minutes.

Ottawa Shuttle Service (**613-680-3313; www.ottawashuttleservice.com; from $25; 10am-10pm**) offers private and shared shuttles from most major hotels.

Blue Line Taxis (**613-238-1111; www.bluelinetaxi.com**) and **Capital Taxi** (**613-744-3333; www.capitaltaxi.com**) offer cab service to and from the airport; the fare is $20 to $30.

Public Transportation

OC Transpo (**613-741-4390, 613-741-6440; www.octranspo.com**) operates buses and a light-rail system known as the O-train. Bus tickets cost $1.50 and most rides require a minimum of two tickets.

BRUCE PENINSULA

The Bruce is a 100km limestone outcrop of craggy shorelines and green woodlands at the northern end of the Niagara Escarpment. The fingerlike protrusion

Inglis Falls Conservation Area, Owen Sound

ANDREW MCLACHLAN/GETTY IMAGES

Bruce Peninsula & Georgian Bay

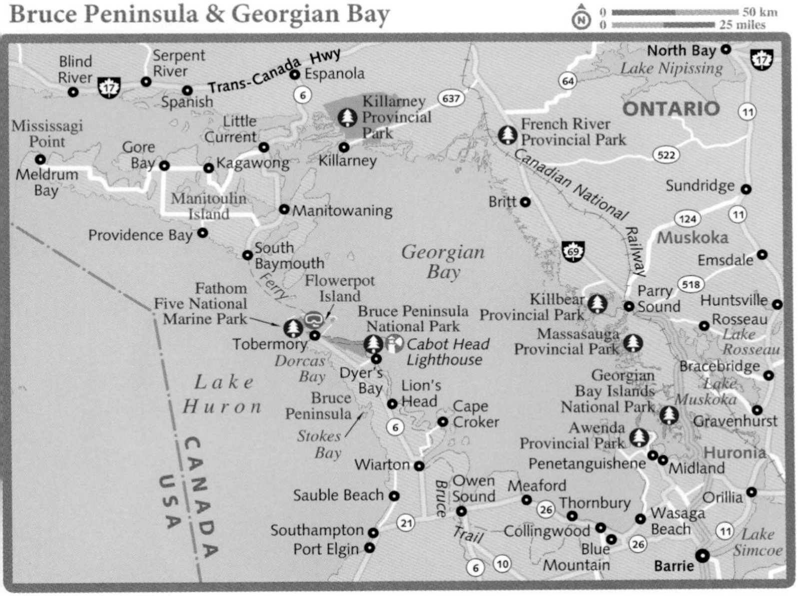

separates the cooler crystal waters of Georgian Bay from warmer Lake Huron. Owen Sound is the largest regional center, while delightful Tobermory is the reward at the tip of the peninsula. Visit www.explorethebruce.com for the latest.

Owen Sound

Owen Sound has a sordid past as a port rife with booze and prostitution. Things got so out of hand that alcohol was banned here for over 60 years – hard to believe, today. By the time the embargo was lifted in 1972, the town had transformed into a thriving artists' colony and remains so today: check out the **Owen Sound Artist's Co-op** (**www.osartistsco-op.com; 279 10th St E; 9:30am-5:30pm Mon-Sat, noon-4pm Sun**) when you're in town.

Sights

Tom Thomson Art Gallery Museum
(**519-376-1932; www.tomthomson.org; 840 1st Ave W; adult/child $5/3; 11am-5pm Mon-Fri, noon-5pm Sat-Sun**) This gallery displays the work of Tom Thomson, granddaddy of modern Canadian landscape painting. His intimate and smoldering portrayal of nature is said to have inspired the formation of the Group of Seven painters. Thomson grew up near Owen Sound and many of his works were composed in nearby thickets of fall leaves.

Waterfalls Waterfall
There are eight scenic waterfalls in the area, four of which are close to downtown. Go to www.visitgrey.ca for a downloadable waterfall tour.

Sleeping & Eating

For a list of area B&Bs, go to www.bbgrey-bruce.com.

Highland Manor B&B **$$**
(**519-372-2699; www.highlandmanor.ca; 867 4th Ave A W; d $120-170;**) This magnificent Victorian mansion (c 1872) has been elegantly furnished by attentive hosts. Decadent, spacious suites all have their own bathrooms. Many have original fireplaces. Highly recommended.

Below: Indian Head Cove, Bruce Peninsula National Park; **Right:** Halfway Log Dump, Bruce Peninsula National Park

(BELOW) LISA STOKES/GETTY IMAGES ©; (RIGHT) HENRY GEORGI/GETTY IMAGES ©

Rocky Racoon Café Fusion **$$**

(**519-376-2232; 941 2nd Ave E; mains $15-23; 11am-11pm Mon-Sat;**) These organic advocates serve up wild boar and Tibetan dumplings, with vegan and vegetarian options. You'll find plenty of South Asian flavors, especially delicious curries.

Owen Sound to Tobermory

The 100km stretch of highway from Owen Sound to Tobermory is monotonous at best. Consider taking a side road or two to get a taste of the scenery that makes the Bruce so special.

From Owen Sound, follow Grey County Rd 1 which winds along the scenic shoreline of staggering pines between Owen Sound and the quaint village of **Wiarton**. Stop here to say hello to **Wiarton Willy**, Canada's version of Punxsutawney Phil, then continue on Hwy 6 to the sleepy and picturesque bay at **Lion's Head**, a great place to stop for lunch.

Heading further north on Hwy 6 for about 25km, you'll reach Dyer's Bay Rd. Turn right and maintain your heading for another 10km to the little village of **Dyer's Bay**, reminiscent of Cape Cod with its pretty clapboard houses and shoreline scenery. From here you must decide if you'll plow on the further 11km to remote **Cabot Head Lighthouse** (**admission by donation; May-Oct**), promising stunning views from the keeper's perch. It's wild and wonderful, but the windy unpaved road is slow going and there's only one way in and out... back to Hwy 6 and north to Tobermory.

Tobermory

Tiny Tobermory is a hippy, nature lover's paradise boasting some of Ontario's most stunning scenery and sunsets. The village centers on the harbor area known as Little Tub, which is bustling during ferry

season (May to late October) and all but deserted in winter.

Sights & Activities

Fathom Five National Marine Park Park
(519-596-2233; www.pc.gc.ca/fathomfive; adult/child $6/3) Established to protect the numerous shipwrecks and islands around Tobermory, this was the first park of its kind in Canada. Aside from the wrecks, the park is known for much loved Flowerpot Island with its top-heavy 'flowerpot' formations, eroded by waves.

Bruce Peninsula National Park Outdoors
(519-596-2233; www.pc.gc.ca/brucepeninsula; day use per vehicle $11.70; May-Oct) Much of the area just south of Tobermory is protected by this national park, flaunting some of Ontario's finest assets: the Niagara Escarpment, 1000-year-old cedars, rare orchids and crystal-clear, limestone refracted waters. Be sure to check in with the visitors center. Must-see locations include **Little Cove**, **the Grotto** and **Singing Sands**, on the other side of Hwy 6.

Bruce Anchor Cruises Cruise
(519-596-2555, 800-591-4254; www.bruceanchorcruises.com; 7468 Hwy 6; adult/child from $37/28; May-Oct) Glass-bottom boat tours over the tops of rusty, barnacled shipwrecks and onward to Flowerpot Island depart from this private dock at the very end of Hwy 6, also a brilliant spot to catch the sunset.

Sleeping & Eating

In summer it's absolutely essential to book accommodations in advance.

Innisfree B&B **$$**
(519-596-8190; www.tobermoryaccommodations.com; 46 Bay St; r $89-154; May-Oct;) Whether it's the scent of fresh blueberry muffins, or the stunning harbor views from the sunroom and large deck,

guests will adore this charming country home.

Blue Bay Motel Motel $$
(519-596-2392; www.bluebay-motel.com; 32 Bay St; d from $95;) Many of this centrally located motel's 16 bright and spacious guest rooms overlook Little Tub Harbour. Fresh and funky, each room is different: choose from double-double, queen and king beds. Some have fireplaces, soaker tubs and LCD TVs. Peek and choose on the website.

Craigie's Fast Food $
(519-596-2867; 4 Bay St; fish & chips $10.50; 7am-7pm May-Oct) This white sea shanty has been serving fish and chips in Tobermory since 1932. Greasy breakfast specials are *the* way to start the day before an early morning ferry or hike into the wilderness.

Bootlegger's Cove Pub $$
(519-596-2219; 236 Big Tub Rd; items $7-25; noon-8pm) Good service, tasty food and a stunning patio overlooking Big Tub Harbour make this joint the local secret we couldn't keep to ourselves. The fun menu includes wraps, quesadillas, pizzas and 'smores!

Information

Tobermory Chamber of Commerce (519-596-2452; www.tobermory.org; Hwy 6; 9am-9pm) As you pull into town (from the south) it's to your right: drop in for the latest updates.

Getting There & Around

From Toronto, **Parkbus** (www.parkbus.ca) offers a limited schedule of express services ($58, five hours) with a number of downtown collection points.

When in Tobermory, the **National Park Shuttle Bus** (519-596-2999; www.tobermoryparkbus.com; adult/senior/child $4.50/2.50/3.50) can take you between Little Tub, the Bruce Peninsula National Park Visitors Centre and Head of Trails.

NORTHERN ONTARIO

If wilderness isn't your thing, move on. Otherwise, bear witness to a stunning, silent expanse where ancient aboriginal canoe routes ignite under the ethereal evening lightshow of the aurora borealis.

Lake Superior Provincial Park

Lake Superior Provincial Park (705-856-2284, 705-882-2026; www.lakesuperiorpark.ca; Hwy 17; day use per vehicle $13, backcountry sites $9.50, campsites $27.25-32.75) protects 1600 sq km of misty fjord-like passages, thick evergreen forest and tranquil sandy coves that feel like they've never known the touch of humankind. The best bits

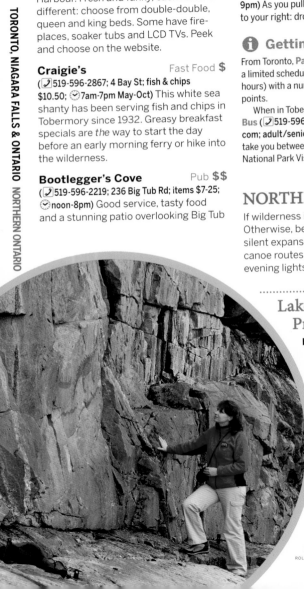

Agawa Rock Pictographs, Lake Superior Provincial Park
ROLF HICKER/GETTY IMAGES ©

of the park require some level of hiking or canoeing to access, but if you're not so inclined or have limited time, there are numerous picture-perfect vistas just off the highway which goes straight through the park. Sights and facilities generally open from May to October.

Your first stop should be the **Agawa Bay Visitors Centre**, 9km in from the park's southern boundary. The interactive museum and park experts will advise you well. There's a smaller information area at **Red Rock Lake**, 53km further north, if you're coming from the other direction.

Katherine Cove picnic area is a must for panoramas of misty sand-strewn shores. Budding anthropologists will appreciate the **Agawa Rock Pictographs**: red-ocher images up to 400 years old. A rugged 500m trail leads you to a rock ledge where, if the lake is calm, the mysterious pictographs can be seen.

Avid hikers will delight in the park's 11 exceptional trails. The **Nokomis Trail** (5km) loops around iconic **Old Woman Bay**, so named because it is said you can see the face of an old woman in the cliffs. Depending on the weather, wispy beard-like fog and shivering Arctic trees exude a distinctly primeval flavor. The diverse **Orphan Lake Trail** (8km) just north of Katherine Cove is a tasting plate of the park's ethereal features: isolated cobble beaches, majestic waterfalls, elevated lookouts and dense maple forests.

Naturally Superior Adventures (705-856-2939, 800-203-9092; www.naturallysuperior.com; RR1 Lake Superior, Wawa; courses from $50, day trips from $95) and **Caribou Expeditions** (800-970-6662; www.caribou-expeditions.com; 1021 Goulais Mission Rd, Goulais Bay; courses from $75, tours from $135) run extensive paddling programs in and around the park.

Wawa is the nearest town with eating and lodging options.

Pukaskwa National Park

At **Pukaskwa** (ext 242 807-229-0801; www.parkscanada.gc.ca/pukaskwa; Hwy 627; day use adult/child $5.80/2.90, backcountry sites $9.80, campsites $15-29), bear hugs are taken literally. Open May through October, the park offers many of the same topographical features as Lake Superior Provincial Park and has an intact predator-prey ecosystem, including a small herd of elusive caribou. There are only 4km of roads in the entire park.

Pukaskwa's frontcountry is based around the only general use campground at **Hattie Cove**, near the park's entrance. Check in with the **visitors center** (807-229-0801; 9am-4pm Jul-Aug) when you arrive: guided hikes and activities depart here most evenings around 7pm.

Three short trails begin at **Hattie Cove**, offering glimpses of the pristine setting. The popular **Southern Headland Trail** (2.2km) is a rocky, spear-shaped route that offers elevated photo-ops of the shoreline and craggy Canadian Shield. Look for the curious stunted trees, so formed by harsh winds blowing off the lake. The **Halfway Lake Trail** (2.6km) loops around a small lake: informative signs offer a scientific perspective on the inner workings of the ecosystem. The **Beach Trail** (1.5km) winds along Horseshoe Bay and Lake Superior revealing sweeping vistas of crashing waves and undulating sand dunes.

If you're not a skilled independent hiker, Naturally Superior Adventures and Caribou Expeditions both offer a variety of guided excursions through Pukaskwa's backcountry.

Jardin Nelson
Jardin Nelson

Montréal & Québec

Once an outpost of Catholic conservatism, an isolated island of *francophonie* languishing in a sea of Anglo culture, Québec province has finally come into its own and has crafted a rich, spirited culture independent of its European motherland. The people of Québec are vibrant and inviting, and the province is strewn with colorful Victorian facades, lush rolling hills and romantic bistros.

Montréal and Québec City are bustling metropolises with a perfect mixture of sophistication, playfulness and history-soaked preserved quarters. Produce from bucolic Charlevoix graces the tables of the region's stellar restaurants. The Laurentians abound with ski resorts and peaks, while the cliffs soaring above the Saguenay River at Tadoussac are equally breathtaking (as are the resident beluga whales). The easygoing, red-tinged Îles de la Madeleine (Magdalen Islands) freckle the sea to the east.

Place Jacques Cartier, Old Montréal

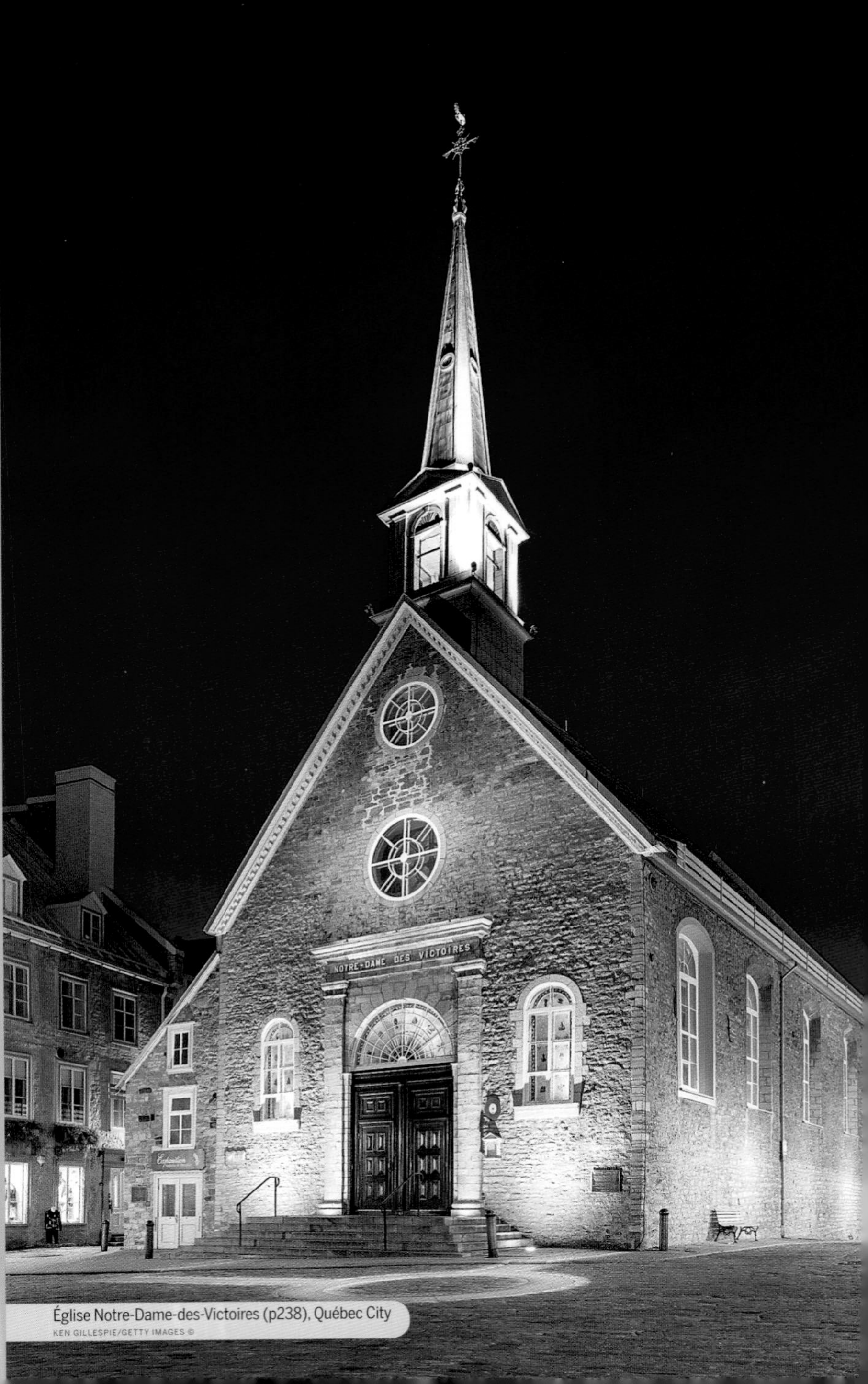

Église Notre-Dame-des-Victoires (p238), Québec City

Montréal & Québec

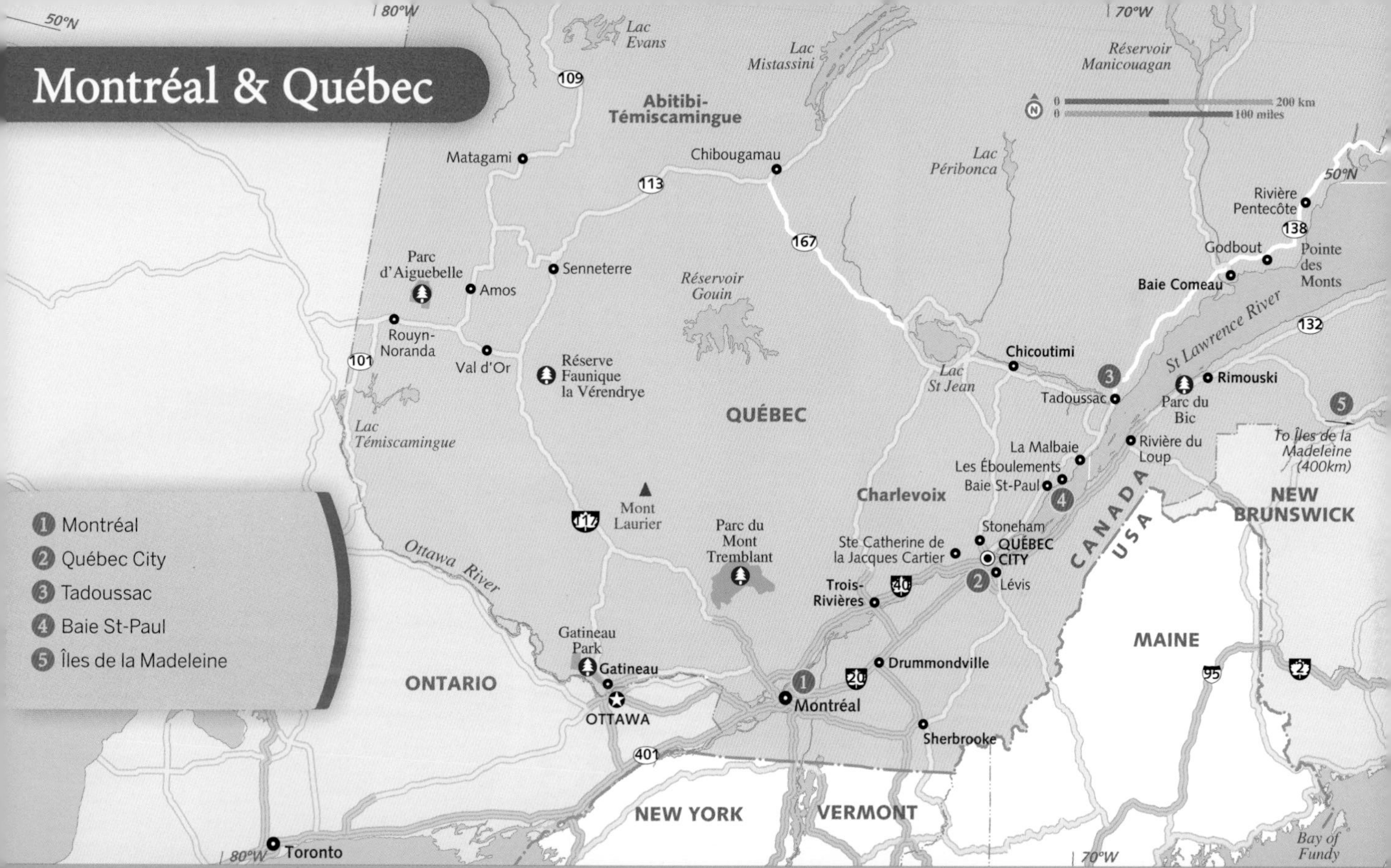

Montréal & Québec's Highlights

Montréal Jazz Festival

Where else can you join more than 2 million music lovers and watch the best jazz-influenced musicians in the world, choosing from 500 shows of which countless are free? BB King, Asto Piazzolla and Michael Bublé are among those who've plugged in at the 11-day bash (p229) during late June. You might want to join them after your free drumming lesson and street-side jam session.

1

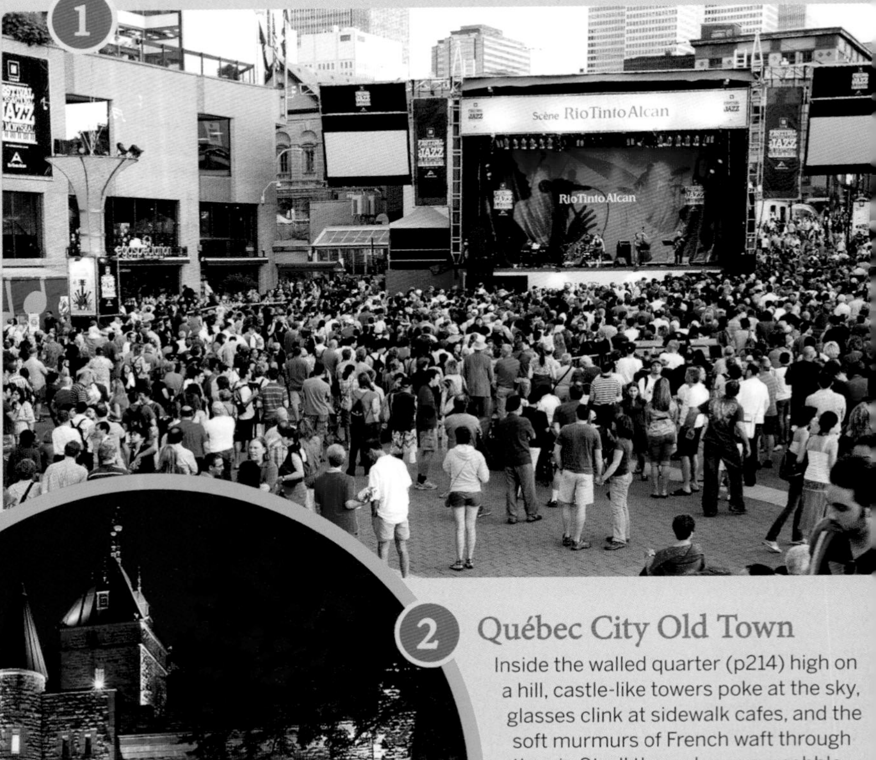

2

Québec City Old Town

Inside the walled quarter (p214) high on a hill, castle-like towers poke at the sky, glasses clink at sidewalk cafes, and the soft murmurs of French waft through the air. Stroll through narrow cobblestone lanes and 400-year-old plazas, and it's easy to believe you're an ocean away from North America. Left: Porte St-Louis (p235)

TRAVEL PICTURES/ALAMY ©

Wet & Wild Tadoussac

3

Whale-watching is Tadoussac's main claim to fame (p249), especially glimpsing the white belugas – the only population outside the Arctic. But it has lots to offer beyond leviathans, such as sea kayaking, 'surfbiking,' hiking in the Saguenay fjord's rugged parks, or simply wandering the local dunes and headlands. Post-adventure, settle into a cafe in the historic, bohemian town, where residents invariably have time for a chat.

ROBERT CHIASSON/GETTY IMAGES ©

4

Îles de la Madeleine

Sunset is prime time on the archipelago (p250), as the sinking orb fires up the islands' ubiquitous red cliffs. Take your pick on Île du Cap Aux Meules (p251): watch atop the bluff at Cap du Phare lighthouse, or cruise to a beachside microbrewery to see the spectacle. Follow up with a lobster dinner and evening mingling with locals at *boîtes à chansons*, the lively small music venues.

5

Baie St-Paul

Stuffed with rustic restaurants and cheerful *gîtes* (B&Bs), Baie St-Paul (p246) is almost impossibly relaxing. While *ateliers* (artists' studios), galleries and boutiques line the town's streets, food is an equally important art. The surrounding flowery farmlands of the Charlevoix region harvest a bounty of organic meat and produce that local chefs transform into sublime cuisine. The local alehouses help wash it all down.

Montréal & Québec's Best...

French Restaurants

L'Express It's so French it could be serving *frites* under the Eiffel Tower. (p226)

Le Lapin Sauté Country cookin' in cozy environs. (p243)

Vices Versa Husband-and-wife chef duo each have their own stove and each cooks half the menu. (p249)

Le Patriarche Nouvelle cuisine and local ingredients amid contemporary art. (p243)

Gathering Spots

Place Jacques Cartier Buskers, vendors and cafes in Old Montréal's heart. (p215)

Place Royale Québec City's atmospheric soul, where it all began 400 years ago. (p237)

Georges Étienne Cartier monument Hit the bongos with the hippies during Tam Tam Sundays. (p219)

Rue St-Jean Bistro- and bar-lined street in Québec City's bohemian St-Jean-Baptiste neighborhood. (p239)

Hotels/B&Bs

Auberge Saint-Antoine Part archaeological site, part boutique hotel with grand views. (p242)

Maison Historique James Thompson The 18th-century residence of a Plains of Abraham veteran. (p241)

Hotel Gault Minimalist, loft-style rooms for design buffs. (p222)

Nature et Pinceaux Mountain-top B&B with four-course breakfast. (p247)

Hôtel Le Germain Sexy rooms with Québec-crafted decor and see-through showers. (p223)

Outdoor Adventures

- **Mont-Tremblant** Whistler-esque skiing in winter, hiking and paddling in summer. (p232)
- **Tadoussac** Get sprayed by whales on a Zodiac or kayak trip. (p249)
- **Îles de la Madeleine** Windsurfing, kitesurfing, cycling, kayaking and cave visits. (p250)
- **Canal de Lachine** Cycle from Old Montréal to its outskirts along the waterway. (p221)

Left: Ville de Mont-Tremblant (p232); **Above:** Low tide at Tadoussac (p249)

Need to Know

ADVANCE PLANNING

- **One month before** In summer book accommodation as soon as possible, especially in festival-crazy Montréal. Same for winter visits to Québec City or the Laurentians.
- **Two weeks before** Purchase theater tickets.
- **One week before** Secure dinner reservations at well-known restaurants in Montréal and Charlevoix.

RESOURCES

- **Tourisme Québec** (☎877-266-5687; www.bonjourquebec.com) Book rooms, show tickets, even car rentals and train tickets.
- **Tourism Montréal** (☎877-266-5687; www.tourisme-montreal.org) Accommodation bookings, videos and a buzzy blog; the last-minute hotel search engine guarantees discounted prices.
- **Tourism Québec City** (www.quebecregion.com) Listings of what to see and do, and where to eat and sleep.
- **Québec Parks** (www.sepaq.com/pq) The low-down for visiting the province's 23 'national' (aka provincial) parks.
- **Cult** (www.cultmontreal.com) Montréal's online alternative magazine has useful music, food and event listings.
- **Montréal Clubs** (www.montreal-clubs.com) Keeps the finger on the pulse of Montréal's latest nightlife hotspots.

GETTING AROUND

- **Fly** Montréal's Trudeau International Airport is Canada's third-busiest and a regional hub. Québec City's airport is much smaller.
- **Car** The Trans-Canada Hwy (Hwy 40 within Québec) runs through Montréal and Québec City. Highways throughout the province are good. Rental cars are readily available.
- **Ferry** Several different ferry services glide across the St Lawrence River, as well as to islands in the Gulf, such as the Îles de la Madeleine.
- **Train** From Montréal, VIA Rail has fast and frequent daily service to Toronto and Québec City, and one train daily to Halifax. There's Amtrak service once daily from New York City to Montréal.

Montréal & Québec Itineraries

Oh la la! Montréal and Québec City wow with romance, history and gastronomic delights. From there the roads hugging the St Lawrence River lead to arts towns, on-the farm restaurants and whales.

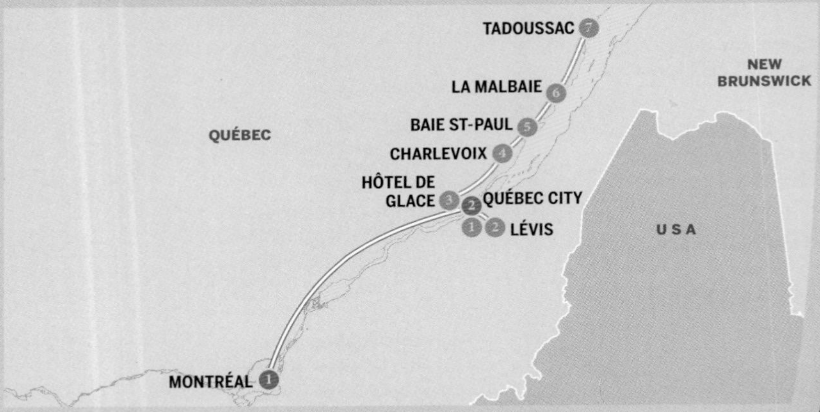

3 DAYS

MONTRÉAL TO QUÉBEC CITY
PROVINCIAL PILLARS

Start in ❶**Montréal** (p214) in the Mile End district, partaking in a local ritual – a long and leisurely brunch. Hike up Mont Royal, stopping to catch your breath and snap the cityscape from the Kondiaronk Lookout before ending up in the boisterous Plateau Mont-Royal for dinner and evening entertainment.

Begin day two by exploring the cobblestoned alleys of Old Montréal. Get a dose of history at Musée d'Archéologie et d'Histoire Pointe-à-Callière, or soak up some culture at Musée des Beaux-Arts. Head to Little Italy for a pasta-wine-espresso dinner, then sample the club scene in the Village.

It's tough to leave such a playful place, but history-drenched ❷**Québec City** (p234) awaits about three hours up the road. Set out on foot through the Old Town's labyrinth of cobbled lanes and squares. Walk over the 400-year-old fortifications; point the camera at turreted Le Château Frontenac; and sip a café au lait in the soulful Place Royale, the cradle of Nouvelle France. Search for the ultimate *table d'hôte* (fixed-price menu) in the Old Lower Town for dinner before tucking into the covers at a romantic inn come nightfall.

5 DAYS

QUÉBEC CITY TO TADOUSSAC
RIVER ROUTE

Rattle around ❶ **Québec City** (p234) for two days, absorbing the historic sites, street performers and jazz-playing corner cafes. If it's summer, hop on the ferry to ❷ **Lévis** (p246) for city views. If it's winter, do a day-trip a half-hour west to see ❸ **Hôtel de Glace** (p242), aka the 'Ice Hotel.'

Begin the journey northeast on Rte 138, following the St Lawrence River as it slices through pastoral ❹ **Charlevoix** (p246). Foodies often make a pilgrimage to this region, known for its organic farms and heavenly eateries. Stop in ❺ **Baie St-Paul** (p246), an arty town packed with galleries, B&Bs, alehouses and, of course, fine French cuisine. About 50km onward along Rte 362, ❻ **La Malbaie** (p248) offers country manors and more rustic restaurants specializing in local fare.

Once you get your fill after a day or two, continue following the river for 70km to ❼ **Tadoussac** (p249). The historic, bohemian town is a top place for whale-watching. Humpbacks, minkes and king-of-the-sea blue whales swim by, as do beluga whales, which otherwise are seen only in the Arctic. Hiking and paddling around the dramatic scenery are the other big draws.

Le Château Frontenac (p238), Québec City

Discover Montréal & Québec

At a Glance

- **Montréal** (p214) Canada's Euro-cool cultural heart.
- **The Laurentians** (p232) Alps-vibed mountain villages.
- **Québec City** (p234) Walled town of unparalleled history and charm.
- **Tadoussac** (p249) Hiking, kayaking and whales big and small.
- **Îles de la Madeleine** (p250) Red cliffs, sand spits and lobster on a breezy archipelago.

Place Jacques Cartier
GARRY BLACK/GETTY IMAGES ©

MONTRÉAL

Historically, Montréal – the only de facto bilingual city on the continent – has been torn right in half, 'The Main' (Blvd St-Laurent) being the dividing line between the east-end Francophones and the west-side Anglos. Today, French pockets dot both sides of the map, a new wave of English-speaking Canadians have taken residence in some formerly French enclaves and thanks to constant waves of immigration, it's not uncommon for Montréalers to speak not one, or two, but three languages in their daily life. With the new generation concerned more with global issues (namely the environment), language battles have become so passé.

One thing not up for debate is what makes Montréal so irresistible. It's a secret blend of French-inspired joie de vivre and cosmopolitan dynamism that has come together to foster a flourishing arts scene, an indie rock explosion, a medley of world-renowned boutique hotels, the Plateau's extraordinary cache of swank eateries and a cool Parisian vibe that pervades every *terrasse* (patio) in the Quartier Latin. It's easy to imagine you've been transported to a distant locale, where hedonism is the national mandate.

Sights

OLD MONTRÉAL

Place d'Armes Historic Site
(Map p218) The twin-towered Notre-Dame Basilica lords over this dignified square, where the early settlers once battled it out with the local Iroquois. A statue of Maison-

neuve stands in the middle of the square, which is surrounded by some of Old Montréal's finest historic buildings. In fact, the **Old Seminary**, next to the basilica, is the city's oldest, built by Sulpician missionaries in 1685 and still occupied today.

Behind the temple-like curtain of columns in the northwest corner lurks the Bank of Montreal. It harbors the head office of Canada's oldest bank, founded in 1817. The opulent marble interior is worth a gander, and there's a small money museum as well.

Place Jacques Cartier & Around — Historic Site

(Map p218) Gently sloped Place Jacques Cartier in the heart of Old Montréal is a beehive of activity, especially in summer, when it's filled with flowers, street musicians, vendors and visitors. The cafes and restaurants lining it are neither cheap nor good, but they do offer front-row seats for the action.

At the square's north end stands the **Colonne Nelson** (Nelson's Column), a monument erected by the British to the general who defeated the French and Spanish fleet at Trafalgar. Nelson faces a small statue of Admiral Vauquelin across the street, put there as a riposte by the French.

The petite palace across the street is the **Château Ramezay**, built in 1705 as the residence of Montréal governor Claude de Ramezay.

There is a tourist office in the northwest corner.

Marché Bonsecours — Market

(Bonsecours Market; Map p218; 350 Rue St-Paul Est; ⌚10am-9pm late Jun-Aug, to 6pm Sep-Mar) The silvery dome standing sentinel over Old Montréal like a glamorous lighthouse belongs to Bonsecours Market. After a stint as City Hall, the neoclassical structure served as the city's main market hall until supermarkets drove it out of business in the 1960s. These days, the flower and vegetable stands have been replaced with fancy boutiques selling arts, crafts and clothing produced in Québec. This is not a bad place to pick up some quality souvenirs.

Montréal Museum Pass

Custom-made for culture buffs, this handy **pass (www.museesmontreal.org; $80)** is valid for three consecutive days and gets you admission to 38 museums, plus unlimited use of the bus and métro system. It's available at tourist offices, major hotels and participating museums. Note that most museums are closed on Monday.

Vieux-Port de Montréal — Park

(Map p218) Montréal's Old Port has morphed into a park and fun zone paralleling the mighty St Lawrence River for 2.5km and punctuated by four grand *quais*. Locals and visitors alike come here for strolling, cycling and in-line skating. Cruise boats, ferries, jet boats and speedboats all depart for tours from various docks. In winter, you can cut a fine figure on an outdoor ice-skating rink.

Historical relics include the striking white **Clock Tower (Map p218; Clock Tower Pier; ⌚10am-9pm mid-May–Sep)** FREE at the northern end of Quai Jacques Cartier. Built in 1922 to honor sailors who died in WWI, it affords commanding views of the river and city.

Centre des Sciences de Montréal — Museum

(Montréal Science Centre; Map p218; www.montrealsciencecentre.com; King Edward Pier; adult/child $14.50/8.50, with IMAX 3-D movie $21.50/14; ⌚9am-5pm) In this sleek, glass-covered science center housing virtual and interactive games, there are plenty of buttons to push, knobs to pull and games to play as you make your way through the high-tech exhibition halls.

Musée d'Archéologie et d'Histoire Pointe-à-Callière — Museum

(Museum of Archaeology & History; Map p218; www.pacmuseum.qc.ca; 350 Place Royale; adult/child $20/7; ⏱10am-5pm Mon-Fri, 11am-5pm Sat & Sun) Housed in a striking contemporary building, this excellent museum sits near the original landing spot of the early settlers and provides a good overview of the city's beginnings. Make time for the multimedia show before plunging underground into a maze of excavated foundations, an ancient sewerage system and vestiges of the first European cemetery. Artifacts and interactive stations help bring the past to life. The **lookout tower** and restaurant can be visited free of charge.

DOWNTOWN

Musée des Beaux-Arts de Montréal — Museum

(Museum of Fine Arts; Map p218; www.mbam.qc.ca; 1380 Rue Sherbrooke Ouest; special exhibitions $20, 5-9pm Wed half-price; ⏱11am-5pm Thu-Tue, to 9pm Wed special exhibition only) FREE A must for art lovers, the Museum of Fine Arts has amassed several millennia worth of paintings, sculpture, decorative arts, furniture, prints, drawings and photographs. European heavyweights include Rembrandt, Picasso and Monet, but the museum really shines when it comes to Canadian art. Highlights include works by Jean-Baptiste Roy-Audy and Paul Kane, landscapes by the Group of Seven, abstractions by Jean-Paul Riopelle and a fair amount of Inuit and aboriginal artifacts.

Montréal City Overview

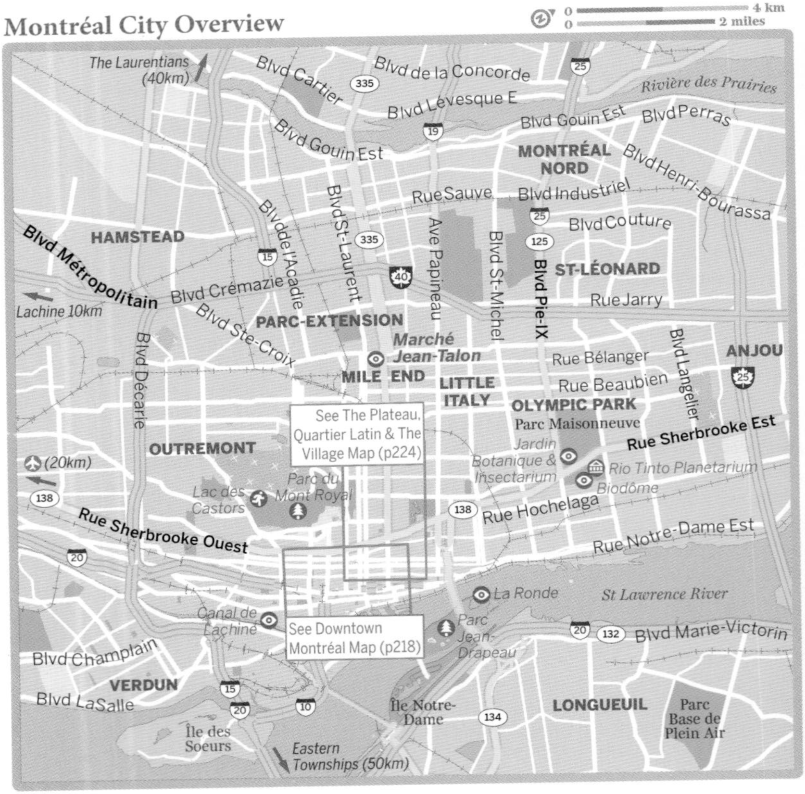

COMPASSANDCAMERA/GETTY IMAGES ©

Don't Miss
Basilique Notre-Dame

Montréal's famous landmark, Notre-Dame Basilica, is a visually pleasing if slightly gaudy symphony of carved wood, paintings, gilded sculptures and stained-glass windows. Built in 1829 on the site of an older and smaller church, it also sports a famous Casavant organ and the Gros Bourdon, said to be the biggest bell in North America. The interior looks especially impressive during an otherwise overly melodramatic **sound and light show**, staged from Tuesday to Saturday night.

NEED TO KNOW

Map p218; www.basiliquenddm.org; 110 Rue Notre-Dame Ouest; adult/child $5/4, sound-and-light show $10/5; 8am-4:30pm Mon-Sat, 12:30-4pm Sun

Chinatown Neighborhood
Although this neighborhood, perfectly packed into a few easily navigable streets, has no sites per se, it's a nice area for lunch or for shopping for quirky knick-knacks. The main thoroughfare, Rue de la Gauchetière, between Blvd St-Laurent and Rue Jeanne Mance, is enlivened with Taiwanese bubble-tea parlors, Hong Kong–style bakeries and Vietnamese soup restaurants. The public square, **Place Sun-Yat-Sen** (Map p218; cnr Rue de la Gauchetière & Rue Clark; underground rail Place-d'Armes), attracts crowds of elderly Chinese and the occasional group of Falun Gong demonstrators.

Musée d'Art Contemporain Museum
(Map p218; www.macm.org; 185 Rue Ste-Catherine Ouest; adult/child $12/free, 5-9pm Wed admission free; 11am-6pm Tue & Thu-Sun, to 9pm Wed) Canada's first major showcase of contemporary art, this museum offers an excellent survey of Canadian, and in particular Québecois, creativity. All the local legends, including Jean-Paul Riopelle,

Downtown Montréal

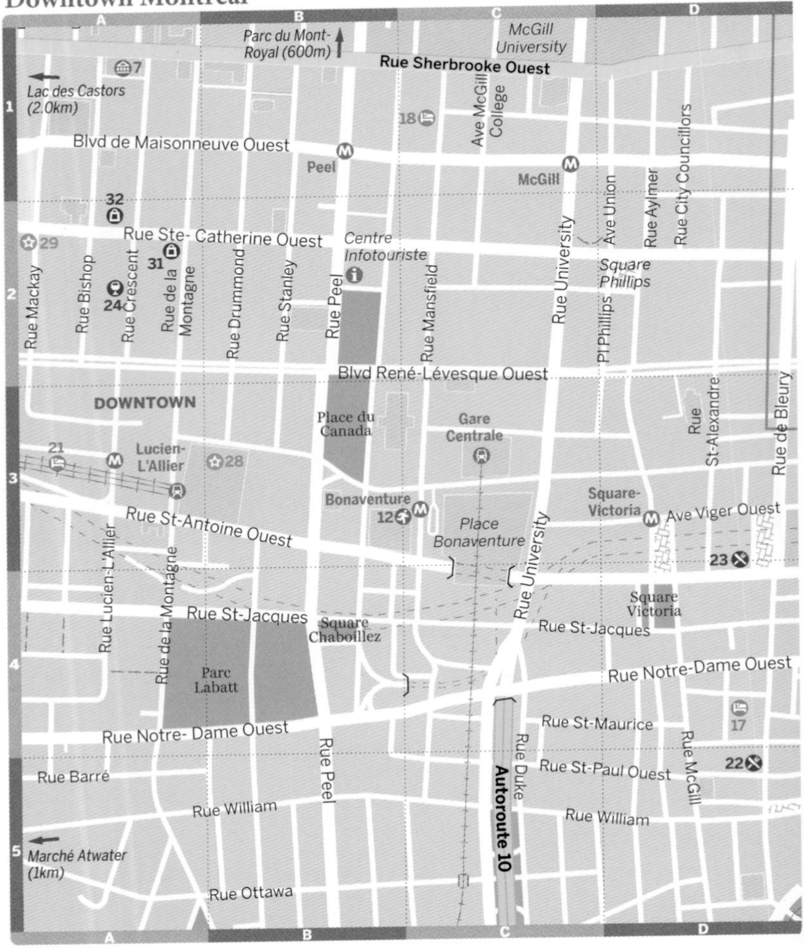

Paul-Émile Borduas and Génévieve Cadieux, are well represented. There are great temporary shows, too. Free English-language **tours** run at 6:30pm Wednesday and at 1pm Sunday.

PARC DU MONT ROYAL AREA

Mont Royal can be entered via the steps at the top of Rue Peel. Buses 80 and 129 make their way from the Place des Arts métro station to the Georges Étienne Cartier monument. Bus 11 from the Mont Royal métro stop traverses the park.

Parc du Mont Royal Park

(Map p216; www.lemontroyal.qc.ca) This 'mountain,' the work of New York Central Park designer Frederick Law Olmsted, is a sprawling, leafy playground that's perfect for cycling, jogging, horseback riding, picnicking and, in winter, cross-country skiing and tobogganing. In fine weather, enjoy panoramic views from the **Kondiaronk Lookout** near **Chalet du Mont-Royal**, a grand old stone villa that hosts big-band concerts in summer, or from the **Observatoire de l'Est**, a favorite

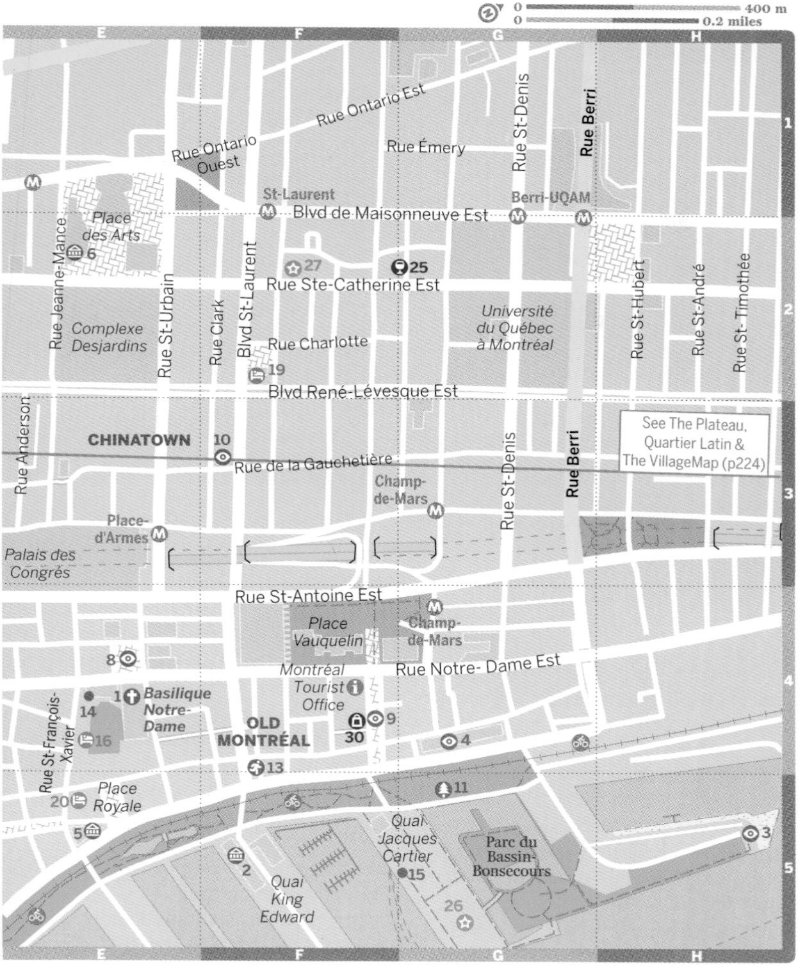

rendezvous for lovebirds. It takes about 30 minutes to walk between the two.

En route you'll spot the landmark 40m-high Cross of Montréal (1924), which is illuminated at night. It's there to commemorate city founder Maisonneuve, who single-handedly carried a wooden cross up the mountain in 1643 to give thanks to God for sparing his fledgling village from flooding.

Georges Étienne Cartier Monument Statue

On the park's northeastern edge, on Ave du Parc, this statue draws hundreds of revelers every Sunday for impromptu drumming and dancing in what has been dubbed 'Tam Tam Sundays' – it's nothing less than an institution. If the noise doesn't lead you all the way there, just follow your nose toward whiffs of 'wacky tabaccy.' This is also a good spot to pick up some unusual handicrafts sold by local artisans.

Downtown Montréal

Don't Miss Sights
1 Basilique Notre-Dame ... E4

Sights
2 Centre des Sciences de Montréal ... F5
3 Clock Tower ... H5
4 Marché Bonsecours ... G4
5 Musée d'Archéologie et d'Histoire Pointe-à-Callière ... E5
6 Musée d'Art Contemporain ... E2
7 Musée des Beaux-Arts de Montréal ... A1
8 Place d'Armes ... E4
9 Place Jacques Cartier & Around ... F4
10 Place Sun-Yat-Sen ... F3
11 Vieux-Port de Montréal ... G5

Activities, Courses & Tours
12 Atrium ... C3
13 Ça Roule Montréal ... F4
14 Guidatour ... E4
15 Le Bateau Mouche ... G5

Sleeping
16 Bonaparte ... E4
17 Hôtel Gault ... D4
18 Hôtel Le Germain ... C1
19 Hotel Zero 1 ... F2
20 Le Petit Hôtel ... E5
21 Les Bons Matins ... A3

Eating
22 Olive + Gourmando ... D5
23 Toqué! ... D3

Drinking & Nightlife
24 Brutopia ... A2
25 Le Ste-Elisabeth ... G2

Entertainment
26 Cirque du Soleil ... G5
27 Metropolis ... F2
28 Montréal Canadiens ... B3
29 Upstairs ... A2

Shopping
30 Galerie Le Chariot ... F4
31 Ogilvy ... A2
32 Parasuco ... A2

PLATEAU MONT-ROYAL

East of Parc du Mont Royal, the Plateau is Montréal's youngest, liveliest and artiest neighborhood.

The main drags are Blvd St-Laurent ('The Main'), Rue St-Denis and Ave du Mont-Royal, all lined with sidewalk cafes, restaurants, clubs and boutiques. Rue Prince Arthur, Montréal's quintessential hippie hangout in the 1960s, and Rue Duluth are alive with BYOW eateries.

QUARTIER LATIN & THE VILLAGE

The Quartier Latin is Montréal's most boisterous neighborhood, a slightly grungy entertainment district made glitzy with an infusion of French panache.

A hotbed of activity, especially during the International Jazz Festival, FrancoFolies and Just for Laughs, the quarter bubbles 24 hours a day in its densely packed rows of bars, trendy bistros, music clubs and record shops.

Over the past decade or so, Montréal's gay community has breathed new life into The Village, a once poverty-stricken corner of the east end. Today, gay-friendly doesn't even begin to describe the neighborhood. People of all persuasions wander Rue Ste-Catherine and savor the joie de vivre in its cafes, bistros and discerning eateries.

LITTLE ITALY & MILE END

The zest of the old country finds its way into the lively Little Italy district, north of the Plateau, where the espresso seems stiffer, the pasta sauce thicker and the chefs plumper. Italian football games seem to be broadcast straight onto Blvd St-Laurent, where the green-white-red flag is proudly displayed. Soak up the atmosphere on a stroll, and don't miss the Marché Jean Talon (p230), which always hums with activity.

Dubbed the 'new Plateau' by the exodus of students and artists seeking a more affordable, less polished haunt, the Mile End district has all the coolness of its predecessor as well as two phenomenal bagel shops, upscale dining along Ave Laurier and tons of increasingly trendy hangouts at its epicenter: Rue St-Viateur and Blvd St-Laurent.

Activities

CYCLING & IN-LINE SKATING

Montréal is a cyclist's haven.

One popular route parallels the Canal de Lachine for 14.5km, starting in Old Montréal and passing a lot of history en route. Picnic tables are scattered along the way, so pick up some tasty victuals at the fabulous **Marché Atwater** (**138 Ave Atwater; 7am-6pm Mon-Wed, to 7pm Thu, to 8pm Fri, to 5pm Sat & Sun; M Atwater**).

Ça Roule Montréal — Bicycle Rental

(**Map p218; www.caroulemontreal.com; 27 Rue de la Commune Est, Old Port; bicycles per hr/24hr $8/35, in-line skates 1st/additional hr $9/4; 9am-8pm Apr-Oct**) Nicely located near the Old Port, Ça Roule Montréal has a wide selection of bicycles, in-line skates, spare parts and a good repair shop.

ICE SKATING

Atrium — Skating

(**Map p218; www.le1000.com; 1000 Rue de la Gauchetière Ouest; adult/child $7.50/5, skate rentals $7; 11:30am-6pm Mon-Fri, 12:30-9pm Sat, to 6pm Sun**) Take to the ice any time the mood strikes at this gigantic, state-of-the-art glass-domed indoor rink in Montréal's tallest tower.

Lac des Castors — Skating

(**Map p216; Parc du Mont Royal; admission free, skate rentals per 2hr $8.50; 9am-9pm Sun-Thu, to 10pm Fri & Sat, weather permitting**) An excellent place for outdoor skating – it's nestled in the woods near a large parking lot and pavilion.

Tours

Le Bateau Mouche — Boat Tour

(**Map p218; 514-849-9952; www.bateau-mouche.ca; 1hr tours adult/child $24/12; 11am, 2:30pm & 4pm May-Oct**) Leaving from Quai Jacques Cartier, hour-long cruises aboard climate-controlled, glass-roofed boats explore the Old Port and Parc Jean-Drapeau. A 90-minute version ($28/15) departs at 12:30pm.

Guidatour — Walking Tour

(**Map p218; 514-844-4021; www.guidatour.qc.ca; tours $12.50-21; May-Oct**) Guidatour's bilingual guides spice up historical tours of Downtown (9:30am and 10:45am), East Old Montréal (11am and 12:30pm)

Quartier Latin

YVES MARCOUX/GETTY IMAGES ©

If You Like… Urban Oases

If you like Parc du Mont Royal, check out these other natural areas in Montréal.

1 **JARDIN BOTANIQUE & INSECTARIUM** (Map p216; www.espacepourlavie.ca; 4101 Rue Sherbrooke Est; adult/child $29.50/15; 9am-6pm; M Pie-IX) Montréal's Botanical Garden is the world's third largest after those in London and Berlin. Approximately 22,000 species of plants grow in 30 outdoor gardens. Highlights include the **First Nations Garden**, the **Insectarium** with its intriguing collection of bugs and the **Butterfly House**. The facility is northeast of central downtown by the Olympic Stadium (Stade Olympique).

2 **PARC JEAN-DRAPEAU** (Map p216; www.parcjeandrapeau.com) The site of the 1967 World's Fair, Parc Jean-Drapeau consists of two islands surrounded by the St Lawrence River: Île Ste-Hélène and Île Notre-Dame. Although nature is the park's main appeal, it's also home to a Vegas-size casino and scream-inducing La Ronde (p223) amusement park. **Ferries** (Quai Jacques Cartier; adult/child $7.50/free; mid-May–mid-Sep) shuttle pedestrians and bicycles to the park from the Old Port.

3 **CANAL DE LACHINE** (Map p216) The waterway stretches for 14.5km from the Old Port to Lac St-Louis. Its banks are a terrific park for cycling and walking.

and West Old Montréal (1:30pm and 3pm) with colorful tales and anecdotes. Tours depart from the Basilique Notre-Dame (p217) for Old Montréal, and from the Centre Infotouriste (p231) for Downtown.

Sleeping

Hotels fill up fast in the summer, when warm weather and festivals galore bring hordes of tourists to Montréal, making reservations essential.

The agencies **BBCanada** (www.bbcanada.com/quebec) and **BedandBreakfast.com** (www.bedandbreakfast.com/montreal-quebec.html), and the **Centre Infotouriste** (www.bonjourquebec.com), can help book accommodations.

OLD MONTRÉAL

Le Petit Hôtel Boutique Hotel **$$**
(Map p218; 514-940-0360, 877-530-0360; www.petithotelmontreal.com; 168 Rue St-Paul Ouest; r $169-299;) This 'small hotel' is indeed tiny, with only 24 small, medium, large and extra-large rooms, but it's *très* chic, with hardwood floors, colorful furniture and plenty of modern electronic gadgets.

Bonaparte Inn **$$**
(Map p218; 514-844-1448; www.bonaparte.com; 447 Rue St-François-Xavier; r $189-240, ste $355;) This elegant property exudes refined, classic European ambience, with wooden floors, Louis-Philippe furniture, French windows – some with views of the Basilique Notre-Dame – and exposed stone walls. After a satisfying three-course breakfast head up to the rooftop patio for snap-worthy views.

Hôtel Gault Boutique Hotel **$$$**
(Map p218; 514-904-1616, 866-904-1616; www.hotelgault.com; 449 Rue Ste-Hélène; r $220-750;) A design aficionado's haven, the Hôtel Gault features a soothing minimalist palette with polished concrete floors and steel accents, original 19th-century cast-iron columns and the occasional splash of warm blondwood. Custom-built beds, decadent linens, iPod docks, flatscreen TVs and heated bathroom floors add warmth and comfort to each of the 30 serenely stark loft-style rooms.

DOWNTOWN

Hotel Zero 1 Hotel **$$**
(Map p218; 514-871-9696; www.zero1-mtl.com; 1 Blvd René-Lévesque Est; r from $139;) This mixed condo/hotel development on the edge of Chinatown and near all the major summertime festivals is the closest Montréal comes to embracing the no-frills capsule-hotel idea. Minimalist

Montréal for Children

Children adore Montréal. The Olympic Park area is the ultimate kid-friendly zone: the **Biodôme** (Map p216; www.espacepourlavie.ca; 4777 Ave Pierre de Coubertin; adult/child $18.75/9.50; 9am-6pm; M Viau), home to porcupines, penguins and other local and exotic critters, is a sure winner, and the creepy crawlies at the Insectarium are sure to provide plenty of gasps and tickles.

Budding scientists will have a field day at the Centre des Sciences de Montréal (p215), which has dozens of interactive stations and video games, and space travelers can catch a show at the **Rio Tinto Planetarium** (Map p216; www.espacepourlavie.ca; 4801 Ave Pierre de Coubertin; adult/child $18.75/9.50; 9:30am-10:30pm). Many museums have special kid-oriented workshops and guided tours.

On nearby Île Ste-Hélène awaits **La Ronde** (Map p216; www.laronde.com; adult/child $49/43; hours vary) amusement park, where the stomach-churning roller coasters and other diversions are especially thrilling for teens.

There's ice skating all year long at the grand Atrium (p221), which offers special kids' sessions on Sundays until 11:30am.

rooms, with sleek black-and-white decor, are teeny tiny, but they don't scrimp on style.

Les Bons Matins B&B **$$**

(Map p218; 514-931-9167, 800-588-5280; www.bonsmatins.com; 1401 Ave Argyle; r $99-119, ste $149-169;) Charming and seductive, with exposed bricks and vibrant colors splashed across bedsheets and wall hangings, this classy establishment fills a series of adjoining turn-of-the-century step-ups. Breakfasts couldn't get better, with gourmet quiche, homemade waffles and Italian-style espresso. Parking is $12 per night.

Hôtel Le Germain Hotel **$$$**

(Map p218; 514-849-2050, 877-333-2050; www.germainmontreal.com; 2050 Rue Mansfield; r from $229;) An air of calm and sophistication greets you at this unassuming hotel just a stone's throw from the McGill University campus. Rooms are sexy, with crisp white linens, dark, attractive Québec-crafted furniture, and see-through showers (with

Canal de Lachine
BRIGITTE MERLE/GETTY IMAGES ©

The Plateau, Quartier Latin & The Village

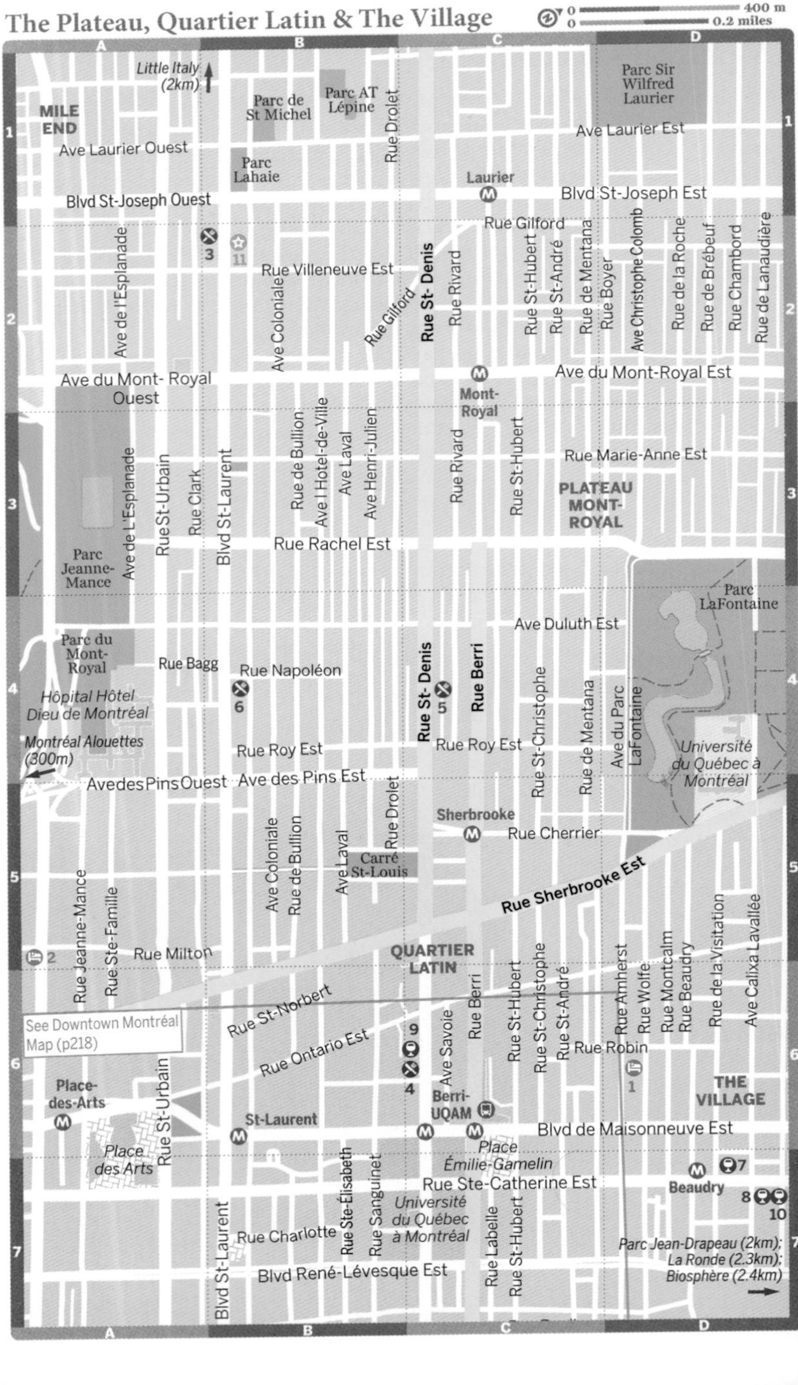

0 400 m
0 0.2 miles
A
B
C
D
1
2
3
4
5
6
7
Little Italy (2km)
MILE END
Parc de St Michel
Parc AT Lépine
Parc Sir Wilfred Laurier
Ave Laurier Ouest
Ave Laurier Est
Parc Lahaie
Rue Drolet
Laurier
Blvd St-Joseph Ouest
Blvd St-Joseph Est
Rue Gilford
3
11
Rue Villeneuve Est
Ave de l'Esplanade
Ave Coloniale
Rue Gilford
Rue St-Denis
Rue Rivard
Rue St-Hubert
Rue St-André
Rue de Mentana
Rue Boyer
Ave Christophe Colomb
Rue de la Roche
Rue de Brébeuf
Rue Chambord
Rue de Lanaudière
Ave du Mont- Royal Ouest
Ave du Mont-Royal Est
Mont-Royal
Rue de Bullion
Ave l Hotel-de-Ville
Ave Laval
Ave Henri-Julien
Rue Rivard
Rue St-Hubert
Rue Marie-Anne Est
Ave de L'Esplanade
Rue St-Urbain
Rue Clark
Blvd St-Laurent
PLATEAU MONT-ROYAL
Rue Rachel Est
Parc Jeanne-Mance
Parc LaFontaine
Ave Duluth Est
Parc du Mont-Royal
Rue Bagg
Rue Napoléon
Rue St-Denis
Rue Berri
Rue St-Christophe
Rue de Mentana
Ave du Parc LaFontaine
6
5
Hôpital Hôtel Dieu de Montréal
Montréal Alouettes (300m)
Rue Roy Est
Rue Roy Est
Université du Québec à Montréal
Ave des Pins Ouest
Ave des Pins Est
Rue Drolet
Sherbrooke
Rue Cherrier
Ave Coloniale
Rue de Bullion
Ave Laval
Carré St-Louis
Rue Sherbrooke Est
Rue Jeanne-Mance
Rue Ste-Famille
2
Rue Milton
QUARTIER LATIN
See Downtown Montréal Map (p218)
Rue St-Norbert
Rue Ontario Est
9
4
Ave Savoie
Rue Berri
Rue St-Hubert
Rue St-Christophe
Rue St-André
Rue Amherst
Rue Wolfe
Rue Montcalm
Rue Beaudry
Rue de la Visitation
Ave Calixa Lavallée
Rue Robin
1
THE VILLAGE
Place-des-Arts
Rue St-Urbain
St-Laurent
Berri-UQAM
Blvd de Maisonneuve Est
Place des Arts
Place Émilie-Gamelin
Rue Ste-Catherine Est
Beaudry
7
8
10
Rue Ste-Élisabeth
Rue Sanguinet
Université du Québec à Montréal
Blvd St-Laurent
Rue Charlotte
Rue Labelle
Rue St-Hubert
Blvd René-Lévesque Est
Parc Jean-Drapeau (2km); La Ronde (2.3km); Biosphère (2.4km)

The Plateau, Quartier Latin & The Village

Sleeping

1 La Loggia Art & Breakfast D6
2 Parc Suites A5

Eating

3 La Sala Rosa B2
4 Les 3 Brasseurs C6
5 L'Express C4
6 Schwartz's B4

Drinking & Nightlife

7 Aigle Noir D7
8 Le Drugstore D7
9 Le Saint Sulpice C6
10 Sky Pub & Club D7

Entertainment

11 Casa del Popolo B2

blinds for shy bathers). The free continental breakfast is a classy affair.

PLATEAU MONT-ROYAL

Parc Suites Hotel **$$**
(Map p224; ☎800-949-8630, 514-985-5656; www.parcsuites.com; 3463 Ave du Parc; ste $149-219; wi-fi) Totally revamped in 2006, these eight modern one-bedroom suites have all the creature comforts – air conditioning, two flatscreen TVs, wi-fi and free long-distance calls within North America. Kitchens are spacious and well-equipped, and thanks to the hotel's location in the heart of the student ghetto, there's a 24-hour grocery store, a 24-hour coffee shop and repertoire theater next door.

QUARTIER LATIN & THE VILLAGE

La Loggia Art & Breakfast B&B **$$**
(Map p224; ☎514-524-2493, 866-520-2493; www.laloggia.ca; 1637 Rue Amherst; r without/with bathroom from $105/145; air-con wi-fi) Although plain-looking from the exterior, the inside of this 19th-century townhouse in the Gay Village is anything but average. The artwork of co-host, Joel, brings the five modern guest rooms alive; a sprawling breakfast buffet prepared by his partner, Rob, is served in a leafy sculpture garden behind the house.

Eating

Downtown and especially the Plateau are a foodie's heaven. More than any other street, Blvd St-Laurent epitomizes the city's gastronomic wealth – from

Les 3 Brasseurs (p227)

RENAULT PHILIPPE/GETTY IMAGES ©

Below: Sandwich at Schwartz's; **Right:** Diners in Old Montréal
(BELOW) TIM DRAPER/GETTY IMAGES ©; (RIGHT) CHRIS CHEADLE/GETTY IMAGES ©

boisterous soup parlors in Chinatown to Schwartz's smoked meat emporium to funky Plateau trendsetters. Still further north looms Mile End, the birthplace of the famous Montréal bagel, and Little Italy, with its comfortable trattoria and not-to-be-missed Marché Jean Talon.

OLD MONTRÉAL

Olive + Gourmando Cafe $
(Map p218; www.oliveetgourmando.com; 351 Rue St-Paul Ouest; mains $5-10; ⏲8am-6pm Tue-Sat; 🌶) Push and shove (if necessary) through thick lunchtime crowds in this corner cafe for a little bit of heaven, as manifested in hot panini and sultry soups made with fresh, often organic produce. Leave room for the infamous chocolate brownies, infused with rich coffee.

Toqué! French $$$
(Map p218; ☎514-499-2084; www.restaurant-toque.com; 900 Place Jean-Paul-Riopelle; tasting menus $110; ⏲11:30am-2pm Tue-Thu, 5:30-10:30pm Tue-Sat) This restaurant is consistently touted as Montréal's top restaurant, with a long list of accolades that add credence to this claim. Chef Normand Laprise's seven-course tasting menu brings fresh Québec produce to the table in a symphony of taste ingenuity and flawless presentation. Reservations essential.

PLATEAU MONT-ROYAL

Schwartz's Sandwiches $
(Map p224; www.schwartzsdeli.com; 3895 Blvd St-Laurent; sandwiches $6-17; ⏲8am-12:30am Sun-Thu, to 1:30am Fri, to 2:30am Sat) Don't be deterred by the line that inevitably forms outside this legendary smoked-meat parlor. Join the eclectic clientele – from students to celebrities – at the communal tables, and don't forget to order the pickles, fries and coleslaw.

L'Express French $$
(Map p224; ☎514-845-5333; 3927 Rue St-Denis; mains $15-29; ⏲8am-2am Mon-Fri, from 10am Sat & Sun) This place is so fantastically

French, you half expect to see the Eiffel Tower out the window, especially after guzzling too much of the excellent wines. The food's classic Parisian bistro – think *steak frites,* bouillabaisse, tarragon chicken – and so is the attitude. Reservations essential.

La Sala Rosa Spanish **$$**
(Map p224; 4848 Blvd St-Laurent; mains $12-15; 5-11pm Tue-Thu & Sun, to midnight Fri & Sat;) Wash down flavorful tapas and every shade of paella with a pitcher of sangria in this unique restaurant, which shares a floor with the Spanish Social Club. Thursdays see free flamenco dance performances.

QUARTIER LATIN & THE VILLAGE

Les 3 Brasseurs Alsatian **$$**
(Map p224; www.les3brasseurs.ca; 1658 Rue St-Denis; mains $11-14; 11:30am-midnight) If you'd like to cap a day of sightseeing with belly-filling fare and a few pints of handcrafted beer, stop by this convivial brewpub, with stylized warehouse looks and a rooftop terrace. The house specialty is *flammekeuche*, a French spin on pizza.

LITTLE ITALY & MILE END

Pastaga Québecois **$$**
(438-381-6389; www.pastaga.ca; 6389 Blvd St-Laurent; small dishes $13-16; 11:30am-2pm Fri, 10am-2pm Sat & Sun & 5-10pm daily) Creative small dishes are great for sharing at this laid-back, yet up-to-the-minute trend-setting restaurant whose name is a play on 'pastis.' There are three dining areas: choose a spot at the front window, sink into a massive banquette in the middle, or perch at a table in the kitchen, in the middle of the action.

Lucca Italian **$$$**
(514-278-6502; 12 Rue Dante; mains $18-36; noon-2:30pm Mon-Fri & 6-10pm Mon-Sat; M De Castelnau) This hot little Italian number is on the speed dial of many Montréal foodies. The menu, put together daily from market-fresh ingredients and

Gay & Lesbian Montréal

Montréal is one of Canada's gayest cities, with the rainbow flag flying especially proudly in The Village along Rue St-Catherine between Rue St-Hubert and Rue Dorion. Dozens of high-energy bars, cafes, restaurants, saunas and clubs flank this strip, turning it pretty much into a 24/7 fun zone. The authoritative guide to the gay and lesbian scene is **Fugues** (www.fugues.com), a free monthly mag found throughout the Village.

Bars and clubs worth checking out include the following:

Sky Pub & Club (Map p224; ☎514-529-6969; 1474 Rue Ste-Catherine Est) Huge place with rooftop terrace complete with Jacuzzi and pool.

Aigle Noir (Map p224; ☎514-529-0040; 1315 Rue Ste-Catherine Est) For the leather-and-fetish crowd.

Le Drugstore (Map p224; ☎514-524-1960; 1360 Rue Ste-Catherine Est) Fun-seekers of every persuasion will be satisfied on at least one of the six multithemed floors.

written on a chalkboard, ranges from classics to adventurous culinary spins. It's *la dolce vita*, Québec style. Rue Dante is just off Blvd St-Laurent, south of Rue Jean-Talon. Reservations recommended.

Drinking & Nightlife

Le Ste-Elisabeth Pub

(Map p218; www.ste-elisabeth.com; 1412 Rue Ste-Elisabeth; ⏲4pm-3am Mon-Fri, from 6pm Sat & Sun) Microbrews, imported Euro beers and quality Scotch sing their sweet siren song to the low-key crowd at this popular pub. It's a pretty place with a lovely garden overlooked by an upstairs terrace.

Brutopia Brewery

(Map p218; www.brutopia.net; 1219 Rue Crescent; ⏲3pm-3am Sat-Thu, noon-3am Fri) Boisterous and brick-lined Brutopia brews its own beer, including its outstanding India Pale Ale, in sparkling copper vats right behind the bar. A friendly young crowd invades nightly, not least for the live bands.

Le Saint Sulpice Pub

(Map p224; www.lesaint-sulpice.ca; 1680 Rue St-Denis; ⏲1pm-3am) On a hot summer night, a cool

Drinkers in a Montréal bar
GUYLAIN DOYLE/GETTY IMAGES ©

place to be is the huge beer garden of this always bustling hangout. There's great people-watching potential here, as well as in the cafe, which has three terraces and a disco. Did we mention the place was huge?

Entertainment

LIVE MUSIC

Casa del Popolo Live Music

(Map p224; www.casadelpopolo.com; 4873 Blvd St-Laurent; noon-late) Low-key and funky, this cafe-bar/art gallery/performance venue usually has several live music and spoken-word events scheduled in three locations. The cafe serves fair-trade coffee and vegetarian fare.

Metropolis Live Music

(Map p218; 514-844-3500; www.montreal-metropolis.ca; 59 Rue Ste-Catherine Est) Of its many faces (a skating rink, a porn movie theater and disco, among others), rock venue suits this 2300-person-capacity concert hall best. The stage was graced by the likes of Radiohead, David Bowie and Coldplay earlier in their careers.

Upstairs Jazz

(Map p218; 514-931-6808; www.upstairsjazz.com; 1254 Rue Mackay; 11:30am-1am Mon-Fri, 5pm-1am Sat, 6:30pm-1am Sun) Some mighty fine talent, both home-grown and imported, has tickled the ivories of the baby grand in this intimate jazz joint. Shows start at 10pm.

THEATER & DANCE

Cirque du Soleil Theater

(Map p218; www.cirquedusoleil.com) For the past two decades, this phenomenally successful troupe has redefined what circuses are all about. Headquartered in Montréal, it usually inaugurates new shows in the city every year or two. Check with the tourist office.

SPORTS

Montréal Canadiens Hockey

(Map p218; 514-932-2582; www.canadiens.com; Bell Centre, 1200 Rue de la Gauchetière Ouest; tickets $29-260) Bell Centre is home base for this National Hockey League team and 24-time Stanley Cup winners (the last time in 1993). Although they have struggled in recent years,

Local Knowledge

Montréal Jazz Festival

RECOMMENDATIONS FROM ANDRÉ MÉNARD, FESTIVAL CO-FOUNDER AND ARTISTIC DIRECTOR

1 GESÙ

My favorite small club to see a show at the festival is **Gesù** (514-861-4378; www.legesu.com; 1200 Bleury Ave). Contemporary jazz is featured there. It's in the stone-walled basement of a church that dates from the mid-19th century. The acoustics are great, and you're close to the stage.

2 METROPOLIS

Metropolis (p229) is a massive rock club that is my favorite big venue. It's an old opera house where we hold reggae and world-music shows. There's a huge dance floor downstage, while the balcony is a different scene with bars, tables and chairs. It has flair combined with excellent sightlines and sound for such a large theater.

3 L'ASTRAL

L'Astral (www.sallelastral.com; 305 Ste-Catherine St Ouest) is the 'house' and meeting place of the festival, where jam sessions and surprise players from the stages show up between midnight and 3am each night. The festival actually owns the venue, and it's open year-round hosting performances.

4 PLACE DES FESTIVALS

This is the main outdoor space for free shows, where up to 100,000 people attend concerts by the likes of the B-52s (in 2011), Rufus Wainwright (in 2012) and Feist (in 2013). We just added the plaza a few years ago, for the festival's 30th anniversary. Here, as elsewhere throughout the event, there is no VIP area. The public is the VIP. It's a very democratic festival!

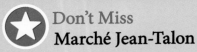

GUYLAIN DOYLE/GETTY IMAGES ©

Don't Miss
Marché Jean-Talon

The gem of Little Italy, this kaleidoscopic market is perfect for assembling a gourmet picnic or for partaking in a little afternoon grazing. A great stop is **Marché des Saveurs**, devoted entirely to Québec specialties such as wine and cider, fresh cheeses, smoked meats and preserves. The market sprawls south of Rue Jean-Talon between Blvd St-Laurent and Rue St-Denis.

NEED TO KNOW

Map p216; 7075 Ave Casgrain; ⏲7am-6pm Mon-Wed & Sat, to 8pm Thu & Fri, to 5pm Sun; M Jean-Talon

Montréalers still have a soft spot for the 'Habs' and games routinely sell out. After the first drop of the puck you might be able to snag a half-price ticket from the scalpers lurking by the entrance.

Shopping

Ogilvy Clothing

(Map p218; www.ogilvycanada.com; 1307 Rue Ste-Catherine Ouest; ⏲10am-6pm Mon-Wed, to 9pm Thu & Fri, 9am-5pm Sat, noon-5pm Sun) Dripping with tradition, this Victorian-era department store stocks all the top international labels. Be sure to visit the historic concert hall on the 5th floor. Since 1927, a kilt-clad bagpiper has roamed the store daily at noon.

Galerie Le Chariot Art

(Map p218; 446 Place Jacques Cartier; ⏲10am-6pm) This three-level gallery specializes in museum-quality Inuit art, primarily soapstone sculptures. Each piece has been authenticated by the Canadian government.

Parasuco Clothing

(Map p218; www.parasuco.com; 1414 Rue Crescent; 9:30am-9pm Mon-Fri, to 6pm Sat, 11am-6pm Sun) Made right here in Montréal, Parasuco has become one of Canada's hottest labels for jeans and casual wear. Its high-energy flagship store stocks all the latest styles.

Information

Centre Infotouriste (Map p218; www.bonjourquebec.com; 1255 Rue Peel; 8:30am-7pm) Free hotel, tour and car reservations, plus currency exchange.

Montréal Tourist Office (Map p218; www.tourism-montreal.org; 174 Rue Notre-Dame Est; 10am-7pm Apr-Oct) Just off bustling Place Jacques Cartier, this little office is always humming and staff are extremely helpful.

Getting There & Away

Air

Both domestic and international airlines land at **Pierre Elliott Trudeau International Airport** (YUL; 514-394-7377, 800-465-1213; www.admtl.com), formerly known as Dorval Airport, about 20km west of downtown.

Bus

Buses to the airports and to Canadian and US destinations depart from the **Station Centrale de l'Autobus** (Central Bus Station; Map p224; 514-842-2281; 505 Blvd de Maisonneuve Est).

Train

Montréal's **Gare Centrale** (Central Train Station; Map p218; 895 Rue de la Gauchetière Ouest) is the local hub for **VIA Rail** (888-842-7245; www.viarail.ca). There are six trains daily to Toronto ($135, 4½ hours) on immaculate trains fitted with wi-fi connection and a beverage service.

Getting Around

To/From the Airport

STM (p232), the city's public transportation system, runs two bus lines from Montréal Trudeau to downtown. Rte 747 (one-way $9 in exact change, one hour) is the express service to downtown, with stops at Lionel-Groulx métro station, the central train station and Berri-UQAM métro station. The service runs every 12 minutes from 8:30am to 8pm, every half-hour from 5:30am to 8:30am and from 8pm to 1am, and hourly between 2am and 5am.

A taxi to/from Trudeau airport costs a flat rate of $40.

Clothing shop in Montréal

CHRIS CHEADLE/GETTY IMAGES ©

If You Like... Mountain Villages

If you like Ville de Mont-Tremblant, stoke your mountain high in these other Laurentian communities.

1 **ST-SAUVEUR**
(www.mssi.ca) St-Sauveur-des-Monts, or St-Sauveur for short, is the busiest village in the Laurentians and is often deluged with day-trippers thanks to its proximity to Montréal (60km). A pretty church anchors Rue Principale, the attractive main street, and is flanked by restaurants, cafes and boutiques. Mont St-Sauveur and four other ski hills provide excellent runs for all levels of expertise. In summer, water park action takes over.

2 **VAL-DAVID**
(www.valdavid.com) Val-David is a pint-size village with an almost lyrical quality and a gorgeous setting along the Rivière du Nord and at the foot of the mountains. Its charms have made it a magnet for artists, whose studios and galleries line the main street, Rue de L'Église. Outfitters rent bicycles, kayaks and canoes, and offer cycle-canoe packages and guided tours on the Rivière du Nord. Rock climbing is also big business.

Public Transportation

Montréal has a modern and convenient bus and métro system run by **STM** **(www.stm.info)**. The métro is the city's subway system and runs quickly and quietly on rubber tires. It operates until at least 12:30am. Some buses provide service all night.

Tickets cost $3 but are cheaper in packages of ten ($24.50). There are also 'Tourist Cards' for $9/18 for one/three days (also valid for the express Rte 747 to the airport).

Note that bus drivers don't give change.

THE LAURENTIANS

The Laurentians, or Les Laurentides in French, are perhaps the best-kept secret of Montréal day-trippers and are just an hour's drive from the city. Here you'll find yourself amid gentle rolling mountains, crystal blue lakes and meandering rivers peppered with towns and villages too cute for words. A visit to this natural paradise is like putting your feet up after a long day.

Nearly all towns in the Laurentians can be accessed via Hwy 15, the Autoroute des Laurentides. Old Rte 117, running parallel to it, is slow but considerably more scenic.

Information

Association Touristique des Laurentides **(Laurentian Tourist Association; ☎450-436-8532, reservation service 450-436-3507; www.laurentides.com; ⏲9am-5pm)** Regional tourist office; can answer questions on the phone, make room bookings and mail out information.

Ville de Mont-Tremblant

The Mont-Tremblant area is the crown jewel of the Laurentians, lorded over by the 968m-high eponymous mountain and dotted with pristine lakes and traversed by rivers. It's a hugely popular four-season playground, drawing ski bums from late October to mid-April, and hikers, bikers, golfers, water sports fans and other outdoor enthusiasts the rest of the year.

The area of Ville de Mont-Tremblant is divided into three sections: **Station Tremblant**, the ski hill and pedestrianized tourist resort at the foot of the mountain; **Mont-Tremblant Village**, a sweet and tiny cluster of homes and businesses about 4km southwest of here; and **St-Jovite**, the main town and commercial center off Rte 117, about 12km south of the mountain.

Sights & Activities

Station Tremblant **(www.tremblant.com; half-/full-day lift tickets $57/76)**, founded in 1938, is among the top-ranked international ski resorts in eastern North America according to *Ski* magazine and legions of loyal fans. The mountain has a vertical drop of 645m and is laced with

95 trails and three snow parks served by 14 lifts, including an express gondola. Ski rentals start at $32 per day.

A summer attraction is the **Skyline Luge** (1/3/5 rides $11/20/26), which snakes down the mountain for 1.4km; daredevils can reach speeds up to 50km/h. The nearby **Activity Centre** (✆891-681-4848; www.tremblantactivities.com; 9am-6pm) can arrange for a wide variety of outdoor pursuits, from fishing to canoeing to horseback riding; inquire here also for more information about the Scandinavian-style spa, dune buggy trails, zip lines, rock climbing, paintball, and helicopter tours.

The southern mountain base spills over into a sparkling **pedestrian tourist village**, with big hotels, shops, restaurants and an amusement park atmosphere.

Sleeping & Eating

Homewood Suites Hotel $$

(✆819-681-0808; www.homewoodsuites.com; 3035 Chemin de la Chapelle; ste from $139;) Smack dab in the middle of the tourist pedestrian village, in the heart of all the action in both summer and winter (the ski gondola is 500m from the door), this homey chain has great-value suites with stunning mountain views, spiffy decor and basic hot breakfasts.

Auberge Le Lupin B&B $$

(✆819-425-5474, 877-425-5474; www.lelupin.com; 127 Rue Pinoteau, Mont-Tremblant Village; r $108-157;) This 1940s log house offers snug digs just 1km away from the ski station, with private beach access to the sparkling Lac Tremblant. The tasty breakfasts whipped up by host Pierre in

Montréal to Québec City & Around

0 50 km
0 25 miles

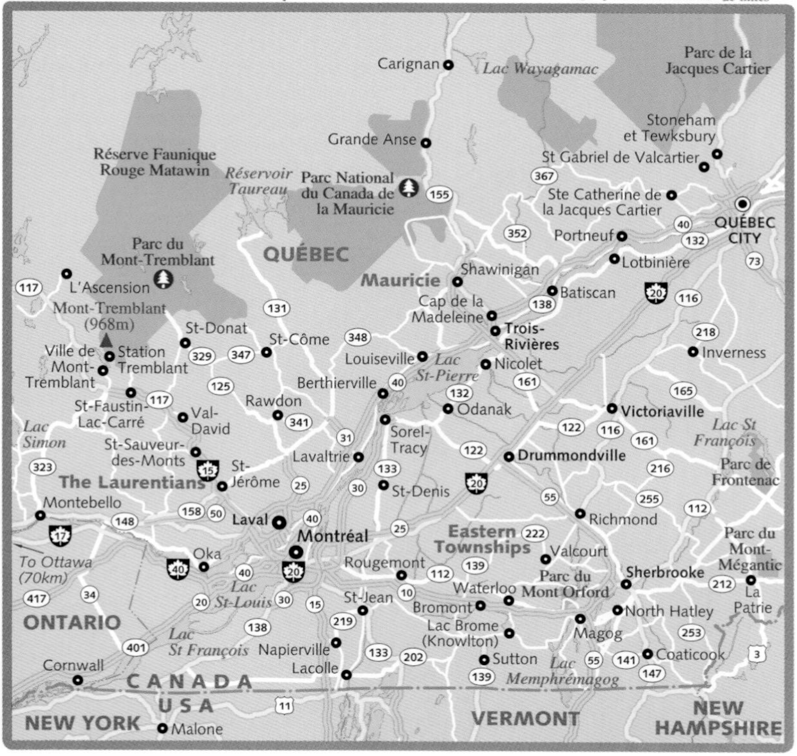

his homey rustic kitchen are a perfect start to the day.

Microbrasserie La Diable Pub **$$**
(www.microladiable.com; Station Tremblant; mains $12-27; ⏲11:30am-2am) After a day of tearing down the mountain, the hearty sausages, burgers and pastas served at this lively tavern at Station Tremblant fill the belly nicely, as do the tasty home brews.

sEb Modern Canadian **$$$**
(☎819-429-6991; www.seblartisanculinaire.com; 444 Rue St-Georges, St-Jovite; mains $27-36, meals from $45; ⏲6-11pm Wed-Sun) Escape the mediocre and get a little taste of what local culinary artisans can create with seasonal, sustainable local ingredients. A flexible, eager-to-please kitchen, an unforgettable menu, and a never-ending wine list enhance the jovial atmosphere here that can be best described as alpine chalet meets globetrotter (think African masks) meets Hollywood chic (Michael Douglas is a regular). Reservations essential.

Information

Mont-Tremblant Tourism (☎819-425-3300; www.tourismemonttremblant.com) St-Jovite (**☎800-322-2932; www.tourismemonttremblant.com; 48 Chemin de Brébeuf**); Mont-Tremblant Village (**☎877-425-2434; www.tourismemonttremblant.com; 5080 Montée Ryan, cnr Rte 327**); Station Tremblant (**☎800-322-2932; www.tourismemonttremblant.com; Place des Voyageurs**).

Getting Around

A shuttle bus ($3) connects Station Tremblant, Mont-Tremblant Village and St-Jovite from 6am to 8pm Sunday to Thursday and 6am to 11pm on Friday and Saturday.

QUÉBEC CITY

Québec, North America's only walled city north of Mexico City, is the kind of place that crops up in trivia questions. Over the centuries, the lanes and squares of the Old Town – a World Heritage site – have seen the continent's first parish church, first museum, first stone church, first Anglican cathedral, first girls' school, first business district and first French-language university.

Once past Le Château Frontenac, the most photographed hotel in the world, you'll find yourself torn between the various neighborhoods' diverse charms. In Old Upper Town, the historical hub, many excellent museums and restaurants hide among the tacky fleur-de-lis T-shirt stores. Old Lower Town, at the base of the steep cliffs, is a labyrinth, where it's a pleasure to get lost among street performers and cozy inns before emerging on the north shore of the St Lawrence River. Leaving

Ville de Mont-Tremblant (p232)
KEN GILLESPIE/DESIGN PICS/GETTY IMAGES ©

Québec City Overview

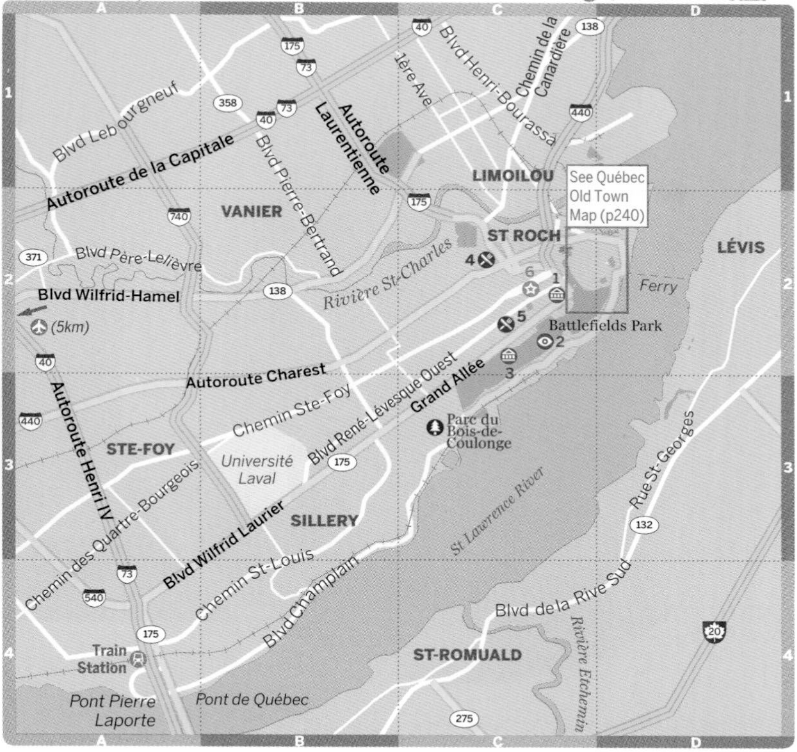

Québec City Overview

Sights

1 Hôtel du Parlement C2
2 Martello Tower 1 .... C2
3 Musée National des Beaux-Arts du Québec C2

Eating

4 Café du Clocher Penché C2
5 Le Cochon Dingue C2

Entertainment

6 Fou-Bar C2

the walled town near the star-shaped Citadelle, hip St-Jean-Baptiste is one of the less historical but still interesting areas, and the epicenter of a vibrant nightlife.

Sights

OLD UPPER TOWN

Fortifications of Québec — Historic Site

(Map p240; www.pc.gc.ca/eng/lhn-nhs/qc/fortifications; Rue d'Auteuil, near Rue St-Louis; guided walks adult/child $10/5; 10am-6pm May-Oct, guided walks 10am & 2pm; 3, 11) The largely restored old wall is a national historic site. You can walk the 4.6km circuit on top of it all around the Old Upper Town, with much of the city's history within easy view. At the old powder magazine beside Porte St-Louis, the **interpretive center** (Map p240; 100 Rue St-Louis; adult/child $4/2, walking tours adult/child $10/5; 10am-6pm May-Oct) examines the city's defenses through displays, models and a short film. The center's

Below: Guard at La Citadelle; **Right:** Québec's Old Town

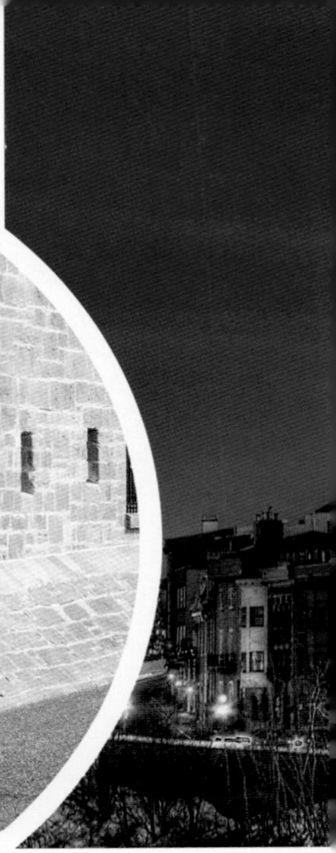

enthusiastic guides run 90-minute **walking tours** from here and the Kiosk Frontenac.

La Citadelle — Fort

(Map p240; ☎418-694-2815; www.lacitadelle.qc.ca; Côte de la Citadelle, Fort; adult/child $10/5.50; ⏰9am-5pm) The Citadelle is the base of Canada's Royal 22s (known in bastardized French as the Van Doos, from the French for 22, vingt-deux). Founded in WWI, the regiment earned three Victoria Crosses in that conflict and in WWII.

The changing of the guard ceremony takes place at 10am each day in the summer months. The beating of the retreat, which features soldiers banging on their drums at shift's end, happens at 7pm on Friday, Saturday and Sunday during July and August.

The dominating Citadelle is North America's largest fort, covering 2.3 sq km. Begun by the French in 1750 and completed by the British in 1850, it served as part of the defense system against an American invasion that never came.

Admission to the site is by one-hour guided tour, which takes in the regimental museum, numerous historical sites and a cannon called Rachel. Tours depart regularly during the summer; from late October to early April, there's only one tour a day, at 1:30pm. A separate tour of the **Governor General's Residence** **(Map p240; ⏰11am-4pm daily Jul & Aug, 10am-4pm Sat & Sun May, Jun, Sep & Oct)** FREE is also available.

LATIN QUARTER

Basilica Notre-Dame-de-Québec — Church

(Map p240; ☎418-694-0665; 16 Rue de Buade; ⏰8:30am-6pm) This cathedral towers above the site of a chapel erected by Samuel de Champlain in 1633. It became one of the continent's first cathedrals in 1674, following the appointment of the first bishop of Québec, Monseigneur de Laval, whose tomb is inside. Ever bigger replacements were constructed over the

centuries, with the last being completed in 1925. The grandiose interior recreates the spirit of the 17th century.

OLD LOWER TOWN

From Upper Town, you can reach this must-see area in several ways. Walk down Côte de la Canoterie from Rue des Ramparts to the Old Port, or edge down the charming and steep Côte de la Montagne. About halfway down on the right, a shortcut, the Break-Neck Stairs (Escalier Casse-Cou) leads down to Rue du Petit-Champlain. You can also take the **funicular** ($2 one-way) from Terrasse Dufferin.

Teeming **Rue du Petit-Champlain** is said to be, along with Rue Sous-le-Cap, the narrowest street in North America, and is the center of the continent's oldest business district. Look out for the murals decorating the 17th- and 18th-century buildings, which, along with numerous plaques, statues and street performers, give this quarter its distinct, history-meets-holiday feel.

Place Royale, Old Lower Town's central, principal square, has had an eventful 402 years. When Samuel de Champlain founded Québec City, he settled this bit of shoreline first. In 1690 cannons placed here held off the attacks of the English naval commander Phips and his men. Today the name 'Place Royale' generally refers to the district.

Built around the old harbor, north of Place Royale, the **Vieux Port** (Old Port) is being redeveloped as a multipurpose waterfront area.

Musée de la Civilisation Museum
(Museum of Civilization; Map p240; ☎418-643-2158; www.mcq.org; 85 Rue Dalhousie; adult/child $15/5, admission free Tue Nov-May & 10am-noon Sat Jan & Feb; ⏰9:30am-6:30pm) This museum offers a dozen exhibitions in its airy halls, including permanent shows on the culture of Québec's 11 Aboriginal peoples, and tells the province's story from the French settlers to today's distinct society. Quirky displays, videos and interactive features bring the weighty subjects to

CHRIS CHEADLE/GETTY IMAGES ©

Don't Miss
Le Château Frontenac

Said to be the world's most photographed hotel, Le Château Frontenac was built in 1893 by the Canadian Pacific Railway (CPR) as part of its chain of luxury hotels. During WWII, Prime Minister MacKenzie King, Winston Churchill and Franklin Roosevelt planned D-Day here. Facing the hotel along Rue Mont-Carmel is **Jardin des Gouverneurs**, with a monument to both Wolfe and Montcalm.

NEED TO KNOW

Map p240; 1 Rue des Carrières

life. The striking building incorporates some pre-existing structures; it shares an early-18th-century wall with Auberge Saint-Antoine.

Église Notre-Dame-des-Victoires Church

(Our Lady of Victories Church; Map p240; ☎418-692-1650; 32 Rue Sous-le-Fort; 🕘9:30am-8:30pm Jul & Aug, to 5pm May & Jun) Our Lady of Victories Church is the oldest stone church in North America, built in 1688 and devastated by cannon fire in 1759. It stands on the spot where Samuel de Champlain set up his 'Habitation,' a small stockade. Inside are copies of works by Rubens and van Dyck.

Centre d'Interprétation de Place-Royale Museum

(Map p240; ☎418-646-3167; 27 Rue Notre-Dame; adult/child $7/2; 🕘9:30am-5pm) This interpretive center touts the area as the cradle of French history in North America with a series of good participatory displays. While here, pick up a brochure on Place Royale's 27 vaulted cellars (ancient stone basements), five of which can be visited for free, including the one right here, complete with costumed barrel-maker.

OUTSIDE THE WALLS

Hôtel du Parlement — Historic Building

(Parliament Building; Map p235; ☎418-643-7239; cnr Ave Honoré Mercier & Grande Allée Est; ⏱9am-4:30pm) FREE Just across from Porte St-Louis is the Parliament Building. The Second Empire structure, dating from 1886, houses the Provincial Legislature, known as the Assemblée Nationale. Its facade is decorated with 22 bronze statues of significant historical Québecois figures, made by much-loved Québecois sculptor Louis-Philippe Hébert. Admission (at door three) is by half-hour tour, available in French, English and Spanish.

Battlefields Park — Historic Site

Though it looks like any urban North American park, this was once a bloody battleground where the course of Canadian history was determined. The part closest to the cliff is known as the **Plains of Abraham**, where the British finally defeated the French in 1759.

Within the park are diverse sites. The reception center at the **Discovery Pavilion** (☎418-648-4071; 835 Ave Wilfrid-Laurier; ⏱8:30am-5:30pm) is a good place to start. It contains a tourist office and the **Canada Odyssey** (adult/child $14/4; ⏱10am-5pm), a 45-minute multimedia spectacle. After covering life before and after the battle, the odyssey concludes with an exhibition on the lot of the soldiers who fought in the battle and on the park itself, used in the 18th and 19th centuries for executions, pistol duels and prostitution. Admission includes a bus tour and entry to **Martello Tower 1** (Map p235; ☎418-648-4071; adult/child $14/4; ⏱9:30am-5:30pm).

Musée National des Beaux-Arts du Québec — Museum

(Map p235; ☎866-220-2150, 418-643-2150; www.mnba.qc.ca; Battlefields Park; adult/child $18/free; ⏱10am-6pm Thu-Tue, to 9pm Wed) Visit this sprawling museum in Battlefields Park to see the province's most important collections of Québecois art and Inuit sculptures, as well as international work.

St-Jean-Baptiste — Neighborhood

Strolling along **Rue St-Jean** is a great way to feel the pulse of this bohemian area. The first thing that strikes you, once you've recovered from crossing busy Ave Honoré Mercier, is the area's down-to-earth attitude. Good restaurants, hip bars and interesting shops, some catering to a gay clientele, line the thoroughfare as far as Rue Racine.

To the southwest, the colorful **Ave Cartier** has exploded in recent years with hip eateries, cafes and boutiques.

St-Jean-Baptiste is about 1km northwest of the Fortifications of Québec interpretive center (p235).

Interior of Église Notre-Dame-des-Victoires
KEN GILLESPIE/DESIGN PICS/GETTY IMAGES ©

Québec Old Town

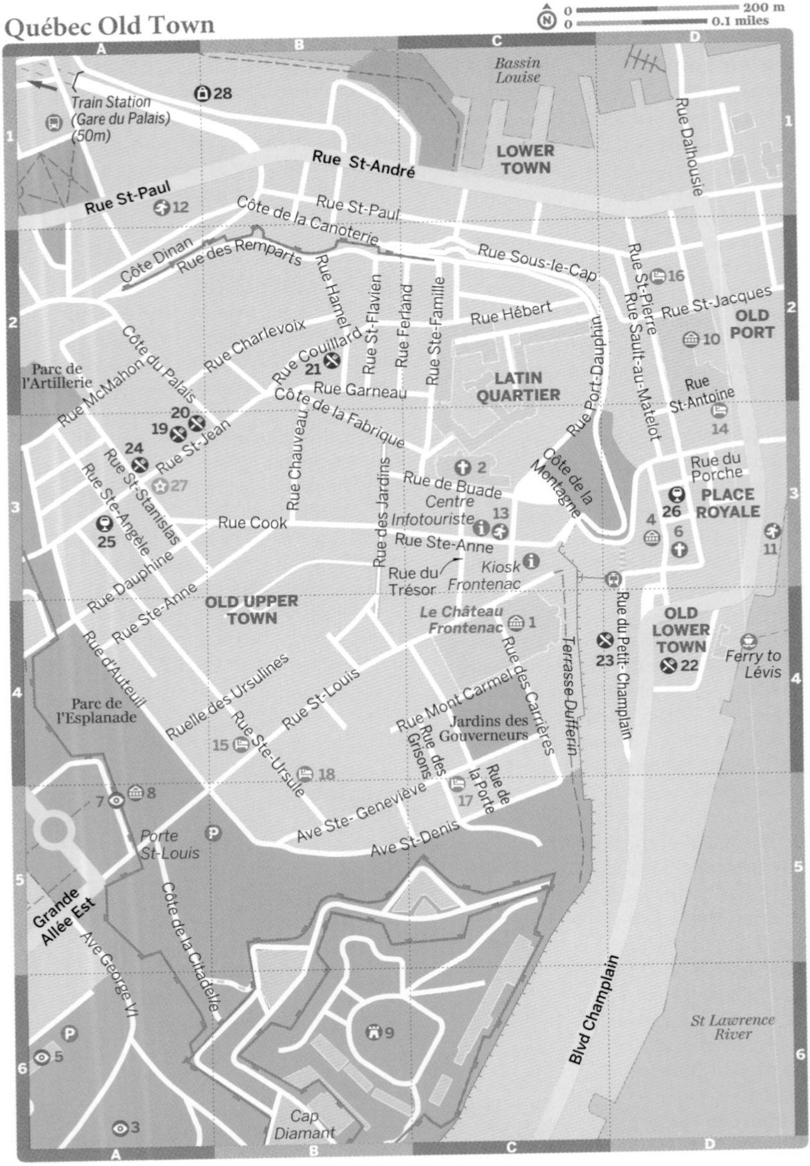

Activities

Cyclo Services Cycling

(Map p240; ☎418-692-4052, 877-692-4050; www.cycloservices.net; 289 Rue St-Paul; bicycles per 2hr/24hr $15/35; ⏰8:30am-8pm) This shop rents bikes and organizes excellent cycle tours of the city and outskirts, available in English. It has good cycling maps covering the vicinity.

Québec Old Town

Tours

Boat Tours Cruise

Operators **Croisières AML** (Map p240; ☎866-856-6668; www.croisieresaml.com; Quai Chouinard) and **Groupe Dufour Croisières** (☎418-692-0222; www.dufour.ca) cruise downriver to Montmorency Falls and Île d'Orléans from near Place Royale.

Les Services Historiques Six Associés Walking Tour

(☎418-692-3033; www.sixassocies.com; 1½-hr walking tours $17) Costumed guides lead excellent walking circuits, such as the ever-popular 'Lust and Drunkenness,' which creaks open the rusty door on the history of alcohol and prostitution in the city. Other tours, offered in English and French, focus on epidemics and crimes. A cheery bunch, they are. Reservations must be made in advance, by phone, email or via an online form.

Sleeping

The best options are the small, European-style hotels scattered around the Old Town.

Look for a room before 2pm or reserve ahead. Midsummer and the winter Carnaval are especially busy times.

OLD UPPER TOWN

Maison Historique James Thompson B&B $$

(Map p240; ☎418-694-9042; www.bedandbreakfastquebec.com; 47 Rue Ste-Ursule; r $75-135) History buffs will get a real kick out of staying in the 18th-century former residence of James Thompson, a veteran of the Battle of the Plains of Abraham. Spacious rooms are bright, with host Guitta's cheerful artwork; and it's easy to while away an afternoon chatting with host Greg, who has a wealth of knowledge on all things Québec and historical.

La Marquise de Bassano Inn $$

(Map p240; ☎418-692-0316, 877-692-0316; www.marquisedebassano.com; 15 Rue des Grisons; r $109-185; @) Rooms sporting canopy beds, claw-foot tubs or a rooftop deck are part of the allure of this serene Victorian house, run by young, gregarious owners. The sweet scent of fresh-baked croissants for breakfast will have you up before the alarm clock.

Detour: Ice Hotel

Located half an hour's drive from central Québec City, the **Hôtel de Glace** (r from $259) first opened its cool, blue doors in 2001, following similar Scandinavian establishments.

Yes, almost everything is made of ice (hot tubs and fireplaces are two understandable exceptions). This architectural feat strikes you, like an ice mallet, as soon as you step into the entrance hall: tall, sculpted columns of ice support a ceiling where a crystal chandelier hangs, and carved sculptures, tables and chairs line the endless corridors. Your bed will also be made of ice, but you can stay cozy and warm thanks to thick Arctic sleeping bags laid on lush deer pelts.

The 3000-sq-meter structure's public areas include exhibition rooms, a chapel, a sugar shack, a slide and an ice bar with DJ. The hotel melts in the spring and has to be rebuilt every winter, a job that takes five weeks, 12,000 tons of snow and 400 tons of ice.

The ice hotel offers several packages, starting at $600 per double, including a welcome vodka, dinner and breakfast. If you're not staying, simply take the tour (adult/child $17.50/8.75). To get to the hotel, take Rte 73 North and get off at Exit 154 toward Rue de la Faune.

Chez Hubert B&B $$
(Map p240; ☎418-692-0958; www.chezhubert.com; 66 Rue Ste-Ursule; s incl breakfast $60-85, d $80-120; @ wi-fi) This dependable choice is in a Victorian townhouse with chandeliers, stained-glass windows and oriental rugs. One of the three tasteful rooms has a view of the Château Frontenac.

OLD LOWER TOWN

Auberge Saint-Antoine Boutique Hotel $$$
(Map p240; ☎418-692-2211; www.saint-antoine.com; 8 Rue St-Antoine; r $199-999; air-con @ wi-fi) History and modernity are ecstatically married in this hotel, where understated contemporary luxuries enhance one of the city's most significant archaeological sites. A daily tour takes in the 700 artifacts on display, discovered when the heated underground car park was installed.

In the original, 250-year-old part of the complex, the rooms and historical suites are stacked with antique furniture and personality.

Hôtel Le Germain-Dominion Boutique Hotel $$$
(Map p240; ☎418-692-2224, 888-833-5253; www.germaindominion.com; 126 Rue St-Pierre; r $189-315; air-con @ wi-fi) This winner by local luxury chain, Groupe Germain, tucked away in a cozy spot in the heart of the Lower Town, hits high notes with fresh, modern decor, a never-ending list of amenities and flawless customer service.

Eating

For the best bargains, get the table d'hôte, especially at lunch.

OLD UPPER TOWN

Chez Temporel Cafe $
(Map p240; ☎418-694-1813; 25 Rue Couillard; mains $11-17; ⏲7am-1:30am Sun-Thu, to 2:30am Fri & Sat) For a sandwich or leisurely breakfast of a perfect café au lait and fresh croissants, you can't beat this Parisian-style hideaway. Later in the day, it's the province of solitary book readers and wistful music.

Casse Crêpe Breton Creperie $

(Map p240; ☎418-692-0438; cassecrepebreton.com; 1136 Rue St-Jean; crepes $4.50-8.75, mains $10; ⏰7am-9:30pm; ☑) Small and unassuming, this find dishes up hot, fresh crepes of every kind. Some diners like to sit at the counter and watch the chef at work.

Chez Ashton Fast Food $

(Map p240; ☎418-692-3055; 54 Côte du Palais; mains $5-10; ⏰11am-11:30pm Sun-Wed, to 4am Thu-Sat) This snack bar is one of the establishments that claims to have invented poutine. It's popular throughout the day and night for all varieties of poutine, burgers and subs.

Le Patriarche Fusion $$$

(Map p240; ☎418-692-5488; www.lepatriarche.com; 17 Rue St-Stanislas; mains $42-50; ⏰5:30-10pm) The nouvelle cuisine at this top-class restaurant is complemented by the contemporary art on the 180-year-old stone walls. On the menu (which is stocked almost entirely with local products), starters include foie gras and buffalo tartare; mains range from New Brunswick salmon fillet to Appalachian deer and Québec lamb.

Poutine, Bien Sûr

Like all fast food, Québec's beloved poutine is perfect if you have a *gueule de bois* (hangover) after a night on the Boréale Blonde. In the calorie-packing culinary Frankenstein, the province's exemplary fries (fresh-cut, never frozen or served limp and greasy) are sprinkled with cheese curds and smothered in gravy. The dish was devised in the early 1980s and spread across Québec like a grease fire.

Chez Ashton in Québec City is a good place to take the poutine challenge.

OLD LOWER TOWN

Le Lapin Sauté French $$

(Map p240; ☎418-692-5325; www.lapinsaute.com; 52 Rue du Petit-Champlain; mains $15-30; ⏰11am-10pm Mon-Fri, 9am-10pm Sat & Sun) If you only splash out once in Québec City, do it at this cozy restaurant specializing in

Poutine, Québec

DARRYL LENIUK/GETTY IMAGES ©

country cooking. Naturally, *le lapin* (rabbit) is available, in lasagna and sausages, among other things, but so are duck, salmon and chicken, and there's maple syrup crème brûlée for dessert. In good weather you can sit on the flowery patio, overlooking tiny Félix Leclerc park.

Le Cochon Dingue French $$
(Map p240; 418-692-2013; www.cochondingue.com; 46 Blvd Champlain; mains $10-28; 8am-11pm) Since 1979 this Gallic gem among touristy eateries has delighted diners with its attentive service and outside seating. A French feel pervades its checkered tablecloths and its dishes, which range from *croque monsieur* to *steak frites*. There's a second branch (p235) with the same menu, in the Ave Cartier district.

OUTSIDE THE WALLS

Café du Clocher Penché French $$
(Map p235; 418-640-0597; 203 Rue St-Joseph Est; mains $20-26; 11:30am-2pm & 5-10pm Tue-Fri, 9am-2pm & 5-10pm Sat, 9am-2pm Sun) This light and airy bistro has a simple, understated design that mimics the unpretentious menu. The happening spot in the St-Roch district is *the* place to pair modern French cuisine with a glass of wine, which you can choose from a vast array of high-quality European vintages.

Drinking & Nightlife

L'Oncle Antoine Pub
(Map p240; 418-694-9176; 29 Rue St-Pierre; 11am-late) In the Old Port area, in the stone cellar of one of the city's oldest surviving houses (dating from 1754), this tavern has several beers on tap (*en fût*) plus Québec microbrews (the coffee-tinted stout is particularly reviving).

Bar Ste-Angèle Bar
(Map p240; 26 Rue Ste-Angèle; 8pm-late) A low-lit, intimate hideaway, where the genial staff will help you navigate the list of cocktail pitchers and local and European bottled beers.

Entertainment

Rue St-Jean, and to a lesser degree Grande Allée and Ave Cartier, are the happening streets.

Fou-Bar Live Music
(Map p235; 418-522-1987; 525 Rue St-Jean; 3pm-3am) Laid-back and with an eclectic mix of bands, this is one of the town's classics for live music. The jazz on Tuesdays from 9pm is a winner.

Les Yeux Bleus Live Music
(Map p240; 1117 Rue St-Jean) The city's best *boîte a chanson* (informal singer/songwriter club), this is the place to catch newcomers, the occasional big-name francophone concert and Québecois classics.

Rue St-Jean, Quartier Latin
CHRIS CHEADLE/GETTY IMAGES ©

Shopping

In the Old Lower Town, **Rue St-Paul** has a dozen shops piled with antiques, curiosities and old Québecois relics.

Marché du Vieux-Port Food
(Map p240; ☎418-692-2517; 160 Quai St André; 9am-6pm Mon-Fri, to 5pm Sat & Sun) Further along, at the waterfront, is this farmers market, where you can stock up on fish, *fromage* (cheese), flowers, foie gras, iced cider and garden gnomes.

Information

Centre Infotouriste (Map p240; ☎418-649-2608, 877-266-5687; www.bonjourquebec.com; 12 Rue Ste-Anne; 8:30am-7:30pm) This busy provincial tourist office also handles city inquiries. Tour operators have counters here.

Kiosk Frontenac (Map p240; 9:30am-5:30pm Jun-Oct) A tourist information booth on Terrasse Dufferin facing Le Château Frontenac; makes reservations for city activities and is the starting point for some tours.

Getting There & Away

Air

Jean Lesage airport (www.aeroportdequebec.com) is west of town off Hwy 40, near where north–south Hwy 73 intersects it.

Bus

The **bus station (☎418-525-3000; 320 Rue Abraham-Martin)** is beside the main train station, Gare du Palais.

Train

In the Lower Town, the renovated and gorgeous **Gare du Palais**, off Rue St-Paul, complete with bar and cafe, is central and convenient. Daily VIA Rail (p231) trains go to Montréal (from $60, three hours) and destinations further west. Bus 800 from Place d'Youville runs to the station.

Another station, across the river in the town of **Charny**, mainly serves eastern destinations.

Getting Around

To/From the Airport

A **Taxi Co-op (☎418-525-5191)** cab between the tourist area and the airport is $34.25.

Local Knowledge

Québec City Old Town

RECOMMENDATIONS FROM RICHARD SÉGUIN, RESIDENT SINCE 1974 AND FORMER TOUR GUIDE

1 PLACE ROYALE
Samuel de Champlain built Québec's first home here in 1608. It's now a beautiful little plaza surrounded by 17th-century stone buildings. Just to be there and look around is a great way to feel the soul of the city. Then stop in Le Cochon Dingue for coffee, a *croque monsieur* and nice desserts. In summer you can grab a seat outdoors.

2 THE FORTIFICATIONS
At the St-Louis gate, in the old powder house, there's an interpretive center. Get a guide there for your walk over the fortifications (p235), because they'll take you to places you wouldn't think of going on your own. They know where all the stairways lead.

3 LE CHÂTEAU FRONTENAC
The historic hotel (p238) is where Churchill and Roosevelt planned D-Day. After visiting it, look for Chez Temporel (p242), down a narrow street nearby. It's a cafe with intimate tables, as in Paris, where writers and artists hang out.

4 PLAINS OF ABRAHAM
The Plains of Abraham (p239) is outside the walls, but it's an important part of the city. The battle of 1759 took place here between generals Montcalm and Wolfe. The Discovery Pavilion is next to it, and you can watch 'Odyssey,' a high-tech show with holograms of the generals and the battle. You can also arrange a tour from the pavilion – the site is huge and best seen by bus.

5 MUSÉE DE LA CIVILISATION
The Museum of Civilization (p237) is especially good for families – a sort of playground with interactive exhibits. There's a real birch-bark canoe, a real teepee and similar displays in the First Nations hall.

Detour: Lévis

On the 1km ferry crossing to the town of Lévis, the best views are undoubtedly on the Québec side of the vessel. The Citadelle, the Château Frontenac and the seminary dominate the clifftop cityscape. Once you disembark, riverside Lévis is a relaxing escape from the intensity of Québec City's Old Town.

Tourisme Lévis (☎418-838-6026; ⏰May-Oct), at the ferry landing, has maps and an Old Lévis package ($9), which includes return ferry and a 30-minute guided bus shuttle to several points of interest.

Near the ferry landing, the **Terrasse de Lévis**, a lookout point inaugurated in 1939 by King George VI and (the then future) Queen Elizabeth II, offers excellent vistas of Québec and beyond from the top of the hill on Rue William-Tremblay.

The **ferry** (☎877-787-7483; www.traversiers.com; car & driver/adult/child one-way $7.75/3.25/2.25) between Québec City and Lévis (10 minutes, frequent between 6am and 2am) provides great views of the river, Le Château Frontenac and the Québec City skyline. The terminal is at Place Royale.

Tour companies **Old Québec Tours** (Map p240; ☎800-267-8687, 418-644-0460; www.toursvieuxquebec.com) and **Dupont Tours** (☎418-649-9226) sometimes run cheaper shuttle buses (by reservation, $22).

Car & Motorcycle

In Old Town, driving isn't really worth the trouble. You can walk just about everywhere, the streets are narrow and crowded, and parking is limited.

Public Transportation

A ride on the city **bus system** (☎418-627-2511) costs $2.75, with transfer privileges, or $7.25 for a day pass. The tourist offices can supply route maps and information.

CHARLEVOIX

For 200 years, this pastoral strip of rolling hills has been a summer retreat for the wealthy and privileged.

Charlevoix is also known as a center for the culinary arts. The Route des Saveurs (Route of Flavors) takes in 16 farms and eateries, including the home of Éboulmontaise lamb and one of Québec's best restaurants. Local menus generally read like inventories of Charlevoix produce.

A driving route to consider taking is the 'River Drive' (Rte 362) one way, through Baie St-Paul, Ste-Irénée and La Malbaie. On the way back you can ride the ear-popping hills of the 'Mountain Drive' (Rte 138) inland and stop in at Parc des Hautes Gorges de la Rivière Malbaie for a hike en route.

Baie St-Paul

The clowning, juggling troupe Cirque du Soleil started out in Baie St-Paul, but most of the entertainment here is of a gentler nature. The small town has some 30 galleries and studios, along with historic houses converted into superb restaurants and *gîtes*.

Sights & Activities

Musée d'Art Contemporain Museum

(www.macbsp.com; 23 Rue Ambroise-Fafard; adult/child $7/free; ⏰10am-5pm Tue-Sun) Across the main drag, this architecturally attention-grabbing gallery houses contemporary art by local artists and some photographic exhibits on loan from the National Gallery of Canada.

Charlevoix, Saguenay & South Shore

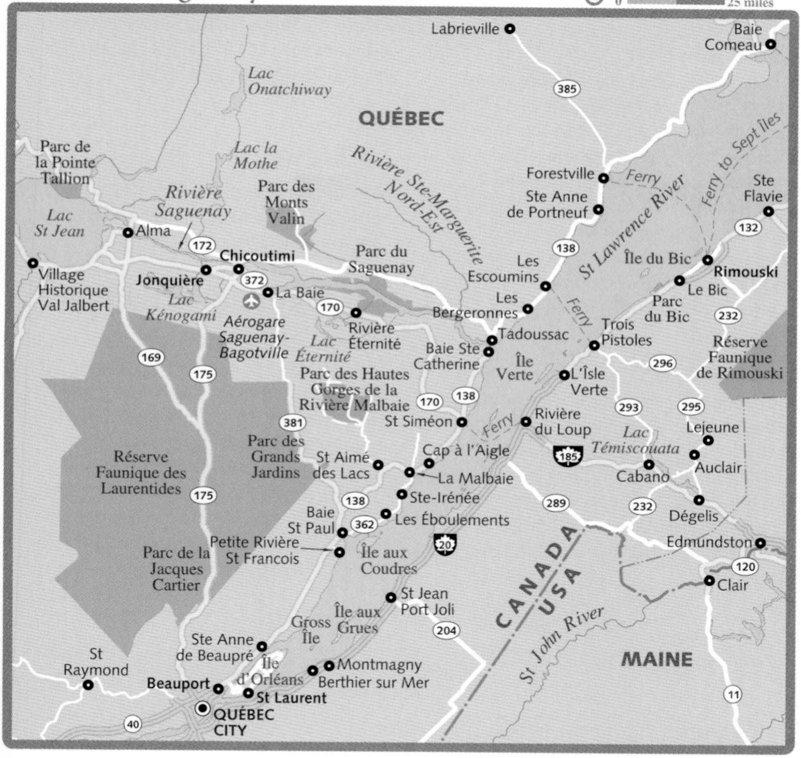

Carrefour Culturel Paul Médéric — Gallery

(4 Rue Ambroise-Fafard; ⏲10am-5pm daily Jun-Oct, 1:30-5pm Thu & Fri, 10am-5pm Sat & Sun Nov-May) FREE This gallery is named after a local priest and writer who founded a youth movement here. Stay a while as it's possible to watch local artisans working in their studios.

Randonnées Nature-Charlevoix — Outdoors

(randonneesnature.com; 11-1 Rue Ambroise-Fafard; adult/child $35.50/15; ⏲1:30pm Jul & Aug) Nonprofit organization Randonnées Nature-Charlevoix runs two-hour tours of the meteor crater. It's based at Boutique Le Cratère, where you can learn about the world's largest inhabited crater by looking at the 3D map and talking to guide François.

Sleeping & Eating

Auberge La Muse — Inn $$

(☎418-435-6839, 800-841-6839; www.lamuse.com; 39 Rue St-Jean-Baptiste; r $79-179; ❄) This cheerful yellow mansion is right in the center of the bustling village. Breakfast is outstanding, but dinner can be hit-or-miss so consider one of the many pubs and bistros within walking distance. Tip: rooms 12, 14, and 15 are the biggest, and room 1 tends to get noisy as it's next to the front door.

Nature et Pinceaux — B&B $$

(☎418-435-2366; www.natureetpinceaux.qc.ca; 33 Rue Nordet; r $95-125; ⏲Apr-Nov) Atop the mountain peeking out over the river below, the views from the spacious rooms at this charming B&B are surpassed only by the phenomenal three-course breakfasts cooked by host Mariette. The house is east of town, signposted off Rte 362.

Le Mouton Noir French $$$
(☎418-240-3030; 43 Rue Ste-Anne; set meals $33-39; ⏰5-10pm Wed-Sun) Since 1978 the rustic-looking Black Sheep has been home to fine French cuisine. Fish – including walleye, the freshwater queen – is on offer when available, as are buffalo, caribou and steak, all enlivened by a deft touch that incorporates wild mushrooms and local produce. The outdoor terrace overlooks the Gouffre River. Reservations advised.

Le Saint Pub Pub $$$
(www.saint-pub.com; 2 Rue Racine; set meals $20-30; ⏰11am-2am) Ale lovers will foam at the mouth in this former brewery, where the dinner menu begins with beers and continues via beer-based sauces, dressings and marinades. For $6 you can sample four regional brews including the local malt.

Information

Charlevoix Tourist Office (www.tourisme-charlevoix.com; 444 Blvd Mgr-de-Laval; ⏰9am-7pm) On Rte 138 just west of town.

La Malbaie

Now encompassing five previously separate villages, La Malbaie was one of Canada's first holiday resorts.

Sights & Activities

Manoir Richelieu Historic Building
The gray country cousin of Québec City's Château Frontenac, this mega-hotel is also owned by the Fairmont chain. Nonetheless, the sprawling, copper-roofed castle-like structure, which was built in 1928, attests to the area's longtime prosperity. Wander the clifftop gardens, have a drink on the terrace and drop by the gallery displaying local art.

Manoir Richelieu, La Malbaie

YVES MARCOUX/GETTY IMAGES ©

Sleeping & Eating

Vices Versa Québecois **$$$**
(☎418-665-6869; 216 Rue St-Étienne, La Malbaie; set meals $65; ⏰6-9:30pm Tue-Sun) The name comes from the split personality menu, on which owner-chefs Danielle and Eric have each created a column of choices. The menu is underpinned by local produce (Éboulmontaise lamb, calf's sweetbreads with Grand-Fonds oyster mushrooms, Cornish stew with Charlevoix beer), but the tangy, peppery sauces keep you guessing exactly which ingredient it is that tastes so good. Reservations essential.

TADOUSSAC

For many visitors to Québec, Tadoussac is the one place in the province they visit outside Montréal and Québec City. What consistently draws the hordes to this small spot is the whales. Not only do Zodiacs zip out in search of the behemoths, but smaller whales such as belugas and minkes can be glimpsed from the shore.

Added to that are activities such as sea kayaking, 'surfbiking,' exploring the fjord by boat or on foot, or simply wandering the dunes and headlands.

Activities

WHALE-WATCHING

From May to November, tourists flock to Tadoussac. The whale-watching is phenomenal, particularly between August and October, when blue whales are spotted. All over town, tickets are available for boat tours, from 12-person Zodiacs to the 600-person *Grand Fleuve*; check out the options carefully.

Otis Excursions (www.otisexcursions.com; 431 Rue du Bateau-Passeur; 2hr Zodiac trips $64, 3hr boat trips $74) is a local company that has been running for 35 years. Its Zodiacs get closest to the waves and offer the most exciting, if roughest, rides. Young children aren't permitted, however.

The Zodiac operated by **Croisières AML** (www.croisieresaml.com; 177 Rue des Pionniers; 2hr Zodiac trips $64, 3hr boat trips $74) is twice the size of the others.

For the adventurous, sea-kayaking supremo **Mer et Monde** (www.mer-et-monde.qc.ca; 148 Rue du Bord de l'Eau; 3hr trips from $52) offers whale-watching expeditions and excursions up the fjord.

HIKING

There are four 1km paths in and around Tadoussac, marked on the map given out by the tourist office. The trails around the peninsulas **Pointe de l'Islet**, by the quay, and, at the other end of the beach, **Pointe Rouge** are the best for spying whales from the shore.

Parc du Saguenay borders the fjord on both sides of the river. The provincial park has over 100km of splendid hiking trails, views down the fjord from atop 350m-plus cliffs, plus trailside refuges where you can spend the night.

Sleeping & Eating

Auberge la Sainte Paix Inn **$$**
(☎418-235-4803; www.aubergelasaintepaix.com; 102 Rue Saguenay; r $98-133) Cheery host Marie is a ray of sunshine in the morning, as are her plentiful, fresh breakfasts. She's happy to help out with tour-planning and sightseeing, and can make good local recommendations. There are only seven rooms, so book well in advance.

Hôtel Tadoussac Hotel **$$**
(☎418-235-4421, 800-561-0718; www.hoteltadoussac.com; 165 Rue du Bord de l'Eau; r from $155; 📶🏊) This 149-room, red-and-white landmark has extensive gardens, a pool overlooking the port, and vintage photos of steamers and the hotel looking considerably smaller in 1870. Somewhat tired and dated bedrooms have plush carpets, ceiling fans and river views.

Maison Clauphi Motel, B&B **$$**
(☎418-235-4303; www.clauphi.com; 188 Rue des Pionniers; B&B/motel rooms $99/139; ⏰May-Oct) The accommodations range from motel and B&B rooms to studios and suites in this building built in 1932 by the

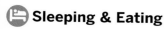

owner's parents. Bikes and waterborne 'surfbikes' can be rented.

Restaurant Le Bateau Québecois $$

(246 Rue des Forgerons; lunch/dinner buffet $12.50/18; 11am-2:30pm & 5-9:30pm May-Oct) A great view comes with the buffet of traditional Québec workers' fare at this friendly restaurant. Fill up on Lac St-Jean meat pie, followed by blueberry, sugar or vinegar pie.

Café Bohème Cafe $$

(239 Rue des Pionniers; set meals $15-20; 8am-10pm May-Oct) The village's hangout of choice is a prime place for a breakfast of fruit and yogurt or a panino, or just to sip fair-trade coffee among the local intellectuals. Later in the day, choose between dishes such as duck confit salad and fresh pasta of the day.

Chez Mathilde Fusion $$$

(227 Rue des Pionniers; set meals from $25; 11am-9:30pm Jun-Oct) The stellar chef at this cute little house utilizes plenty of local produce in his creative, though limited, menu. The innovative dishes, cooked to perfection, are served up alongside a view of the port from an airy patio.

Information

Tourist Information Office (418-235-4744, 866-235-4744; www.tadoussac.com; 197 Rue des Pionniers; 8am-9pm) In the middle of town, with very patient staff that can help with accommodations.

Getting There & Away

The 24-hour, 10-minute ferry from Baie Ste-Catherine in Charlevoix is free. The terminal is at the end of Rue du Bateau Passeur.

Tadoussac is off Rte 138.

ÎLES DE LA MADELEINE

Everything about the Magdalen Islands, a stringy archipelago that resembles a Mandelbrot set on maps, is head-turning. The islands are 105km north of Prince Edward Island (PEI), and the six largest are connected by the 200km-long, classically named Rte 199. Between the islands' 350km of beach are iron-rich, red cliffs, molded by wind and sea into anthropomorphic forms and caves just crying out to be explored by kayak.

The islands are teeming with artists, often encountered looking for inspiration in a *pot-en-pot* (a local specialty, with mixed fish, seafood and sauce baked in a pie crust) or a Pas Perdus (one of three beers brewed on Cap aux Meules).

The islands fall in the Atlantic Time Zone, one hour ahead of mainland Québec.

Parc du Saguenay (p249), Tadoussac

Getting There & Around

The airport is on the northwest corner of Île du Havre aux Maisons.

The cheapest and most common arrival method is by ferry from Souris, Prince Edward Island, to Île du Cap aux Meules. CTMA Ferries (418-986-3278, 888-986-3278; www.ctma.ca; adult/child/bicycle/car $48.75/24.50/11.75/91) makes the five-hour cruise year-round. Ferries depart daily from July to early September; every day but Monday in May, June and September; and from October to April, two or three times a week. In midsummer, reservations are strongly recommended. There are discounts between mid-September and mid-June.

Between June and October, CTMA also operates a two-day cruise from Montréal via Québec City, Tadoussac and Chandler (one-way/return from $435/1000). It's a great way of seeing the St Lawrence River, and you could always take your car ($287) and return by road.

There is no public transportation. Le Pédalier (418-986-2965; 545 Chemin Principale; rental 1hr/4hr/1 week $6/18/85), in Cap aux Meules, rents bicycles.

Île du Cap aux Meules

With more than half the archipelago's population and its only Tim Hortons, the islands' commercial center is disappointingly developed compared with its neighbors. Nonetheless, it's still 100% Madelinot and, with its amenities, accommodations and lively nightlife, it makes an ideal base.

Sights & Activities

On the west side of the island, you can see the red cliffs in their glory. Their patterns of erosion can be glimpsed from the clifftop path between La Belle Anse and Fatima. Southwest, the lighthouse at **Cap du Phare** (Cap Hérissé) is a popular place to watch sunsets, and a cluster of bright boutiques and cafes overlooks a shipwreck at **Anse de l'Étang du Nord**. In the middle of the island, signposted on Chemin de l'Église near the junction with Rte 199, **Butte du Vent** offers views along the sandbanks running north and south.

À l'Abri de la Tempête Brewery
(418-986-5005; 286 Chemin Coulombe; tours $6.50; tours 11am-7pm May-Oct) Finish the day at this microbrewery on the beach.

Aerosport Carrefour d'Aventures Kayaking
(418-986-6677; www.aerosport.ca; 1390 Chemin Lavernière) Young, enthusiastic thrill-seekers run this company, which offers kayak expeditions and cave visits. When the wind is right, you'll have an unforgettable experience if you opt for the power-kite-buggy ride.

Vert et Mer Kayaking
(418-986-3555; www.vertetmer.com; 84 Chemin des Vigneau) This eco-outfit offers guided walks and sea-kayaking excursions. You can choose from half-day, full-day or overnight trips as far away as Île Brion, an uninhabited ecological preserve at the northern end of the Magdalen archipelago, where yurt lodgings are provided.

Sleeping & Eating

Pas Perdus Inn, Pub $$
(Not Lost; 418-986-5151; 169 Chemin Principale; s/d $45/90, mains $12-20; 11am-8pm) Munching on a shark burger on the terrasse at Pas Perdus, or in the red interior among curvy mirrors, is a sure way to feel the islands' bohemian pulse. You can actually get a decent night's sleep in the bright bedrooms above the restaurant now that the musical entertainment has shifted next door.

This venue hosts live acts most summer nights; on Monday, a free jam session (10pm); and on Friday (11pm) local DJs. Everyone drops by to surf the internet or sip a Pas Perdus from the nearby microbrewery.

Pas Perdus is on the east side of the island, just west of the tourist office.

La Factrie Seafood $$
(521 Chemin du Gros Cap; mains $15-30; 8am-7pm Mon-Sat, 1-6pm Sun May-Sep) Top-notch seafood in a cafeteria above a lobster-processing plant: only in Îles de la Madeleine! Try lobster in salad, boiled, thermidore, sandwich or crepe form.

Below: Kiteboarder, Îles de la Madeleine; **Right:** La Belle Anse, Île du Cap aux Meules (p251)

Café la Côte Cafe **$$**
(499 Chemin Boisville Ouest; mains $9-20; 11am-10pm Jun-Sep) Near the fishers statue in L'Etang du Nord, this beach-hut-like place is perfect for breakfast or a quick lunch of seafood or pasta. The adjoining *boîte à chansons* puts on outdoor Acadian music shows on summer evenings.

Information

The main tourist office (418-986-2245, 877-624-4437; www.tourismeilesdelamadeleine.com; 128 Chemin Principale; 8am-8pm Jul & Aug, 9am-8pm Jun & Sep, 9am-5pm Oct-May), near the ferry terminal, is a helpful source of information about all the islands.

Île du Havre Aubert

Heading south from Cap aux Meules to the archipelago's largest island, Rte 199 glides between dunes backed by the blue Atlantic and Baie-du-Havre-aux-Basques, popular with kite surfers.

The liveliest area of **Havre Aubert** town is La Grave, where the rustic charm of a fishing community remains in the old houses, small craft shops and restaurants. Beyond, walk along the **Sandy Hook** to feel like you're at the end of the world (except during the sand castle contest in late August).

The excellent **Musée de la Mer** (1023 Rte 199; adult/child $8/5; 10am-6pm) covers Madelinot history from Jacques Cartier's impressions of walruses onwards.

At **Le Site d'Autrefois** (3106 Chemin de la Montagne; adult/child $10/4; 9am-5pm Jun-Aug, 10am-4pm Sep), flamboyant fisher Claude preserves Madelinot traditions through storytelling, singing and a model village.

Café de la Grave (969 Rte 199; mains $9-15; 9am-3am late Apr-Oct) is more than a local institution – it's one of the

islands' vital organs. *Pot-en-pot*, *croque monsieur*, soups and cakes meet an appreciative crowd in the former general store.

Économusée **Artisans du Sable** (907 Rte 199; 10am-9pm) sells chessboards, candlesticks and other souvenirs...all made of sand.

Île du Havre aux Maisons

The home of the airport is one of the most populated islands but certainly doesn't feel it. The area to the east of Rte 199 is probably the most scenic, and is best seen from Chemin des Buttes, which winds between green hills and picture-perfect cottages. A short climb from the car park on Chemin des Échoueries near Cap Alright, the cross-topped **Butte Ronde** has wonderful views of the lumpy coastline.

Sleeping & Eating

La Butte Ronde B&B **$$**

(418-969-2047, 866-969-2047; www.labutteronde.com; 70 Chemin des Buttes; r incl breakfast $120-165) With ticking clocks, classical music, beautiful rooms decorated with photos of Tuareg nomads, and a sea-facing conservatory, this grand home in a former schoolhouse has a calming, library-like air.

Domaine du Vieux Couvent Hotel **$$$**

(418-969-2233; www.domaineduvieuxcouvent.com; 292 Rte 199; r incl breakfast $150-275; Mar-Dec, restaurant 5-9pm May-Dec;) Smack-dab in the middle of the archipelago, the Domaine has the swankiest digs in Îles de la Madeleine. Every room overlooks the ocean through a wall of windows. The very popular restaurant is a must-visit for adventurous foodies, who can sample local dishes made with seafood, veal, boar, wild fruits and cheeses from the islands (set meals from $27).

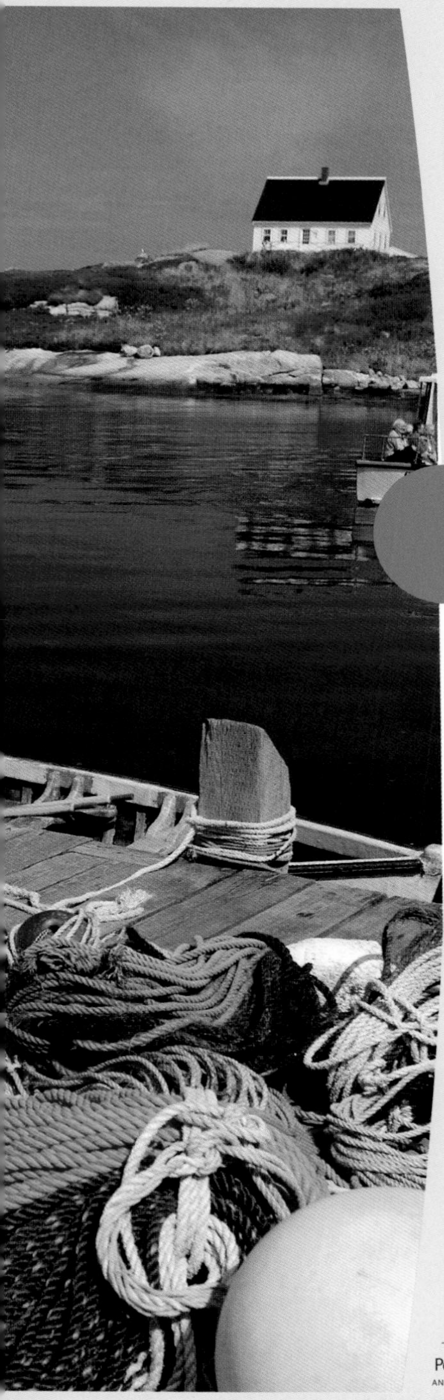

Nova Scotia & Maritime Canada

At first glance, Nova Scotia appears as sweet as a storybook. Its lupin-studded fields, gingerbread-like houses, picture-perfect lighthouses and lightly lapping waves on sandy shores make you want to wrap it all up and give it to a kid as a Christmas gift. Then another reality creeps up on you: this is also the raw Canada, of fisherfolk braving icy seas, of coal miners, of moose, of horse-flies and of hockey.

Here and throughout the Maritimes, it's easy to discover empty coastal beach trails and vistas doused with briny breezes. Celtic and Acadian communities dot the landscape, and their crazy-fiddlin' music vibrates through local pubs.

New Brunswick shows off its best side from its capital Fredericton down to the Fundy shore. And little Prince Edward Island (PEI), personified by Anne Shirley, LM Montgomery's spunky red-headed star of the Green Gables series, is as sweet and pretty as it is portrayed in the books.

Peggy's Cove (p269), Nova Scotia
ANDREW BAIN/GETTY IMAGES ©

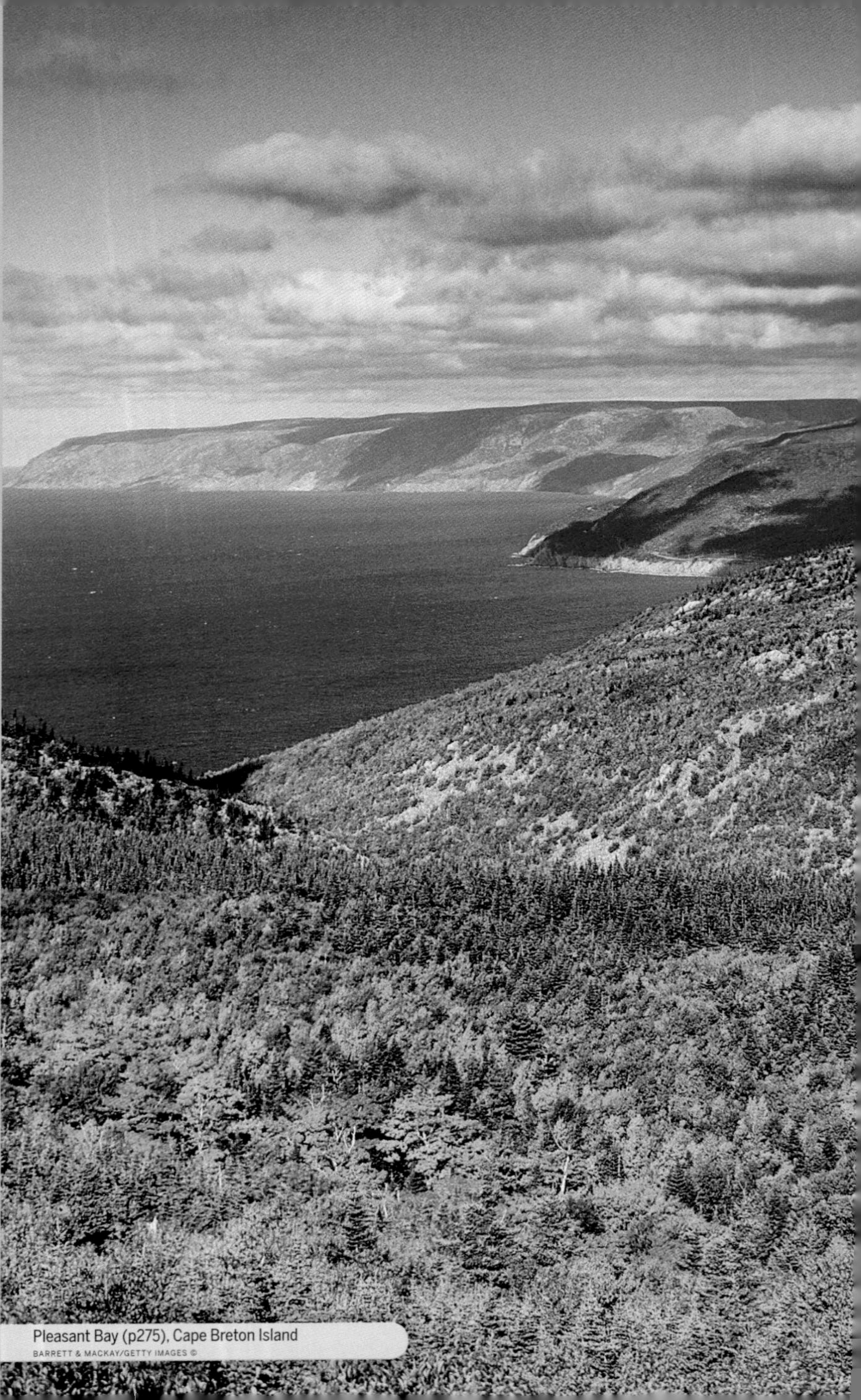

Pleasant Bay (p275), Cape Breton Island
BARRETT & MACKAY/GETTY IMAGES ©

Nova Scotia & Maritime Canada

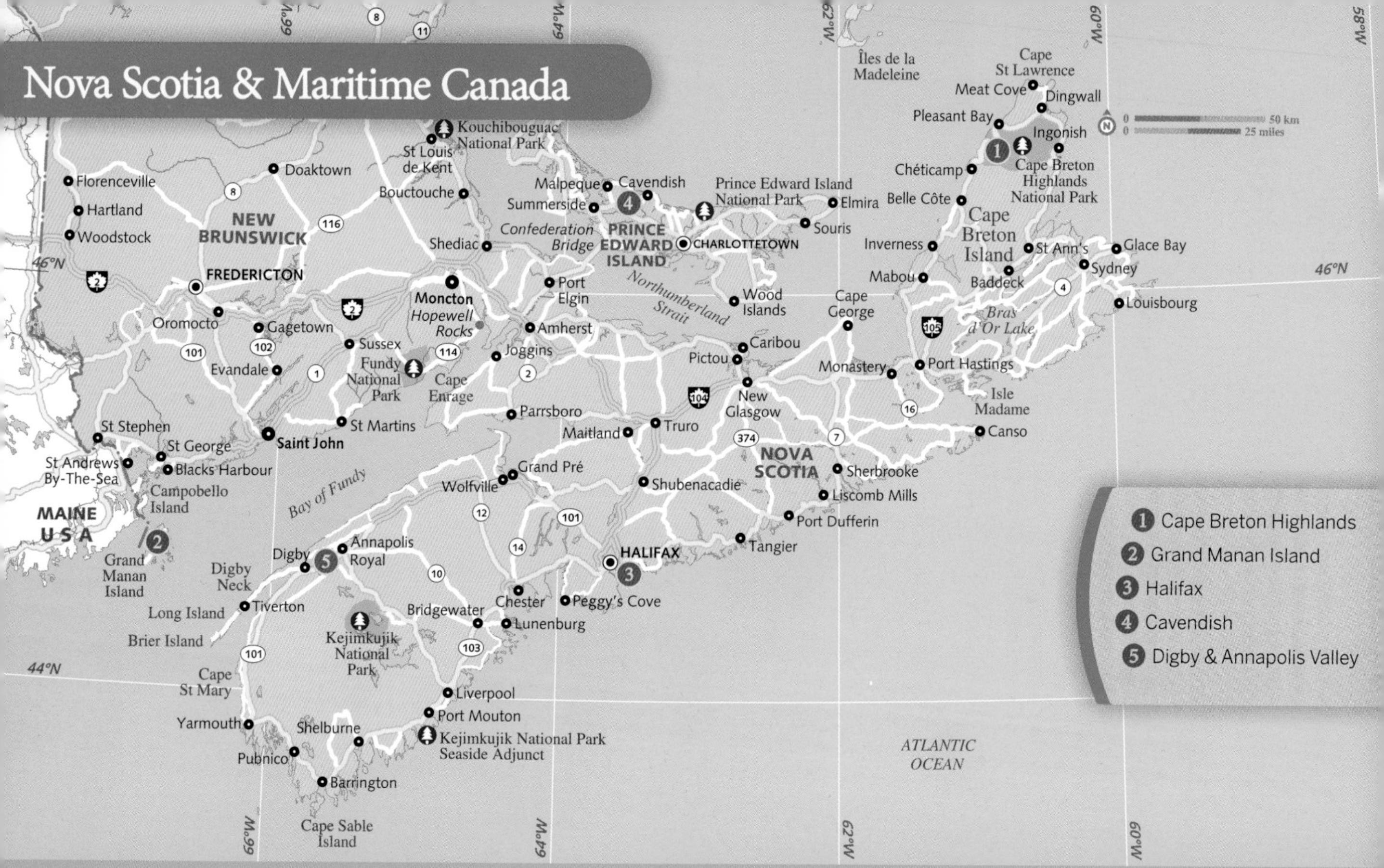

Nova Scotia & Maritime Canada's Highlights

Cape Breton Highlands

Driving the 300km Cabot Trail through the highlands (p273) is a singular, brake-smoking journey. The road winds and climbs over coastal mountains, with sea views at every turn, whales visible just offshore, moose nibbling roadside and plenty of paths to stop and hike. Be sure to tote your dancing shoes – Celtic and Acadian communities pepper the region, and their high-energy fiddles blow the roof off local pubs.

1

2

Grand Manan Island

Grand Manan (p279) is a fine place to absorb clifftop lighthouses, clapboard fis ing hamlets and other requisite Maritime scenery. But the island's unique geography ups the ante. Located in the Bay of Fundy, it's slapped by the world's most extreme tides. And those tides stir up serious food for whales. Fin, humpback, scarce North Atlantic right whales and mega-huge blue whales swim in to feast making a whale-watch here extraordinary

Left: Swallowtail Lighthouse (p279)

ANDREW BAIN/GETTY IMAGES ©

Halifax

With heritage buildings, art galleries and cosmopolitan eateries sloping down to the waterfront, Halifax (p264) lets you soak up Maritime culture at its finest. By day it is Nova Scotia's historic-site-studded capital, offering everything from a spooky citadel to *Titanic* exhibits to pirates' old stomping grounds for exploration. By night it morphs into a music center, where rockin' indie bands plug in for crowds. Right: Maritime Museum of the Atlantic (p265)

3

HENRY GEORGI/GETTY IMAGES ©

4

Cavendish

You know how spunky Anne Shirley, Lucy Maud Montgomery's immortal heroine of *Anne of Green Gables,* wins over everyone in her path? So it is with Cavendish (p286), the wildly popular little town that inspired the book. It'll charm even the biggest skeptic – eventually. Past the water parks and wax museums lie pink-sand beaches, a green patchwork of rolling fields and tidy seaside villages every bit as pastoral as in the storybook. Above: House of Green Gables (p287)

5

Digby & Annapolis Valley

Digby Neck (p271) is another Bay of Fundy hot spot for whale watching. It's often cited as the Maritimes' best, since the leviathans swim close to shore. The thrill of spotting a whale's spout, followed by its giant tail flukes arching and descending, can't be beat. All the action will stoke your hunger; Digby is the world's scallop capital, so dinner is ready-made. Above: Digby harbour

Nova Scotia & Maritime Canada's Best...

Dining

- **Edna** A Halifax delight that stirs up a whopping Atlantic bouillabaisse. (p268)
- **Chanterelle Country Inn** They don't forage for their own mushrooms at St Ann's Bay for nothing. (p275)
- **St Ann's Lobster Supper** Top place to don a bib and get crackin'. (p285)
- **Lot 30** Creative takes on local seafood, with masterful wine pairings in Charlottetown. (p285)

Lighthouses

- **Peggy's Cove** Picture-perfect, red-and-white tower sends cameras clicking. (p269)
- **Swallowtail** Looms atop a moss-covered cliff with seals swimming below. (p279)
- **Cape Enrage** Presides over the highest, meanest tides in the world (hence the name). (p281)
- **East Quoddy Head** Lookout for whales on Campobello Island's north end. (p281)

Live Music

- **Red Shoe Pub** World-renowned Celtic fiddlers scorch the strings in Mabou. (p274)
- **Baddeck Gathering Ceilidhs** Nightly fiddling and dancing at the local parish hall. (p276)
- **Benevolent Irish Society** Another rowdy place to catch a ceilidh, in Charlottetown. (p285)
- **Lower Deck** Bands rock Halifax's most sociable pub nightly. (p269)

Wildlife-Watching

- **Digby Neck** Endangered North Atlantic right whales, humpbacks and perhaps blue whales if you're lucky. (p271)
- **Grand Manan Island** Add puffins to the humpback and right whale mix. (p279)
- **Pleasant Bay** Whales, seals and a bonus Tibetan monastery. (p275)
- **Cape Breton Highlands National Park** More moose than you can shake a shrub at on the Cabot Trail. (p274)

Humpback whale, Grand Manan Island (p279); **Above:** Tiverton, Long Island (p271)

(LEFT & ABOVE) BARRETT & MACKAY/GETTY IMAGES ©

Need to Know

ADVANCE PLANNING

- **One month before** For summer book accommodation and rental cars as soon as possible.
- **Two weeks before** Book cycling and whale-watching excursions; make ferry reservations.
- **One week before** Get binoculars, motion-sickness pills ready.

RESOURCES

- **Tourism Nova Scotia** (www.novascotia.com) Links to attractions, tour operators and accommodations.
- **Studio Map** (www.studiorally.ca) Guide to Nova Scotia's art and craft studios, plus a shortlist of eateries and B&Bs.
- **Tourism New Brunswick** (www.tourismnewbrunswick.ca) Info on scenic drives and other trip-planning resources.
- **Tourism PEI** (www.tourismpei.com) The low-down on local foods, Confederation Trail cycling, beaches and *Anne of Green Gables* sights.
- **Bay Ferries** (www.ferries.ca) Reservations for ferries between Saint John, New Brunswick, and Digby, Nova Scotia.
- **Northumberland Ferries** (www.ferries.ca) Reservations between Wood Islands, Prince Edward Island (PEI), and Caribou, Nova Scotia.
- **Wines of Nova Scotia** (www.winesofnovascotia.ca) Information on vineyards and festivals across the province.

GETTING AROUND

- **Fly** Halifax International Airport is the hub for travel across the region; services to/from Charlottetown, PEI, and Fredericton, New Brunswick.
- **Car** Road conditions are good, and driving distances are manageable. The longest drives most people will do are Halifax to Cape Breton Island, and Halifax to Charlottetown – both four hours.
- **Ferry** Common transport mode between Saint John, New Brunswick, and Digby, Nova Scotia; and between Wood Islands, PEI, and Caribou, Nova Scotia.
- **Train** Once daily VIA Rail train from Halifax to Montréal (21 hours).

Nova Scotia & Maritime Canada Itineraries

With three days, hopscotch through Nova Scotia's wine country; the intrepid can whale-watch at Digby Neck, where behemoths congregate like nowhere else. With five days, take a bite of all the Maritime provinces.

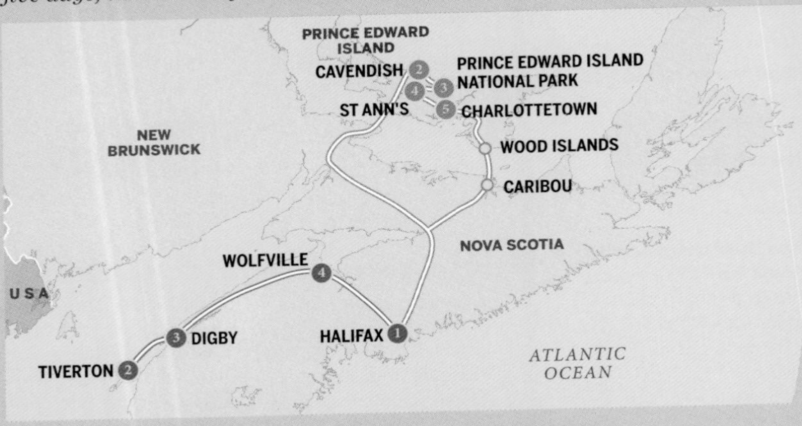

3 DAYS — HALIFAX TO HALIFAX
WHALES & WINE

Spend the first day in ❶ **Halifax** (p264). Wander the waterfront and its historic properties, making sure to check out the Halifax Seaport Farmers Market and the *Titanic* exhibits at the Maritime Museum. When night falls, fork into one of downtown's hip restaurants, then see what's on for live music at the local pubs.

On day two motor west to ❷ **Tiverton** (p271) on Digby Neck, a 275km drive. Yes, it's a long haul, but Ocean Explorations Whale Cruises is worth it. Buckle into a tangerine-colored flotation suit and hold on tight as you get up close and personal with humpbacks and rare North Atlantic right whales. Eat like a whale afterwards in ❸ **Digby** (p270), famous worldwide for the buttery scallops plucked from its waters.

Depart Digby on day three, backtracking to ❹ **Wolfville** (p272), a university town ringed by wineries. Pull over for sparkling pours at L'Acadie Vineyards, or sweet ice wines at Gaspereau Vineyards, one of the region's star grape crushers. You can spend the night here in the star-filled valley – there are several inns, and some of the wineries host guests – or return to Halifax, an hour down the road.

5 DAYS

HALIFAX TO HALIFAX

HEART OF THE MARITIMES

This 650km loop circles through Nova Scotia, New Brunswick and PEI.

Eat and drink in ❶ **Halifax** (p264) for a day or two, then make a break northwest to New Brunswick. Give the province a quick kiss hello and goodbye, then barrel over the 12.9km Confederation Bridge that links New Brunswick to PEI. Voila – you're in Anne's Land (Anne being the fictional red-headed orphan of Green Gables fame), and ❷ **Cavendish** (p286) is the wildly developed town that pays homage to her.

Continue the red theme by exploring the sandstone bluffs at ❸ **Prince Edward Island National Park** (p286), where there's bird watching, beach walking and swimming. There's also lobster eating: spurting shellfish all over your shirt at a 'lobster supper' initiates you into the local lifestyle, and the church basement in nearby ❹ **St Ann's** (p285) hosts an excellent venue to get juicy. It's easy to while away a few days in this area around Cavendish.

Spend a day in PEI's compact, colonial capital ❺ **Charlottetown** (p282) before taking the ferry from Wood Islands to Caribou back in Nova Scotia. From there, it takes about two hours to return to Halifax.

Stanhope Beach, Prince Edward Island National Park (p286)

Discover Nova Scotia & Maritime Canada

At a Glance

- **Halifax** (p264) Good-time, historic city where the Maritimes' heart beats.
- **Cape Breton Island** (p273) Pulse-igniting coastal views and foot-tapping music.
- **Fredericton** (p276) New Brunswick's graceful, red-brick capital.
- **Grand Manan Island** (p279) Lighthouses, fishing villages, and puffin- and whale-watching tours.
- **Prince Edward Island** (p282) Pastoral landscape with pink-sand beaches.

Alexander Keith's Nova Scotia Brewery

ROLF HICKER PHOTOGRAPHY/GETTY IMAGES ©

HALIFAX

Halifax is the kind of town that people flock to, not so much for the opportunities, but for the quality of life it has to offer. Sea breezes off the harbor keep the air clean, and parks and trees nestle between heritage buildings, cosmopolitan eateries and arty shops. Stroll the historic waterfront, catch some live music and enjoy the best of what the Maritimes have to offer.

Sights

DOWNTOWN

Historic Properties Notable Building

(www.historicproperties.ca) The Historic Properties are a group of restored buildings on Upper Water St, built between 1800 and 1905. Originally designed as huge warehouses for easy storage of goods and cargo, they now house boutiques, restaurants and bars and are connected by waterfront boardwalks. Artisans, merchants and buskers do business around the buildings in the summer.

Alexander Keith's Nova Scotia Brewery Brewery

(☎902-455-1474; www.keiths.ca; Brewery Market, 1496 Lower Water St; adult/child $16/8; ⏲11am-8pm Mon-Thu, to 9pm Fri & Sat, noon-4pm Sun) A tour of this brewery takes you to 19th-century Halifax via costumed thespians, quality brew and dark corridors. Finish your hour-long tour with a party in the basement pub with beer on tap and ale-inspired yarns. Note that you'll need your ID. Kids are kept happy with lemonade.

Maritime Museum of the Atlantic — Museum

(902-424-7490; http://maritimemuseum.novascotia.ca/; 1675 Lower Water St; adult/child $9.25/5; 9:30am-5pm Wed-Mon, to 8pm Tue) Part of this fun waterfront museum used to be a chandlery, where all the gear needed to outfit a vessel was sold. You can smell the charred ropes, cured to protect them from saltwater. There's a wildly popular display on the *Titanic* and another on the Halifax Explosion. The 3-D film about the *Titanic* costs $5. Outside at the dock you can explore the CSS *Acadia*, a retired hydrographic vessel from England.

Citadel Hill National Historic Site — Historic Site

(902-426-5080; off Sackville St; adult/child $11.70/5.80; 9am-6pm) Canada's most visited national historic site, the huge and arguably spooky Citadel, is a star-shaped fort atop Halifax' central hill. Construction began in 1749 with the founding of Halifax; this version of the Citadel is the fourth, built from 1818 to 1861. Guided tours explain the fort's shape and history.

Art Gallery of Nova Scotia — Gallery

(902-424-7542; www.artgalleryofnovascotia.ca; 1723 Hollis St; adult/child $12/5; 10am-5pm Wed, Fri & Sat, to 9pm Thu, noon-5pm Sun) Don't miss the permanent, tear-jerking Maud Lewis Painted House exhibit that includes the 3m-by-4m house that Lewis lived in most of her adult life. The main exhibit in the lower hall changes regularly, featuring anything from ancient art to the avant-garde.

Tours

Tall Ship Silva — Boat Tour

(902-429-9463; www.tallshipsilva.com; Queen's Wharf, Prince St; cruises adult/child $22/15; noon, 2pm, 4pm, 6pm & 10:30pm daily May-Oct) Lend a hand or sit back and relax while taking a 1½-hour daytime cruise or a two-hour evening party cruise on Halifax' square-masted tall ship.

Local Knowledge

Maritime Art

RECOMMENDATIONS FROM SARAH FILLMORE, CHIEF CURATOR OF THE ART GALLERY OF NOVA SCOTIA AND CURATOR OF THE SOBEY ART AWARD

1 MARITIME'S LARGEST ART COLLECTION

The Art Gallery of Nova Scotia has the largest collection, with locations in both Halifax and Yarmouth. Well-known artists include realist Alex Colville (1920-2013) and Maud Lewis (1903-1970). Lewis is Nova Scotia's most renowned folk artist. Her tiny painted house is on permanent display in the Halifax gallery.

2 ATTRACTING ARTISTS

The unique quality of the light here, coupled with the breathtaking and rugged scenery, has long lured artists. The creative economy is alive and well in the region: galleries and multifaceted businesses that support artists are becoming more in number and more resourceful in how they show artists' work.

3 GALLERY-RICH TOWNS

A drive around the provinces will allow you ample opportunities to encounter the rich artistic output. In Nova Scotia, for example, explore the galleries of South Shore towns like Mahone Bay, Lunenburg and Chester, as well as the artist-run centers of the Annapolis Valley and Antigonish.

4 CAPE BRETON CRAFTS

Cape Breton is an art-lover's wonderland. The **Cape Breton Centre for Craft and Design** (www.capebretoncraft.com; 322 Charlotte St) in Sydney offers a wide range of local artists' work, specializing in craft. It also houses handsome and expansive studios.

Halifax

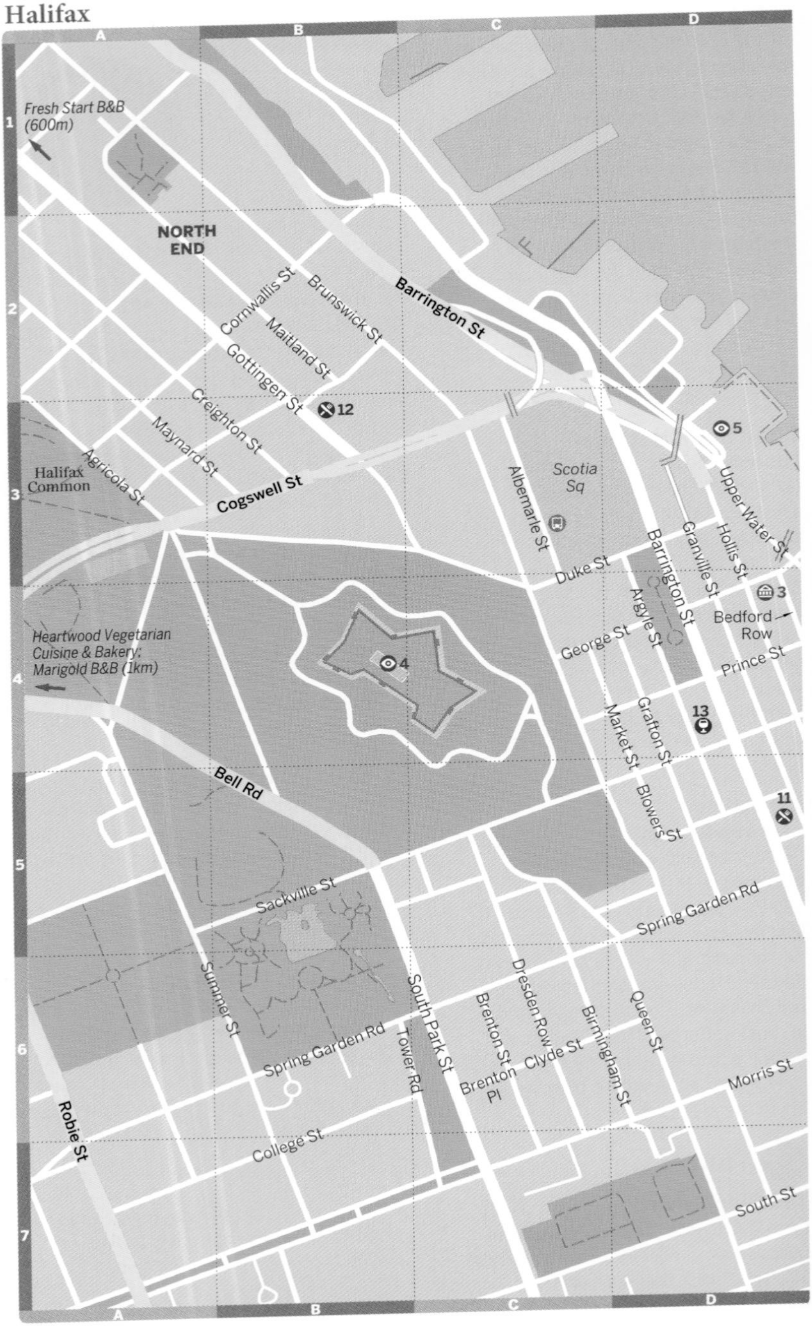

A
B
C
D
1
2
3
4
5
6
7
Fresh Start B&B (600m)
NORTH END
Cornwallis St
Brunswick St
Barrington St
Maitland St
Gottingen St
Creighton St
12
Maynard St
Agricola St
Halifax Common
Cogswell St
5
Scotia Sq
Albermarle St
Upper Water St
Barrington St
Granville St
Hollis St
Duke St
Argyle St
3
Bedford Row
George St
Prince St
4
Heartwood Vegetarian Cuisine & Bakery; Marigold B&B (1km)
13
Market St
Grafton St
Bell Rd
Blowers St
11
Sackville St
Spring Garden Rd
Summer St
South Park St
Dresden Row
Brenton St
Birmingham St
Queen St
Tower Rd
Spring Garden Rd
Clyde St
Brenton Pl
Morris St
Robie St
College St
South St

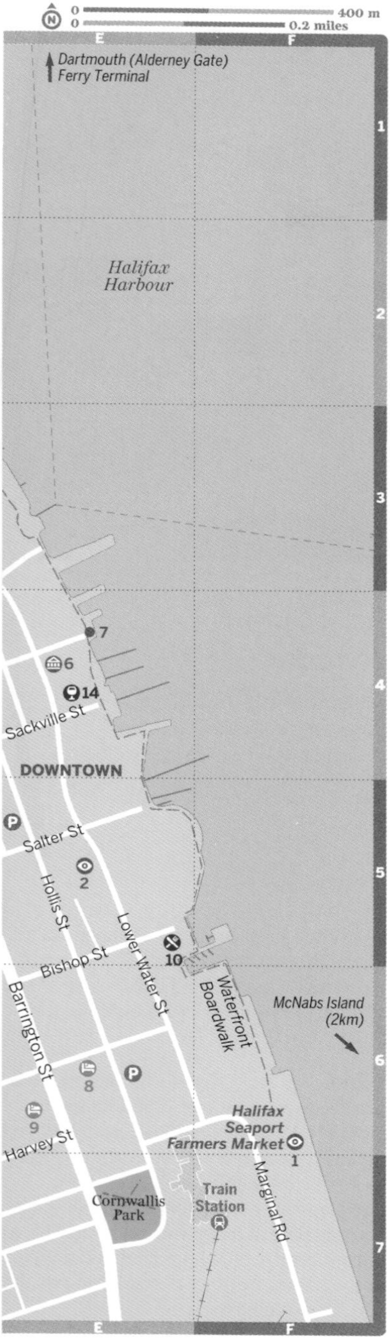

Halifax

Don't Miss Sights
1 Halifax Seaport Farmers Market F6

Sights
2 Alexander Keith's Nova Scotia Brewery E5
3 Art Gallery of Nova Scotia D4
4 Citadel Hill National Historic Site B4
5 Historic Properties D3
6 Maritime Museum of the Atlantic E4

Activities, Courses & Tours
7 Tall Ship Silva E4

Sleeping
8 Halliburton E6
9 Waverley Inn E6

Eating
10 Bicycle Thief E5
11 Chives Canadian Bistro D5
12 Edna B3

Drinking & Nightlife
13 Economy Shoe Shop D4
14 Lower Deck E4

Sleeping

Waverley Inn — Inn $$

(902-423-9346, 800-565-9346; www.waverleyinn.com; 1266 Barrington St; d incl breakfast $135-235;) Every room here is furnished uniquely and nearly theatrically with antiques and dramatic linens. Both Oscar Wilde and PT Barnum once stayed here and probably would again today if they were still living. The downtown location can't be beat.

Fresh Start B&B — B&B $$

(902-453-6616, 888-453-6616; www.bbcanada.com/2262.html; 2720 Gottingen St; r $110-130; @) Run by two retired nurses, this majestic yet lived-in-feeling Victorian is in a gay-friendly part of the North End. Rooms with en-suite bathrooms are the best value.

Marigold B&B — B&B $$

(902-423-4798; www.marigoldbedandbreakfast.com; 6318 Norwood St; s/d $75/85;) Feel at home in this artist's nest full of bright floral paintings and fluffy cats. It's

ISLAND IMAGES/ALAMY ©

Don't Miss
Halifax Seaport Farmers Market

The old Halifax Brewery Farmers Market was so popular that this larger edifice was built to expand the fun. Find over 250 vendors selling everything from artisanal soaps to fresh carrots and baked goods. The market is biggest on Friday, Saturday and Sunday, but it's a great lunch stop anytime it's open.

NEED TO KNOW

www.halifaxfarmersmarket.com; Marginal Rd; 10am-5pm Tue-Sun

in a tree-lined residential area with easy public transport access.

Halliburton Inn $$$
(**902-420-0658; www.thehalliburton.com; 5184 Morris St; r $159-350;**) Pure, soothing class without all that Victorian hullabaloo can be found at this exceedingly comfortable and well-serviced historic hotel right in downtown.

Eating

Heartwood Vegetarian Cuisine & Bakery Vegetarian $
(**902-425-2808; 6250 Quinpool Rd; light meals from $5; 10am-8pm Mon-Sat;**) Try the local organic salad bar or amazing baked goods, along with a cup of fair-trade coffee. Heartwood is about 1.5km west of the citadel; take Bell Rd, cross Robie St and head down Quinpool Rd.

Edna Modern Canadian $$
(**www.ednarestaurant.com; 2053 Gottingen St; mains $14-22; from 5pm Tue-Sun**) Everything here is delicious, from the Southern fried rock hen to the filled-with-everything-good-from-the-sea Atlantic bouillabaisse. You can dine at a big wooden table where guests from everywhere chat and mingle, at the bar for a little less socializing or at a regular old table for two.

Detour: Peggy's Cove

Peggy's Cove is one of the most visited fishing towns in Canada and for a good reason: the rolling granite cove highlighted by a perfect red-and-white lighthouse exudes a dreamy seaside calm, even through the parading tour buses. Most visitors hop off their air-con bus, snap a few pictures, then get right back on the bus. If you stick around, you'll find it surprisingly easy to chat with the friendly locals (there are only 45 of them) and settle into fishing-village pace. At 43km west of Halifax on Hwy 333, it makes a mellow day trip from the city.

It's best to visit before 10am in the summer, as tour buses arrive in the middle of the day and create one of the province's worst traffic jams. There's a free parking area with washrooms and a **tourist office** (☎902-823-2253; 109 Peggy's Cove Rd; ⏰9am-7pm May-Oct) as you enter the village. Free 45-minute walking tours are led from the tourist office daily from mid-June through August.

Bicycle Thief Modern Canadian **$$**
(☎902-425-7993; 1475 Lower Water St; lunch mains $14-18, dinner mains $15-29; ⏰11.30am-late Mon-Fri, 5:30pm-late Sat) Named for the 1948 classic Italian film, this shabby-chic waterfront restaurant has won similar critical acclaim by local foodies – and with good reason. Start with regional oysters or polenta with wild mushroom ragout, then continue with dishes like pistachio-honey roasted salmon or pancetta wrapped pork tenderloin.

Brooklyn Warehouse Canadian **$$**
(☎902-446-8181; www.brooklynwarehouse.ca; 2795 Windsor St; lunch mains $8-15, dinner mains around $20; ⏰11:30am-10pm Mon-Sat;) This North End hot spot is loaded with vegetarian and vegan options – the eggplant moussaka stack is excellent. It has a huge beer and cocktail menu, and an atmosphere that feels like a modern, hip version of *Cheers* – but with way better food.

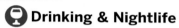

Chives Canadian Bistro Canadian **$$$**
(☎902-420-9626; 1537 Barrington St; mains $17-35; ⏰5-9:30pm) The menu changes with what's seasonably available and uses mostly local ingredients. The food is fine dining, while the low-lit cozy ambience is upscale casual.

Drinking & Nightlife

Lower Deck Pub
(☎902-422-1501; 1869 Lower Water St) A first stop for a real Nova Scotian knee-slapping good time. Think pints in frothy glasses, everyone singing, and live music all spilling out over the sidewalks on summer nights. When someone yells 'sociable!' it's time to raise your glass.

Economy Shoe Shop Pub
(☎902-423-8845; 1663 Argyle St) This has been the 'it' place to drink and people-watch in Halifax for well over a decade. On weekend nights, actors and journalists figure heavily in the crush.

Information

Destination Halifax (www.halifaxinfo.com) Halifax' official tourism site has information on everything from events to package bookings.

Getting There & Away

Air

Most air services in Nova Scotia go to/from Halifax and there are multiple daily flights to Toronto, Calgary and Vancouver.

Train

One of the few examples of monumental Canadian train station architecture left in the Maritimes is found at 1161 Hollis St. Options with **VIA Rail** (www.viarail.ca) include overnight service to Montréal (21 hours, daily except Tuesdays).

Getting Around

To/From the Airport

Halifax International Airport is 40km northeast of town on Hwy 102 toward Truro. The cheapest way to get there is by Metro Transit public bus 320, which runs half-hourly to hourly between 5am and midnight from the Metro X bus stop on Albemarle St between Duke and Cogswell Sts. If you arrive in the middle of the night, as many flights do, your only choice is a taxi, which costs $56 to downtown Halifax.

Public Transportation

Metro Transit (902-490-6600; www.halifax.ca/metrotransit; one-way fare $3.25) runs the city bus system and the ferries to Dartmouth.

Fred is a free city bus that loops around downtown every 30 minutes in the summer.

DIGBY & ANNAPOLIS VALLEY

Digby

Known for its scallops, mild climate and daily ferry to Saint John, New Brunswick, Digby (www.digby.ca) is nestled in a protected inlet off the Bay of Fundy.

Digby has been a tourist mecca for more than a century and it's a pleasant and convenient base from which to explore Digby Neck and some beautiful, lesser-known hiking trails in the area (hint: get out to Point Prim).

Sleeping & Eating

Bayside Inn B&B B&B $$

(902-245-2247, 888-754-0555; www.baysideinn.ca; 115 Montague Row; r $64-108; wi-fi) In continuous operation since the late 1800s, the historic 11-room Bayside is Digby's oldest inn. Centrally located in

Annapolis Valley Wine Tour

This tour of our favorite wineries starts at Blomidon Estate Winery in Canning North of Highway 1. From here go into downtown Wolfville and turn inland on Gaspereau Dr across from Tim Hortons. Follow the signs to the next three vineyards.

Blomidon Estate Winery (902-582-7565; www.blomidonwine.com; 10318 Hwy 221; tastings $4; 10am & 6pm Jun-Sep) The sparkling wines and Tidal Bay are probably the best, but the oaky red is worth a try.

Gaspereau Vineyards (902-542-1455; www.gaspereauwine.com; 2239 White Rock Rd; 10am-5pm May-Oct, tours noon, 2pm & 4pm) This is one of the province's best-known wineries, with award-winning ice wine. The tasting room in a big red barn is posh on the inside and the staff is extra friendly.

L'Acadie Vineyards (902-542-8463; www.lacadievineyards.ca; 310 Slayter Rd; cottages $150; 10am-5pm May-Oct) Overlooking Gaspereau Valley, this geothermally powered winery grows certified-organic grapes to make traditional-method sparkling and dried-grape wines.

Luckett Vineyards (www.luckettvineyards.com; 1293 Grand Pre Rd, Wolfville; tastings $7, lunch mains $9-15; 10am-5pm May-Oct) This is one of the best destination wineries in the region, with palatial views over the vines and hillsides down to the Bay of Fundy cliffs.

town, it has views over the scallop fleet and Fundy tides. The cheaper rooms have shared bathrooms.

Boardwalk Café Cafe $
(☎902-245-5497; 40 Water St; lunch mains $8-15; ⏰11am-2pm & 5-8pm Mon-Fri, noon-3pm Sat) This little waterfront cafe serves delicious light mains, such as chicken rappie pie and shrimp jambalaya. Dinner is a more upscale experience, with mains around $18.

Getting There & Away

Digby is also the port for Bay Ferries (☎888-249-7245; www.bayferries.com; adult/child/car/bicycle $43/28/81/10) boats to New Brunswick.

Digby Neck

Craning out to take a peek into the Bay of Fundy, Digby Neck is a giraffe's length strip of land that's a haven for whale- and seabird-watchers.

Two ferries connect Long and Brier Islands to the rest of Digby Neck. The *Petit Passage* ferry leaves East Ferry (on Digby Neck) 25 minutes after the hour and Tiverton (on Long Island) on the hour; ferries are timed so that if you drive directly from Tiverton to Freeport (18km) there is no wait for the *Grand Passage* ferry to Westport (on Brier Island). Both ferries operate hourly, 24 hours a day, year-round. Round-trip passage on each ferry is $5.50 for a car and all passengers. Pedestrians ride free.

Long Island

Most people head straight to Brier Island, but Long Island has better deals on whale-watching, as well as a livelier community. At the northeastern edge of Long Island, **Tiverton** is an active fishing community.

Local Knowledge

Whale Watching

RECOMMENDATIONS FROM TOM GOODWIN, BIOLOGIST, GUIDE AND OWNER OF OCEAN EXPLORATIONS IN TIVERTON, NOVA SCOTIA

1 **DIGBY NECK**
Digby Neck and its islands are the best place to see big whales in the Maritimes. Fin, humpback and minke are the most common types that swim close to shore. The Fundy tides create the perfect conditions for their food source, such as herring and krill, which is what draws them. Further out in the bay we often see the North Atlantic right whale. We have sporadic blue whale sightings, too – they're the biggest of the species. To see one is like winning the lottery.

2 **GRAND MANAN ISLAND**
Grand Manan in New Brunswick is another top place for whale-watching, and one of the few other locations where you can see the rare North Atlantic right whale.

3 **CAPE BRETON HIGHLANDS**
The Cape Breton Highlands is the best area to view whales from the shore, though they're likely to be pilot whales, a smaller kind.

4 **THE BACK-UP PLAN**
People need a backup plan in case of bad weather. For instance, at Digby Neck, there is lots of fog in the summer and wind in the fall. Though conditions are poor here, and we don't go out, the weather might be totally fine 30 to 60 minutes up the road at, say, Annapolis Royal, where there are old forts and historic sites. Schedule an extra day, and take advantage of the region's other attractions.

5 **SEAFOOD AFTER THE TOUR**
You have to get fresh seafood – especially scallops – when you're in Digby. The town is famous for them. Try the Boardwalk Cafe, which is by the wharf and where you'll see fleets hauling in their catch.

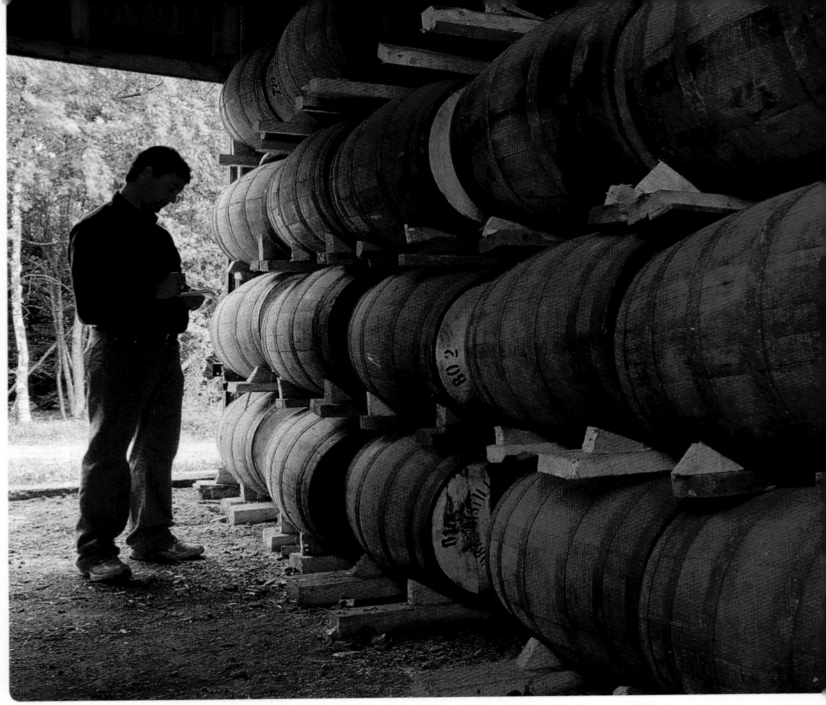

One of the best whale-watching tours in the province is found just near the Tiverton ferry dock. **Ocean Explorations Whale Cruises** (877-654-2341, 902-839-2417; www.oceanexplorations.ca; half-day tours adult/child $59/40; Jun-Oct), led by biologist Tom Goodwin, has the adventurous approach of getting you down low to whale level in a Zodiac. Shimmy into an orange coastguard-approved flotation suit and hold on tight!

At the southwestern end of Long Island, **Freeport** is central for exploring both Brier and Long Islands.

Wolfville

Wolfville has a perfect blend of old college-town culture, small-town homeyness, and the fine food and drink scene that's grown around the surrounding wine industry. Just outside town, you'll find Acadian dikes, scenic drives and some of the best hiking along the Fundy Coast.

Sleeping & Eating

Garden House B&B B&B **$$**

(902-542-1703; www.gardenhouse.ca; 220 Main St; r $65-110;) This antique house retains its old-time feel in the most comfortable way. Creaky floors, a rustic breakfast table decorated with wildflowers, and that everyone is encouraged to take off their shoes creates a lived-in vibe you instantly feel a part of. Bathrooms are shared.

Front & Central Fusion **$$**

(866-542-0588; 117 Front St; small plates $8-15; lunch Thu-Sun, dinner Tue-Sun;) Choose creative small plates, from a delicious vegetarian 'faux pho' to scallops with a maple glazed pork belly. Share the plates, mix and match and have fun with it. Light eaters may find one is enough, while big appetites may devour four or more.

Left: Glenora Inn & Distillery (p273), Mabou;
Below: Baddeck (p275), Cape Breton Island
(LEFT) JOHN SYLVESTER/ALAMY ©; (BELOW) BARRETT & MACKAY/GETTY IMAGES ©

Information

Wolfville **(www.wolfville.info)** Information on Wolfville, Acadia University and exploring Nova Scotia.

CAPE BRETON ISLAND

Floating over the rest of Nova Scotia like an island halo, Cape Breton is a heavenly, forested realm of bald eagles, migrating whales, palpable history and foot-tapping music. Starting up the Ceilidh Trail along the western coastline, Celtic music vibrates through the pubs and community centers, eventually reaching the Cabot Trail where more eclectic Acadian-style tunes ring out around Chéticamp.

The 300km Cabot Trail continues around Cape Breton Highlands National Park. It winds and climbs around and over coastal mountains, with heart-stopping ocean views at every turn, moose on the roads (watch out!) and plenty of trails to stop and hike.

Mabou

Although it looks unlikely at first glance, micro Mabou is the not-so-underground hot spot of Cape Breton's Celtic music scene.

Sights & Activities

Glenora Inn & Distillery Distillery
(☎902-258-2662, 800-839-0491; www.glenora-distillery.com; Hwy 19; guided tours incl tasting $7; ⏱tours hourly 9am-5pm Jun-Oct) Take a tour and taste the rocket fuel at the only distillery making single malt whiskey in Canada. Then, stop for an excellent meal at the gourmet pub (there are daily lunchtime and dinner ceilidhs) or even for the night. It's 9km north of Mabou.

Sleeping & Eating

Red Shoe Pub Pub $$

(☎902-945-2996; www.redshoepub.com; 11533 Hwy 19; mains $9-22; ⏰11:30am-11pm Mon-Wed, to 2am Thu-Sat, noon-11pm Sun) Straddling the spine of the Ceilidh Trail, this pub is the beating heart of Mabou. Gather round a local fiddle player (often from the Rankin family) while enjoying a pint and a superb meal. The desserts, including the gingerbread with rum-butterscotch sauce and fruit compote, are divine.

Chéticamp

While Mabou is the center of Celtic music, lively Chéticamp throws in some folky notes and French phrases to get your feet moving to Acadian tunes.

Sleeping & Eating

Acadian Crafts & Cuisine Acadian $$

(☎902-224-2170; 15067 Main St; mains $10-15; ⏰9am-9pm) This Acadian-only restaurant serves home-style dishes, such as Laurette's meat pie (an Acadian-style pork pie) or get a sample plate to try a bit of everything.

Entertainment

Doryman's Beverage Room Live Music

(☎902-224-9909; 15528 Cabot Trail) This drinking establishment hosts 'sessions' (cover $8), with a fiddler and piano players from Mabou each Saturday (2pm to 6pm), and an acoustic Acadian group at 8pm Sunday, Tuesday, Wednesday and Friday.

Cape Breton Highlands National Park

One-third of the Cabot Trail runs through this extensive **park** (www.pc.gc.ca/capebreton; adult/child/vehicle & passengers $7.80/3.90/19.60) of woodland, tundra, bog and startling sea views.

There are two park entrances: one at Chéticamp and one at Ingonish. Purchase an entry permit at either park entrance. A one-day pass is good until noon the next day.

Alexander Graham Bell National Historic Site, Baddeck

ROLF HICKER PHOTOGRAPHY/GETTY IMAGES ©

Pleasant Bay

A perfect base for exploring the park, Pleasant Bay is a carved-out bit of civilization hemmed in on all sides by wilderness. It's an active fishing harbor known for its whale-watching tours and Tibetan monastery.

Sights & Activities

Gampo Abbey Monastery
(**902-224-2752; www.gampoabbey.org; tours 1:30-3:30pm Mon-Fri Jun-Sep**) This abbey, 8km north of Pleasant Bay past the village of Red River, is a monastery for followers of Tibetan Buddhism. You can visit the grounds any time during the day, but you get a more authentic experience with a tour – a friendly monk escorts you.

Captain Mark's Whale & Seal Cruise Boat Tour
(**902-224-1316, 888-754-5112; www.whaleandsealcruise.com; adult $35-44, child $15-22; May-Sep**) Depending on the season, two to five daily tours can be taken in the lower-priced 'Cruiser' motorboat or closer to the action in a Zodiac. Captain Mark promises not only guaranteed whales, but also time to see seabirds and seals, as well as Gampo Abbey. Tours leave from the wharf next to the Whale Interpretive Centre.

Around St Ann's Bay

Settle into the artsy calm of winding roads, serene lakes, eagles soaring overhead and a never-ending collection of artists' workshops that dot the trail like Easter eggs.

Sleeping & Eating

Chanterelle Country Inn & Cottages Inn $$
(**902-929-2263, 866-277-0577; www.chanterelleinn.com; 48678 Cabot Trail, North River; r $145-225, restaurant mains $20 to $28, 4-course set menu veg/nonveg $38/45; May-Nov;**) Unparalleled as an environmentally friendly place to stay, the house and cabins are on 60 hectares overlooking rolling pastures and bucolic bliss. Meals (breakfast and dinner) are served on the screened-in porch. If you're not staying, you can reserve for dinner at the highly reputed **restaurant**.

Baddeck

An old resort town in a pastoral setting, Baddeck is on the north shore of Bras d'Or Lake, halfway between Sydney and the Canso Causeway. It's the most popular place to stay for those who intend to do the Cabot Trail as a one-day scenic drive.

Sights & Activities

Alexander Graham Bell National Historic Site Museum
(**902-295-2069; www.parkscanada.gc.ca; 559 Chebucto St; adult/child $7.80/3.90; 9am-6pm**) The inventor of the telephone is buried near his summer home, Beinn Bhreagh, which is visible across the bay from Baddeck. The excellent museum of the Alexander Graham Bell National Historic Site, at the eastern edge of town, covers all aspects of his inventions and innovations.

Sleeping & Eating

Broadwater Inn & Cottages Inn $$
(**902-295-1101, 877-818-3474; www.broadwater.baddeck.com; 975 Bay Rd; r $95-150, ste $225, cottages $105-225; May-Nov;**) In a tranquil spot 1.5km east of Baddeck, this c 1830 home once belonged to JAD McCurdy, who worked with Alexander Graham Bell on early aircraft designs. The rooms in the inn are full of character, have bay views and are decorated with subtle prints and lots of flair. Modern self-contained cottages are set in the woods and are great for families.

Highwheeler Cafe & Deli Cafe $
(486 Chebucto St; sandwiches $9; 6am-8pm;) This place bakes great bread and goodies (some gluten-free), makes big tasty sandwiches (including vegetarian), quesadillas, soups and more. Finish off on the sunny deck licking an ice-cream cone. Box lunches for hikers are also available.

Entertainment

Baddeck Gathering Ceilidhs Live Music
(902-295-2794; www.baddeckgathering.com; St Michael's Parish Hall, 8 Old Margaree Rd; adult/child $10/5; 7:30pm Jul & Aug) Nightly fiddling and dancing. The parish hall is just opposite the VIC right in the middle of town.

Louisbourg

Louisbourg, 37km southeast of Sydney, is famous for its historic fortress. The town itself has plenty of soul, with its working fishing docks, old-timers and a friendly vibe.

Sleeping & Eating

Cranberry Cove Inn Inn $$
(902-733-2171, 800-929-0222; www.cranberrycoveinn.com; 12 Wolfe St; r $105-160; May-Nov;) From the dark pink facade to the period-perfect interior of mauves, dusty blues and antique lace, you'll be transported back in time through rose-colored glasses at this stunning inn. Each room is different and several have Jacuzzis and fireplaces.

Beggar's Banquet Seafood $$$
(888-374-8439; Point of View Suites, 15 Commercial St Extension; meals $38; 6-8pm Jul-Sep) Finally, here's a chance for you to get into period costume and gorge on a feast of local seafood in a replicated 18th-century tavern. There's a choice of four delicious and copious mains including crab and lobster. It's located at the Point of View Suites.

NEW BRUNSWICK

Fredericton

This sleepy provincial capital does quaint very well. On warm weekends, 'The Green,' as it's known, looks like something out of a watercolor painting – families strolling, kids kicking soccer balls, couples picnicking.

Sights

Beaverbrook Art Gallery Museum
(www.beaverbrookartgallery.org; 703 Queen St; adult/child $10/5, pay as you wish Thu after 5pm; 10am-5pm Mon-Wed, Fri & Sat, to 9pm Thu, noon-5pm Sun) This relatively small but excellent gallery was one of Lord Beaverbrook's gifts to the town. The exceptional collection includes works by international heavyweights and is well worth an hour or so. Among others you will see Constable, Dali, Gainsborough and Turner, Canadian artists Tom Thompson, Emily Carr and Cornelius Kreighoff as well as changing contemporary exhibits of Atlantic art.

Officers' Square Historic Site
(www.downtownfredericton.ca; btwn Carleton & Regent Sts; ceremonies 11am & 4pm daily & 7pm Tue & Thu Jul & Aug) Once the military parade ground, the Garrison District's Officers' Square now hosts a full-uniform changing of the guard ceremony in summertime. Also in summer the Calithumpians Outdoor Summer Theatre performs daily at 12:15pm weekdays and 2pm weekends. The free historical skits are laced with humor.

Tours

Heritage Walking Tours Walking Tour
(10am, 2:30pm & 5pm daily Jul & Aug, 4pm Jun & Sep-Nov) FREE Enthusiastic young people wearing historic costumes lead good, free hour-long tours of the river, the government district or the Historic Garrison District, departing from City Hall.

ROLF HICKER PHOTOGRAPHY/GETTY IMAGES ©

Don't Miss
Louisbourg National Historic Site

Budget a full day to explore this extraordinary historic site that faithfully re-creates Fortress Louisbourg as it was in 1744, right down to the people – costumed thespians take their characters and run with them. Built to protect French interests in the region, it was also a base for cod fishing and an administrative capital.

Free guided tours around the site are offered throughout the day. Be prepared for lots of walking, and bring a sweater and raincoat even if it's sunny when you start out.

Though the scale of the reconstruction is massive, three-quarters of Louisbourg is still in ruins. The 2.5km **Ruins Walk** guides you through the untouched terrain and out to the Atlantic coast.

Three restaurants in the site serve food typical of the time. **Hotel de la Marine** and the adjacent **L'Épée Royale** (grilled cod with soup $14, 3-course meal $20) are where sea captains and prosperous merchants would dine on fine china with silver cutlery. Servers in period costume also dish out grub at **Grandchamps House** (meals $9-15), a favorite of sailors and soldiers. Wash down beans and sausage with hot buttered rum ($4).

NEED TO KNOW

902-733-2280; 259 Park Service Rd; adult/child $17.60/8.80; 9am-5:30pm

Sleeping

Carriage House Inn B&B **$$**
(506-452-9924, 800-267-6068; www.carriagehouse-inn.net; 230 University Ave; r incl breakfast $105-139;) In a shady Victorian neighborhood near the Green, this beautifully restored 1875 Queen Anne was built for a lumber baron and former Fredericton mayor. The grand common room

Detour: Fredericton to Fundy Shore

Start on the north side of the river in Fredericton, and follow Rte 105 south through Maugerville to Jemseg. At Exit 339, pick up Rte 715 South which will take you to the **Gagetown ferry landing** (24hr year-round) FREE. This is the first of a system of eight free cable ferries that crisscross the majestic St John River en route to the city of Saint John. You will never have to wait more than a few minutes for the crossing, which generally takes five to 10 minutes.

From Gagetown, head south on Rte 102, known locally as 'Old River Road.' The hilly 42km piece of road between Gagetown and the **Evandale ferry landing** (24hr year-round) FREE is especially picturesque, with glorious panoramic views of fields full of wildflowers, white farmhouses and clots of green and gold islands set in the intensely blue water of the river.

A hundred years ago, tiny Evandale was a bustling little place, where a dance band would entertain riverboat passengers stopping off for the night at the **Evandale Resort** (506-468-2222; ferry landing; r $139-199), now restored to its Victorian grandeur. On the other side of the water, Rte 124 takes you the short distance to the **Belleisle ferry** (24hr year-round) FREE. The ferry deposits you on the rural Kingston Peninsula, where you can cross the peninsula to catch the **Gondola Point Ferry** (signposted off Hwy 1 at Exit 141) FREE and head directly into Saint John.

has polished hardwood floors, antiques, comfy sofas, fireplaces and a grand piano. Upstairs, the guest rooms have high ceilings, four-posters, period wallpapers and vintage artwork.

Brennan's B&B B&B $$
(506-455-7346; www.bbcanada.com/3892.html; 146 Waterloo Row; r incl breakfast $95-135;) Built for a wealthy merchant family in 1885, this turreted white riverfront mansion is now a handsome four-room B&B. The better rooms have hardwood floors and water views.

Eating

WW Boyce Farmers Market Market $
(www.boycefarmersmarket.com; 665 George St; 6am-1pm Sat) This Fredericton institution is great for picking up fresh fruit, vegetables, meat, cheese, handicrafts, dessert and flowers. Many of the 150 or so stalls recall the city's European heritage, with everything from German-style sausages to French duck pâtés to British marmalade. There is also a restaurant where Frederictonians queue to chat and people-watch.

Blue Door Fusion $$$
(506-455-2583; www.thebluedoor.ca; 100 Regent St; mains $14-28; 11:30am-2pm Tue-Fri, 5-9pm Mon-Sat) This local hot spot serves upscale fusion dishes like Gorgonzola bruschetta, maple-miso cod and chicken curry in a dim, urban-chic dining room. Retro cocktails like Singapore slings and Harvey Wallbangers are real favorites.

Drinking & Nightlife

Lunar Rogue Pub Pub
(www.lunarrogue.com; 625 King St; 10am-late Mon-Sat, 11am-10pm Sun) This jolly locals' joint has a good beer selection and a fine assortment of single malts. The patio is wildly popular during the warmer weather.

Information

Visitors Center (888-888-4768, 506-460-2129; www.tourismfredericton.ca; City Hall, 397 Queen St; 9am-8pm) Free city parking passes provided here.

Getting There & Away

Air

Fredericton International Airport (YFC; www.yfcmobile.ca) is on Hwy 102, 14km southeast of town.

Car & Motorcycle

Cars with out-of-province license plates are eligible for a free three-day parking pass for downtown Fredericton May to October, available at the visitors center at City Hall.

Getting Around

A taxi to the airport costs $18 to $22.

Bicycle rentals are available at **Radical Edge** (506-459-3478; www.radicaledge.ca; 386 Queen St; rental per day $25).

Grand Manan Island

Grand Manan is a peaceful, unspoiled place. There are no fast-food restaurants, no trendy coffeehouses or nightclubs, no traffic lights and no traffic. Just a ruggedly beautiful coastline of high cliffs and sandy coves interspersed with spruce forest and fields of long grass.

The ferry disembarks at the village of North Head at the north end of the island. The main road, Rte 776, runs 28.5km down the length of the island along the eastern shore. You can drive from end to end in about 45 minutes.

Sights

Swallowtail Lighthouse Lighthouse

Whitewashed Swallowtail Lighthouse (1860) is the island's signature vista, cleaving to a rocky promontory about 1km north of the ferry wharf. Access is via steep stairs and a slightly swaying suspension bridge. Since the light was automated in 1986, the site has been left to the elements. Nevertheless, the grassy bluff is a stupendous setting for a picnic. It has a wraparound view of the horizon and seals raiding the heart-shape fishing weirs (an ancient type of fishing trap made from wood posts) below.

Seal Cove Historic Site

Seal Cove is the island's prettiest village. Much of its charm comes from the fishing boats, wharves and herring-smoking sheds clustered around the tidal creek mouth. For a century, smoked herring was king on Grand Manan. A thousand men and women worked splitting, stringing and drying fish in 300 smoke-houses up and down the island. The last

Wharf at Seal Cove
BARRETT & MACKAY/GETTY IMAGES ©

smokehouse shut down in 1996. Today, the sheds house an informal **Sardine Museum** (admission by donation; 11am-4pm Tue-Sat).

Activities

Sea Watch Tours Birdwatching

(506-662-8552, 877-662-8552; www.sea-watchtours.com; Seal Cove fisherman's wharf; adult/child $86/48; Mon-Sat Jul & Aug) Make the pilgrimage out to isolated Machias Seal Island to see the Atlantic puffins waddle and play on their home turf. Access is limited to 15 visitors a day, so reserve well in advance.

Whales-n-Sails Adventures Boat Tour

(506-662-1999, 888-994-4044; www.whales-n-sails.com; North Head fisherman's wharf; adult/child $66/46; Jul-Sep) A marine biologist narrates these exhilarating whale-watching tours aboard the sailboat *Elsie Menota*. You'll often see puffins, razorbills, murre and other seabirds.

Hiking Trails Hiking

Grab the comprehensive guide to the *Heritage Trails and Footpaths on Grand Manan* ($5), available at most island shops.

For an easy hike, try the 1.6km shoreline path from Long Pond to Red Point (about one hour round-trip; suitable for children).

Sleeping

Shorecrest Lodge Inn $$

(506-662-3216; www.shorecrestlodge.com; 100 Rte 776, Seal Cove; r $90-135;) Near the ferry landing, this big, comfy farmhouse has 10 sunny rooms with quilts and antique furniture. A rec room has a TV and a toy train set for the kids. The Austrian owners cook up fresh seafood dinners (mains $18 to $28) and takeout lunches; nonguests can call ahead to order.

Inn at Whale Cove Inn $$

(506-662-3181; www.whalecovecottages.ca; Whistle Rd, North Head; s/d incl breakfast $135/145; May-Oct) 'Serving rusticators since 1910,' including writer Willa Cather, who wrote several of her novels here in the 1920s and '30s. The main lodge (built in 1816) and half a dozen vine-covered and shingled cottages retain the charm of

Hopewell Rocks, New Brunswick

LASZLO PODOR PHOTOGRAPHY/GETTY IMAGES ©

that earlier era. They are fitted with polished pine floors and stone fireplaces, antiques, chintz curtains and well-stocked bookshelves. Some have kitchens.

Eating

Reservations are essential for dinner due to limited table space island-wide.

North Head Bakery Bakery $
(www.northheadbakery.ca; 199 Rte 776, North Head; baked goods $1-5; 6:30am-5:30pm Tue-Sat May-Oct) Scrumptious Danish pastries, fruit pies and artisanal breads made with organic flour make this cheerful red-and-white bakery the first stop for many folks just off the ferry. Sit at the lunch counter with a coffee and sandwich and watch the parade.

Inn at Whale Cove Modern Canadian $$$
(506-662-3181; www.whalecovecottages.ca; Whistle Rd, North Head; mains $22-28; 5-9pm) Absolutely wonderful food in a relaxed country setting on the cove. The menu changes daily, but includes mouth-watering upscale meals such as Provençal-style rack of lamb, scallop ravioli and a to-die-for hazelnut crème caramel for dessert. Come early and have a cocktail by the fire in the cozy, old-fashioned parlor.

Shopping

Roland's Sea Vegetables Market
(www.rolandsdulse.com; 174 Hill Rd; 9am-6pm) Grand Manan is one of the few remaining producers of dulse, a type of seaweed that is used as a snack food or seasoning in Atlantic Canada and around the world. Dark Harbour, on the west side of the island, is said to produce the world's best. Buy some at this little roadside market, which sells various types of edible local seaweeds from nori to sea lettuce to Irish moss.

If You Like… Coastal Scenery

If Grand Manan Island floats your boat, check out these other highlights along the Fundy Coast.

1 **ST ANDREWS BY-THE-SEA**
(www.townofstandrews.ca) A genteel summer resort town of inns, spas and pubs, St Andrews is where folks come to dine on lobster and windowshop with an ice cream cone. High tea or afternoon gin at the castle-like Algonquin Resort is de rigueur.

2 **CAMPOBELLO ISLAND**
(www.visitcampobello.com) Campobello feels as much a part of the USA as of Canada; it connects to Lubec, Maine via bridge. Franklin D Roosevelt spent significant time here, and the island's southern half is an international park preserving the wild landscape he loved. Look for whales offshore from East Quoddy Head Lighthouse.

3 **FUNDY NATIONAL PARK**
(www.pc.gc.ca/fundy; daily permits adult/child/family $7.80/3.90/19.60) One of the country's most popular national parks, its highlights include the world's highest tides, irregularly eroded sandstone cliffs and 120km of walking trails.

4 **CAPE ENRAGE**
(www.capenrage.ca; off Rte 905; adult/child $5/3; 9am-8pm) The 150-year-old clifftop lighthouse provides dramatic views. There's an on-site climbing and rappelling school and excellent meals in the lightkeeper's house.

5 **HOPEWELL ROCKS**
(www.thehopewellrocks.ca; off Hwy 114; adult/child/family $9/6.75/24, shuttle per person $2; 8am-8pm;) Some look like arches, others like massive stone mushrooms. People come from all over the world to marvel at the rocks' Dr Seussian vibe. Be prepared for crowds.

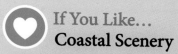

Below: Confederation Chamber, Province House National Historic Site;
Right: North River Rd, Charlottetown
(BELOW & RIGHT) BARRETT & MACKAY/GETTY IMAGES ©

Information

Tourist Office (www.grandmanannb.com; 130 Rte 776, North Head; 8am-4pm Mon-Fri, 9am-noon Sat)

Getting There & Around

The only way to get on and off the island from Blacks Harbour on the mainland to North Head on Grand Manan is by the **government ferry** (506-662-3724; www.coastaltransport.ca; adult/child/car/bicycle $12/6/33/4; ticket office at North Head ferry terminal). The crossing takes 1½ hours, and there are seven departures daily in summer. Service is first-come, first-served at Blacks Harbour; plan on arriving at least 45 minutes before departure. Watch for harbor porpoises and whales en route.

PRINCE EDWARD ISLAND

Charlottetown

PEI's capital is just about the perfect size, with a collection of stylish eateries and a lively cultural scene. Couple this with quiet streets for strolling, abundant greenery and a well-preserved historical core, and you have plenty of small-town appeal.

Sights

Province House National Historic Site Historic Site
(902-566-7626; http://www.pc.gc.ca/lhn-nhs/pe/provincehouse/index.aspx; 165 Richmond St; admission $3.40; 8:30am-5pm) It was

here in 1864, within the Confederation Chamber, that 23 representatives of Britain's North American colonies first discussed the creation of Canada. Along with being the 'birthplace of Canada,' the site is home to Canada's second-oldest active legislature.

Several rooms have been restored, and in July and August actors in period garb wander the halls and regularly come together to perform reenactments of the famous conference.

Tours

Confederation Players Walking Tour

(**☎800-565-0278; 6 Prince St; adult/child $15/8; ⏲daily Jul & Aug**) There is no better way to tour Charlottetown. Playing the fathers and ladies of Confederation, actors garbed in 19th-century dress educate and entertain through the town's historic streets.

Peake's Wharf Boat Cruises Boat Cruise

(**☎902-566-4458; www.peakeswharfboattours.com; 1 Great George St; 70min cruise $20; ⏲2:30pm, 6:30pm & 8pm Jun-Aug**) Observe sea life, hear interesting stories and witness a wonderfully different perspective of Charlottetown from the waters of its harbor. An excellent seal-watching trip ($28) departs at 2:30pm, returning at 5pm.

Sleeping

Charlotte's Rose Inn Inn $$

(**☎902-892-3699, 888-237-3699; www.charlottesrose.ca; 11 Grafton St; r incl breakfast $120-195, apt $195; ❄📶**) Miss Marple must be around here somewhere. This decadent Victorian has true English flair with bodacious rose-printed wallpaper, lace canopies, big fluffy beds and grand bathrooms. There's a fire in the parlor for guests to enjoy along with complimentary tea and cakes.

Detour: Prince Edward Island Distilleries

Two distinctly different distilleries operate on Prince Edward Island (PEI), echoing the province's fame for bootlegging during prohibition.

Prince Edward Distillery (902-687-2586; www.princeedwarddistillery.com; Rte 16, Hermanville; 11am-6pm) specializes in potato vodka that, even in its first year of production, has turned international heads (some calling it among the finest of its class). Stop in for tours of the immaculate distillery and to taste the different vodkas (potato, grain and blueberry) as well as the newer products such as bourbon, rum, whiskey, pastis and a very interesting and aromatic gin.

Myriad View Distillery (902-687-1281; www.straightshine.com; 1336 Rte 2, Rollo Bay; 11am-6pm Mon-Sat, 1-5pm Sun) produces Canada's first and only legal moonshine. The hardcore Straight Lightning Shine is 75% alcohol and so potent it feels like liquid heat before it evaporates on your tongue. Take our advice and start with a micro-sip! A gulp could knock the wind out of you. The 50% alcohol Straight Shine lets you enjoy the flavor a bit more. Tours and tastings are free and the owner is happy to answer any questions.

The distilleries are 75km east of Charlottetown. It's about a 10-minute drive on Hwy 307 between the two places.

Fairholm Inn B&B **$$$**
(902-892-5022, 888-573-5022; www.fairholm.pe.ca; 230 Prince St; ste incl breakfast $129-289;) This historic inn was built in 1838 and is a superb example of the picturesque movement in British architecture. Take tea while enjoying the morning sun in the beautiful conservatory, wander the gardens or hole up with a book in the library. Luxurious English fabrics, beautiful PEI artwork and grand antiques fill each suite.

Great George Inn **$$$**
(902-892-0606, 800-361-1118; www.thegreatgeorge.com; 58 Great George St; d incl breakfast $175-219, ste $269-899;) This colorful collage of celebrated buildings along Charlottetown's most famous street has rooms ranging from plush and historic to bold and contemporary – but all are simply stunning. It's both gay- and family-friendly.

Lobster

Eating

Leonard's Cafe $

(University Ave; sandwiches from $5; ⏲9am-5pm Tue-Sat) Find absolute comfort in this little cafe full of cushioned seating and soothing country-style muted hues. Treat yourself to excellent German pastries, salads and creative sandwiches as well as all-day breakfasts made with free-range eggs, a great cheese selection and cold cuts like Black Forest ham.

Water Prince Corner Shop Seafood $$

(☎902-368-3212; 141 Water St; meals $10-27; ⏲9:30am-8pm) When locals want seafood they head to this inconspicuous, sea-blue eatery near the wharf. It is deservedly famous for its scallop burgers, but it's also the best place in town for fresh lobster. You'll probably have to line up for a seat, otherwise order takeout lobster, which gets you a significant discount.

Lot 30
Modern Canadian $$$

(☎902-629-3030; 151 Kent St; mains $22-55; ⏲from 5pm Tue-Sun) Anyone who's anyone goes to Lot 30, but show up unknown and in jeans and you'll be treated just as well.

For a treat, try the excellent-value five-course tasting menu ($60) – small servings of a starter, three mains and a dessert sampler.

Drinking

Gahan House Pub

(☎902-626-2337; 126 Sydney St; ⏲11am-10pm or 11pm Sun-Thu, to midnight or 1am Fri & Sat) Within these homey, historic walls the pub owners brew PEI homegrown ales. Sir John A's Honey Wheat Ale is well worth introducing to your insides, as is the medium- to full-bodied Sydney Street Stout. The food here is also great – enjoy with friends old and new.

If You Like… Seafood

If you like Water Prince Corner Shop, head to these seafood hot spots, all within an hour of Charlottetown and a half-hour from Cavendish.

1 **NEW GLASGOW LOBSTER SUPPER**
(☎902-964-2870; Rte 258; lobster dinners $32; ⏲4-8:30pm) You can make a right mess with the lobster here, while also gorging on an endless supply of great chowder, mussels, salads, breads and homemade desserts.

2 **ST ANN'S LOBSTER SUPPER**
(☎902-621-0635; Rte 224; lobster dinners $32; ⏲4:30-8:30pm) Crack into a crustacean in this quintessential PEI church basement, complete with chowder, steamed blue mussels and melted butter. Many islanders' rank it as their favorite lobster supper.

3 **MALPEQUE OYSTER BARN**
(Malpeque Wharf; 6 oysters $14; ⏲11am-9pm Mon-Sat, noon-9pm Sun) The hamlet of Malpeque is where the namesake oysters come from, famed for their moist, briny taste that's perfect with a beer. This atmospheric cafe sits in the top of a fisherman's barn overlooking the bay.

Entertainment

Benevolent Irish Society Live Music

(☎902-963-3156; 582 North River Rd; admission $10; ⏲8pm Fri) On the north side of town, this is a great place to catch a ceilidh. Come early, as seating is limited.

Information

Visitors Centre (☎888-734-7529, 902-368-4444; www.peiplay.com; 6 Prince St; ⏲9am-10pm Jul & Aug, reduced hours Sep-Jun) It has all the answers, a plethora of brochures and maps, and free internet access.

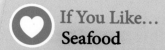

Getting There & Away

Air

Charlottetown Airport (YYG; ☎902-566-7997; www.flypei.com) is 8km north of the city center at Brackley Point and Sherwood Rds. A taxi to/from town costs $12, plus $3.50 for each additional person.

Getting Around

Bicycle

Riding is a great way to get around this quaint town. **MacQueen's Bicycles** (☎902-368-2453; www.macqueens.com; 430 Queen St; per day/week $25/125) rents a variety of quality bikes.

Car & Motorcycle

The municipal parking lots near the tourist office and Peak's Wharf charge $6 per day.

Prince Edward Island National Park

Heaving dunes and red sandstone bluffs provide startling backdrops for some of the island's finest stretches of sand; welcome to **Prince Edward Island National Park** (☎902-672-6350; www.pc.gc.ca/pei; day pass adult/child $7.80/3.90).

The park is open year-round, but most services only operate between late June and the end of August.

Sights & Activities

Beaches lined with marram grasses and wild rose span almost the entire length of the park's 42km coastline. In most Canadians' minds, the park is almost synonymous with these strips of sand. **Dalvay Beach** sits to the east, and has some short hiking trails through the woods. The landscape flattens and the sand sprawls outward at **Stanhope Beach**. Here, a boardwalk leads from the campground to the shore. Backed by dunes, and slightly west, is the expansive and popular **Brackley Beach**. On the western side of the park, the sheer size of **Cavendish Beach** makes it the granddaddy of them all. A beautiful bike lane runs all the way along this coast.

Cavendish

Anyone familiar with *Anne of Green Gables* might have lofty ideas of finding Cavendish as a quaint village bedecked in flowers and country charm; guess again. While the Anne and Lucy Maud Montgomery sites are right out of the imagination-inspiring book pages, Cavendish itself is a mishmash of manufactured attractions with no particular town center. The junction of Rte 6 and Hwy 13 is the tourist center and the area's commercial hub.

To really get a feel for the *Anne of Green Gables* scenery get out and walk the green, gentle creek-crossed woods that Lucy Maud herself knew like the back of her hand. The best way is to start at the Lucy Maud Montgomery's Cavendish Homestead where you can buy a combo ticket that includes the House of Green Gables for $8.50. Then walk the 1.1km return trail to the House of Green Gables through the 'Haunted Wood.'

Sights

Lucy Maud Montgomery's Cavendish Homestead Historic Site

(☎902-963-2231; Rte 6; adult/child $4/2; 9am-6pm) This is considered hallowed ground to Anne fans worldwide. Raised by her grandparents, Lucy Maud lived in this house from 1876 to 1911 and it is here that she wrote *Anne of Green Gables*. You'll find the old foundation of the house, many interpretive panels about Lucy Maud, a small on-site museum and a bookshop.

Avonlea Village Amusement Park

(☎902-963-3050; www.avonlea.ca; Rte 6; adult/family $19/70; 10am-5pm) Delve deeper into Anne fantasy at this theme park where costumed actors portray characters from the book and perform dramatic moments and scenes from Green Gable chapters.

BARRETT & MACKAY/GETTY IMAGES ©

Don't Miss
House of Green Gables

Cavendish is the home town of Lucy Maud Montgomery (1874–1942), author of *Anne of Green Gables*. Here she is simply known as Lucy Maud or LM. Owned by her grandfather's cousins, the now-famous House of Green Gables and its Victorian surrounds inspired the setting for her fictional tale.

In 1937 the house became part of the national park and it's now administered as a national heritage site, celebrating Lucy Maud and Anne with artifacts (pictured above), exhibits and audio-visual displays.

NEED TO KNOW

902-672-7874; Rte 6; adult/child $6.30/3.15; 10am-5pm Mon-Sat

Sleeping & Eating

Parkview Farm Tourist Home & Cottages B&B $

(902-963-2027, 800-237-9890; www.peionline.com/al/parkview; 8214 Rte 6; r with shared bathroom incl light breakfast $65-70, 2-bedroom cottages $165-265;) This fine choice is set on a working dairy farm, 2km east of Cavendish. Ocean views, bathrooms and the prerequisite flowered wallpaper and frills abound in this comfortable and roomy tourist home.

Kindred Spirits Country Inn & Cottages Inn $$

(902-963-2434, 800-461-1755; www.kindred-spirits.ca; Rte 6; d $85-320, cottages $105-500;) A huge, immaculate complex, this place has something for everyone from a storybook-quality inn-style B&B to deluxe suites. Rooms are every Anne fan's dream, with dotty floral prints, glossy wood floors and fluffy, comfy beds.

Carr's Oysters Seafood **$$**
(☎902-886-3355; Stanley Bridge Wharf, Rte 6; mains $14-32; ⏰10am-7pm) Dine on oysters straight from Malpeque Bay or lobster, mussels and seafood you've never even heard of like quahogs from this place's saltwater tanks. There are also plenty of fish on offer from salmon to trout. The setting over the bay is sociable and bright and there's also an on-site market selling fresh and smoked sea critters.

Pearl Modern Canadian **$$$**
(☎902-963-2111; 7792 Cavendish Rd; mains $22-32, brunch $8-12; ⏰from 4:30pm daily, 10am-2pm Sun) This shingled house just outside Cavendish, is surrounded by flowers and is an absolutely lovely place to eat. There are plenty of unusual and seasonally changing options like ice wine–infused chicken liver pâté on a Gouda brioche for starters and locally inspired mains such as delicious butter-poached scallops.

ℹ Information

Cavendish Visitor Centre (☎902-963-7830; cnr Rte 6 & Hwy 13; ⏰9am-9pm)

Best of the Rest

Yukon Territory (p290)
Rugged northern region with a frontier flavor and spectacular scenery

Manitoba (p293)
Prairie heartland with polar-bear watching and a bustling main city

Newfoundland & Labrador (p296)
Rustic east-coast communities teeming with stories and characters

Top: Polar bear cubs, Manitoba; **Left:** Palace Grand Theatre (p292), Dawson City, Yukon Territory

Yukon Territory

HIGHLIGHTS

1. **Klondike National Historic Sites** (p292) Collection of fascinating Dawson City heritage buildings.
2. **MacBride Museum** Illuminates the region's gold-rush past; you can even try panning for riches yourself.
3. **Bombay Peggy's** (p292) Snooze and/or booze in a former brothel.

Miles Canyon, Whitehorse

WHITEHORSE

The leading city and capital of the Yukon, Whitehorse will likely have a prominent role in your journey. The territory's two great highways, the Alaska and the Klondike, cross here. You'll find all manner of outfitters and services for explorations across the territory.

Sights

MacBride Museum Museum

(**☎867-667-2709; www.macbridemuseum.com; cnr 1st Ave & Wood St; adult/child $10/5; ⏲9:30am-5pm**) The Yukon's attic covers the gold rush, Aboriginal peoples, intrepid Mounties and more. Old photos vie with old stuffed critters; daily special events like gold-panning are fun.

Tours

Yukon Historical & Museums Association Walking Tour

(**☎867-667-4704; 3126 3rd Ave; admission $6; ⏲11am-6pm Mon-Sat Jun-Aug**) Offers quirky and interesting downtown walking tours four times daily.

Sleeping

Coast High Country Inn Hotel **$$**

(**☎867-667-4471, 800-554-4471; www.highcountryinn.yk.ca; 4051 4th Ave; r $100-220; ❄@📶**) Towering over Whitehorse (four stories!), the High Country is popular with business travelers and high-end groups. The pub is a favourite.

Eating & Drinking

Klondike Rib & Salmon Canadian **$$**

(**☎867-667-7554; 2116 2nd Ave; mains $12-25; ⏲4-9pm May-Sep**) It looks touristy and it seems touristy and it *is* touristy, but the food is excellent at this sprawling casual place with two decks.

Burnt Toast

Bistro $$

(☎867-393-2605; 2112 2nd Ave; mains $10-25; ⌚9am-9pm) Brunch is excellent at this smart bistro (try the French toast) and lunch and dinner specials abound. Food is local and seasonal; consult the blackboard.

Information

VIC (☎867-667-3084; 100 Hanson St; ⌚8am-8pm) Essential; has territory-wide information.

Getting There & Away

Air

Erik Nielsen Whitehorse International Airport (YXY; ☎867-667-8440; www.gov.yk.ca/yxy/airports/yxy) Five minutes west of downtown off the Alaska Hwy.

Bus

White Pass & Yukon Route (☎867-633-5710; www.wpyr.com; Whitehorse ticket office, 1109 1st Ave; ⌚9am-5pm Mon-Sat mid-May–mid-Sep) Offers a jaw-dropping scenic 10-hour rail and bus connection to/from Skagway via Carcross, BC (one-way to Skagway adult/child $185/92.50). Service is not daily. Also offers one-day tours from Whitehorse that include a train ride.

Northern Lights in NWT

Head to Yellowknife in the Northwest Territories (NWT) for one of Canada's most memorable sights. Commonly called the northern lights, the mysterious aurora borealis stripes the night sky with a kaleidoscope of breathtaking colors that impresses mightily. Best viewing is from December to March and local operators include **Aurora Village** (☎867-669-0006; www.auroravillage.com). Its viewing vehicles have heated seats ($120) but they also offer dog-sledding ($95) and snowshoeing ($95) alternatives.

Yellowknife can be reached by air from Edmonton in Alberta and Whitehorse.

Aurora borealis in the sky above Yellowknife, Northwest Territories

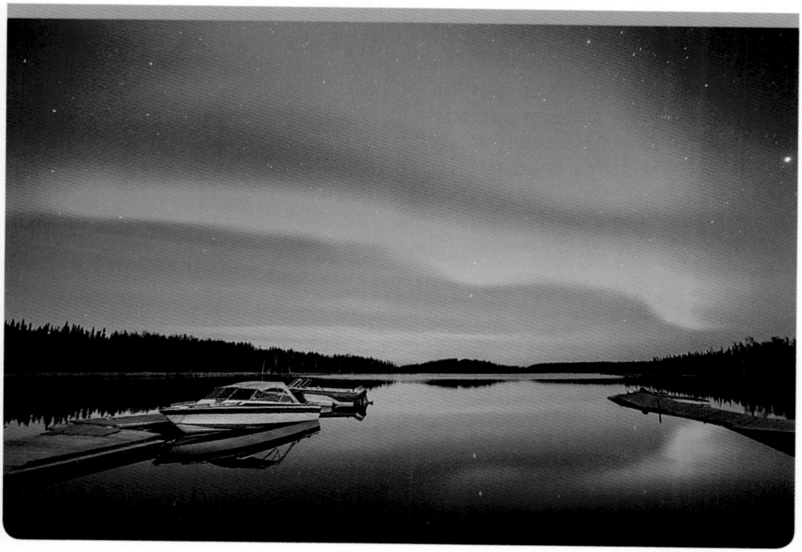

WAN RU CHEN/GETTY IMAGES ©

DAWSON CITY

If you didn't know its history, Dawson would be an atmospheric place to pause for a while, plunging into its quirky culture and falling for its seductive, funky vibe. That it's one of the most historic and evocative towns in Canada is like gold dust on a cake: unnecessary but damn nice.

Sights

Klondike National Historic Sites Historic Site
(www.pc.gc.ca/dawson; passes adult $7-32) It's easy to relive the gold rush at myriad preserved and restored places. Parks Canada tries its best with limited resources. Various restored buildings such as the Palace Grand Theatre **(King St)** are open on a sporadic and rotating basis, usually 10am to 1pm.

Jack London Interpretive Centre Museum
(Firth St; adult/child $5/free; 11am-6pm May-Aug) In 1898 Jack London lived in the Yukon, the setting for his most popular stories, including *Call of the Wild* and *White Fang*. At the writer's cabin there are daily interpretive talks.

Tours

Goldbottom Tours Gold Rush Tour
(867-993-5750; www.goldbottom.com; ticket office Front St; with/without transport from Dawson $55/45; May-Sep) Run by the legendary Millar mining family. Tour their placer mine 15km up Hunker Creek Rd, which meets Hwy 2 just north of the airport. The three-hour tours include a gold-panning lesson; you get to keep what you find.

Sleeping

Bombay Peggy's Inn $$
(867-993-6969; www.bombaypeggys.com; cnr 2nd Ave & Princess St; r $95-210; Mar-Nov;) At this renovated former brothel, Peggy's allure is its period furnishings and spunky attitude. The bar is a classy oasis.

Klondike Kate's Lodge $$
(867-993-6527; www.klondikekates.ca; cnr King St & 3rd Ave; cabins $140-200; Apr-Sep; @) The 15 cabins behind the excellent restaurant of the same name are rustic without the rusticisms.

Eating

Drunken Goat Taverna Greek $$
(867-993-5800; 2nd Ave; mains $14-25; noon-9pm) Follow your eyes to the flowers, your ears to the Aegean music and your nose to the superb Greek food, run 12-months-a-year by the wonderful Tony Dovas.

Entertainment

Diamond Tooth Gertie's Gambling Hall Casino
(867-993-5575; cnr Queen St & 4th Ave; admission $10; 7pm-2am Mon-Fri, 2pm-2am Sat & Sun May-Sep) This popular re-creation of an 1898 saloon is complete with small-time gambling, a honky-tonk piano and dancing girls. The casino helps promote the town and fund culture.

Getting There & Away

Dawson City is 527km from Whitehorse. Should you fly in, there are no rental cars.

Dawson City Airport (YDA; Klondike Hwy) About 19km east of Dawson.

Manitoba

HIGHLIGHTS

1. **Winnipeg Art Gallery** Breathtaking Inuit art collection in a funkier-than-you-think city.
2. **Fort Prince of Wales National Historic Site** (p294) Hulking old-stone fort from the 1700s.
3. **Great White Bear Tours** (p295) Tundra coaches roll out to view lumbering polar bears.

Hudson Bay, Churchill (p294)

WINNIPEG

Rising above the prairie, it's a metropolis where you least expect it. Cultured, confident and captivating, it's more than just a pit stop on the Trans-Canada haul, but a destination in its own right.

Sights & Activities

DOWNTOWN

Winnipeg Art Gallery Gallery
(WAG; ☎204-786-6641; www.wag.ca; 300 Memorial Blvd; adult/child $12/6; ⏰11am-5pm Tue, Wed & Fri-Sun, to 9pm Thu) This ship-shaped gallery plots a course for contemporary Manitoban and Canadian artists, including the world's largest collection of Inuit work.

THE FORKS

Forks National Historic Site Historic Site
(☎204-983-6757; www.parkscanada.ca/forks) In a beautiful riverside setting, modern amenities for performances and interpretive exhibits outline the area's history. Footpaths line the riverbank; plaques offer historical context.

Tours

Historic Exchange District Walking Tours Walking Tour
(☎204-942-6716; www.exchangedistrict.org; Old Market Sq; adult/child $8/free; ⏰9am-4:30pm Mon-Sat Jun-Aug) Themed and history tours departing from Old Market Sq. Book in advance.

Sleeping

Place Louis Riel Suite Hotel Hotel $$
(☎204-947-6961; www.placelouisriel.com; 190 Smith St; r $120-250; ❄📶🐾) In a renovated 23-story building downtown, the 302 rooms here all include large, stylish kitchens.

Fort Garry Hotel Hotel $$
(☎800-665-8088, 204-942-8251; www.fortgarryhotel.com; 222 Broadway Ave; r $130-200; ❄@📶🏊) Winnipeg history radiates

from this locally owned 1913 limestone legacy that's like something out of a movie.

Eating

News Cafe Cafe **$**
(www.winnipegfreepress.com/cafe; 237 McDermot Ave; mains $7-12; 8am-6pm Sat-Thu, to 10pm Fri;) This great corner cafe is run by Winnipeg's major daily newspaper, the *Free Press*. Besides great breakfasts and lunches that include a famous pulled pork sandwich, there's a definite newsy vibe.

Deer + Almond Bistro **$$**
(204-504-8562; 85 Princess St; mains $12-25; 11am-3pm & 5-11pm Mon-Sat) This fabulous recent addition to the Exchange District has a creative and ever-changing menu that features a Canadian accent on comfort food.

Drinking & Nightlife

King's Head Pub Pub
(204-957-7710; www.kingshead.ca; 120 King St; 11am-2am) Vaguely British, the gregarious sidewalk tables are the place to be in the Exchange District on a balmy evening.

Getting There & Away

Air

Winnipeg International Airport (YWG; www.waa.ca) has a flash terminal a convenient 10km west of downtown.

Train

VIA Rail's transcontinental *Canadian* departs **Union Station** (123 Main St) two or three times weekly in each direction. Trains also head north to Churchill.

CHURCHILL

Churchill lures people to the shores of Hudson Bay for polar bears, beluga whales, a huge old stone fort and endless Subarctic majesty.

Sights

Fort Prince of Wales National Historic Site Historic Site
Parks Canada (www.parkscanada.ca; Jul & Aug) administers three sites in the area documenting Churchill's varied history.

It took 40 years to build and its cannons have never fired a shot, but the star-shaped stone Fort Prince of Wales has been standing prominently on rocky Eskimo Point across the Churchill River since the 1770s.

Forks National Historic Site (p293), Winnipeg

Four kilometers south of the fort, **Sloop's Cove** was a harbor for European vessels during Churchill's harsh winters.

Cape Merry, at the national historic site, has a lone cannon and crumbling walls but the location astounds with vistas across the bay and river.

Tours

POLAR BEAR TOURS

Great White Bear Tours Adventure Tour

(☎866-765-8344, 204-487-7633; www.greatwhitebeartours.com; 266 Kelsey Blvd; from $400 per day; ⊙Oct & Nov) Uses tundra coaches but only operates day tours; guests sleep in town.

LAND & SEA TOURS

Sea North Tours Adventure Tour

(☎204-675-2195; www.seanorthtours.com; 39 Franklin St; tours from $105; ⊙Jul & Aug) Summer beluga whale tours use a custom viewing boat, zodiac inflatables and kayaks.

Lazy Bear Lodge Adventure Tour

(☎866-687-2327, 204-675-2869; www.lazybearlodge.com; 313 Kelsey Blvd; tours from $135; ⊙Jul & Aug) Summer day tours include kayaking with belugas.

Sleeping

Tundra Inn Motel $$

(☎204-675-2850, 800-265-8563; www.tundrainn.com; 34 Franklin St; r from $135, bear season from $235; @ 🛜) The 31 motel-style rooms are large and comfortable with fridges and microwaves.

Polar Inn Motel $$

(☎204-675-8878; www.polarinn.com; 153 Kelsey Blvd; r incl breakfast from $120, bear season from $200; 🛜) Basic motel-style units come with fridges. There are also studios with small kitchens and full apartments.

Eating & Drinking

Gypsy's Bakery Canadian $$

(☎204-675-2322; 253 Kelsey Blvd; mains $7-25; ⊙7am-9pm; 🛜) Luscious baked goods await in display cases and you can order from a full cafeteria-style menu.

Information

Town of Churchill (www.churchill.ca)

Getting There & Away

There is no road to Churchill; access is by plane or train only.

Air

Churchill Airport (YYQ; ☎204-675-8868) is 11km east of town; most accommodations offer drop-off/pickup, a taxi is a pricey $20.

Train

Via Rail's Churchill train is slow; it runs two to three times per week and takes upwards of 45 hours from Winnipeg and 16 from Thompson.

Newfoundland & Labrador

HIGHLIGHTS

1. **Signal Hill National Historic Site** Landmark waterfront site with amazing views.
2. **Duke of Duckworth** Friendly party pub in the heart of St John's.
3. **Gros Morne National Park** Hike the mountains and kayak the fjord-like lakes.

Cabot Tower, Signal Hill National Historic Site, St John's

ST JOHN'S

Encamped on the steep slopes of a harbor, with jelly-bean-colored row houses popping up from hilly streets, St John's is often described as looking like a mini San Francisco.

Highlights include view-gaping from Signal Hill and listening to live music and hoisting a pint (or shot of rum) in George St's pubs.

Sights

Signal Hill National Historic Site — Historic Site

(☎709-772-5367; www.pc.gc.ca/signalhill; ⏰grounds 24hr) The tiny castle atop the hill is Cabot Tower (⏰8:30am-5pm Apr-Nov), built in 1900 to honor both John Cabot's arrival in 1497 and Queen Victoria's Diamond Jubilee.

An awesome way to return to downtown is along the **North Head Trail** (1.7km) which connects Cabot Tower with the harborfront Battery neighborhood. The walk departs from the tower's parking lot and traces the cliffs, imparting tremendous sea views and sometimes whale spouts.

Tours

Iceberg Quest — Boat Tour

(☎709-722-1888; www.icebergquest.com; Pier 6; 2hr tour adult/child $60/28) Departs from St John's harbor and makes a run down to Cape Spear in search of icebergs in June, and whales in July and August.

Sleeping

Chef's Inn — B&B $$

(☎709-753-3180, 877-753-3180; www.thechefsinn.ca; 29 Gower St; r $140-170; 🚭❄📶) The four rooms are done up in modern, minimalist decor, and each has an en suite bathroom.

Narrows B&B — B&B $$

(☎709-739-4850, 866-739-4850; www.thenarrowsbb.com; 146 Gower St; r $130-175; 🚭📶) Warm colors mix with elegant trims and large wooden beds in the rooms of this welcoming B&B.

Eating

Reluctant Chef Modern Canadian $$$
(☎709-754-6011; www.facebook.com/TheReluctantChefRestaurant; 281 Duckworth St; set menu $60; ⏲noon-3:30pm Wed-Fri, 5pm-midnight Mon-Sat) Perhaps it should be renamed the 'passionate chef,' given the lovingly prepared, eight-course (give or take) menu that hits the toasty tables here.

Chinched Modern Canadian $$$
(☎709-722-3100; www.chinchedbistro.com; 7 Queen St; mains $30-35; ⏲6-9:30pm Tue-Sat) Chinched is St John's first real foodie restaurant, the kind that offers megaquality dishes but without the white-tablecloth pretense. So belly up in the warm, dark-wood room for octopus tacos or Newfoundland wild mushroom risotto.

Drinking & Nightlife

Duke of Duckworth Pub
(www.dukeofduckworth.com; McMurdo's Lane, 325 Duckworth St; ⏲noon-late; wi-fi) 'The Duke,' as it's known, is an unpretentious English-style pub that represents all that's great about Newfoundland and Newfoundlanders.

Getting Around

To/From the Airport

St John's International Airport is 6km north of the city on Portugal Cove Rd (Rte 40).

GROS MORNE NATIONAL PARK

This **national park** (☎709-458-2417; www.pc.gc.ca/grosmorne; adult/child/family per day $9.80/4.90/19.60) stepped into the world spotlight in 1987, when Unesco granted it World Heritage designation. The park's stunning flat-top mountains and deeply incised waterways are supernatural playgrounds.

The hiking, kayaking, camping, wildlife-spotting and boat tours are fantastic.

Centrally located Rocky Harbour is the largest village and most popular place to stay. Nearby Norris Point and further-flung Woody Point also make good bases.

Tours

Bon Tours Boat Tour
(☎709-458-2016; www.bontours.ca; Ocean View Motel, Main St, Rocky Harbour) Bon runs the phenomenal Western Brook Pond boat tour (2hr trip per adult $53-60, child $20-26) every hour between 10am and 5pm.

Gros Morne Adventures Guided Tour
(☎709-458-2722, 800-685-4624; www.grosmorneadventures.com; Norris Point wharf) It offers daily guided sea kayak tours (two/three hours $55/65) in Bonne Bay, plus full-day and multiday kayak trips and various hiking tours.

Sleeping

Aunt Jane's Place B&B B&B $
(☎709-453-2485; www.grosmorne.com/victorianmanor; Water St, Woody Point; d without/with bathroom $75/85; ⏲May-Oct; non-smoking) This historic house oozes character. It sits beachside, so you may be woken early in the morning by the heavy breathing of whales.

Middle Brook Cottages Cabin $$
(☎709-453-2332; www.middlebrookcottages.com; off Rte 431, Glenburnie; cabins $115-149; ⏲Mar-Nov; non-smoking, wi-fi) These all-pinewood, spick-and-span cottages are both perfectly romantic and perfectly kid-friendly. They have kitchens and TVs, and you can splash around the swimming hole and waterfalls behind the property.

Eating

Old Loft Restaurant Seafood $$
(☎709-453-2294; www.theoldloft.com; Water St, Woody Point; mains $15-21; ⏲11:30am-9pm Jul & Aug, to 7pm May, Jun & Sep) Set on the water in Woody Point, this tiny place is popular for its traditional Newfoundland meals.

Information

Western Newfoundland Tourism (www.gowesternnewfoundland.com)

Getting There & Around

Deer Lake Airport (YDF; www.deerlakeairport.com) is 71km south of Rocky Harbour.

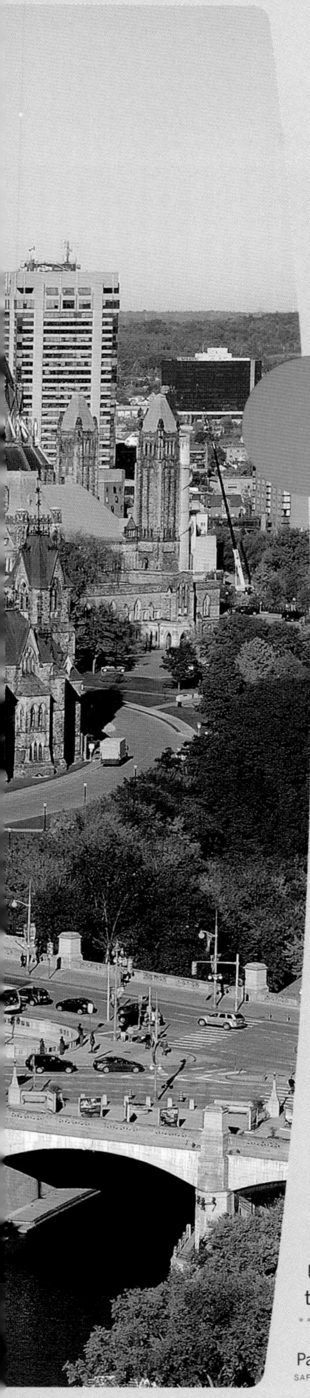

Canada In Focus

Parliament Hill (p189), Ottawa

Canada Today

> *To many citizens, a free, portable health-care system is at the very root of what makes Canada great.*

belief systems
(% of population)

if Canada were 100 people

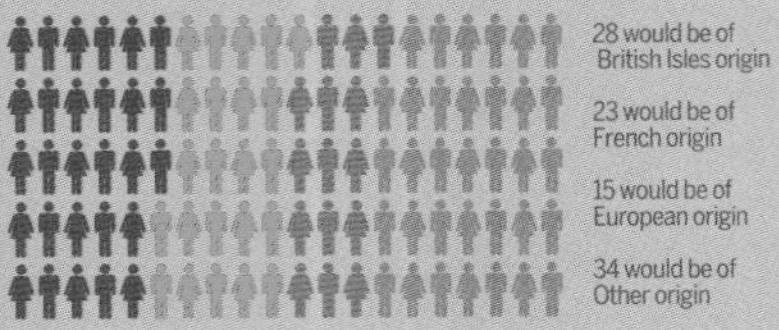

population per sq km

Peace Bridge, Calgary (p143)

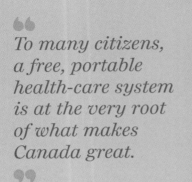

Economy

Compared to its international brethren, Canada has weathered the global financial crisis pretty well. Yes, the economy dropped into a recession, and Ottawa posted its first fiscal deficit in 2009 after 12 years of surplus, but Canadian banks bounced back, thanks to their tradition of conservative lending. The International Monetary Fund predicted Canada would be the only one of the seven major industrialized democracies to return to surplus by 2015, and the current federal government – led by the Conservatives – is focused on making this a reality. Federal job cuts are impacting on departments such as Parks Canada and Aboriginal Affairs, among many others. While the Conservatives say they're removing inefficiencies, with most cuts coming from back-office jobs, the opposition says the cuts are affecting front-line services, and imperiling natural and historic sites.

WITOLD SKRYPCZAK/GETTY IMAGES ©

Table Talk

The nation's much-cherished but ailing universal health-care system sparks serious table talk. Although no one will admit it, a two-tiered system is in place, and those with deep pockets can access additional, often quicker care in private facilities. Still, a free, portable health-care system that's available to everyone is quite a feat. To many citizens, it's at the very root of what makes Canada great. So are progressive views on same-sex marriage, immigration and marijuana use.

Climate change is another hot topic. A recent poll showed 53% of Canadians believed climate change caused the 2013 floods that put much of Calgary, Alberta, under water.

Oil Between Neighbors

Voltaire may have written off Canada as 'a few acres of snow' back in the mid-18th century, but those 'few acres' have yielded vast amounts of oil, timber and other natural resources, and propelled Canada to an enviable standard of living.

Extracting and developing resources comes with an ecological price, however. Oil in particular is a conundrum. Northern Alberta's Athabasca Oil Sands (or Tar Sands, depending which side of the ecofence you're on) are the world's second-biggest oil reserves, and they've done an excellent job boosting the economy. They also produce 5% of Canada's greenhouse gas emissions, according to Environment Canada. The pro-industry camp says improvements are being made and, when compared to other oil producers such as Saudi Arabia and Venezuela, the oil sands measure up, especially when human-rights issues and decreased transportation distances are considered (most of Canada's oil goes to the US).

Politics

In 2006, the Conservative Party took over from the Liberals for the first time in 12 years. Managing the economy (a Conservative tenet) and strengthening social services and health care (policies of the Liberals and left-leaning groups) were among the main issues. Stephen Harper became the new prime minister, but he led Canada's smallest minority government since Confederation.

The 2011 election held some surprises. The Conservatives won and picked up enough seats (166) to form a majority. But the big story was the surge of the New Democratic Party, a leftist group that had long been on the fringe, until it upped its seat count from 37 to 103 in 2011. It did so at the expense of the center-left Liberals. Canada's next federal election is scheduled for 2015, and it's pretty much up for grabs.

History

Old Town (p235), Québec City

HENRY GEORGI/GETTY IMAGE

The human story of Canada begins around 15,000 years ago when Aboriginal locals began carving thriving communities from the abundant wilderness. Everything changed, though, when the Europeans rolled in from the late 15th-century onwards, staking claims that triggered rumbling conflicts and eventually shaped a vast new nation. Much of this colorful heritage is accessible to visitors, with 956 national historic sites covering everything from forts to battlefields to famous homes.

Early Locals & Viking Visitors

The first Canadians most likely came from Asia, chasing down caribou and bison across the one-time land link between Siberia and Alaska and eventually settling throughout the Americas. The north proved particularly popular for its abundance of tasty fish and seal dinners, and these early Aboriginal communities eventually spread to four main regions

Circa 15,000 BC

Humans arrive via a land bridge from Siberia, following herds of caribou and bison.

in what would become Canada: the Pacific, the Plains, southern Ontario/St Lawrence River and the northeast woodlands.

About 2500 BC, a second major wave of migration from Siberia brought the ancestors of the Inuit to Canada. These early Inuit were members of the Dorset Culture, named after Cape Dorset on Baffin Island, where its remains were first unearthed. Around AD 1000, a separate Inuit cultural group – the whale-hunting Thule of northern Alaska – began making its way east through the Canadian Arctic. As these people spread, they overtook the Dorset Culture. The Thule are the direct ancestors of Canada's modern-day Inuit.

These original communities lived and thrived for thousands of years before anyone else turned up and stayed. Around AD 1000, Viking explorer Leif Eriksson and his hairy posse poked ashore on the east coast, sticking around long enough to establish winter settlements and a few hardy outposts. Life was tough for these interlopers and the hostile reception from the locals eventually sent them back where they came from. Without a glowing recommendation from these first European visitors, it was several centuries before anyone else bothered to make the epic journey across the Atlantic.

The Best... Historic Sites

1 Fortifications of Québec (p235), Québec City

2 Louisbourg (p277), Nova Scotia

3 Klondike National Historic Sites (p292), Yukon

4 Craigdarroch Castle (p88), British Columbia

5 Province House National Historic Site (p282), Prince Edward Island

Return of the Europeans

After Christopher Columbus made heading west from Europe across the ocean fashionable again with his 1492 expedition in search of Asia, avaricious European monarchs began queuing up to sponsor expeditions. In 1497 Giovanni Caboto – better known as John Cabot – sailed under a British flag as far west as Newfoundland and Cape Breton. His great discovery turned out to be a surfeit of cod stocks, triggering a hungry rush of boats from Europe, including Spanish whaling vessels.

King François I of France looked over the fence at his neighbors, stroked his beard, and ordered Jacques Cartier to appear before him. By this time, the hunt was on not only for the fabled Northwest Passage route but also for gold, given the shiny discoveries made by Spanish conquistadors among the Aztec and Inca civilizations.

AD 1000
Viking Leif Eriksson lands his crew on the east coast, setting up winter encampments.

1497
Sailing from Britain, John Cabot lands in Newfoundland, sparking a hungry rush for local cod.

1534
Jacques Cartier sails into what is now Québec, claiming the land for France.

What's in a Name?

Explorer Jacques Cartier is said to have picked up the name 'Kanata' from two Huron-Iroquois youths. It means 'settlement' in the Huron-Iroquois language and the lads were showing him the way to the village of Stadacona – later known as Québec City – rather than referring to an entire country. But the name stuck and Cartier used it in his journals to define the large 'new' region he had hit upon. As the known area grew, the name stayed the same: maps from 1547 designated everything north of the St Lawrence River as 'Canada.'

But upon arrival in Labrador, Cartier found only 'stones and horrible rugged rocks.' He kept exploring, though, and soon went ashore on Québec's Gaspé Peninsula to claim the land for France. The local Iroquois thought he was a good neighbor at first, until he kidnapped two of the chief's sons and took them to Europe. Rather surprisingly, Cartier returned them a year later when sailing up the St Lawrence River.

Fur: the New Gold

While these early explorers were always looking for gold to please their royal sponsors back home, it eventually become clear that the riches of the new land were not quite so sparkly. With fur the latest fashion of the French court, the New World's lustrous and abundant pelts were suddenly in huge demand across Europe.

In 1588 the French crown granted the first trading monopoly in Canada, only to have other merchants promptly challenge the claim. And so the race for control of the fur trade was officially on. The economic value of this enterprise and, by extension, its role in shaping Canadian history, cannot be underestimated. It was the main reason behind the country's European settlement, at the root of the struggle for dominance between the French and the British, and the source of strife and division between various Aboriginal groups.

To support their claims, French pioneers established a tentative foothold on Île Ste-Croix (a tiny islet in the river on the present US border with Maine) in 1604. They soon moved to Port Royal (today's Annapolis Royal) in Nova Scotia. Exposed and difficult to defend, neither site was ideal for controlling the inland fur trade. As the would-be colonists moved up the St Lawrence River, they came upon a spot their leader, Samuel de Champlain, considered prime real estate – where today's Québec City now stands. It was 1608 and 'New France' had landed.

1608

Samuel de Champlain establishes the first permanent settlement of 'New France.'

Right: Statue of Samuel de Champlain

1670

King Charles II creates Hudson's Bay Company to shore up fur trade for the Brits.

Brits Take Over

While the French enjoyed their plush fur monopoly for several decades, the Brits mounted a challenge in 1670 when King Charles II formed the Hudson's Bay Company. He granted it a trade monopoly over a vast northern area that would today encompass about 40% of Canada.

As both countries reaffirmed and expanded their claims, skirmishes broke out between groups of colonizers, mirroring the wars that were engulfing Europe in the first half of the 18th century. Things came to a head with the Treaty of Utrecht, which forced the French to recognize British claims in the region.

But the enmity and military skirmishes between the two continued for several decades, culminating in a 1759 battle on Québec's Plains of Abraham that is remembered today as one of Canada's most important military events. Besieging the city in a surprise and bloody attack that left both commanding generals dead, the Brits eventually won the day and the French were forced to hand over control of Canada in the resulting 1763 Treaty of Paris.

Managing their newly acquired territory was a tricky challenge for the Brits, who had to contend with aboriginal uprisings as well as resentment from French Canadians. Next, the restless American colonies started rumbling from the south. To keep the French Canadians on side, the Québec Act of 1774 confirmed the French Canadians' right to their religion, allowed them to assume political office and restored the use of French civil law. It worked: during the American Revolution (1775–83), most French Canadians refused to take up arms in support of the American cause.

After the revolution, the English-speaking population exploded when some 50,000 settlers from the newly independent USA migrated north. Called United Empire Loyalists due to their presumed allegiance to Britain, the majority ended up living in Nova Scotia and New Brunswick, while a smaller group settled along the northern shore of Lake Ontario and in the Ottawa River Valley (forming the nucleus of what became Ontario). About 8000 settlers moved to Québec, creating the first sizeable Anglophone community in the French-speaking bastion.

The Best... Historic Neighborhoods

1 Gastown, Vancouver (p63)

2 Québec City Old Town (p235)

3 Old Montréal (p214)

4 Downtown Halifax (p264)

1759
Famous Plains of Abraham battle for Québec City. France loses to Britain.

1763
Treaty of Paris boots France out of Canada, cementing British rule over the region.

1775
American Revolution rebels try enticing Québec to join the revolt against the British; Québec refuses.

The Maple Leaf Symbol

It's on the penny, on Air Canada planes, on Toronto hockey jerseys – you can't escape the maple leaf, considered a national symbol for almost two centuries. In 1836 *Le Canadien*, a newspaper published in Lower Canada, called it a suitable emblem for the nation. Ontario and Québec both were using it on their coat of arms by 1868. The Canadian Armed Forces used it during the world wars. Finally, after much wrangling over the design (one leaf? three leaves? 13 points?), the current 11-point leaf was granted national symbol status and went on the flag in 1965.

Canada Splits…then Unites

Accommodating the interests of Loyalist settlers, the British government passed the Constitutional Act of 1791, which divided the colony into Upper Canada (today's southern Ontario) and Lower Canada (now southern Québec). Lower Canada retained French civil laws, but both provinces were governed by the British criminal code.

These divisions didn't help matters, with rising tensions and arguments caused by the clear dominance of the British over the French in administrative matters across the two regions. Two French rebellions kicked off in the 1830s and although each was swiftly quelled, it was an indication that the ill-conceived division was unsustainable. The Brits then tried a different approach.

The Union Act of 1840 sought to crush French nationalism by legislating that British laws, language and institutions were superior across both regions, now joined together as the Province of Canada. If anything, the union's clear underlying objective of destroying French identity made Francophones cling together even more tenaciously – the wounds can still be seen in Canada today.

With the rise of the USA after the American Civil War (1861–65), fragile Canada, whose border with the USA was established on the 49th parallel in 1818, sought to further solidify its status and prevent annexation. In 1864 Charlottetown, Prince Edward Island (PEI), became the birthing room for modern Canada when the 'Fathers of Confederation' – a group of representatives from Nova Scotia, New Brunswick, PEI, Ontario and Québec – got together and hammered out the framework for a new nation. The British North America Act was passed in 1867, creating a modern, self-governing nation originally known as the Dominion of Canada. The day the act became official, July 1, is now celebrated across the country as Canada's national holiday.

1793

Explorer Alexander Mackenzie makes the first transcontinental journey across the land.

1858

Prospectors discover gold along BC's Fraser River, spurring thousands of get-rich-quick dreamers to head north.

1864

The Fathers of Confederation meet in Charlottetown, molding a new country called Canada.

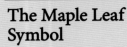

Creating Confederation

Under Canada's first prime minister, John A Macdonald, land and colonies were slowly added to the confederation. The government acquired a vast northern swathe, now called the Northwest Territories (NWT), in 1869 for the paltry sum of £300,000 – about $11.5 million in today's money – from the Hudson's Bay Company. The land was sparsely populated, mostly by Plains First Nations and several thousand Métis (may-*tee*), a racial blend of Cree, Ojibwe or Saulteaux and French-Canadian or Scottish fur traders, who spoke French as their main language. Their biggest settlement was the Red River Colony around Fort Garry (today's Winnipeg).

The Canadian government immediately clashed with the Métis people over land-use rights, causing the latter to form a provisional government led by the charismatic Louis Riel. He sent the Ottawa-appointed governor packing and, in November 1869, seized control of Upper Fort Garry, thereby forcing Ottawa to the negotiating table. However, with his delegation already en route, Riel impulsively executed a Canadian prisoner he was holding at the fort.

Province House National Historic Site (p282), Charlottetown, Prince Edward Island

1896
Klondike Gold Rush kicks off in the Yukon; 40,000 hopefuls roll into Dawson City.

1913
Immigration crests, with more than 400,000 embracing the maple leaf, mostly Americans and Eastern Europeans.

1933
Three out of 10 people are unemployed, as Canada struggles through the Great Depression.

The Best... History Museums

1 Maritime Museum of the Atlantic (p265), Halifax

2 Canadian War Museum (p187), Ottawa

3 Musée d'Archéologie et d'Histoire Pointe-à-Callière (p216), Montréal

4 Royal BC Museum (p87), Victoria

5 Glenbow Museum (p143), Calgary

Although the murder caused widespread uproar in Canada, the government was so keen to bring the west into the fold it agreed to most of Riel's demands, including special language and religious protections for the Métis. As a result, the then-pint-sized province of Manitoba was carved out of the NWT and entered the dominion in July 1870. Macdonald sent troops after Riel but he narrowly managed to escape to the USA. He was formally exiled for five years in 1875.

Rail Link to the West

Despite the progress toward confederation, the west coast remained a distant and forbidding frontier. British Columbia (BC), created in 1866 by merging the colonies of New Caledonia and Vancouver Island, finally joined in 1871 in exchange for the Canadian government assuming all its debt and promising to link it with the east within 10 years via a vast transcontinental railroad.

The Canadian Pacific Railway's construction is one of the most impressive and decisive chapters in Canada's history. Though essential in uniting the nation, it was a costly proposition, made even more challenging by the rough and rugged terrain the tracks had to traverse. To entice investors, the government offered major benefits, including massive land grants in western Canada. Workers drove the final spike into the track at Craigellachie, BC, on November 7, 1885.

Canada rang in the 20th century on a high note. Industrialization was in full swing, prospectors had discovered gold in the Yukon, and Canadian resources – from wheat to lumber – were increasingly in demand. In addition, the new railroad opened the floodgates to immigration. Between 1885 and 1914 about 4.5 million people arrived in Canada. This included large groups of Americans and Eastern Europeans, especially Ukrainians, who went to work cultivating the prairies.

By the time the guns of WWI fell silent in 1918, most Canadians were fed up with sending their sons and husbands to fight in distant wars for Britain. Under the government of William Lyon Mackenzie King, Canada made it clear that Britain could no longer automatically draw upon the Canadian military and even sent its own ambassador to Washington. This forcefulness led to the Statute of Westminster, passed by the British Parliament in 1931. It formalized the independence of Canada

1961
Saskatchewan introduces the first universal health-care plan, an idea that soon spreads across Canada.

1963
Trans-Canada Hwy completed, spanning 7821km from St John's, Newfoundland, to Victoria, BC.

1982
Queen Elizabeth II signs the Canada Act, giving Canada complete sovereignty.

and other Commonwealth nations, although Britain retained the right to pass amendments to those countries' constitutions – a right only removed with the 1982 Canada Act. The British monarch remains Canada's head of state, although this is predominantly a ceremonial role and does not diminish the country's sovereignty.

Modern-Day Canada

The period after WWII brought another wave of economic expansion and immigration, especially from Europe. The one province left behind during the 1950s boom years was Québec, caught in the grip of ultraconservative leader Maurice Duplessis. Only after his death did the province finally start getting up to speed during the 'Quiet Revolution' of the 1960s. Still, progress wasn't swift enough for radical nationalists who claimed independence was the only way to ensure Francophone rights. Québec has spent the ensuing years flirting with separatism, culminating in a cliffhanger 1994 referendum when a majority of less than 1% voted that the province should remain a part of Canada.

In 1960 Canada's Aboriginal peoples were finally granted Canadian citizenship. Issues involving land rights and discrimination played out in the decades that followed. In 1985 Canada became the first country in the world to pass a national multicultural act. Today, more than 20% of Canada's population is foreign-born.

The new millennium has been kind to Canada. The Canadian dollar took off around 2003 – thanks to oil, diamonds and other natural resources fueling the economy – and tolerance marches onward, with medical marijuana and gay marriage both legalized. The country showed off its abundant assets to the world when it successfully hosted the 2010 Winter Olympics in Vancouver.

1998

Government apologizes to Aboriginal peoples for 'attitudes of racial and cultural superiority...'

2010

Vancouver and Whistler showcase Canada's cool when hosting the Winter Olympics.

Right: Ski jumper at Whistler

RANDY LINCKS/GETTY IMAGES ©

Family Travel

Whistler (p81), British Columbia

RANDY LINCKS/GETTY IMAGES

There are so many experiences in Canada guaranteed to leave your kids wide-eyed with wonder: the challenge is choosing what to focus on. Consider their interests when you decide between the wow factor of watching a whale slide by, ziplining along a mountain canyon, exploring 18th-century forts or beachcombing among shiny purple starfish. And you can expect a warm welcome: Canada is one of the world's most kid-friendly countries.

When to Go

Canada is a year-round destination but if you're planning to bring your children to highlights such as Montréal, Québec or Toronto in winter make sure they have plenty of thick clothing: temperatures can dip to -20°C (-4°F) in these cities and if you're not prepared, your kids will be miserable.

Beyond that, Canada's weather welcomes children of all ages. The school vacation summer season is popular with families, since there's always plenty of outdoor action to be had and there are hundreds of festivals and community events across the country, many with a dedicated family focus – a favorite is the Vancouver International Children's Festival (www.childrensfestival.ca). It offers storytelling, performances and activities on Granville Island in late May.

Of course, summer season is the peak for most hotel accommodation prices, so consider spring or fall: if you can wrest them from the clutches of school you can save a packet.

The second most popular time for family travel is winter – especially December to February – when parents bring older children and teenagers to ski resorts across the country. Your usually sullen teens might even smile and thank you profusely if you give them the best snowboarding experience of their lives. And if you come in time for Christmas, you'll also enjoy some seasonal treats – such as Santa Claus parades and festive light displays – that will make your visit unforgettable.

For more tips and tricks on hitting Canada with your kids, see Lonely Planet's *Travel with Children*.

The Best... Children's Attractions

1 Vancouver Aquarium (p61), Vancouver

2 Canada Agricultural Museum (p194), Ottawa

3 Centre des Sciences de Montréal (p215)

4 Avonlea Village (p286), Cavendish, Prince Edward Island

5 Royal Ontario Museum (p161), Toronto

6 La Citadelle ceremonies (p236), Québec City

Where to Go

It's a big place and you're spoilt for choice, so put some thought into which regions your kids (and you) might enjoy most. Hit Vancouver for beaches and snow sports on the same day; look out for elk, moose or wolves in the Rocky Mountains; dive into the rich history and cobbled streets of old Québec; or take a splashtastic boat tour at Niagara Falls.

Most kids will enjoy a visit to a museum or two on their trip and many in Canada are dedicated to children: there are space and science centers (as well as aquariums) across the country. Even 'stuffy' galleries or history museums have made great strides in recent years to cater to children: check ahead on their websites for kid-friendly events and programming.

Many of these attractions offer free entry to under-fives as well as reduced rates for older children and school students. Also, make sure you ask about family tickets, a special group rate that's offered at many attractions in Canada.

For information on travel with children in Canada's major cities, see p61 (Vancouver), p164 (Toronto), p194 (Ottawa) and p223 (Montréal).

What to Do

If your kids are an active bunch, consider hiring bikes for them: you'll find many city parks have great trails – Vancouver's Stanley Park may be the best. BC's traffic-free Kettle Valley Trail offers dramatic canyon scenery along a converted railbed; outfitters around Kelowna provide wheels. Mountain biking teens can test their mettle at downhill bike parks such as the summer facility in Whistler.

Horseback riding is a very Canadian alternative – especially if you combine it with a visit to cowboy country around the Rocky Mountains. Or get on the water for a marine wildlife-viewing trip – the east or west coasts are ideal for whale-watching. If your kids would rather be *in* the water, Tofino on Vancouver Island has surf schools galore.

Children can also hit the slopes with skiing or snowboarding lessons at one of Canada's excellent, family-friendly winter resorts, such as Whistler or the facilities around Banff.

Need to Know

Changing facilities Found in most stores, malls and cinemas

Cots Available at most mid- to high-end accommodations

Highchairs Generally available, especially in midrange restaurants

Kids' menus Offered at many midrange restaurants

Nappies (diapers) Widely available

Strollers Cities and towns are generally stroller friendly

Transport Fully accessible to children; under-fives usually travel free

Beside skiing, there are often gentler activities such as snowshoeing expeditions, where you can tramp through the snow between the icicle-covered 'Christmas trees.'

Sleeping & Eating

Hotels and motels typically have rooms with two double beds. Most can also bring in rollaways or cots, usually for a small charge.

Some properties offer 'kids stay free' promotions and some – usually resorts or larger hotels – have special kids clubs with scheduled activities. B&Bs are often pickier, so make sure you clarify who you're bringing with you when you book: some B&Bs are adult-only, while others will roll out the red carpet for your offspring.

If you're concerned about the costs of eating out with a large group at every meal (or just aware of that ultrapicky young eater you have traveling with you), consider a hotel room with a kitchen or even a self-catering apartment: either will enable you to keep dining costs down and please everyone's palate at the same time. Tourism bureaus across the country will be able to help you find this type of accommodation easily, especially in larger cities.

Children are welcome at the vast majority of restaurants across Canada, the exceptions being some high-end eateries. Many restaurants – especially in the midrange – have dedicated children's menus. If they don't, ask for a half-order and you'll find that most eateries will happily oblige. Easy-to-find Canadian foods that kids will love include poutine (French fries topped with brown gravy and cheese), fish and chips, and pancakes or French toast with maple syrup.

What to Pack

Aside from the aforementioned winter clothing, layers are the key to successfully packing for your kids here: it can get spontaneously cool in Canada during the summer months. And relentlessly rainy days (we're talking about you, British Columbia) can make everyone miserable, so make sure the youngsters have some good rain gear if traveling outside the peak summer period. Don't worry too much about packing, though: Canada is well-stocked with shops and department stores and children's clothing is generally well priced.

Sunscreen, of course, is a must and bug spray is a good idea if you're going to be in the great outdoors for any length of time. If you're planning any long drives – and Canada is the home of the long drive – bring every activity you can think of to keep the kids occupied.

Arts & Culture

Montréal Jazz Festival (p43)

DAN HERRICK/GETTY IMAGES ©

Looking specifically at artistic output, overseas visitors might be forgiven for thinking that culture in Canada simply means Celine Dion, William Shatner, Margaret Atwood and a few totem poles. But while Canadians rarely shout about it, the country's creative and artistic scenes are rich and vibrant across the nation, offering a deep well of creativity for visiting culture vultures to sink their beaks into.

Literature

Canada's earliest inhabitants built their cultures on storytelling, passing important tales from generation to generation. Later authors created a written body of Canadian literature – the phrase 'Canlit' is still used here – that defined the struggles of creating a new life in a vast, sometimes barren wilderness. These often deeply affecting novels are the ideal accompaniment for an epic train ride across the prairies. Recommended authors for the long haul include Margaret Laurence and Robertson Davies, while many will also enjoy Lucy Maud Montgomery's *Anne of Green Gables*.

But if you want to hit an adult pageturner during your travels, there are three main authors to focus on. If you read Mordecai Richler's *The Apprenticeship of Duddy Kravitz* while hanging around in Montréal's Plateau district, you'll almost feel the story on the streets around you (his later epic,

Aboriginal Artists

There was little outside recognition of the art produced by aboriginal communities until the 20th century. But over the last 50 years or so, there's been a strong and growing appreciation of this body of work, led initially by the paintings, sculptures and carvings of revered Haida artist Bill Reid (1920–98), whose work appears on the back of the $20 bill. Also look out for colorful paintings by Norval Morrisseau; mixed-media works by Saskatchewan-born Edward Poitras; and challenging younger artists, such as Marianne Nicolson and Brian Jungen, who explore political and environmental themes in their art.

Barney's Version, was made into a 2010 movie). Short-story writer Alice Munro won the 2013 Nobel Prize for Literature. Her work often focuses on small-town life in western Ontario. *The View from Castle Rock* provides a good sampler. And a trip to Canada that doesn't include a Margaret Atwood novel is like visiting a bar without having a drink. Consider top titles such as *Oryx and Crake*, *The Blind Assassin* or *The Handmaid's Tale* or dive into *Surfacing*, an enigmatic story where the Canadian wilderness is a character in itself.

Other Canadian authors to look out for in the local bookstore include Carol Shields, Douglas Coupland, William Gibson and Michael Ondaatje. If you time your visit well, you can join the local bookworms at literary events including the Vancouver Writers Fest (www.writersfest.bc.ca), Toronto's International Festival of Authors (www.ifoa.org) and the annual five-city Word on the Street (www.thewordonthestreet.ca).

Visual Arts

Canada's artistic bent was founded thousands of years ago when early Aboriginal inhabitants began adorning their homes with visual representations of the natural world. Later, European painters continued to use nature as their muse, often adding images of the mysterious Aboriginal locals to their canvases.

But the most famous artistic school in Canadian cultural history is the Group of Seven, a clutch of painters who banded loosely together in the early 1920s, creating bold, stylized representations of the striking Canadian landscape that still seem fresh and vibrant today. Members of the group – which included famed luminaries such as Tom Thomson, Lawren Harris and Arthur Lismer, and which later expanded beyond the original seven – would often disappear into the wilderness for months on end. It's during one of these trips that Thomson met his demise, drowning in a lake in 1917, just as he was at the height of his creative powers.

While Group of Seven paintings still attract huge prices and exhibitions of their work typically lure large crowds, Canada also has an energetic contemporary art scene. Internationally renowned latter-day stars include photoconceptualist Jeff Wall, painter and sculptor Betty Goodwin and painter and avant-garde filmmaker Michael Snow – look out for their works at galleries across the country. And don't forget to check out the celebrated public-art scenes on the streets of Vancouver, Toronto and Montréal.

Music

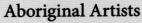

Ask visitors to name a few Canadian musicians and they'll stutter to a halt after Justin Bieber, Celine Dion, Bryan Adams and perhaps Leonard Cohen. But ask the locals to do the same and they'll hit you with a roster of performers you've probably never heard of as well as a few that you always assumed were US-born. For the record, this is the homeland of classic legends such as Neil Young and Joni Mitchell as well as modern superstars such as Rush, Arcade Fire, Drake, Michael Buble and Diana Krall.

Working their list into a lather, it won't be long before most Canadians also mention the Tragically Hip, Barenaked Ladies, Blue Rodeo, Guess Who, Feist, New Pornographers, Sarah McLachlan, Oscar Peterson, Great Big Sea, Gordon Lightfoot and Bruce Cockburn: seminal Canadian musicians past and present that define the country's musical soundscape yet often have little profile outside the country. The Hip, for example, can easily pack stadiums in Canada while they'd struggle to fill a midsized venue in most other countries.

To tap into the scene on your visit, drop into a local independent record store and ask for some recommendations. They'll likely point you to the area's best live-music venues and offer you some tips on who to look out for. And if you're a true die-hard traveling muso, consider timing your visit for a music festival. The Montréal Jazz Festival (www.montrealjazzfest.com) is one of the biggest in the world, while Toronto's North by Northeast (www.nxne.com) draws music industry executives hoping to find the rock stars of tomorrow.

The Best... Art Galleries

1 National Gallery of Canada (p192), Ottawa

2 Art Gallery of Ontario (p158), Toronto

3 Musée des Beaux-Arts de Montréal (p216)

4 Vancouver Art Gallery (p61), Vancouver

5 Art Gallery of Alberta (p141), Edmonton

Film

There are two distinct sides to Canada's burgeoning movie industry. As a production hot spot, it's often used as a visual stand-in for US cities, which means you usually don't know you're watching a Canadian-made flick when you sit down to *X-Men* or *Twilight: New Moon*. But aside from being a busy back-lot for Hollywood – the nickname Hollywood North is frequently used here – there's a healthy independent Canadian movie-making scene with a flavor all its own.

Celebrated films made here over the years (and which are about as far from Hollywood blockbusters as you can imagine) include *Incendies* (2010, directed by Denis Villeneuve), *Away from Her* (2006, directed by Sarah Polley), *The Sweet Hereafter* (1997, directed by Atom Egoyan), *Thirty Two Short Films About Glenn Gould* (1993, directed by Francois Girard) and *The Red Violin* (1998), co-written by Don McKellar, who has often seemed like a one-man movie industry unto himself. Guy Maddin is another well-known local filmmaker. He typically films around his hometown of Winnipeg; see *Keyhole* (2011) for an example of his offbeat style.

You can dip into both sides of the Canadian film industry at the country's two main movie festivals. The Toronto International Film Festival (www.tiff.net) is a glitzy affair where Hollywood megastars drop by to promote their new offerings. In contrast, the Vancouver International Film Festival (www.viff.org) showcases art-house and independent flicks from Canada and around the world.

Food, Wine & Microbrews

Cooked lobsters, Nova Scotia

PRAXISPHOTOGRAPHY/GETTY IMAGES

Canadian cuisine has moved well beyond the doughnut, and cities such as Montréal, Toronto and Vancouver now offer world-leading dining scenes. Regions across the country have rediscovered distinctive local ingredients produced on their doorsteps, and chefs transform these into an impressive plateful. The approach has also spread to drink: celebrated wines are produced in the Okanagan, Niagara and beyond, while microbrewed beer has added local flavor to pub nights.

Local Flavors

From East Coast lobster to prairie pierogis (dumplings) and West Coast spot prawns, distinctive dishes define Canada's regions. These provincial soul foods reflect local ingredients and the diverse – often immigrant – influences of their cooks.

Starting from the east, the main dish of the Maritimes is lobster – boiled in the pot and served with a little butter – and the best place to get stuck into it is a town hall or church basement alongside chatty locals. Try some hearty seafood chowder while waiting for your meal to arrive, but don't eat too much; you'll need room for the mountainous fruit pie coming your way afterwards.

Visitors to Nova Scotia should save their appetites for butter-soft Digby scallops and rustic Lunenberg sausage, while the favored food of nearby Newfoundland and Labrador combines rib-sticking cod cheeks and sweet snow crab.

Along with broiled Atlantic salmon, French-influenced New Brunswick serves up *poutine râpée*, potatoes stuffed with pork and boiled for a few hours. It's been filling the bellies of locals here for decades and is recommended if you haven't eaten for a week or two.

Over in the even more French-influenced province of Québec, fine food is a way of life. Cosmopolitan Montréal has long claimed to be the nation's fine-dining capital, but there's an appreciation of food here at all levels that includes hearty pea soups, exquisite cheeses and tasty pâtés sold at bustling markets. In addition, there's poutine – irresistible dark golden fries topped with gravy and cheese curds – and huge, bulging smoked meat sandwiches that will fill you for a week.

Ontario – especially Toronto – is a microcosm of Canada's melting pot of cuisines. Like Québec, maple syrup is a super-sweet flavoring of choice here, found in desserts such as beavertails (sugary pastries with rich toppings) and on fluffy breakfast pancakes the size of Frisbees.

Canada's Aboriginal people have many fascinating culinary traditions. Reliant on meat and seafood – try a juicy halibut stew on British Columbia's (BC) Haida Gwaii – there's also a tradition of bannock (pan-fried bread) that was imported by the Scots and appropriated by Canada's first locals.

In contrast, the central provinces of Manitoba, Saskatchewan and Alberta have their own culinary ways. The latter is the nation's beef capital – you'll find top-notch Alberta steak on menus here and across the country. Pierogis, introduced by Ukrainian immigrants, are a staple across the border in Manitoba, while Saskatchewan serves up striking Saskatoon berry pies to all who pass through.

In the far west, British Columbians have traditionally fed themselves from the sea and the fertile farmlands of the interior. Okanagan Valley peaches, cherries and blueberries are the staple of many summer diets. But it's the seafood that attracts the lion's share of culinary fans. Tuck into succulent wild salmon, juicy Fanny Bay oysters and velvety regional scallops and you may (rightfully) think you've found foodie nirvana.

The Best... Restaurants

1 Hawksworth (p73), Vancouver

2 Lee (p170), Toronto

3 Le Lapin Sauté (p243), Québec City

4 Vices Versa (p249), La Malbaie

5 Hudson's on First (p96), Duncan, BC

6 Edna (p268), Halifax

Top Dining Districts

Ask anyone in Toronto, Montréal or Vancouver to name Canada's leading foodie city and they'll likely inform you that you've just found it. But while each of the big three claims to be at the head of the top table, their strengths are so diverse that they're more accurately defined as complementary courses in one great meal.

First dish on the table is Montréal, which was Canada's dine-out capital long before the upstarts threw off their doughnut-based shackles. Renowned for introducing North America's finest French-influenced cuisine, it hasn't given up its crown lightly. Chefs here are often treated like rock stars as they challenge Old World conventions with daring, even artistic approaches. You should also expect a great restaurant experience: Montréalers have a bacchanalian love for eating out, from cozy old-town

Extreme Cuisine

Unique foods for traveling taste-trippers include Prince Edward Island's (PEI) Solomon Gundy, a marinated herring and chopped-meat combo, and geoduck (pronounced 'gooey duck'), a giant saltwater clam that's a popular British Columbian (BC) Chinese dish. In Alberta, search out some 'prairie oysters' for your fellow travelers, then sit back and watch them tuck into a plate of bull's testicles. In Newfoundland, seal flipper pie appears on menus; the flavor is strong and gamey, in case you're wondering. Backcountry foraging is also big in Canada: BC is a popular mushroom-picking spot, while New Brunswick is ideal for fiddleheads (edible fern fronds). Just be sure to consult a mushroom field guide or go with an experienced forager.

restaurants to the animated patios of Rue Prince Arthur and the sophisticated, often funky eateries of the Plateau.

If Montréal is an ideal starter, that makes Toronto the main course – although that's a reflection of its more recent elevation rather than its preeminence. Fusion is the default approach in Canada's largest city, with contemporary immigration adding modern influences from Asia to a foundation of British, Greek and Italian cuisines. With 7000 restaurants to choose from, though, it can be a tough choice figuring out where to unleash your appetite. Your best approach is to hit the neighborhoods: the Financial District and Old York areas are studded with swanky eateries, while eclectic, affordable joints fill Chinatown, Baldwin Village and Queen West.

And while that appears to make Vancouver the dessert, it could be argued that this glass-towered metropolis is the best of the bunch. Some of the country's most innovative chefs have set up shop here, inspired by a distinctive local larder of unique ingredients and Canada's most cosmopolitan – especially Asian – population. Fusion is the starting point in fine-dining districts such as Yaletown and Kitsilano. But there's also a high level of authentic ethnic dining across the city: sushi bars and Japanese *izakaya* jostle for attention with superb Vietnamese and Korean eateries. And if you want to discover what Pacific Northwest or West Coast cuisine means, this is the place to tuck in and conduct some lip-smacking field research.

Wine Regions

While international visitors are often surprised to learn that wine is produced here, their suspicions are tempered after a drink or two. Canada's wines have gained ever-greater kudos in recent years and while smaller-scale production and the industry dominance of other wine regions means they'll never be a global market leader, there are some tasty treats waiting for thirsty grape lovers.

And since the best way to sample any wine is to head straight to the source – where you can taste the region in the glass – consider doing some homework and locating the nearest vineyards on your visit. Don't miss the top table wineries in Ontario's Niagara region or BC's Okanagan Valley – the country's leading producers – but a visit to the charming boutique operations of Nova Scotia's Annapolis Valley and Vancouver Island's Cowichan Valley can be just as rewarding.

Wherever your tipple-craving takes you, drink widely and deeply and prepare to be surprised. And make sure you have plenty of room in your suitcase – packing materials are always available, if you can avoid drinking everything before you make it to the airport.

For background and further information, check the website of Wines of Canada (www.winesofcanada.com) and visit the blog Canadian Wine Guy (www.canadianwineguy.com).

Here for the Beer?

Canadians don't only drink wine, of course – beer is at least as important as a national beverage here. And while you'll soon come across the mass-produced fizz of brewing behemoths Labatt and Molson, a little digging uncovers a thriving regional microbrewing scene dripping with fantastic ales, bitters and lagers.

Midsized breweries such as Moosehead in New Brunswick, Alexander Keith's in Nova Scotia, Sleemans in Ontario, Big Rock in Alberta and Okanagan Springs in BC produce some easy-to-find, highly quaffable tipples. It's worth noting that several of these have been taken over by the two big boys in recent years, although they haven't changed much about these successful operations.

It's at the local level where you'll find the real treats. Canada is suffused with a foamy head of small-batch brewers and visiting beer geeks should search these out by asking for the local brew wherever they find themselves. Highlights include Québec's Boréale, Alberta's Wild Rose Brewery and Nova Scotia's Propeller Brewing. In Ontario, keep your tongue alert for beers from Wellington Brewery, Great Lakes Brewery and Steam Whistle Brewing. And in BC, it's all about Phillips Brewing, Driftwood Brewing, Townsite Brewing and Central City Brewing, among many others. Cheers!

Food Festivals

Canada has loads of palate-pleasing food and wine events, which makes it especially important to check the dates of your trip: they're among the best ways to hang out, get to know the locals and experience some fantastic cuisine.

Starting in the east, recommended events – large and small – include PEI's International Shellfish Festival (www.peishellfish.com) in mid-September, New Brunswick's Shediac Lobster Festival (www.shediaclobsterfestival.ca) in mid-July and Nova Scotia's Fall Wine Festival (www.winesofnovascotia.ca) from mid-September to mid-October.

Québec-bound visitors should hit the Eastern Townships' Magog-Orford area (near Montréal) for the Fête des Vendanges (www.fetedesvendanges.com), which is held in early September and focuses on regional food and wine. Chocoholics might prefer the nearby Fête du Chocolat de Bromont (www.feteduchocolat.ca) held in mid-May.

On the BC Farm Trail

Ask Vancouverites where the food on their tables comes from and most will point vacantly at a nearby supermarket, but others will tell you about the Fraser Valley. This lush interior region starts about 30km from the city and is studded with busy farms. Now, farmers and the people they feed are getting to know one another on a series of Circle Farm Tours. These self-guided driving treks take you around several food-producing communities, highlighting recommended pit stops – farms, markets, wineries and dining suggestions – along the way. Download free tour maps at www.circlefarmtour.com.

Across the border in Ontario, Niagara stages more than one annual event to celebrate its wealth of wine, including January's Icewine Festival, June's New Vintage Festival and September's giant, two-week Niagara Wine Festival. For information on these events, visit www.niagarawinefestival.com.

If you're still hungry and thirsty by the time you make it out to the west coast, it's hard to miss one of the Okanagan Valley's four main wine festivals – one for each season. They include the 10-day Fall Wine Festival, staged in October, and the highly enjoyable Winter Wine Festival in January, which focuses on ice wine. For more information on these events, visit www.thewinefestivals.com.

Those who'd rather sample all those BC microbrewed beers instead should drop into Vancouver Craft Beer Week (www.vancouvercraftbeerweek.com) in May. Better yet, head across the water to Vancouver Island for Victoria's Great Canadian Beer Festival (www.gcbf.com) in September. Both are great places to mingle with fellow hop-heads and tip back tasty regional suds. March's Vancouver Wine Festival (www.vanwinefest.ca) has also become quite the to-do.

Cheeses on display at Marché Jean-Talon (p230), Montréal
CHRIS CHEADLE/GETTY IMAGES ©

Outdoors

Rocky Mountains, Alberta

MICHAEL INTERISANO/DESIGN PIC/GETTY IMAGES ©

While the great Canadian outdoors looks undeniably pretty on postcards, the wild wilderness here is not just about good looks. Locals have been jumping in head first – sometimes literally – for decades, with activities ranging from hiking and kayaking to biking and climbing. For visitors, there are countless operators across the country that can help you gear up and get out there.

Skiing & Snowboarding

While it might have taken the 2010 Winter Olympics in Vancouver to show the world just how special Canada's snow sports facilities are, it was certainly no secret to the locals. From Québec to Ontario and from Alberta to British Columbia (BC), this is the country where it seems like almost everyone was born to ski. Visitors will find world-renowned resorts here, but it's also worth asking the locals where they like to hit the slopes: for every big-time swanky resort, there are several smaller spots where the terrain and the welcome can be even better.

Québec boasts some big slopes – Le Massif, near Québec City, has a vertical drop of 770m – located handily close to the cities. Most of these nonalpine hills, such as Mont-Tremblant, are a day's drive from Toronto and around an hour from Québec City and Montréal. Ski areas in Québec's

The Best... Day Hikes

1 Sunshine Meadows (p129), Banff

2 Lake Louise (p130), Banff

3 Stanley Park (p61), Vancouver

4 Bruce Trail (p180), Ontario

5 Nokomis Trail, Lake Superior Provincial Park (p203), Ontario

Eastern Townships offer renowned gladed runs – runs that weave through a thinned forest.

Head west and you'll hit the big mountains and vast alpine terrains. Glide down gargantuan slopes at Whistler-Blackcomb, which has North America's highest vertical drop *and* most impressive terrain variation. You'll also slide through stunning postcard landscapes in the Canadian Rockies, especially at Sunshine Meadows in Banff National Park.

In BC's Okanagan Valley, resorts such as Apex and Big White boast good snow year after year (no droughts here). Snowpack ranges from 2m to 6m-plus, depending on how close the resort is to the Pacific Ocean.

For cross-country skiing, Alberta offers some popular trails that were part of that other Canadian Winter Olympics, Calgary in 1988.

For further information and resources covering the national scene, check the website of the Canadian Ski Council (www.skicanada.org).

Hiking

You don't have to be a hiker to hike in Canada. While there are plenty of multiday jaunts for those who like tramping through the wilderness equipped only with a small Swiss Army knife, there are also innumerable opportunities for those whose idea of a hike is a gentle stroll around a lake with a pub visit at the end.

The country's hiking capital is Banff National Park, crisscrossed with stunning vistas accessible to both hard and soft eco-adventurers. In the park's Sunshine Meadows area, for example, you can wind through landscapes teeming with alpine flora – as bald eagles circle overhead – and enjoy mountain panoramas arguably unmatched in Canada. Also in the Rockies region, areas near Jasper offer breathtaking glacier views.

In BC's provincial parks system (www.bcparks.ca) you'll have a choice of more than 100 parks, each with distinct landscapes to hike through, including ancient volcanoes. And since you're in BC, head over to Grouse Mountain and hit the Grouse Grind, a steep forest hike that's known as 'mother nature's Stairmaster.' You'll understand why by the time you get to the top (*if* you get to the top).

Out east, awe-inspiring trails stripe the landscape. In southern Ontario, the Bruce Trail (www.brucetrail.org) tracks from Niagara Falls to Tobermory. It's the oldest and longest continuous footpath in Canada and spans more than 800km. Though portions are near cities such as Hamilton and Toronto, it's surprisingly serene. In contrast, Newfoundland's trails make for fantastic shoreline hiking and often provide whale views.

And don't forget the cities. Canada's major metropolises offer some great urban hikes, an ideal way to get to know the communities you're visiting. Slip into your runners for a stroll (or a jog) with the locals in Montréal's Parc du Mont Royal or Vancouver's gem-like Stanley Park, where the idyllic seawall winds alongside towering trees and lapping ocean. It's the kind of breathtaking, vista-packed stroll that gives hiking a good name.

Cycling & Mountain Biking

Mountain biking is a big deal in Canada. While cycling enthusiasts in other countries might be into trundling around town or along a gentle riverside trail, in Canada you're more likely to find them hurtling down a mountainside covered in mud and punishing their bike as if they were riding a bucking bronco. Given the landscape, of course, it was just a matter of time before the wheels hit the off-road here.

If you need to ease yourself in, start gently with BC's Kettle Valley Trail (www.kettlevalleyrailway.ca), near Kelowna. This dramatic segment of converted railbed barrels across picturesque wooden trestle bridges and through canyon tunnels.

Looking for more of an adrenalin rush? In North Vancouver (see www.nsmba.ca), you can ride on much narrower and steeper 'trestles.' Birthplace of 'freeride' mountain biking (which combines downhill and dirt jumping), this area offers elevated bridges, log rides and skinny planks that loft over the wet undergrowth. It's a similar story up at Whistler where the melted ski slopes are transformed into a summertime bike park that draws thousands every year – especially during the Crankworx Mountain Bike Festival (www.crankworx.com/whistler) in July.

For road touring, Canada's east coast, with more small towns and less emptiness, is a fantastic place to pedal, either as a single-day road ride or a multiday trip. In Québec province, try any part of the 4000km Route Verte (www.routeverte.com), the longest network of bicycle paths in the Americas. Or follow bucolic red roads on Prince Edward Island's (PEI) (www.tourismpei.com/pei-cycling), including the 279km Confederation Trail that extends across the province from east to west. The trail passes by idyllic villages where riders can stop for a bite to eat or to rest for the night.

If you're in one of Canada's big cities and you feel like stretching your legs, consider renting a bike for a half-day trundle: Vancouver and Victoria in BC have particularly good city-spanning bike trails.

Fishing

Built on its aboriginal and pioneer past, Canada has a strong tradition of fishing and you can expect to come across plenty of opportunities to hook walleye, pike, rainbow or lake trout on your travels. Among the best fishing holes to head for are Lunenburg (west of Halifax) in Nova Scotia and the Miramichi River in New Brunswick. And while salmon are the usual draw on the Pacific coastline, hopping aboard a local vessel for some sea fishing off Haida Gwaii can deliver the kind of giant catches you'll be bragging about for years to come.

Climbing

All those inviting crags you've spotted on your trip are an indication that Canada is a major climbing capital, ideal for short scales or multiday crampon-picking jaunts.

BC's Squamish region, located between Vancouver and Whistler, is a climbing center, with dozens of accessible (and not so accessible) peaks. Tap into the scene via Squamish Rock Guides (www.squamishrockguides.com). If mountaineering is more your thing, the Rockies are the recommended first stop. The area near Banff is an ideal destination for climbers, no matter what your skill level. Yamnuska (www.yamnuska.com) is one company that offers ice and other climbs in this region.

Windsurfing Wonders

It seems that Québec's Îles de la Madeleine – a small chain in the Gulf of St Lawrence, accessible by ferry from Québec or Prince Edward Island – were made for wind sports. It's the kind of place so blessed that if the wind is blowing the wrong way, you can drive a few minutes down to another beach where it's just perfect. Sheltered lagoons offer safe learning locations for testing kiteboards or seeking shelter during heavy days.

If you prefer the European approach, the Matterhorn of Canada is BC's Mt Assiniboine, located between the Kootenay and Banff national parks. Other western classics include Alberta's Mt Edith Cavell, in Jasper; and Garibaldi Peak, in Garibaldi Provincial Park, near Whistler. If you need a guide, check in with the excellent Alpine Club of Canada (www.alpineclubofcanada.ca).

If your trip takes you out southeast instead, Ontario's favorite climbing havens dot the Bruce Peninsula.

Kayaking & Canoeing

If you're on a tight schedule and don't have time for some of Canada's multiday sea kayaking odysseys – think remote Canadian Arctic or the west coast wilderness of Vancouver Island – there are plenty of other, more accessible ways to get your paddling fix here. Big cities such as BC's Vancouver and Victoria offer tours and lessons near town, while the province's Sunshine Coast and Salt Spring Island offer crenulated coastlines combined with tranquil sea inlets.

As old as kayaking, and equally as Canadian, is the canoe. Experienced paddlers can strike out on one of 33 Canadian Heritage Rivers (www.chrs.ca). Some of the best include the Athabasca River in the Rockies and Vancouver Island's Cowichan River. Ontario parks such as Lake Superior Provincial Park and Algonquin Provincial Park are also paddling paradises.

White-water rafting enthusiasts can take to the rapids in Jasper National Park. Calmer float trips are also available on the local waterways.

Surfing

If you're aiming to become a temporary beach bum on your Canada trip, head to the wild west coast of BC's Vancouver Island and hang out on the beaches around Tofino. Surfing schools and gear rental operations stud this region and you'll have an awesome time riding the swells or just watching everyone else as you stretch out on the sand. Backed by verdant rain forest, it's an idyllic spot to spend some time.

June to September is the height of the season here but serious surfers also like to drop by in winter to face down the lashing waves. Check Surfing Vancouver Island (www.surfingvancouverisland.com) for a taste of what to expect.

Some 6000km away, the east coast of Nova Scotia can also dish out some formidable swells. The US south coast's hurricane season (August to November) brings Canadians steep fast breaks, snappy right and left point breaks, and offshore reef and shoal breaks in areas just outside Halifax, as well as the entire south shore region. There are also a couple of surf schools in the province. Scotia Surfer (www.scotiasurfer.com) has the lowdown.

Spectator Sports

Ice hockey players near Banff Town (p122), Alberta

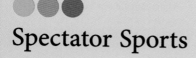

PHILIP AND KAREN SMITH/GETTY IMAGES ©

While Canadians have a solid reputation for being mild-mannered, that all changes when it comes to watching sports. Meek and peace-loving most of the time, locals will paint their faces, down a few too many Molsons and chant, scream and sing at the top of their lungs at hockey games that somehow seem to define their existence. For visitors, watching sports with these passionate locals is an eye-opening cultural experience.

Hockey

While Canada is a multifaith country, there's one religion that rises above all others. Hockey – don't even bother calling it *ice* hockey here – rouses rabid emotions in die-hard fans and can trigger group hugging and uncontrollable sobbing at the drop of a puck, especially when the local team has just lost (like they have always done lately) in the annual Stanley Cup play-offs.

Canada has seven teams in the elite, US-dominated National Hockey League (NHL): the Vancouver Canucks, Calgary Flames, Edmonton Oilers, Ottawa Senators, Montréal Canadiens, Winnipeg Jets and Toronto Maple Leafs (don't make the mistake of calling them 'the Leaves'). CBC television's website (www.cbc.ca/sports/hockey/nhl) has the details.

But although it's the country's national sport and Wayne Gretzky – its most famous

The Best... Professional Sports Teams

1 Toronto Maple Leafs (p174; hockey)

2 Vancouver Canucks (p78; hockey)

3 Montréal Canadiens (p229; hockey)

4 Ottawa Senators (p197; hockey)

5 Toronto Blue Jays (p174; baseball)

former player – is Canadian, no team north of the border has won that illusive cup since 1993. It's a touchy subject here, which might explain why riots have ensued in some cities when another annual run at the trophy comes to naught.

While tickets for games in some areas can be hard to come by – Vancouver Canucks games routinely sell out, for example, and booking as far ahead as possible for the September to June season is essential – you don't have to hit a stadium to catch a game. For a glimpse at what it feels like to be unreservedly in love with a Canadian hockey side, head to any local pub on game night and you'll be swept up in the emotion. And the beer will be better than the overpriced plastic cups of fizz on offer at the games themselves.

After the game, make sure you ask your new beer buddies about the 2010 Winter Olympics in Vancouver. Their faces will light up as they regale you with the story of the US versus Canada men's hockey gold medal battle, a movie-style epic in which the local boys scored a nail-biting 3-2 overtime win. On the night, the entire country rose as one to hug each other and cheer.

Minor pro teams and junior hockey clubs also fill arenas with rabid fans. Check the Canadian Hockey League (www.chl.ca) and American Hockey League (www.theahl.com) for local stick wielders.

Football

We're not talking about soccer and we're not even talking about American Football here. With eight major teams across the country, the Canadian Football League (CFL) is second only to hockey in the hearts and minds of many north-of-the-border sports nuts. And while it's similar to American Football – think hefty padding, an egg-shaped ball and the kind of crunching tackles that would stop a grizzly bear – the Canadian version involves teams of 12 players and is fought out on a larger pitch.

Like hockey, the main annual aim of the Hamilton Tiger-Cats, Montréal Alouettes, Toronto Argonauts, Winnipeg Blue Bombers, Saskatchewan Roughriders, Calgary Stampeders, Edmonton Eskimos and BC Lions is to win that elusive trophy, this one called the Grey Cup. Play-off games trigger raucous street celebrations in host cities, with fans from visiting teams parading around in team shirts hollering their undying love for their side.

Established in 1958, the fortunes of the CFL have ebbed and flowed over the decades but recent years have seen solid popularity and the improvement of stadium facilities as well as the awarding of a franchise: the as-yet unnamed Ottawa team will be the third CFL team the city has had and they are expected to debut in 2014.

For visitors, tickets for Grey Cup games can be hard to get hold of but regular matches during the June to November season are much more accessible: expect a family atmosphere and a partylike vibe with cheerleaders and noisy crowd interaction. For more information on the league, check out its official website at www.cfl.ca.

Soccer

Canada's most popular participation sport, soccer – you won't get very far calling it football here – has traditionally mirrored the US experience by never quite reaching the heights of the continent's more established professional sports. But you can't keep a good pastime down, and while they struggled with early attempts at building support here (by importing fading stars from Europe and South America), recent leagues are on a much more solid footing.

The three biggest Canadian professional teams are Toronto FC, the Montréal Impact and the Vancouver Whitecaps. All have entered the sport's US-based top level Major League Soccer (MLS) class. The Canadian Soccer League (www.canadiansoccerleague.com) occupies a lower rung on the sport's ladder. It's dominated by teams from Ontario, including the North York Astros and Windsor Stars.

Soccer is growing in popularity as a spectator sport in Canada, but tickets for top-level games are still relatively easy to buy – book ahead via club websites, though, if you have a particular date in mind.

Roller Derby

Vancouver's hottest alternative sports league, Terminal City Rollergirls (www.terminalcityrollergirls.com) pits all-female amateur flat-track roller derby teams against each other as they whistle around the track at breakneck speeds. The bouts are between teams with names such as Riot Girls and Bad Reputations. But you don't have to be in Vancouver to catch the action: roller derby leagues are growing across Canada and you can check out the options near to where you are at www.rollerderbycanada.ca.

Baseball

Following the 2004 relocation of the Montréal Expos to Washington (they're now called the Washington Nationals), Canada's only Major League Baseball (MLB) team is the Toronto Blue Jays, a member of the American League's Eastern Division. Founded in 1977 and playing in the city's cavernous downtown SkyDome – now known as the Rogers Centre – they are the only non-US team to win the World Series (in 1993). Follow the team and check out ticket options for the April to early October season at www.bluejays.com.

There is also one professional minor league side in Canada: the Vancouver Canadians (www.milb.com), affiliated with the Blue Jays and playing in the Northwest League. Their recently refurbished outdoor stadium with mountain views is one of the best diamonds in Canada, so hit the bleachers and feel the nostalgic ambiance of old-school summertime baseball.

Additional lower level teams across the country – including the Edmonton Capitals (www.capsbaseball.ca) and Winnipeg Goldeyes (www.goldeyes.com) – offer a similar family-friendly feel, while college teams are also popular if you want to catch the atmosphere of a game without paying Blue Jay prices.

Wildlife

Khutzeymateen Grizzly Bear Sanctuary, British Columbia

RICHARD WEAR/DESIGN PICS/GETTY IMAGES

On land, in the water and in the air, Canada is teeming with the kind of camera-worthy critters that make visitors wonder if they haven't stepped into a safari park by mistake. And when we say 'critters,' we're not talking small fry: this is the home of grizzlies, wolves, moose and bald eagles, as well as a perfect viewing spot for a roll call of whales.

Grizzly Bears & Black Bears

The main wildlife viewing target for many Canada-bound visitors, grizzly bears – *ursus arctos horribilis* to all you Latin scholars out there – are most commonly found in the Rocky Mountain regions of British Columbia (BC) and Alberta. Standing up to 3m tall, you'll know them by their distinctive shoulder hump. Solitary animals with no natural enemies (except us), they enjoy crunching on elk, moose or caribou but they're usually content to fill their bellies with berries and – if they're available – juicy fresh salmon. Keep in mind that you should never approach any bear. And in remote areas, be sure to travel in groups.

Just to confuse you, grizzlies are almost black, while their smaller relation, the black bear, is sometimes brown. More commonly spotted in the wild than grizzlies, Canada is home to around half a million black bears and they're spread out across the country, except for Prince Edward Island (PEI), southern Alberta and southern Saskatchewan. In regions such as northern BC as well as Banff and Jasper National Parks, seeing black bears feasting on berries as you drive past on the highway is surprisingly common.

In 1994, coastal BC's Khutzeymateen Grizzly Bear Sanctuary (near the northern town of Prince Rupert) was officially designated for protected status. More than 50 grizzlies currently live on this 45,000-hectare refuge. Visit www.env.gov.bc.ca/bcparks/explore/parkpgs/khutzeymateen/ for details. A few ecotour operators have permits for viewing these animals if you want to check them out face-to-face.

The Best... Bear & Moose Viewing

1 Jasper National Park (p122), Alberta

2 Algonquin Provincial Park (p197), Ontario

3 Icefields Parkway (p134), Alberta

4 Churchill (p294), Manitoba

5 Cape Breton Island (p273), Nova Scotia

Polar Bears

Weighing less than a kilogram at birth, the fiercest member of the bear clan is not quite so cute when it grows up to be a hulking 600kg. But these mesmerizing animals still pack a huge visual punch for visitors. If your visit to Canada won't be complete until you've seen one, there's really only one place to go: Churchill, Manitoba, on the shores of Hudson Bay (late September to early November is the viewing season). About 900 of the planet's roughly 20,000 white-furred beasts prowl the tundra here.

Operators will tour you around the Polar Bear Capital of the World in elevated tundra buggies. Just don't step out: these carnivorous, ever-watchful predators are not cuddly cartoon critters and will view you as an easy take-out dinner. Unlike grizzlies and black bears, polar bears actively prey on people, whether or not they have cameras.

While Churchill is a polar-bear-watcher magnet, it's not Canada's only potential viewing spot. The animals occasionally show up in Newfoundland and Labrador, coming ashore from drifting pack ice. And while northern Nunavut is home to nearly half of the world's polar bear population, its bear-rich spots such as Ukkusiksalik National Park are notoriously difficult and expensive to visit.

Moose

Canada's iconic shrub-nibbler, the moose is a massive member of the deer family that owes its popularity to a distinctively odd appearance: skinny legs supporting a humungous body and a cartoonish head that looks permanently inquisitive and clueless at the same time. And then there are the antlers: males grow a spectacular rack every summer, only to discard them come November.

Adding to their *Rocky & Bullwinkle* appeal, a moose can move at more than 50km per hour and easily out-swim two men paddling a canoe – all on a vegetarian diet comprised mostly of leaves and twigs.

You'll spot moose foraging for these yummy treats near lakes, muskegs and streams, as well as in the forests of the western mountain ranges in the Rockies and the Yukon. Newfoundland is perhaps the moosiest place of all. In 1904 the province imported and released four beasts into the wild. They enjoyed the good life of

The Effect of Climate Change

Climate change is impacting Canada's creatures. In Churchill, Manitoba, polar bears are arriving sooner and staying later each year, and are more plentiful near town. Shorter winters mean the polar ice melts sooner and freezes later, making the bears' seal hunting season shorter.

Some sections of British Columbia have seen moose populations drop between 20% and 70%. Scientists think warmer weather may be playing a role by inducing stresses (such as ticks and other parasites) that make the moose vulnerable to disease and habitat decline.

shrub-eating and hot sex, ultimately spawning the 120,000 inhabitants that now roam the woods.

Generally not aggressive, moose will often stand stock still for photographs. They can be unpredictable, though, so don't startle them. During mating season (September), the giant males can become belligerent, so keep your distance: great photos are not worth an antler charge from 500kg of angry moose.

Elk, Deer & Caribou

Moose are not the only animals that can exhibit a Mr Hyde personality change during rutting season. Usually placid, male elk have been known to charge vehicles in Jasper National Park, believing their reflection in the shiny paintwork to be a rival for their harem of eligible females. It's rare, though, and Jasper is generally one of the best places in Canada to see this large deer species wandering around on the edge of town.

White-tailed deer can be found anywhere from Nova Scotia's Cape Breton to the Northwest Territories' Great Slave Lake. Its bigger relative, the caribou, is unusual in that both males and females sport enormous antlers. Barren-ground caribou feed on lichen and spend most of the year on the tundra from Baffin Island to Alaska. Woodland caribou roam further south, with some of the biggest herds trekking across northern Québec and Labrador. These beasts, which have a reputation for not being especially smart, also show up in the mountain parks of BC, Alberta and Newfoundland, which is where many visitors catch a glimpse of them.

Wolves

It's fitting that wolves follows elk, deer and caribou in this section since that's what they spend much of their time doing in the wild. Perhaps the most intriguing and mysterious of all Canada's wild animals, they hunt cleverly and tenaciously in packs and have no qualms about taking on prey much bigger than themselves – although human attacks are extremely rare.

Clearly wary of human contact, they're also not the easiest animals to spot. If you are lucky enough to catch sight of one – perhaps in the Rockies – it will likely be from a distance.

Fairly common in sparsely populated areas throughout the country, you may also hear wolves howling at the moon if you're out in the bush. In Ontario's Algonquin Provincial Park, you can actually take part in a public 'howl.' Wolves will readily respond to human imitations of their calls, so the park's staff conducts communal sessions on various summer evenings to give visitors a 'wail' of an experience.

The Best... Whale Watching

1 Digby Neck (p271), Nova Scotia

2 Victoria (p89), British Columbia

3 Tofino (p100), British Columbia

4 Tadoussac (p249), Québec

5 Grand Manan Island (p271), New Brunswick

Whales

More than 22 species of whale and porpoise lurk offshore in Atlantic Canada, including camera-hogging superstars such as the humpback whale, which averages 15m and 36 tons; the North Atlantic right whale, the world's most endangered leviathan, with an estimated population of just 350; and the mighty blue whale, the largest animal on earth at 25m and around 100 tons. Then there's the little guy, the minke, which grows to 10m and often approaches boats, delighting with acrobatics as it shows off. Whale-watching tours are very popular throughout the region.

You can also spot humpbacks and gray whales off the west coast. But it's the orca – or killer whale – that dominates viewing here. Their aerodynamic bodies, signature black-and-white color and incredible speed (up to 40km/h) make them the Ferraris of the aquatic world and their diet includes seals, belugas and other whales (hence the 'killer whale' tag). The waters around Vancouver Island, particularly in the Johnstone Strait, teem with orcas every summer. Whale-watching tours depart from points throughout this region: Tofino and Victoria are particularly hot spots for operators.

Belugas glide in Arctic waters to the north. These ghostly white whales are one of the smallest members of the whale family, typically measuring no more than 4m and weighing about one ton. They are chatty fellows who squeak, groan and peep while traveling in close-knit family pods. If you tire of the polar bears in Churchill, Manitoba, you can also view belugas here via a boat or kayak tour. The more adventurous can also don a wetsuit and go snorkeling with them. Tadoussac, Québec is the only place to see belugas outside the Arctic, as the krill-rich waters of the Saguenay River host a hungry population of the little white whales.

Birds

Canada's wide skies are home to 462 bird species, with BC and Ontario boasting the greatest diversity. The most famous feathered resident is the common loon, Canada's national bird – if you don't spot one in the wild, you'll see it on the back of the $1 coin. Rivaling it in the ubiquity stakes are Canada geese, hardy fowls that can fly up to

1000km per day and seem to have successfully colonized parks throughout the world, usually to the chagrin of park wardens who have to clean up after them.

The most visually arresting of Canada's birds are its eagles, especially the bald variety. The bald eagle wingspan can reach up to 2m and, like wolves, they provide a spine tingling experience for anyone lucky enough to see one in the wild. Good viewing sites include Brackendale, between Vancouver and Whistler in BC, where up to 4000 eagles nest in winter. Also train your camera on Bras d'Or Lake in Cape Breton, Nova Scotia, and on Vancouver Island's southern and western shorelines.

Seabirds flock to Atlantic Canada to breed. You'll be able to feast your eyes upon razorbills, kittiwakes, arctic terns, common murres and, yes, puffins. Everyone loves these cute little guys, a sort of waddling penguin-meets-parrot with black-and-white feathers and an orange beak. They nest around Newfoundland, in particular.

The seabird colonies can be up to one million strong, their shrieks deafening and their smell, well, not so fresh. Still, it's an amazing sight to behold. The preeminent places to get feathered are New Brunswick's Grand Manan Island and Newfoundland's Witless Bay and Cape St Mary's (both on the Avalon Peninsula near St John's). The best time is May through August, before the birds fly away for the winter.

Moose, Alberta
PHILIPPE WIDLING/DESIGN PICS/GETTY IMAGES ©

Survival Guide

Snow-plowed road, British Columbia
ROBERT MCGOUEY/GETTY IMAGES ©

A-Z Directory

Sleeping Price Ranges

The following price ranges refer to a double room with private bathroom in high season, unless stated otherwise. Tax (which can be up to 17%) is not included in prices listed.

$ less than $80 ($100 in major cities)

$$ $80-180 ($100-250 in major cities)

$$$ more than $180 ($250 in major cities)

Accommodations

Provincial tourist offices publish comprehensive directories of accommodations, and some take bookings online.

Seasons

- Peak season is summer, basically June through August, when prices are highest.
- It's best to book ahead during summer, as well as during ski season at winter resorts, and during holidays and major events, as rooms can be scarce.
- Some properties close down altogether in the off-season.

Amenities

- At many budget properties (campgrounds, hostels, simple B&Bs) bathrooms are shared.
- Midrange accommodations, such as most B&Bs, inns (*auberges* in French), motels and some hotels, generally offer the best value for money. Expect a private bathroom, cable TV and in some cases, free breakfast.
- Top-end accommodations offer an international standard of amenities, with fitness and business centers and on-site dining.
- Most properties offer in-room wi-fi. It's typically free in budget and midrange lodgings, while top-end hotels often charge a fee.
- Many smaller properties, especially B&Bs, ban smoking. Marriott and Westin brand hotels are 100% smoke free. Other properties have rooms set aside for nonsmokers. We use the nonsmoking icon (🚭) to mean that *all* rooms within a property are nonsmoking.
- Air-conditioning is not a standard amenity at most budget and midrange places. If you want it, be sure to ask about it when you book.

Book Your Stay Online

For more accommodations reviews by Lonely Planet authors, check out www.lonelyplanet.com/hotels. You'll find independent reviews, as well as recommendations on the best places to stay. Best of all, you can book online.

Discounts

- In winter, prices can plummet by as much as 50%.
- Membership in the American Automobile Association (AAA) or an associated automobile association, American Association of Retired Persons (AARP) or other organizations also yields modest savings (usually 10%).
- Check hotel websites for special online rates. The usual suspects also offer discounted room prices throughout Canada:

Priceline (www.priceline.com)

Hotwire (www.hotwire.com)

Expedia (www.expedia.com)

Travelocity (www.travelocity.com)

B&Bs

- **Bed & Breakfast Online** (www.bbcanada.com) is the main booking agency for properties nationwide.
- In Canada, B&Bs (*gîtes* in French) are essentially converted private homes whose owners live on-site. People who like privacy may find B&Bs too intimate, as

walls are rarely soundproof and it's usual to mingle with your hosts and other guests.

- Standards vary widely, sometimes even within a single B&B. The cheapest rooms tend to be small with few amenities and a shared bathroom. Nicer ones have added features such as a balcony, a fireplace and an en suite bathroom. Breakfast is always included in the rates (though it might be continental instead of a full cooked affair).
- Not all B&Bs accept children.
- Minimum stays (usually two nights) are common, and many B&Bs are only open seasonally.

Hotels & Motels

Most hotels are part of international chains, and the newer ones are designed for either the luxury market or businesspeople. Rooms have cable TV and wi-fi; many also have swimming pools and fitness and business centers. Rooms with two double or queen-sized beds sleep up to four people, although there is usually a small surcharge for the third and fourth person. Many places advertise that 'kids stay free' but sometimes you have to pay extra for a crib or a rollaway (portable bed).

In Canada, like the USA (both lands of the automobile), motels are ubiquitous. They dot the highways and cluster in groups on the outskirts of towns and cities. Although most motel rooms won't win any style awards, they're usually clean and comfortable and offer good value for travelers. Many regional motels remain your typical 'mom and pop' operations, but plenty of North American chains have also opened up around the region.

Chain Hotels

BUDGET

Econo Lodge (☎ 877-424-6423; www.econolodge.com)

Howard Johnson (☎ 800-446-4656; www.hojo.com)

Quality Inn & Suites (☎ 877-424-6423; www.qualityinn.com)

Super 8 (☎ 800-800-8000; www.super8.com)

Travelodge/Thriftlodge (☎ 800-578-7878; www.travelodge.ca)

MIDRANGE

Best Western (☎ 800-780-7234; www.bestwestern.com)

Comfort Inn (☎ 877-424-6423; www.comfortinn.com)

Days Inn (☎ 800-329-7466; www.daysinn.com)

Fairfield Inn (☎ 800-228-2800; www.fairfieldinn.com)

Hampton Inn (☎ 800-426-7866; www.hamptoninn.com)

Holiday Inn (☎ 888-465-4329; www.holidayinn.com)

TOP END

Delta (☎ 877-814-7706; www.deltahotels.com)

Fairmont (☎ 800-257-7544; www.fairmont.com)

Hilton (☎ 800-445-8667; www.hilton.com)

Hyatt (☎ 888-591-1234; www.hyatt.com)

Marriott (☎ 888-236-2427; www.marriott.com)

Radisson (☎ 888-201-1718; www.radisson.com)

Ramada (☎ 800-272-6232; www.ramada.com)

Sheraton (☎ 800-325-3535; www.sheraton.com)

Westin (☎ 800-937-8461; www.westin.com)

Climate

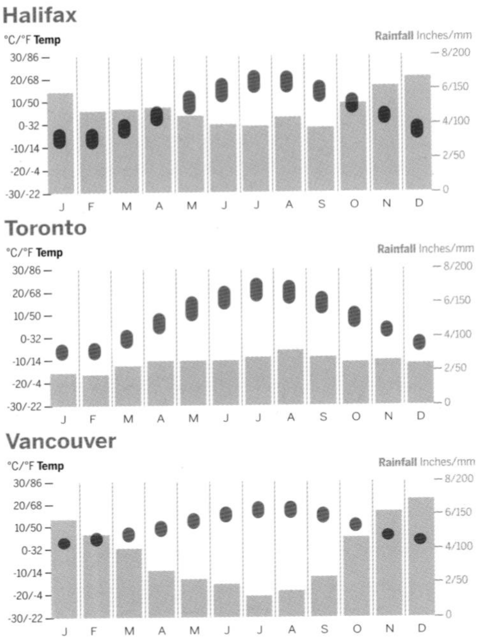

Customs Regulations

The **Canada Border Services Agency** (CBSA; www.cbsa.gc.ca) has the customs lowdown. A few regulations to note:

- **Alcohol** You can bring in 1.5L of wine, 1.14L of liquor or 24 355mL beers duty free.
- **Gifts** You can bring in gifts totaling up to $60.
- **Money** You can bring in/take out up to $10,000; larger amounts must be reported to customs.
- **Personal effects** Camping gear, sports equipment, cameras and laptop computers can be brought in without much trouble. Declaring these to customs as you cross the border might save you some hassle when you leave, especially if you'll be crossing the US–Canadian border multiple times.
- **Pets** You must carry a signed and dated certificate from a veterinarian to prove your dog or cat has had a rabies shot in the past 36 months.
- **Prescription drugs** You can bring in/take out a 90-day supply for personal use (though if you're taking it to the USA, know it's technically illegal, but overlooked for individuals).
- **Tobacco** You can bring in 200 cigarettes, 50 cigars, 200g of tobacco and 200 tobacco sticks duty free.

Discount Cards

Discounts are commonly offered for seniors, children, families and people with disabilities, though no special cards are issued (you get the savings on-site when you pay). AAA and other automobile association members can also receive various travel-related discounts.

International Student Identity Card (ISIC; www.isic.org) Provides students with discounts on travel insurance and admission to museums and other sights. There are also cards for those who are under 26 but not students, and for full-time teachers.

Parks Canada Discovery Pass (www.pc.gc.ca/ar-sr/lpac-ppri/ced-ndp.aspx; adult/child/family $68/33/136) Provides access to more than 100 national parks and historic sites for a year. Can pay for itself in as few as seven visits over daily entry fees; also provides quicker entry into sites.

Electricity

120V/60Hz

120V/60Hz

Food

For information on food, see the Cuisines of Canada chapter. The following price ranges are for main dishes:

$ less than $12

$$ $12-25

$$$ more than $25

Gay & Lesbian Travelers

Canada is tolerant when it comes to gays and lesbians, though this outlook is more common in the big cities than in rural areas. Same-sex marriage is legal throughout the country (Canada is one of only 15 nations worldwide that permits this).

Montréal, Toronto and Vancouver are by far Canada's gayest cities, each with a humming nightlife scene, publications and lots of associations and support groups. All have sizeable Pride celebrations, too, which attract big crowds.

Attitudes remain more conservative in the northern regions. Throughout Nunavut, and to a lesser extent in the aboriginal communities of the Northwest Territories, there are some retrogressive attitudes toward homosexuality. The Yukon, in contrast, is more like British Columbia (BC), with a live-and-let-live west coast attitude.

The following are good resources for gay travel; they include Canadian information, though not all are exclusive to the region:

Damron (www.damron.com) Publishes several travel guides, including *Men's Travel Guide, Women's Traveller* and *Damron Accommodations;* gay-friendly tour operators are listed on the website, too.

Gay Canada (www.gaycanada.com) Search by province or city for queer-friendly businesses and resources.

Out Traveler (www.outtraveler.com) Gay travel magazine.

Purple Roofs (www.purpleroofs.com) Website listing queer accommodations, travel agencies and tours worldwide.

Queer Canada (www.queercanada.ca) A general resource.

Xtra (www.xtra.ca) Source for gay and lesbian news nationwide.

Health

Before You Go

Insurance

Canada offers some of the finest health care in the world. However, unless you are a Canadian citizen, it can be prohibitively expensive. It's essential to purchase travel health insurance if your regular policy doesn't cover you when you're abroad. Check www.lonelyplanet.com/travel-insurance for supplemental insurance information.

Bring medications you may need clearly labeled in their original containers. A signed, dated letter from your physician that describes your medical conditions and medications, including generic names, is also a good idea.

Practicalities

- **Newspapers & Magazines** The most widely available newspaper is the Toronto-based *Globe and Mail*. Other principal dailies are the *Montréal Gazette, Ottawa Citizen, Toronto Star* and *Vancouver Sun*. *Maclean's* (www.macleans.ca) is Canada's weekly news magazine.

- **Radio & TV** The Canadian Broadcasting Corporation (CBC) is the dominant nationwide network for both radio and TV. The CTV Television Network (CTV) is the major competition.

- **Smoking** Banned in all restaurants, bars and other public venues nationwide.

- **Weights & Measures** Canada officially uses the metric system, but imperial measurements are used for many day-to-day purposes.

Medical Checklist

- acetaminophen (eg Tylenol) or aspirin
- anti-inflammatory drugs (eg ibuprofen)
- antihistamines (for hay fever and allergic reactions)
- antibacterial ointment (eg Neosporin) for cuts and abrasions
- steroid cream or cortisone (for poison ivy and other allergic rashes)
- bandages, gauze, gauze rolls
- adhesive or paper tape
- safety pins, tweezers
- thermometer
- DEET-containing insect repellent for the skin
- permethrin-containing insect spray for clothing, tents and bed nets
- sunblock
- motion-sickness medication

Recommended Vaccinations

No special vaccines are required or recommended for travel to Canada. All travelers should be up to date on routine immunizations.

Websites

Government travel-health websites are available for **Australia** (www.smarttraveller.gov.au), the **United Kingdom** (www.nhs.uk/healthcareabroad) and the **United States** (www.cdc.gov/travel/).

MD Travel Health (www.mdtravelhealth.com) General health resources.

Public Health Agency of Canada (www.phac-aspc.gc.ca) Canadian health resources.

World Health Organization (www.who.int) General health resources.

In Canada

Availability & Cost of Health Care

Medical services are widely available. For emergencies, the best bet is to find the nearest hospital and go to its emergency room. If the problem isn't urgent, call a nearby hospital and ask for a referral to a local physician, which is usually cheaper than a trip to the emergency room (where costs can be $500 or so before any treatment).

Pharmacies are abundant, but prescriptions can be expensive without insurance. However, Americans may find Canadian prescription drugs to be cheaper than drugs at home. You're allowed to take out a 90-day supply for personal use (it's technically illegal to bring them into the USA, but overlooked for individuals).

Infectious Diseases

Most are acquired by mosquito or tick bites, or environmental exposure. The Public Health Agency of Canada has details on all listed below.

- **Giardiasis** Intestinal infection. Avoid drinking directly from lakes, ponds, streams and rivers.

- **Lyme Disease** Occurs mostly in southern Canada. Transmitted by deer ticks in late spring and summer. Perform a tick check after you've been outdoors.

- **Severe Acute Respiratory Syndrome (SARS)** At the time of writing, SARS had been brought under control in Canada.

- **West Nile Virus** Mosquito-transmitted in late summer and early fall. Prevent by keeping covered (wear long sleeves, long pants, hats, and shoes rather than sandals) and apply a good insect repellent, preferably one containing DEET, to exposed skin and clothing.

Environmental Hazards

- **Cold exposure** This can be a significant problem, especially in the northern regions. Keep all body surfaces covered, including the head and neck. Watch out for the 'Umbles' – stumbles, mumbles, fumbles and grumbles – which are signs of impending hypothermia.

- **Heat exhaustion** Dehydration is the main contributor. Symptoms include feeling weak, headache, nausea and sweaty skin. Lay the victim flat with their legs raised, apply cool, wet cloths to the skin, and rehydrate.

Insurance

Make sure you have adequate travel insurance, whatever the length of your trip. At a minimum you need coverage for medical emergencies and treatment, including hospital stays and an emergency flight home. Medical treatment for non-Canadians is very expensive.

Also consider insurance for luggage theft or loss. If you already have a home-owners or renters policy, check what it will cover and only get supplemental insurance to protect against the rest. If you have prepaid a large portion of your vacation, trip cancellation insurance is worthwhile.

Worldwide travel insurance is available at www.lonelyplanet.com/travel-insurance. You can buy, extend and claim online at any time – even if you're already on the road. Also check the following providers:

Insure.com (www.insure.com)

Travel Guard (www.travelguard.com)

Travelex (www.travelex.com)

Internet Access

- It's easy to find internet access. Libraries and community agencies in practically every town provide free wi-fi and computers for public use. The only downsides are that usage time is limited (usually 30 minutes), and some facilities have erratic hours.

- Internet cafes are limited to the main tourist areas, and access generally starts around $2 per hour.

- Wi-fi is widely available. Most lodgings have it (in-room, with good speed), as do many restaurants, bars and Tim Hortons coffee shops. We've identified sleeping, eating, drinking and other listings that have wi-fi (whether free or fee-based) with a (wi-fi icon). We've denoted lodgings that offer internet terminals with a (internet icon).

- For a list of wi-fi hot spots around Canada, visit **Wi-Fi Free Spot** (www.wififreespot.com).

Legal Matters

Police

If you are arrested or charged with an offense, you have the right to keep your mouth shut and to hire any lawyer you wish (contact your embassy for a referral, if necessary). If you cannot afford one, ask to be represented by public counsel. There is a presumption of innocence.

Drugs & Alcohol

- The blood-alcohol limit is 0.08% and driving cars, motorcycles, boats and snowmobiles while drunk is a criminal offense. If you are caught, you may face stiff fines, license suspension and other nasty consequences.

- Consuming alcohol anywhere other than at a residence or licensed premises is also a no-no, which puts parks, beaches and the rest of the great outdoors off limits, at least officially.

- Avoid illegal drugs, as penalties may entail heavy fines, possible jail time and a criminal record. The only exception is the use of marijuana for medical purposes, which became legal in 2001. Meanwhile, the decriminalization of pot possession for personal use remains a subject of ongoing debate among the general public and in parliament.

Other Legal Issues

- Abortion is legal.
- Travelers should note that they can be prosecuted under the law of their home country regarding age of consent, even when abroad.

Money

- All prices quoted are in Canadian dollars ($), unless stated otherwise.
- Canadian coins come in 5¢ (nickel), 10¢ (dime), 25¢ (quarter), $1 (Loonie) and $2 (toonie or twoonie) denominations. The gold-colored Loonie features the loon, a common Canadian water bird, while the two-toned toonie is decorated with a polar bear. Canada started phasing out its 1¢ (penny) coin in 2012.
- Paper currency comes in $5 (blue), $10 (purple), $20 (green) and $50 (red) denominations. The $100 (brown) and larger bills are less common. The newest bills in circulation – which have enhanced security features – are actually a polymer-based material; they feel more like plastic than paper.
- The Canadian dollar has seen fluctuations over the last decade, though since 2007 it has tracked quite closely to the US dollar.
- For changing money in the larger cities, currency exchange offices may offer better conditions than banks.
- See Need to Know for exchange rates and costs.

ATMs

- Many grocery and convenience stores, airports, and bus, train and ferry stations have ATMs. Most are linked to international networks, the most common being Cirrus, Plus, Star and Maestro.
- Scotiabank, common throughout Canada, is part of the Global ATM Alliance. If your home bank is a member, fees may be less if you withdraw from Scotiabank ATMs.

Cash

Most Canadians don't carry large amounts of cash for everyday use, relying instead on credit and debit cards. Still, carrying some cash, say $100 or less, comes in handy when making small purchases. In some cases, cash is necessary to pay for rural B&Bs and shuttle vans; inquire in advance to avoid surprises. Shops and businesses rarely accept personal checks.

Credit Cards

Major credit cards such as MasterCard, Visa and American Express are widely accepted in Canada, except in remote, rural communities where cash is king. You'll find it difficult or impossible to rent a car, book a room or order tickets over the phone without having a piece of plastic. Note that some credit card companies charge a 'transaction fee' (around 3% of whatever you purchased); check with your provider to avoid surprises.

For lost or stolen cards, these numbers operate 24 hours:

American Express (☎ 866-296-5198; www.americanexpress.com)

MasterCard (☎ 800-307-7309; www.mastercard.com)

Visa (☎ 800-847-2911; www.visa.com)

Taxes & Refunds

Canada's federal goods and services tax (GST), variously known as the 'gouge and screw' or 'grab and steal' tax, adds 5% to just about every transaction. Most provinces also charge a provincial sales tax (PST) on top of it. Several provinces have combined the GST and PST into a harmonized sales tax (HST). Whatever the methodology, expect to pay 10% to 15% in most cases. Unless otherwise stated, taxes are not included in prices given.

You might be eligible for a rebate on some of the taxes. If you've booked your accommodations in conjunction with a rental car, plane ticket or other service (ie if it all appears on the same bill from a 'tour operator'), you should be eligible to get 50% of the tax refunded from your accommodations. Fill out the GST/HST Refund Application for Tour Packages form available from the **Canada Revenue Agency** (☎ 902-432-5608, 800-668-4748; www.cra-arc.gc.ca/E/pbg/gf/gst115).

Tax Rates By Province

Percentages represent federal and provincial taxes combined:

Alberta 5%

British Columbia 12%

Manitoba 13%

New Brunswick 13%

Newfoundland 13%

Northwest Territories 5%

Nova Scotia* 14%

Nunavut 5%

Ontario 13%

Prince Edward Island 14%

Québec 15%

Saskatchewan 10%

Yukon 5%

* rate to increase 1% in 2015

Tipping

Tipping is a standard practice. Generally you can expect to tip:

Restaurant waitstaff 15% to 20%

Bar staff $1 per drink

Hotel bellhop $1 to $2 per bag

Hotel room cleaners From $2 per day (depending on room size and messiness)

Taxis 10% to 15%

Opening Hours

The list below provides general opening hours for businesses. Reviews throughout the book show specific hours. Note that hours can vary by season. Our listings depict peak season operating times. Opening hours often decrease during off-peak months and a number of businesses close altogether.

Banks 10am to 5pm Monday to Friday; some open 9am to noon Saturday

General office hours 9am to 5pm Monday to Friday

Museums 10am to 5pm daily, sometimes closed Monday

Restaurants breakfast 8am to 11am, lunch 11:30am to 2:30pm Monday to Friday, dinner 5pm to 9:30pm daily; some open 8am to 1pm Saturday and Sunday

Bars 5pm to 2am daily

Clubs 9pm to 2am Wednesday to Saturday

Shops 10am to 6pm Monday to Saturday, noon to 5pm Sunday, some open to 8pm or 9pm Thursday and/or Friday

Supermarkets 9am to 8pm, some open 24 hours

Public Holidays

Canada observes 10 national public holidays and more at the provincial level. Banks, schools and government offices close on these days.

National Holidays

New Year's Day January 1

Good Friday March or April

Easter Monday March or April

Victoria Day Monday before May 25

Canada Day July 1; called Memorial Day in Newfoundland

Labour Day First Monday of September

Thanksgiving Second Monday of October

Remembrance Day November 11

Christmas Day December 25

Boxing Day December 26

Provincial Holidays

Some provinces also observe local holidays, with Newfoundland leading the pack.

Family Day Third Monday of February in Alberta, Ontario, Saskatchewan and Manitoba (second Monday in British Columbia); known as Louis Riel Day in Manitoba

St Patrick's Day Monday nearest March 17

St George's Day Monday nearest April 23

Uniquely Canadian Celebrations

National Flag Day (February 15) Commemorates the first time the maple-leaf flag was raised above Parliament Hill in Ottawa, at the stroke of noon on February 15, 1965.

Victoria Day (late May) This day was established in 1845 to observe the birthday of Queen Victoria and now celebrates the birthday of the British sovereign who's still Canada's titular head of state. Victoria Day marks the official beginning of the summer season (which ends with Labour Day on the first Monday of September). Some communities hold fireworks.

National Aboriginal Day (June 21) Created in 1996, it celebrates the contributions of Aboriginal peoples to Canada. Coinciding with the summer solstice, festivities are organized locally and may include traditional dancing, singing and drumming; storytelling; arts and crafts shows; canoe races; and lots more.

Canada Day (July 1) Known as Dominion Day until 1982, Canada Day was created in 1869 to commemorate the creation of Canada two years earlier. All over the country, people celebrate with barbecues, parades, concerts and fireworks.

Thanksgiving Day (mid-October) First celebrated in 1578 in what is now Newfoundland by explorer Martin Frobisher to give thanks for surviving his Atlantic crossing, Thanksgiving became an official Canadian holiday in 1872 to celebrate the recovery of the Prince of Wales from a long illness. These days, it's essentially a harvest festival involving a special family dinner of roast turkey and pumpkin, very much as it is practiced in the US.

National Day Monday nearest June 24 in Newfoundland; June 24 in Québec (aka St-Jean-Baptiste Day)

Orangemen's Day Monday nearest July 12 in Newfoundland

Civic Holiday First Monday of August everywhere *except* Newfoundland, Québec and Yukon Territory

Discovery Day Third Monday of August in Yukon Territory

School Holidays

Kids break for summer holidays in late June and don't return to school until early September. University students get even more time off, usually from May to early or mid-September. Most people take their big annual vacation during these months.

Telephone

Canada's phone system is almost identical to the USA's system.

Domestic & International Dialing

- Canadian phone numbers consist of a three-digit area code followed by a seven-digit local number. In many parts of Canada, you must dial all 10 digits preceded by 1, even if you're calling across the street. In other parts of the country, when you're calling within the same area code, you can dial the seven-digit number only, but this is slowly changing.
- For direct international calls, dial 011 + country code + area code + local phone number. The country code for Canada is 1 (the same as for the USA, although international rates still apply for all calls made between the two countries).
- Toll-free numbers begin with 800, 877, 866 or 855 and must be preceded by 1. Some of these numbers are good throughout Canada and the USA, others only work within Canada, and some work in just one province.

Emergency Numbers

Dial 911. This is *not* the emergency number in the Yukon, Northwest Territories or Nunavut.

Cell Phones

- Local SIM cards can be used in European and Australian phones. Other phones must be set to roaming.
- If you have a European, Australian or other type of unlocked GSM phone, buy a SIM card from local providers such as **Telus** (www.telus.com), **Rogers** (www.rogers.com) or **Bell** (www.bell.ca).
- US residents can often upgrade their domestic cell phone plan to extend to Canada. **Verizon** (www.verizonwireless.com) provides good results.
- Reception is poor in rural areas no matter who your service provider is.

Public Phones

Coin-operated public pay phones are fairly plentiful. Local calls cost 50¢; many phones also accept prepaid phonecards and credit cards. Dialing the operator (0) or directory assistance (411 for local calls, 1 + area code + 555-1212 for long-distance calls) is free of charge from public phones; it may incur a charge from private phones.

Phonecards

- Prepaid phonecards usually offer the best per-minute rates for long-distance and international calling. They come in denominations of $5, $10 or $20 and are widely sold in drugstores, supermarkets and convenience stores. Beware of cards with hidden charges such as 'activation fees' or a per-call connection fee.
- A surcharge ranging from 30¢ to 85¢ for calls made from public pay phones is common.

Time

- Canada spans six of the world's 24 time zones. The Eastern zone in Newfoundland is unusual in that it's only 30 minutes different from the adjacent zone. The time difference from coast to coast is 4½ hours.
- Canada observes daylight saving time, which comes into effect on the second Sunday in March, when clocks are put forward one hour, and ends on the first Sunday in November. Saskatchewan and small pockets of Québec, Ontario and BC are the only areas that do not switch to daylight saving time.
- In Québec especially, times for shop hours, train schedules, film screenings etc are usually indicated by the 24-hour clock.

Tourist Information

- The **Canadian Tourism Commission** (www.canada.travel) is loaded with general information, packages and links.
- All provincial tourist offices maintain comprehensive websites packed with information helpful in planning your trip. Staff also field telephone inquiries and, on request, will mail out free maps and directories about accommodations, attractions and events. Some offices can also help with making hotel, tour or other reservations.
- For detailed information about a specific area, contact the local tourist office, aka visitors center. Just about every city and town has at least a seasonal branch with helpful staff, racks of free pamphlets and books and maps for sale.

Provincial tourist offices:

Newfoundland & Labrador Tourism (☎ 800-563-6353; www.newfoundlandlabrador.com)

Northwest Territories (NWT) Tourism (☎ 800-661-0788; www.spectacularnwt.com)

Time Differences Between Cities

When it's 3pm in Vancouver, it's:

- 6pm in Montréal
- 6pm in New York City
- 7:30pm in St John's (Newfoundland)
- 11pm in London, England

Nunavut Tourism (☎ 866-686-2888; www.nunavuttourism.com)

Ontario Tourism (☎ 800-668-2746; www.ontariotravel.net)

Prince Edward Island Tourism (☎ 800-463-4734; www.peiplay.com)

Tourism British Columbia (☎ 800-435-5622; www.hellobc.com)

Tourism New Brunswick (☎ 800-561-0123; www.tourismnewbrunswick.ca)

Tourism Nova Scotia (☎ 800-565-0000; www.novascotia.com)

Tourism Saskatchewan (☎ 877-237-2273; www.sasktourism.com)

Tourisme Québec (☎ 877-266-5687; www.bonjourquebec.com)

Travel Alberta (☎ 800-252-3782; www.travelalberta.com)

Travel Manitoba (☎ 800-665-0040; www.travelmanitoba.com)

Yukon Department of Tourism (☎ 800-661-0494; www.travelyukon.com)

Travelers with Disabilities

Canada is making progress when it comes to easing the everyday challenges facing people with disabilities, especially the mobility impaired.

- Many public buildings, including museums, tourist offices, train stations, shopping malls and cinemas, have access ramps and/or lifts. Most public restrooms feature extra-wide stalls equipped with hand rails. Many pedestrian crossings have sloping curbs.
- Newer and recently remodeled hotels, especially chain hotels, have rooms with extra-wide doors and spacious bathrooms.
- Interpretive centers at national and provincial parks are usually accessible, and many parks have trails that can be navigated in wheelchairs.
- Car rental agencies offer hand-controlled vehicles and vans with wheelchair lifts at no additional charge, but you must reserve them well in advance.
- For accessible air, bus, rail and ferry transportation check **Access to Travel** (www.accesstotravel.gc.ca), the federal government's website. In general, most transportation agencies can accommodate people with disabilities if you make your needs known when booking.

Other organizations specializing in the needs of travelers with disabilities:

Access-Able Travel Source (www.access-able.com) Lists accessible lodging, transport, attractions and equipment rental by province.

Mobility International (www.miusa.org) Advises travelers with disabilities on mobility issues and runs an educational exchange program.

Society for Accessible Travel & Hospitality (www.sath.org) Travelers with disabilities share tips and blogs.

Visas

Citizens of dozens of countries – including the USA, most Western European nations, Australia, New Zealand, Japan and South Korea – do not need visas to enter Canada for stays of up to 180 days. US permanent residents are also exempt. **Citizenship & Immigration Canada** (www.cic.gc.ca) has the details.

Nationals of other countries – including China, India and South Africa – must apply to the Canadian visa office in their home country for a temporary resident visa (aka visitor visa). A separate visa is required if you plan to study or work in Canada.

Single-entry visas ($75) are usually valid for a maximum stay of six months from the date of your arrival in Canada. Multiple-entry visas ($150) allow you to enter Canada from all other countries multiple times while the visa is valid (up to 10 years), provided no single stay exceeds six months. Note you don't need a multiple-entry visa for repeated entries into Canada from the USA, unless you have visited a third country.

Visiting the USA

Admission requirements are subject to rapid change. The **US State Department** (www.travel.state.gov) has the latest information, or check with a US consulate in your home country.

Under the US visa-waiver program, visas are not required for citizens of 36 countries – including most EU members, Australia and New Zealand – for visits of up to 90 days (no extensions allowed), as long as you can present a machine-readable passport and are approved under the **Electronic System for Travel Authorization** (ESTA; www.cbp.gov/esta). Note you must register at least 72 hours before arrival, and there's a $14 fee for processing and authorization.

Canadians do not need visas, though they do need a passport or document approved by the **Western Hemisphere Travel Initiative** (www.getyouhome.gov). Citizens of all other countries need to apply for a US visa in their home country before arriving in Canada.

All foreign visitors (except Canadians) must pay a US$6 'processing fee' when entering at land borders.

Women Travelers

Canada is generally a safe place for women to travel, even alone and even in the cities. Simply use the same common sense as you would at home.

In bars and nightclubs, solo women are likely to attract a lot of attention, but if you don't want company, most men will respect a firm 'no thank you.' If you feel threatened, protesting loudly will often make the offender slink away – or will at least spur other people to come to your defense. Note that carrying mace or pepper spray is illegal in Canada.

Physical attack is unlikely, but if you are assaulted, call the police immediately (911 except in the Yukon, Northwest Territories and Nunavut) or contact a rape crisis center. A complete list is available from the **Canadian Association of Sexual Assault Centres** (☎604-876-2622; www.casac.ca). Hotlines in some of the major cities:

- **Calgary** (☎403-237-5888)
- **Halifax** (☎902-425-0122)
- **Montréal** (☎514-934-4504)
- **Toronto** (☎416-597-8808)
- **Vancouver** (☎604-255-6344)

Resources for women travelers include:

Her Own Way (www.travel.gc.ca/travelling/publications/her-own-way) Published by the Canadian government for Canadian travelers, but contains a great deal of general advice.

Journeywoman (www.journeywoman.com)

Transport

Getting There & Away

Flights, tours and rail tickets can be booked online at www.lonelyplanet.com/bookings.

Entering the Country

Entering Canada is pretty straightforward. First, you will have to show your passport (and your visa if you need one). The border officer will ask you a few questions about the purpose and length of your visit. After that, you'll go through customs. See **Going to Canada** (www.goingto-canada.gc.ca) for details.

Note that questioning may be more intense at land border crossings and your car may be searched.

For updates (particularly regarding land-border crossing rules), check the websites for the **US State Department** (www.travel.state.gov) and **Citizenship & Immigration Canada** (www.cic.gc.ca).

Climate Change & Travel

Every form of transport that relies on carbon-based fuel generates CO_2, the main cause of human-induced climate change. Modern travel is dependent on airplanes, which might use less fuel per mile per person than most cars but travel much greater distances. The altitude at which aircraft emit gases (including CO_2) and particles also contributes to their climate change impact. Many websites offer 'carbon calculators' that allow people to estimate the carbon emissions generated by their journey and, for those who wish to do so, to offset the impact of the greenhouse gases emitted with contributions to portfolios of climate-friendly initiatives throughout the world. Lonely Planet offsets the carbon footprint of all staff and author travel.

Passport

Most international visitors require a passport to enter Canada. US citizens at land and sea borders have other options, such as an enhanced driver's license or passport card. See the **Western Hemisphere Travel Initiative** (www.getyouhome.gov) for approved identification documents.

Visitors from certain countries also require a visa to enter Canada; see p344.

Air

Airports & Airlines

Toronto is far and away the busiest airport, followed by Vancouver. The international gateways you're most likely to use:

Calgary (YYC; www.calgaryairport.com)

Edmonton (YEG; www.flyeia.com)

Halifax (YHZ; www.hiaa.ca)

Montréal (Trudeau | YUL; www.admtl.com)

Ottawa (YOW; www.ottawairport.ca)

St John's (YYT; www.stjohnsairport.com)

Toronto (Pearson | YYZ; www.torontopearson.com)

Vancouver (YVR; Map p62; www.yvr.ca)

Winnipeg (YWG; www.waa.ca; 2000 Wellington Ave)

Land

Border Crossings

There are around 25 official border crossings along the US-Canadian border, from New Brunswick to British Columbia.

The website of the **Canadian Border Services Agency** (www.cbsa-asfc.gc.ca/bwt-taf/menu-eng.html) shows current wait times at each. You can also access it via Twitter (@CBSA_BWT).

In general, waits rarely exceed 30 minutes, except during the peak summer season, and on Friday and Sunday afternoons, especially on holiday weekends. Some entry points are especially busy:

- Windsor, Ontario, to Detroit, Michigan
- Fort Erie, Ontario, to Buffalo, New York
- Niagara Falls, Ontario, to Niagara Falls, New York
- Québec to Rouse's Point/Champlain, New York
- Surrey, British Columbia, to Blaine, Washington

When returning to the USA, check the website for the **US Department for Homeland Security** (http://apps.cbp.gov/bwt) for border wait times.

All foreign visitors (except Canadians) must pay a $6 'processing fee' when entering the USA by land; credit cards are not accepted.

Bus

Greyhound (www.greyhound.com) and its Canadian equivalent, **Greyhound Canada** (www.greyhound.ca), operate the largest bus network in North America. There are direct connections between main cities in the USA and Canada, but you usually have to transfer to a different bus at the border (where it takes a good hour for all passengers to clear customs/immigration). Most international buses have free wi-fi on board.

Other notable international bus companies (with free wi-fi) include:

Megabus (www.megabus.com) Runs between Toronto and US cities, including New York City, Philadelphia and Washington DC; usually cheaper than Greyhound. Tickets can only be purchased online.

Quick Coach (www.quickcoach.com) Runs between Seattle and

Vancouver; typically a bit quicker than Greyhound.

Car & Motorcycle

The highway system of the continental USA connects directly with the Canadian highway system at numerous points along the border. These Canadian highways then meet up with the east–west Trans-Canada Hwy further north. Between the Yukon Territory and Alaska, the main routes are the Alaska, Klondike and Haines Hwys.

If you're driving into Canada, you'll need the vehicle's registration papers, proof of liability insurance and your home driver's license. Cars rented in the USA can usually be driven into Canada and back, but make sure your rental agreement says so. If you're driving a car registered in someone else's name, bring a letter from the owner authorizing use of the vehicle in Canada.

Train

Amtrak (www.amtrak.com) and **VIA Rail Canada** (www.viarail.ca) run three routes between the USA and Canada: two in the east and one in the west. Customs inspections happen at the border, not upon boarding.

Sea

Ferry

Various ferry services on the coasts connect the US and Canada.

- Bar Harbor, Maine to Yarmouth, Nova Scotia: Service halted in recent years but supposedly it will start again with a new operator.
- Seattle to Victoria, British Columbia: **Victoria Clipper** (www.clippervacations.com).

Getting Around

Air

Airlines in Canada

Air Canada operates the largest domestic-flight network, serving some 150 destinations.

The Canadian aviation arena also includes many independent regional and local airlines, which tend to focus on small, remote regions, mostly in the North. Depending on the destination, fares in such noncompetitive markets can be high.

Air Canada (☎ 888-247-2262; www.aircanada.com) Nationwide flights.

Air North (☎ in Canada 867-668-2228, in USA 800-661-0407; www.flyairnorth.com) Flies from the Yukon to British

Greyhound Bus Routes & Fares

Route	Duration (hr)	Frequency (daily)	Fare (US$)
Boston-Montréal	7-8	4	85
Detroit-Toronto	5-6	5	73
New York-Montréal	8-9	6-10	84
Seattle-Vancouver	4	3-5	38

Train Routes & Fares

Route	Duration (hr)	Frequency (daily)	Fare (US$)
New York-Toronto *(Maple Leaf)*	13	1	125
New York-Montréal *(Adirondack)*	11	1	65
Seattle-Vancouver *(Cascades)*	4	2	52

Columbia, Alberta, Northwest Territories and Alaska.

Calm Air (☎ 800-839-2256, 204-778-6471; www.calmair.com) Flights throughout Manitoba and Nunavut.

Central Mountain Air (☎ 888-865-8585; www.flycma.com) Destinations throughout British Columbia and Alberta.

Harbour Air (☎ 800-665-0212; www.harbour-air.com) Seaplane service from the city of Vancouver to Vancouver Island, Gulf Islands and the Sunshine Coast.

Hawkair (☎ 866-429-5247; www.hawkair.ca) Serves northern British Columbia from Vancouver and Victoria.

Pacific Coastal Airlines (☎ 800-663-2872; www.pacific-coastal.com) Vancouver-based airline with service to many British Columbia locales.

Porter Airlines (☎ 888-619-8622; www.flyporter.com) Turboprop planes from eastern Canadian cities to Toronto's quicker, more convenient Billy Bishop City Airport downtown.

Provincial Airlines (☎ 800-563-2800; www.provincialairlines.ca) St John's–based airline with service throughout Newfoundland and to Labrador.

Seair Seaplanes (☎ 800-447-3247, 604-273-8900; www.seairseaplanes.com) Flies from Vancouver to Nanaimo and the Southern Gulf Islands in British Columbia.

West Coast Air (☎ 800-347-2222; www.westcoastair.com) Seaplane service from Vancouver city to Vancouver Island and the Sunshine Coast.

WestJet (☎ 888-937-8538, 800-538-5696; www.westjet.com) Calgary-based low-cost carrier serving destinations throughout Canada.

Air Passes

Star Alliance (www.staralliance.com) members Air Canada, United Airlines and US Airways have teamed up to offer the North American Airpass, which is available to anyone not residing in the USA, Canada, Mexico, Bermuda or the Caribbean. It's sold only in conjunction with an international flight operated by any Star Alliance member airline. You can buy as few as three coupons (from US$399) or as many as 10.

Bicycle

Much of Canada is great for cycling. Long-distance trips can be done entirely on quiet back roads, and many cities (including Edmonton, Montréal, Ottawa, Toronto and Vancouver) have designated bike routes.

- Cyclists must follow the same rules of the road as vehicles, but don't expect drivers to always respect your right of way.
- Helmets are mandatory for all cyclists in British Columbia, New Brunswick, Prince Edward Island and Nova Scotia, as well as for anyone under 18 in Alberta and Ontario.
- The Better World Club (p349) provides emergency roadside assistance. Membership costs $40 per year, plus a $12 enrollment fee, and entitles you to two free pickups, and transport to the nearest repair shop, or home, within a 50km radius of where you're picked up.

Transportation

- By air: most airlines will carry bikes as checked luggage without charge on international flights, as long as they're in a box. On domestic flights they usually charge between $30 and $65. Always check details before you buy the ticket.
- By bus: you must ship your bike as freight on Greyhound Canada. In addition to a bike box ($10), you'll be charged according to the weight of the bike, plus an oversize charge ($30) and GST. Bikes only travel on the same bus as the passenger if there's enough space. To ensure that yours arrives at the same time as (or before) you do, ship it a day early.
- By train: VIA Rail will transport your bicycle for $25, but only on trains offering checked-baggage service (which includes all long-distance and many regional trains).

Rental

- Outfitters renting bicycles exist in most tourist towns.
- Rentals cost around $15 per day for touring bikes and $25 per day for mountain bikes. The price usually includes a helmet and lock.
- Most companies require a security deposit of $20 to $200.

Boat

Ferry services are extensive, especially throughout the Atlantic provinces and in British Columbia.

Walk-ons and cyclists should be able to get aboard at any time, but call ahead for vehicle reservations or if you require a cabin berth. This is especially important during summer peak season and holidays. Main operators:

Bay Ferries (888-249-7245; www.ferries.ca) Year-round service between Saint John, New Brunswick, and Digby, Nova Scotia.

BC Ferries (888-223-3779, 250-386-3431; www.bcferries.com) Huge passenger-ferry systems with 25 routes and 47 ports of call, including Vancouver Island, the Gulf Islands, the Sechelt Peninsula along the Sunshine Coast and the islands of Haida Gwaii – all in British Columbia.

Coastal Transport (506-662-3724; www.coastaltransport.ca) Ferry from Blacks Harbour to Grand Manan in the Fundy Isles, New Brunswick.

CTMA Ferries (888-986-3278, 418-986-3278; www.ctma.ca) Daily ferries to Québec's Îles de la Madeleine from Souris, Prince Edward Island.

Marine Atlantic (800-341-7981; www.marine-atlantic.ca) Connects Port aux Basques and Argentia in Newfoundland with North Sydney, Nova Scotia.

Northumberland Ferries (888-249-7245, 902-566-3838; www.ferries.ca) Connects Wood Islands, Prince Edward Island and Caribou, Nova Scotia.

Bus

Greyhound Canada (p346) is the king, plowing along an extensive network in central and western Canada, as well as to/from the USA. Regional carriers pick up the slack, especially in the east.

Buses are generally clean, comfortable and reliable. Amenities may include onboard toilets, air-conditioning (bring a sweater), reclining seats, free wi-fi and onboard movies. Smoking is not permitted. On long journeys, buses make meal stops every few hours, usually at highway service stations.

Coach Canada (800-461-7661; www.coachcanada.com) Scheduled service within Ontario and from Toronto to Montréal.

Intercar (888-861-4592; www.intercar.qc.ca) Connects Québec City, Montréal and Tadoussac, among other towns in Québec.

Malaspina Coach Lines (877-227-8287; www.malaspinacoach.com) Service between Vancouver and the Sunshine Coast communities of British Columbia.

Maritime Bus (902-429-2029; www.maritimebus.com) For New Brunswick, Prince Edward Island and Nova Scotia.

Megabus (www.megabus.com) Service between Toronto and Montréal via Kingston; tickets can only be purchased online.

Orléans Express (888-999-3977; www.orleansexpress.com) Service to eastern Québec.

Pacific Coach Lines (250-385-4411, 800-661-1725; www.pacificcoach.com) Service between Victoria, Vancouver and Whistler.

Parkbus (800-928-7101; www.parkbus.ca) Runs from Toronto to Algonquin, Killarney and other Ontario parks.

Red Arrow (www.redarrow.ca) Serves all the major cities in Alberta, with free wi-fi, snacks, drinks and plug-ins.

Car & Motorcycle

Automobile Associations

Auto-club membership is a handy thing to have in Canada. The **Canadian Automobile Association** (CAA; 800-268-3750; www.caa.ca) offers services, including 24-hour emergency roadside assistance, to members of international affiliates such as AAA in the USA, AA in the UK and ADAC in Germany. The club also offers trip-planning advice, free maps, travel-agency services and a range of discounts on hotels, car rentals etc.

The **Better World Club** (866-238-1137; www.betterworldclub.com), which donates 1% of its annual revenue to environmental cleanup efforts, has emerged as an alternative. It offers service throughout the USA and Canada, and has a roadside-assistance program for bicycles.

Bring Your Own Vehicle

There's minimal hassle driving into Canada from the USA as long as you have your vehicle's registration papers, proof of liability insurance and your home driver's license.

Driving Licenses

In most provinces visitors can legally drive for up to three months with their home driver's license. In some, such as British Columbia, this is extended to six months.

If you're spending considerable time in Canada, think about getting an International Driving Permit (IDP), which is valid for one year. Your automobile association at home can issue one for a small fee. Always carry your home license together with the IDP.

Fuel

Gas is sold in liters. Prices are higher in remote areas, with Yellowknife usually setting the national record; drivers in Calgary typically pay the least for gas.

Fuel prices are usually lower in the USA, so fill up south of the border.

Insurance

Canadian law requires liability insurance for all vehicles, to cover you for damage caused to property and people.

- The minimum requirement is $200,000 in all provinces except Québec, where it is $50,000.
- Americans traveling to Canada in their own car should ask their insurance company for a Nonresident Interprovince Motor Vehicle Liability Insurance Card (commonly known as a 'yellow card'), which is accepted as evidence of financial responsibility anywhere in Canada. Although not mandatory, it may come in handy in an accident.
- Car-rental agencies offer liability insurance. Collision Damage Waivers (CDW) reduce or eliminate the amount you'll have to reimburse the rental company if there's damage to the car itself. Some credit cards cover CDW for a certain rental period if you use the card to pay for the rental and decline the policy offered by the rental company. Always check with your card issuer to see what coverage it offers in Canada.
- Personal accident insurance (PAI) covers you and any passengers for medical costs incurred as a result of an accident. If your travel insurance or your health-insurance policy at home does this as well (and most do, but check), then this is one expense you can do without.

Rental

CAR

To rent a car in Canada you generally need to:

- be at least 25 years old (some companies will rent to drivers between the ages of 21 and 24 for an additional charge)
- hold a valid driver's license (an international one may be required if you're not from an English- or French-speaking country)
- have a major credit card

You should be able to get an economy-size vehicle for about $35 to $65 per day. Child safety seats are compulsory (reserve them when you book) and cost about $13 per day.

Major international car-rental companies usually have branches at airports, train stations and in city centers.

In Canada, on-the-spot rentals often are more expensive than pre-booked packages (ie cars booked with a flight).

Avis (☎ 800-437-0358; www.avis.com)

Budget (☎ 800-268-8900; www.budget.com)

Dollar (☎ 800-800-4000; www.dollar.com)

Enterprise (☎ 800-261-7331; www.enterprise.ca)

Hertz (☎ 800-263-0600; www.hertz.com)

National (☎ 877-222-9058; www.nationalcar.ca)

Practicar (☎ 800-327-0116; www.practicar.ca) Formerly known as Rent a Wreck, Practicar often has lower rates. It's also affiliated with Backpackers Hotels Canada and Hostelling International.

Thrifty (☎ 800-847-4389; www.thrifty.com)

MOTORCYCLE

Several companies offer motorcycle rentals and tours. A Harley Heritage Softail Classic costs about $210 per day, including liability insurance and 200km mileage. Some companies have minimum

Road Distances (Km)

	Banff	Calgary	Edmonton	Halifax	Inuvik	Jasper	Montréal	Ottawa	Québec City	St John's	Toronto	Vancouver	Whitehorse	Winnipeg
Calgary	130													
Edmonton	410	290												
Halifax	4900	4810	4850											
Inuvik	3440	3515	3220	8110										
Jasper	280	415	370	5250	3150									
Montréal	3700	3550	3605	1240	6820	3950								
Ottawa	3450	3340	3410	1440	6620	3770	200							
Québec City	3900	3800	3880	1020	7060	4210	250							
St John's	6200	6100	6150	1480	9350	6480	2530	2730	2310					
Toronto	3400	3400	3470	1790	6680	3820	550	450	800	3090				
Vancouver	850	970	1160	5880	3630	790	4580	4350	4830	7130	4360			
Whitehorse	2210	2290	2010	6830	1220	1930	5620	5390	5840	8150	5450	2400		
Winnipeg	1450	1325	1330	3520	4550	1670	2280	2140	2520	4820	2220	2290	3340	
Yellowknife	1800	1790	1510	6340	3770	1590	5050	4900	5350	7620	4950	2370	2540	2800

These distances are approximate only.

rental periods, which can be as much as seven days. Riding a hog is especially popular in British Columbia.

Coastline Motorcycle (250-335-1837, 866-338-0344; www.coastlinemc.com) Tours and rentals out of Victoria and Vancouver in British Columbia.

McScoots Motorcycle & Scooter Rentals (250-763-4668; www.mcscoots.com) Big selection of Harleys; also operates motorcycle tours. It's based in Kelowna, British Columbia.

Open Road Adventure (250-494-5409; www.canadamotorcyclerentals.com) Rentals and tours out of Summerland, near Kelowna, British Columbia.

Harley-Davidson Laval (877-459-2950; www.harleydavidsonlaval.com) Rentals by half-day, full day, weekend or longer out of suburban Montréal.

Recreational Vehicles

The RV market is biggest in the west, with specialized agencies in Calgary, Edmonton, Whitehorse and Vancouver. For summer travel, book as early as possible. The base cost is roughly $160 to $265 per day in high season for midsize vehicles, although insurance, fees and taxes add a hefty chunk to that. Diesel-fueled RVs have considerably lower running costs.

Canadream Campers (403-291-1000, 800-461-7368; www.canadream.com) Based in Calgary, with rentals (including one-way rentals) in eight cities, including Vancouver, Whitehorse, Toronto and Halifax.

Cruise Canada (800-671-8042; www.cruisecanada.com) Offers three sizes of RVs. Locations in Halifax, and in central and western Canada; offers one-way rentals.

Road Conditions & Hazards

Road conditions are generally good, but a few things to keep in mind:

- Fierce winters can leave potholes the size of landmine craters. Be prepared to swerve. Winter travel in general can be hazardous due to heavy snow and ice, which may cause roads and bridges to close periodically. **Transport Canada** (800-387-4999;

www.tc.gc.ca/road) provides links to road conditions and construction zones for each province.

- If you're driving in winter or in remote areas, make sure your vehicle is equipped with four-season radial or snow tires, and emergency supplies in case you're stranded.
- Distances between service stations can be long in sparsely populated areas such as the Yukon, Newfoundland or northern Québec, so keep your gas topped up whenever possible.
- Moose, deer and elk are common on rural roadways, especially at night. There's no contest between a 534kg bull moose and a Subaru, so keep your eyes peeled.

Road Rules

- Canadians drive on the right-hand side of the road.
- Seat belt use is compulsory. Children under 18kg must be strapped in child-booster seats, except infants, who must be in a rear-facing safety seat.
- Motorcyclists must wear helmets and drive with their headlights on.
- Distances and speed limits are posted in kilometers. The speed limit is generally **40km/h to 50km/h in cities** and **90km/h to 110km/h outside town**.
- Slow down to 60km/h when passing emergency vehicles (such as police cars and ambulances) stopped on the roadside with their lights flashing.
- Turning right at red lights after coming to a full stop is permitted in all provinces (except where road signs prohibit it, and on the island of Montréal, where it's always a no-no). There's a national propensity for running red lights, however, so don't assume 'right of way' at intersections.
- Driving while using a hand-held cell phone is illegal in British Columbia, Newfoundland, Nova Scotia, Ontario, Prince Edward Island, Québec and Saskatchewan.
- Radar detectors are not allowed in most of Canada (Alberta, British Columbia and Saskatchewan are the exceptions). If you're caught driving with a radar detector, even one that isn't being operated, you could receive a fine of $1000 and your device may be confiscated.
- The blood-alcohol limit for drivers is 0.08%. Driving while drunk is a criminal offense.

Local Transportation

Bicycle

Cycling is a popular means of getting around during the warmer months, and many cities have hundreds of kilometers of dedicated bike paths. Bicycles typically can be taken on public transportation (although some cities have restrictions during peak travel times). All the major cities have shops renting bikes. Toronto and Montréal have bike-share programs; Vancouver will launch a bike share program in 2014.

Bus

Buses are the most common form of public transportation, and practically all towns have their own systems. Most are commuter oriented, and offer only limited or no services in the evenings and on weekends.

Train

Toronto and Montréal are the two Canadian cities with subway systems. Vancouver's version is mostly an above-ground monorail. Calgary, Edmonton and Ottawa have efficient light-rail systems. Route maps are posted in all stations.

Taxi

Most of the main cities have taxis. They are usually metered, with a flag-fall fee of roughly $2.70 and a per-kilometer charge around $1.75. Drivers expect a tip of between 10% and 15%. Taxis can be flagged down or ordered by phone.

Tours

Tour companies are another way to get around this great big country. Some reliable companies operating in multiple Canadian provinces:

Arctic Odysseys (☎ 206-325-1977, 800-574-3021; www.arcticodysseys.com) Experience Arctic Canada close up on tours chasing the northern lights in the Northwest Territories, heli-skiing on Baffin Island or polar-bear spotting on Hudson Bay.

Backroads (☎ 510-527-1555, 800-462-2848; www.backroads.com) Guided cycling, walking and/or paddling tours in the

Rockies, Nova Scotia and Québec.

Moose Travel Network (☎ in eastern Canada 888-816-6673, in western Canada 888-244-6673; www.moosenetwork.com) Operates backpacker-type tours in small buses throughout British Columbia, Alberta and beyond.

Nahanni River Adventures (☎ 800-297-6927; www.nahanni.com) Operates rafting and kayaking expeditions in the Yukon, British Columbia and Alaska, including trips on the Firth, Alsek and Babine Rivers, as well as down the Tatshenshini-Alsek watershed.

Road Scholar (☎ 800-454-5768; www.roadscholar.org) Formerly known as Elderhostel, the nonprofit organization offers study tours in nearly all provinces for active people over 55, including train trips, cruises, and bus and walking tours.

Routes to Learning (☎ 613-530-2222, 866-745-1690; www.routestolearning.ca) From walking in the steps of Newfoundland's Vikings to exploring New Brunswick's Acadians or Nova Scotia's lighthouses, this nonprofit group has dozens of educational tours throughout Canada.

Salty Bear Adventure Tours (☎ 902-202-3636; www.saltybear.ca) Backpacker-oriented van tours through the Maritimes with jump-on/jump-off flexibility. There's a three-day circuit around Cape Breton, Nova Scotia, and a five-day route that goes into Prince Edward Island.

Trek America (☎ in UK 0870-444-8735, in USA 800-221-0596; www.trekamerica.com) Active camping, hiking and canoeing tours in small groups, geared primarily at people between 18 and 38, although some are open to all ages.

Train

VIA Rail (☎ 888-842-7245; www.viarail.ca) operates most of Canada's intercity and transcontinental passenger trains, chugging over 14,000km of track. In some remote parts of the country, such as Churchill, Manitoba, trains provide the only overland access.

- Rail service is most efficient in the corridor between Québec City and Windsor, Ontario – particularly between Montréal and Toronto, the two major hubs.
- The rail network does not extend to Newfoundland, Prince Edward Island or the Northern Territories.
- Free wi-fi is available on most trains.
- Smoking is prohibited on all trains.

Classes

There are four main classes:

- Economy class buys you a fairly basic, if indeed quite comfortable, reclining seat with a headrest. Blankets and pillows are provided for overnight travel.
- Business class operates in the southern Ontario/Québec corridor. Seats are more spacious and have outlets for plugging in laptops. You also get a meal and priority boarding.
- Sleeper class is available on shorter overnight routes. You can choose from compartments with upper or lower pullout berths, and private single, double or triple roomettes, all with a bathroom.

Long-Distance Train Routes

Route	Duration (hr)	Frequency	Fare
Toronto–Vancouver *(Canadian)*	83	3 weekly	from $590
Winnipeg–Churchill *(Hudson Bay)*	44	2 weekly	from $170
Halifax–Montréal *(Ocean)*	21	1 daily (Wed-Mon)	from $151
Jasper–Prince Rupert	33	3 weekly	from $163

- Touring class is available on long-distance routes and includes sleeper class accommodations plus meals, access to the sightseeing car and sometimes a tour guide.

Costs

Taking the train is more expensive than the bus, but most people find it a more comfortable way to travel. June to mid-October is peak season, when prices are about 40% higher. Buying tickets in advance (even just five days before) can yield significant savings.

Long-Distance Routes

VIA Rail has several classic trains (see also p353):

- **Canadian** A 1950s stainless-steel beauty between Toronto and Vancouver, zipping through the northern Ontario lake country, the western plains via Winnipeg and Saskatoon, and Jasper in the Rockies over three days.
- **Hudson Bay** From the prairie (slowly) to the Subarctic: Winnipeg to polar-bear hangout Churchill.
- **Ocean** Chugs from Montréal along the St Lawrence River through New Brunswick and Nova Scotia.
- **Jasper to Prince Rupert** An all-daylight route from Jasper, Alberta, to coastal Prince Rupert, British Columbia; there's an overnight stop in Prince George (you make your own hotel reservations).

Privately run regional train companies offer additional rail-touring opportunities:

Royal Canadian Pacific (☎ 877-665-3044; www.royalcanadianpacific.com) Another cruise-ship-like luxury line between and around the Rockies via Calgary.

Rocky Mountaineer Railtours (www.rockymountaineer.com; 2 days from $1000) Gape at Canadian Rockies scenery on swanky trains between Vancouver, Kamloops and Calgary.

White Pass & Yukon Route (www.wpyr.com; round-trip $160) Gorgeous route paralleling the original White Pass trail from Whitehorse, Yukon, to Fraser, British Columbia.

Rail Passes

VIA Rail offers a couple of passes that provide good savings:

- The Canrailpass-System is good for seven trips on any train during a 21-day period. All seats are in economy class; upgrades are not permitted. You must book each leg at least three days in advance (doable online). Costs start at $1008/630 in high/low season.
- The Canrailpass-Corridor (from $360) is good for seven trips during a 10-day period on trains in the Québec City–Windsor corridor (which includes Montréal, Toronto and Niagara).

Reservations

Seat reservations are highly recommended, especially in summer, on weekends and around holidays. During peak season (June to mid-October), some of the most popular sleeping arrangements are sold out months in advance, especially on long-distance trains such as the *Canadian*. The *Hudson Bay* often books solid during polar-bear season (around late September to early November).

Language

The sounds used in spoken French can almost all be found in English. There are a couple of exceptions: nasal vowels (represented in our pronunciation guides by 'o' or 'u' followed by an almost inaudible nasal consonant sound 'm', 'n' or 'ng'), the 'funny' *u* sound ('ew' in our guides) and the deep-in-the-throat *r*. Bearing these few points in mind and reading our pronunciation guides below as if they were English, you'll be understood just fine.

To enhance your trip with a phrasebook, visit **lonelyplanet.com**. Lonely Planet iPhone phrasebooks are available through the Apple App store.

Basics

Hello./Goodbye.
Bonjour./Au revoir. — bon·zhoor/o·rer·vwa

How are you?
Comment allez-vous? — ko·mon ta·lay·voo

I'm fine, thanks.
Bien, merci. — byun mair·see

Excuse me./Sorry.
Excusez-moi./Pardon. — ek·skew·zay·mwa/par·don

Yes./No.
Oui./Non. — wee/non

Please.
S'il vous plaît. — seel voo play

Thank you.
Merci. — mair·see

That's fine./You're welcome.
De rien. — der ree·en

Do you speak English?
Parlez-vous anglais? — par·lay·voo ong·glay

I don't understand.
Je ne comprends pas. — zher ner kom·pron pa

How much is this?
C'est combien? — say kom·byun

Accommodations

I'd like to book a room.
Je voudrais réserver une chambre. — zher voo·dray ray·zair·vay ewn shom·brer

How much is it per night?
Quel est le prix par nuit? — kel ay ler pree par nwee

Eating & Drinking

I'd like ..., please.
Je voudrais ..., s'il vous plaît. — zher voo·dray ... seel voo play

That was delicious!
C'était délicieux! — say·tay day·lee·syer

Bring the bill/check, please.
Apportez-moi l'addition, s'il vous plaît. — a·por·tay·mwa la·dee·syon seel voo play

I'm allergic (to peanuts).
Je suis allergique (aux cacahuètes). — zher swee a·lair·zheek (o ka·ka·wet)

I don't eat ...
Je ne mange pas de ... — zher ner monzh pa de ...

fish	*poisson*	pwa·son
(red) meat	*viande (rouge)*	vyond (roozh)
poultry	*volaille*	vo·lai

Emergencies

I'm ill.
Je suis malade. — zher swee ma·lad

Help!
Au secours! — o skoor

Call a doctor!
Appelez un médecin! — a·play un mayd·sun

Call the police!
Appelez la police! — a·play la po·lees

Directions

I'm looking for (a/the) ...
Je cherche ... — zher shairsh ...

bank
une banque — ewn bongk

... embassy
l'ambassade de ... — lam·ba·sahd der ...

market
le marché — ler mar·shay

museum
le musée — ler mew·zay

restaurant
un restaurant — un res·to·ron

toilet
les toilettes — lay twa·let

tourist office
l'office de tourisme — lo·fees der too·rees·mer

Behind the Scenes

Author Thanks

Karla Zimmerman

Thanks to all the local knowledge interviewees who took the time to talk about their favorite places. Thanks to stalwart LP colleagues Celeste Brash and John Lee whose good humor didn't fail when I hit them up for info. Thanks most to Eric Markowitz, partner-for-life supremo, who fed me and brought me beer during the write-up phase. You top my Best List.

Acknowledgments

Climate map data adapted from Peel MC, Finlayson BL & McMahon TA (2007) 'Updated World Map of the Köppen-Geiger Climate Classification', Hydrology and Earth System Sciences, 11, 163344.

Transit map: Vancouver TransLink Map © TransLink 2013.

Illustration pp68-69 by Michael Weldon.

Cover photographs
Front: Sunrise in the Rocky Mountains, David Sucsy / Getty Images; Back: Lile-aux-Puces Island, New Brunswick, Philippe Renault / Alamy

This Book

This 2nd edition of *Discover Canada* was researched and written by Karla Zimmerman, Celeste Brash, John Lee, Sarah Richards, Brendan Sainsbury, Caroline Sieg, Ryan Ver Berkmoes and Benedict Walker. This guidebook was commissioned in Lonely Planet's Oakland office, and produced by the following:

Commissioning Editor Korina Miller
Coordinating Editors Elizabeth Jones, Fionnuala Twomey
Senior Cartographer Mark Griffiths
Book Designer Clara Monitto
Senior Editors Catherine Naghten, Karyn Noble
Assisting Editor Jenna Myers
Cover Research Naomi Parker
Language Content Branislava Vladisavljevic
Thanks to Brendan Dempsey, Ryan Evans, Samantha Forge, Indra Kilfoyle, Valentina Kremenchutskaya, Marsha Leitzel, Fabiano Portilho Lencioni, Martine Power, Angela Tinson, Saralinda Turner, Tony Wheeler

SEND US YOUR FEEDBACK

Things change – prices go up, schedules change, good places go bad and bad places go bankrupt. So if you find things better or worse, recently opened or long since closed, or you just want to tell us what you loved or loathed about this book, please get in touch and help make the next edition even more accurate and useful. We love to hear from travelers – your comments keep us on our toes and our well-traveled team reads every word. Although we can't reply individually to postal submissions, we always guarantee that your feedback goes straight to the appropriate authors, in time for the next edition. Each person who sends us information is thanked in the next edition – the most useful submissions are rewarded with a selection of digital PDF chapters.

Visit lonelyplanet.com/contact to submit your updates and suggestions or to ask for help. Our award-winning website also features inspirational travel stories, news and discussions.

Note: We may edit, reproduce and incorporate your comments in Lonely Planet products such as guidebooks, websites and digital products, so let us know if you don't want your comments reproduced or your name acknowledged. For a copy of our privacy policy visit lonelyplanet.com/privacy.

Index

000 Map pages

C

D

E

000 Map pages

000 Map pages

N

O

P

000 Map pages

Q

R

S

000 Map pages

Y

Z

How to Use This Book

These symbols give you the vital information for each listing:

- Telephone Numbers
- Opening Hours
- Parking
- Nonsmoking
- Air-Conditioning
- Internet Access
- Wi-Fi Access
- Swimming Pool
- Vegetarian Selection
- Family-Friendly
- Pet-Friendly
- Bus
- Ferry
- Metro
- Subway
- Train
- Tram

All reviews are ordered in our authors' preference, starting with their most preferred option. Additionally:

Sights are arranged in the geographic order that we suggest you visit them, and within this order, by author preference.

Eating and Sleeping reviews are ordered by price range (budget, mid-range, top end) and within these ranges, by author preference.

Look out for these icons:

FREE No payment required

A green or sustainable option

Our authors have nominated these places as demonstrating a strong commitment to sustainability – for example by supporting local communities and producers, operating in an environmentally friendly way, or supporting conservation projects.

Map Legend

Sights
- Beach
- Buddhist
- Castle
- Christian
- Hindu
- Islamic
- Jewish
- Monument
- Museum/Gallery
- Ruin
- Winery/Vineyard
- Zoo
- Other Sight

Activities, Courses & Tours
- Diving/Snorkelling
- Canoeing/Kayaking
- Skiing
- Surfing
- Swimming/Pool
- Walking
- Windsurfing
- Other Activity/Course/Tour

Sleeping
- Sleeping
- Camping

Eating
- Eating

Drinking
- Drinking
- Cafe

Entertainment
- Entertainment

Shopping
- Shopping

Information
- Post Office
- Tourist Information

Transport
- Airport
- Border Crossing
- Bus
- Cable Car/Funicular
- Cycling
- Ferry
- Monorail
- Parking
- S-Bahn
- Taxi
- Train/Railway
- Tram
- Tube Station
- U-Bahn
- Underground Train Station
- Other Transport

Routes
- Tollway
- Freeway
- Primary
- Secondary
- Tertiary
- Lane
- Unsealed Road
- Plaza/Mall
- Steps
- Tunnel
- Pedestrian Overpass
- Walking Tour
- Walking Tour Detour
- Path

Boundaries
- International
- State/Province
- Disputed
- Regional/Suburb
- Marine Park
- Cliff
- Wall

Population
- Capital (National)
- Capital (State/Province)
- City/Large Town
- Town/Village

Geographic
- Hut/Shelter
- Lighthouse
- Lookout
- Mountain/Volcano
- Oasis
- Park
- Pass
- Picnic Area
- Waterfall

Hydrography
- River/Creek
- Intermittent River
- Swamp/Mangrove
- Reef
- Canal
- Water
- Dry/Salt/Intermittent Lake
- Glacier

Areas
- Beach/Desert
- Cemetery (Christian)
- Cemetery (Other)
- Park/Forest
- Sportsground
- Sight (Building)
- Top Sight (Building)